BORN TO LOSE

EUGENE ROSOW

BORN TO LOSE

THE GANGSTER FILM IN AMERICA

New York   OXFORD UNIVERSITY PRESS   1978

Library of Congress Cataloging in Publication Data
Rosow, Eugene.
Born to lose.
Bibliography: p.
Filmography: p.
Includes index.
1. Gangster films—History and criticism.
2. Moving-pictures—United States. I. Title.
PN1995.9.G3R6   791.43'0909'352   78-4942   ISBN 0-19-502382-X

Printed in the United States of America

This book is dedicated with love and gratitude to my parents
H. Michael Rosow and Leda Werier Rosow,
and to all the people who are struggling for a world
in which gangsters will not be glorified.

PREFACE

My interest in gangster pictures grew out of my curiosity as a film maker-historian about why these movies have so gripped our American imagination and culture. I believe that gangster films help to tell us who we are as Americans, and beyond that, who we are as human beings confronting the problems of an advanced urban-industrial capitalist society.

My own enjoyment of gangster movies has been clouded by a sense of danger. The danger lay beyond that stern lesson tacked on to many a movie that gangsters must come to a bad end. I believe that gangster pictures project the exciting, energetic, and egalitarian qualities of American life. At the same time they evoke other, more distressing, dimensions of American life—dimensions that we should examine in our efforts to travel down a truly democratic road. I have rooted the study of gangster movies in American social history in order to reach a better understanding of how and why gangster films became a significant force in our culture. I have also concentrated on the formal and technical evolution of gangster movies in order to give as complete a picture as possible of the origin and development of a film genre.

I have tried to view every film mentioned in this book twice. For those films for which I could not find prints I had to rely on reviews, records of censorship boards, film scripts, and distributors' descriptions—fortunately, nearly all of these films were in the 1912–1930 period.

Research for this book was conducted at the Academy of Motion Picture Arts and Sciences, the American Film Institute, the British Film Institute, the Cinémathèque Française, the Pacific Film Archive, the Wisconsin State Historical Society, the Museum of Modern Art (New York), the Library of Congress, UCLA, the Lincoln Center for the Performing Arts, and in the living rooms of a number of film collectors. A grant from the American Film Institute and the Max Farrand Travelling Fellowship in American History helped make this research possible.

As a documentary film maker I have tried to illustrate this book in such a way that the reader will also become a viewer. I would like each reader/viewer to come away from this book with a *visual* understanding of the genre which will be useful in his or her future viewing of gangster pictures. The necessity of using publicity stills—as opposed to frame enlargements—has imposed a static quality on what should ideally be a fluid visual experience. I hope that future film scholars will find it possible to use actual film material and that teachers who use this book will be able to rent as many films as possible to accompany it. In the future, video discs or film casettes should accompany film books such as this one.

I would like to express my appreciation and deep gratitude to a number of people who have helped make this book possible. Hugh Gray, Lawrence Levine, and Leon Litwack have given me valuable encouragement and criticism that has considerably strengthened this work. Bruce Barthol, Barbara Bedway, Lowell Bergman, Jeff Gerth, Michael Goldin, Colin McArthur, Henri Langlois, Tom Luddy, Mara Sabinson, Joel Siegel, Jerzy Toeplitz, Miriam Ziegelaub, and especially Linda Post have helped at critical times in different ways. The cooperation and help of a number of people in several picture archives have contributed to the difficult task

of illustrating this book. They include Bonnie Rothbart, Terry Roach, Sam Gill, Debbi Bergman, Mary Olivarez, Cheryl Behnke, and Bob Kushman of the Academy of Motion Picture Arts and Sciences Library; Susan Dalton of the Wisconsin State Historical Society Film and Theater Collection; Mrs. Malkin and Roger Nadelman of UCLA; Esther Brumberg of the Museum of the City of New York; Mary Corliss and Carol Carey of the Museum of Modern Art; and George M. Barringer of the Quigley Photographic Archive, Georgetown University.

I am also grateful to Sheldon Meyer of Oxford University Press for seeing this book through some difficult times and for his support, suggestions, and encouragement throughout the process. Pat Golin, Leona Capeless, Leslie Phillips, and Frederick Schneider of Oxford also deserve my thanks for their patience and contributions.

Read and enjoy.

New York   E. R.
April 1978

"The gangster may play all sorts of pranks with the ballot box, but in its own good time the latter will get even by kicking the gangster into the gutter."

Columbus Dispatch, 10 April 1896
(first use of the word "gangster"
in print in America)

CONTENTS

INTRODUCTION

Maybe these gangsters will put up a lot of factories and use all the water in our creeks for power and our trees for paper pulp and our kids to run the machines for them! Maybe if we pay 'em enough they'll put up a lot of tall buildings so we can't see the sun for the smoke from chimneys! And all the cowboys left in this country'll get jobs driving trucks.

Cowboy character in *Gunsmoke*
(Paramount, 1931)

The story of gangster movies is as American as apple pie, a story that could have been taken from today's headlines. Robert War-show, one of the most perceptive critics of popular culture, was the first to note the deeper mythic dimensions and dramatic importance of gangster pictures for Americans when he wrote, "The experience of the gangster as an experience of art is universal to America. There is almost nothing we understand better or react to more readily or with quicker intelligence."

People have mythologized bandits for centuries in folklore, literature, and art. The American movie gangster is part of this tradition; within it, he is closer to the bandits of ballads than to those of books. Like ancient storytellers, wandering minstrels, and popular poets, film makers have reached out to the largest possible audience with stories of heroes and heroines that they thought would strike the most responsive chord with the public. As Hollywood movie makers became increasingly successful in catering to audience demands, they relied on certain conventions for presenting characters, stories, and settings. When a set of conventions proved consistently popular with audiences, the film industry repeated them and crystallized them into genres. By the start of the sound film era at the end of the twenties, most Westerns, gangster pictures, musicals, horror movies, and thrillers were hammered out on studio assembly lines according to loose convention formulas. This book focuses on the development of a specific film genre in the belief that genre provides the best approach to understanding the origins of gangster films in American culture and the reasons for their continued popularity.

The movies that make up the gangster genre are more than simple action-packed dramas about violent criminals driven by dreams of success. The recurring characters, stories, themes, motifs, and iconography of gangster movies represent a superstructure of values and ideas that make up a self-image of America's advanced capitalist society. Movie genres provide a self-image capable of evolution in response to social tensions and dislocations. Each new addition and embellishment has a cumulative effect on the further development of the genre, so that a movie genre becomes a dynamic, living form for the reproduction of cultural myths and values—a form that allows for the transfer of a culture from generation to generation. The gangster genre as a vehicle for myths has proven more durable than the various studios, styles, and directors that created it. Film genres themselves have been able to survive television's assumption of film's role in generating myths that are required by—and illuminate—America's social and economic system.

Modern societies require myth as much as primitive societies, despite the widely accepted view that science has rendered such modes of thought obsolete. (The faith in the scientific method itself verges on a type of mythology.) Myths are not merely faulty representations of objects and social reality. They are products of the mind's attempt to understand and interpret these realities with ''an intellectual construction that fuses concept and emotion into an image.''[1] Such images and what they represent, as with the cowboy and the gangster, can become a form of shorthand for historical processes that are difficult for those people living through them to accept or comprehend. According to the work of anthropologist Claude Levi-Strauss, myths are symbolic languages that mediate between actual conditions and the unrealized hopes and goals of a culture; they function as methods of conceptual transformation for collective thought.[2] In many ways, gangster movies have provided an apt mytho-metaphor for the experience of a society in the throes of accepting its industrialization and urbanization. American society, whose economic system was exalted and seemingly justified by spectacular success during the 1920's, only to be severely challenged by the Depression, wars, and economic dislocation that followed, and the increasing domination of multinational corporations.

Gangster pictures recapitulate the events of social history that produced them. We can regard the evolution of the gangster genre as a continuing documentary in which the images and sounds of American history, from the turn of the Century on, are dramatized in gangster movies: the story begins with the movie gangster as an immigrant city boy in the first decade of film narrative, before and after 1910. As a young man, the movie gangster went off to World War I to make the world safe for democracy. A veteran returning to the America of the Roaring Twenties, he became a high-rolling bootlegger in tune with the dollar decade and the spectacular success of the movie industry. After the crash, as the country sank deeper into the Depression, the movie gangster was lionized as a fearless and ambitiously ruthless gunman rising to the heights of financial success and respectability. Soon the gangster became a scapegoat who was gunned down during the New Deal, after which he was quickly re-incarnated as a G-man. G-men and movie gangsters were called up for the World War II effort to fight Nazis and were later called on for cold war patriotic duty against communist spies. During the fifties and sixties, movie gangsters joined crime syndicates as the reality of growing nationwide syndicate activity was revealed by government investigations. As American society became increasingly impersonal under the domination of large, faceless corporations, gangster films turned to nostalgic biographies and films involving their heroes' ethnic backgrounds. Movie gangsters again surged to the forefront of movie popularity in the troubled era of the Vietnam war and the Watergate scandals.

The popularity and mythic importance of gangster movies have replaced those of Western movies as an intriguing index of how we think and feel. They are as lively and colorful as the legends of ancient peoples, and they are a mythical mode of thinking that will seem as ancient and barbaric in a more socially and economically democratic future as the stone age seems to us today. For the present, the durability of the gangster genre is also an indication of the growth of a cancer in the American mind—a pervasive criminal mentality that is a threat to our self-concept as a nation founded on democratic liberty, justice, and equality.

PART I

THE ORIGINS OF THE MOVIE GANGSTER

1

ROBIN HOODS AND ROBBER BARONS

Behind every great fortune there lies a crime.

Balzac

Today the private ownership of the collective tool is a crime. This crime is at the foundation of every other that disfigures society. And from it issues the festering stenches of our sweatshop civilization.

Eugene Debs

Gangster vs. Cowboy

The 1932 Monogram production *Broadway to Cheyenne* begins with rolling presses and a headline screaming, "GANGLAND ON THE SPOT." A district attorney tells a gangster, "You've been dishing it out for a long time and now you're going to take it; . . . you're a candidate for the hot seat in the big house!" Meanwhile, at the Back Door Club two rival gangs shoot it out for control of the Bronx. The cop/cowboy hero, known as Breezy (Rex Bell), happens to be at the club and gets shot through the arm. He wants revenge, but his chief sends him out of the city for a vacation. He goes back home to Cheyenne, Wyoming, and upon arriving wrecks his car and jumps on a horse. A bunch of his old pals grab him, rip off his city clothes, and give him a Western outfit. After these rites of repassage, Breezy is ready to take on the gangsters, who coincidentally show up in Cheyenne to hide out from the law in the Bronx and try to work a protection racket by machine-gunning cattle. This film presents in starkest terms the conflict between cowboy and gangster for the allegiance of Americans as mythic hero. When the gangster kills the cowboy's father and tries to rape the heroine, Breezy (on his horse) heads the gangster (in his car) off at the pass, rides him down in the desert, lassoes the machine gun, and after winning a furious fist fight tells the gangster, "You can dish it out but you can't take it. There's no lawyers here to pull a habeas corpus, but there's a gang here to pull a rope." The posse rides up and the gangster begs, "Gimme a break!" An old-timer in the posse tells him, "Sure, we'll give you a break. We'll give you a rope and tree we never used before." But before they can lynch him, the gangster commits suicide. The cowboy is still champion and, of course, gets the girl as a prize.

Breezy's victory reaffirmed the image of the cowboy as an American hero in 1932— the year that gangster films were at the height of their popularity and Western films at a low

American edition of English outlaw novel

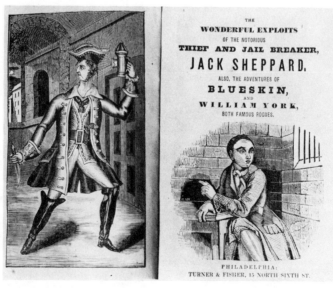

Robin Hoods: Billy the Kid (*left*), and young Jesse James (*right*)

point.[1] This vivid and crude reaffirmation of a traditional American hero in *Broadway to Cheyenne* can be seen as one reaction to Depression conditions, an attempt to allay the nagging doubts and fearful assault on America's traditional faith and optimism in its political and economic systems. If, as Robert Warshow wrote, "the gangster is the 'no' to that great American 'yes' which is stamped so big over our official culture and yet has so little to do with the way we really feel about our lives," the cowboy is the "yes," and the West is the land of America's faith in itself.[2]

Outlaws have always been popular in American folklore and some of the mythic gangster's roots are intertwined with those of the Western hero, whose drama has been the dominant mythical expression in American popular culture. To Howard Hawks, who has directed some of the best Westerns and gangster films, the heroes of both genres are basically the same character—a man with a gun.[3] In gangster and Western films, as in the stories of most mythic fighting men, the weapon has an iconographic importance, an aura of power and a phallic function, that defines the hero's manhood.[4] But as a man with a gun, the gangster for the most part is a descendant of Western outlaws rather than cowboy heroes; for the most popular characterization of American outlaws that has emerged from folk traditions and dime novels is that of a Robin Hood.[5]

In America, as in other countries, bandit heroes have appeared in response to certain basic conditions with a common core of institutionalized injustice and widespread poverty. Those in power corrupt laws which are supposed to guarantee justice; the entire social and economic system favors the wealthiest. Bandit heroes who steal from the rich become champions of the poor.[6] According to legend, the Jesse James gang robbed banks and railroads in Missouri but not farmers. Billy the Kid "was like Robin Hood; he'd steal from the white people and give it to the Mexicans, so they thought he was all right."[7] Sam Bass shared the loot he stole from the Union Pacific with the sharecroppers and poor farmers of East Texas, and Pretty Boy Floyd burned unregistered mortgages of poor Oklahoma farmers whenever he robbed a bank. Folklorists have pointed out that the actual outlaws were not as noble and selfless as their legends indicate; that the durability of the bandit-hero tradition reveals a strong desire and need for such heroes among the folk cultures and media audiences that idolize them.[8] Accord-

The Great Train Robbery

The horizontal world of the Western

ing to E.J. Hobsbawm, who has studied bandit heroes and traditions of different historical periods and cultures, such outlaws, in general, express a proto-revolutionary consciousness of the necessity of widespread social change and a symbolic cry for justice. They can also represent a nostalgic yearning for a more simple and democratic past.[9] In **The Great Train Robbery** (1903), the first American Western, the gang stops the train of America's onrushing industrial future as if to thwart the destruction of rural, pre-industrial America. The mythic gangster of the twenties and early thirties was rooted in the Robin Hood tradition of America's legendary Western outlaws, but the gangster and his world are essentially alien to the mythology and meaning of the West.

The setting of the Western genre contrasts sharply with that of the gangster film. At first, the popular culture image of the West was one of lush, green virgin forests and rugged mountains. In such settings, woodsmen and mountain men molded their characters through direct contact with nature or with the native Americans, who taught them how to live with nature (without having to exploit it feverishly, ignorantly, or destructively).[10] In contrast, the mythic gangster is a character out of touch with a natural setting. When he does look up toward the sky, as in **Underworld** or **Scarface,** it is to see a neon sign—not a sunset—that reminds him, "The world is yours."

The movies have established the wide open spaces, the immense sky, and the fiercely dramatic landscapes of Monument Valley in Arizona as the basic physical setting for the Western.[11] This movie landscape is a horizontal one. Except for occasional stunt jumps from high cliffs and steep rides down slopes, the Western movie hero moves through a horizontal plane that suggests repose and reassuring contact with the ground. The gangster's setting, on the other hand, is dominated by the vertical planes of a city, which is appropriate to the story of his rise and fall.

The mythic West is also a place beyond the boundaries of the legal and social restraints of civilization. The untamed wilderness demanded a self-reliance that makes the West viable dramatically and suitable for heroic quests in which mythological heroes must go beyond the civilized world.[12]

In the Western the environment is seen as a positive, democratic, and moral vision, while the gangster film depicts an urban capitalist, industrial reality that is eroding this vision. This was the mythic West of the American Dream—the West as frontier and garden.

The frontier, according to the historian Frederick Jackson Turner, was a guarantor of demographic and social mobility that gave American society its open and democratic flavor. The supposed individualistic and democratic nature of frontier settlements echoed and—with each movement West—re-echoed the mythic identity of Amercia as a land of freedom and equality. Should the tensions arising out of the dynamic and often violent growth of American society prove too great, the frontier could act as a safety valve that would lower the pressures that could otherwise explode America's democratic self-image.[13] The blazing sunsets of Western stories continually pointed to horizons of new beginnings toward which the cowboy and his horse could ride, bearing the grail of American progress.

Progress associated with the Western fron-

tier meant a geographic movement away from the decaying civilization of Europe and toward the fresh possibilities offered by the wilderness—an optimistic march away from the past and toward the future. The new civilization that followed the frontier was idealized as a yeoman republic that had been so enthusiastically described by Jefferson and Crèvecœur in the eighteenth century.[14] The West would be a garden republic of independent equal yeoman farmers who would know God directly through tilling the soil and would cultivate morality along with their crops and children. In this Western garden of the American dream every tree, river, and country church would bear witness to the growth of the agrarian republic. The Western hero would find the path and clear the way.

In *Broadway to Cheyenne,* Breezy tells the gangster that he has twenty-four hours to get out of town: "This Cheyenne country isn't big enough to hold you and me. I'm staying. If you stay you're on the spot." This is the same message the Western hero has for Indians and outlaws, and it is characteristic of his role as "tamer" of the Wild West—a chevalier riding against "savagery" in the name of "civilization."[15]

Yet the Western hero always rides into the sunsets farther West because he is ill at ease with the civilization he so strenuously defends. The Western hero's sidekicks are usually friendly Indians or scruffy old-timers—not shopkeepers, bankers, or railroad officials. Implicit in these friendships is a preference for those closest to nature and the freedom beyond the frontier, rather than the townspeople and their society.

Most writers who describe the Western hero's ambivalence refer to such polarities as nature and society, or savagery and civilization, and present the hero as a man caught in a kind of dilemma between total freedom and

The gangster's vertical world

law and order.[16] The hero's predicament has also been viewed in Freudian terms as being one of having to repress an unbridled sexuality in society which he will obscenely enjoy as soon as he gets over the horizon.[17] Common to all these interpretations is the picture of the Western hero as a "natural man" who must act as an agent for advancing a society in which there is little room for natural men. An anarchist for law and order, the Western hero vicariously gratifies our desires for total freedom and spontaneity while at the same time re-affirming the necessity of a society of laws. The gangster functions in a similar way, but the historical moment of his drama is bleaker, and he must die to re-affirm the laws of society.

One key factor that is ignored in analyses of the Western hero is that of private property. When the cowboy rides farther west, he heads for land owned by no human and toward people who listen to the wind and animals instead of the jingling of their money. The civilization and law and order of the frontier towns of both myth and historic fact were rooted in private property. Bank robbers, stage robbers, train robbers, horse thieves, cattle rustlers, and Indians trying to get back their land are usually the Western hero's antagonists—and yet, in general, the

Robber Baron

Western hero owns no property.[18] The "primitive" freedom of the Indians that the Western hero seems to want to share is one of nomads not bound by possessive attitudes toward the land they farmed or moved through. Even the oldest culture in North America to have continuously settled in one place—the Hopi Indians—did not regard themselves as owning the land. Their relation to the land was that of stewards and caretakers in partnership with other forms of life.[19] But the West was divided up into private parcels, and the land and Indians were contained, as if in concentration camps, by the six-gun and repeating rifle and barbed wire—products of an industrial capitalist society that the gangster figure came to represent.

The gangster's origins in industrial America can be found in the actions and attitudes of men like Cornelius Vanderbilt, Jim Fisk, Jay Gould, Andrew Carnegie, John D. Rockefeller, and J.P. Morgan—the captains of capital who dominated America's age of enterprise. "Meteoric as was Rico's rise from the gutter it was inevitable that he should return there,"[20] proclaims the last newspaper article in the film **Little Caesar.** Robber Baron Jim Fisk's life was similarly described as "the sweep of a fiery meteor, or a great comet . . . plunging with terrific velocity and dazzling brilliance across the horizon, whirling into its blazing train broken fortunes, raving financiers, corporations, magnates and public officers, civil and military judges, priests, and presidents."[21] The Robber Barons, the richest and most powerful men in America, were so named by journalist E.L. Godkin because they behaved like the feudal German noblemen who extorted money from passersby and acted as a law unto themselves. They were strongly etched in the public imagination as models of successful Americans. "A popular and ele-

gant orator of the day [1869], Mayor Oakey Hall of Tweed Ring fame, likened Vanderbilt to Franklin, Jackson and Lincoln, as 'a remarkable prototype of that rough-hewn American character which can carve the way of every humbly-born boy to national eminence. . . .' "[22] National eminence among a people who, according to Henry Adams, held a self-image as "a restless, pushing, energetic, ingenious race" demanded first of all that Robber Barons be clever.

" 'Rico's a smart guy! Everything's going to be all right,' whispers Otero to Tony as Little Caesar tells the gang his plans for a holdup. 'Well, Sir, he is a smart man,' was the repeated defense made of the famous persons who had so quickly pre-empted railroads, ore fields and harbor rights. Jay Gould was universally envied for his smartness and so was Jim Fisk smart; and though Beecher thundered at him as the 'glaring meteor, abominable in his lusts, and flagrant in his violation of public decency,' the age admired him without stint, at his worst 'he had only done what others would have done in his place.' "[23] What Fisk did, like other Robber Barons, was to amass a fortune as quickly and ruthlessly as possible. An article in *The Nation* described Vanderbilt's ascent as presented in a monument that the Commodore commissioned to commemorate his millions:

There are the railroads and the river-boats, which are witnesses to an energy and a business sagacity which before now have bought whole legislatures, debauched courts, crushed out rivals, richer or poorer, as the unmoral, unsentimental forces of nature grind down whatever opposes their blind force, and which have given Mr. Fisk and other gentlemen a lesson, which even they have not yet wholly mastered, in watering stock to the discomfiture of small stockholders of all ages and both sexes. In short there, in the glory of brass, are portrayed, in a fashion

THE "BRAINS"

THAT ACHIEVED THE TAMMANY VICTORY AT THE ROCHESTER DEMOCRATIC CONVENTION.

quite good enough, the trophies of a lineal successor of the mediaeval baron that we read about, who may have been illiterate, indeed; and who was not humanitarian; and not finished in his morals; and not, for his manners, the delight of the refined society of his neighborhood; nor yet beloved by his dependents; but who had a keen eye for roads, and had the heart and hand to levy contribution to all who passed by his way."[24]

The opening shot of the gangster film **Quick Millions** is of a train bustling through the country toward Chicago. In American literature and popular culture, the train has represented the technological assault on a pastoral self-image. Hawthorne wrote of being startled out of an 1844 meditation on nature: "But, Hark! There is a whistle of the locomotive—the long shriek harsh above all other harshness, for the space of a mile cannot nullify it into harmony. It talks a story of busy men, citizens from the hot street, who have come to spend a day in a country village, men of business; in short, of all unquietness; and no wonder that it gives such a startling shriek, since it brings the noisy world into the midst of our slumbrous peace."[25] The train was a product of the real machines tearing up America's garden of pastoral innocence—the Robber Barons, gangs, rings, and corporations. A cartoon of Vanderbilt as an outlaw astride a locomotive is closer to the railroad reality that touched the lives of Americans than the harsh shriek disrupting Hawthorne's reverie.

Making transportation a racket is an important theme linking Robber Barons, movie gangsters, and actual racketeers. Cornelius Vanderbilt began his career by operating a ferry between Staten Island and Manhattan, and then he moved into shipping lines and railroads. In **Public Enemy,** Tom Powers rises from truck driver to gangster. In 1921 Meyer Lansky, one of the key figures in organized crime, was working as an automobile mechanic, souping up getaway cars; years later, the crime syndicate of which he is reported to have been the brains used a teamster pension fund to finance part of a gambling empire.[26] When Bugs Moran (Spencer Tracy) in **Quick Millions** approaches another trucker with a deal, he proposes a scheme that was a basic corporate strategy of the Robber Baron:

BUGS: "I'll tell you what I was thinking, Nails. Now if I controlled . . . that is, I mean if we, if we controlled all the trucks we could put this town in our vest pocket. You know that, don't you?"
NAILS: "Yeah, sure."

THE MODERN COLOSSUS OF (RAIL) ROADS.

John D. Rockefeller

BUGS: "Just a question of big business—you know—organization."

For a Robber Baron, as for a gangster, the first step was to organize and centralize the corporation. A climate of secrecy prevailed. Rockefeller demanded that prospective members sign a pledge worthy of a movie Mafia ritual:

"I, ——— ———, do solemnly promise upon my honor and faith as a gentleman that I will keep secret all transactions which I may have with the corporation known as the South Improvement Company; that should I fail to complete any bargains with the said company, all the preliminary conversations shall be kept strictly private; and finally that I will not disclose the price for which I dispose of my products or any other facts which may in any way bring to light the internal workings or organization of the company. All this I do freely promise."[27]

One basic scene that has come to define the gangster genre is a meeting in which an ambitious boss calls together all the independent gangsters and tells them they are about to form a combination to avoid ruinous competition and run the bootlegging industry more efficiently. Protests are met with a quick beating on the spot or threats of death. The same scene fits right into the story of the Standard Oil Company, in which Rockefeller, by controlling transportation, first absorbed twenty-five rival refineries in Cleveland and then went after the rest of the oil industry. In one meeting Rockefeller told other oil men, "Let us, who see what a combination strictly carried out will effect, unite secretly to accomplish it. Let us become the nucleus of a *private* company which gradually shall acquire control of all refineries everywhere. . . ."[28] Those who stood in the way understood the consequences as clearly as if they had been punched to the floor in **Scarface.** The owner of one rival refinery told the Hepburn congressional committee (in 1876): "There was pressure brought to bear upon my mind and upon almost all citizens of Cleveland engaged in the oil business to the effect that unless we went into the South Improvement Co. we were virtually killed as refiners; that if we did not sell out we should be crushed out. . . . We sold at a sacrifice, and we were obliged to. There was only one buyer in the market, and we had to sell on their terms or be crushed out, as it was represented to us."[29]

At the same time, Robber Barons who controlled corporations felt no responsibility to the stockholders, whom they regarded as pawns in their financial maneuverings. A stockholder in one of the first corporations complained that those in control "can outrage right and common decency, and then

Troops shoot strikers in Ludlow, Colorado

J.P. Morgan

with impunity defy their employees, owners, and all the world."[30] When Rico takes over Sam Vettori's mob in **Little Caesar,** he warns the gang and the gangster he has just deposed that, if they don't obey his orders, "my gun's gonna speak its piece!" Robber Barons threatened workers in much the same way. As Jay Gould put it: "I can hire one half of the working class to kill the other half." Robber Barons meant to keep their employees in line by using armed thugs—strikebreakers, saboteurs, *agents provocateurs,* armies of vigilantes, or National Guard troops if necessary. Like movie gangsters, Robber Barons would kill when their property was threatened, and the history of industrial unionization in America resembles gang warfare—on a much larger and more vicious scale.

A car screeches around the corner on two wheels. A body flies out and crumples in the gutter. The corpse has a message around the neck to Tony Camonte in **Scarface:** "Stay out of the North Side." The scene could easily have been from the Robber Barons' territorial battles. In bitter railroad wars between Vanderbilt and the Erie Ring (comprised of Gould, Drew, and Fisk), armies of hired thugs fought pitched battles with rifles and cannon. Trains were derailed and sabotaged, and at one point the Erie Ring with their army fled New York City in the middle of the night for New Jersey, carrying their millions with them. The harsh shrieks of train whistles that shattered pastoral tranquility were accompanied by the gunshots of Robber Baron warfare.

The Robber Barons saw nothing unusual or extreme in eliminating competition by any means necessary; that was the very nature of doing business in America. Chauncey Depew defended the railroads' tactics before the Hepburn committee by asserting: "Every manufacturer in the State of New York existed by violence and lived by discrimination. . . . By secret rates and deceiving their competitors as to what their rates were and by evading all laws of trade these manufacturers exist."[31] Al Capone had a similar rationalization in the twenties, and his attitude toward laws was the same.

After Tony Camonte's lawyer gets him out

of jail with a writ of habeas corpus in **Scarface,** the movie gangster tells him to get lots of "those writs of 'Hocus Pocus' " J.P. Morgan expressed the same attitude toward laws when he told his lawyer, who warned him that a plan might be illegal, "Well, I don't know as I want a lawyer to tell me what I cannot do. I hire him to tell me how to do what I want to do."[32] Vanderbilt was more blunt: "What do I care about the law. H'ain't I got the power?" Robber Barons also used politicians as a club for beating down rivals and organized workers. The captains of capital meant politicians to be their agents. Railroad magnate Collis Huntington wrote to a henchmen, "We should be very careful to get a U.S. Senator from California that *will be disposed to use us fairly,* and then *have the power to help us. . . .*"[33]

The Senate at this time—the late nineteenth century—was known as "the Millionaires' Club," and according to one congressman, "The House of Representatives was like an auction room where more valuable considerations were disposed of under the speaker's hammer than in any other place on earth."[34] In both political parties, according to one contemporary account, "the source of power and cohesive force is the desire for office and for office as a means of gain."[35] Most politicians clearly understood their duties and the special interest functions they were meant to perform. When a greenhorn Republican prosecuting attorney began a suit against Standard Oil in Ohio, Senator Mark Hanna quickly filled him in on the rules when he wrote, "You have been in politics long enough to know that no man in public office owes the public anything."[36] In California the Railroad Barons made it so clear to whom politicians owed their allegiance that "petty job seekers in their naiveté had gone to railroad headquarters believing simply that the state capitol was really located

there."[37] Problems arose when competitive bribery drove up the price per legislator, as in the bidding for the New York legislature between the Erie Ring and Vanderbilt, or when politicians went into business for themselves. Robber Barons sought "men in office who will not steal but who will not interfere with those who do."[38]

In the first gangster film, **The Musketeers of Pig Alley** (1912), which was made in the wake of a scandal involving corrupt city officials, a mysterious hand gives the Snapper Kid a wad of money after the title card reading "Links in the System." (In most prints of **Musketeers** this scene is missing.) The Robber Baron legacy of political corruption has been depicted in gangster films ever since, and it has been regularly attacked by the censors as offensive. The examiners for the New York Motion Picture Commission, after viewing the 1928 film **Me Gangster,** ordered the removal of one title that read, "Before I was nineteen, graft and crooked politics had made Pop a big power in the district," and demanded that a title reading, "No more work for me now—I've got a politician's job" be changed to "Good news. A politician's got me a real job."[39] And most of the twenty-five changes the censors ordered in **The Racket** concerned gangsters bribing police and public officials, and fixed elections. Robber Barons, like movie gangsters, kept politicians well- paid, so that, as one offending title in **The Racket** put it, "Government of the professionals—by the professionals—and for the professionals—shall not perish from the earth!"[40]

The Robber Barons began to build their empires by controlling transportation. They achieved their ultimate success and political influence through financial control. At age thirteen or fourteen, Rockefeller believed that "it was a good thing to let the money be my slave and not make myself a slave to

"The Bosses of the Senate"

money."[41] Bankers like J.P. Morgan entered corporate management of railroads to protect investments and loans that were threatened by the uncertainty of competition. The "money trust" combined rival companies and directed corporate policies solely on the basis of their financial interests, restricting output and growth, and causing bankruptcy when advantageous. These private bankers considered themselves more powerful than the federal government, to which they loaned money. When Teddy Roosevelt made threatening gestures toward the Morgan banking interests in 1902, J.P. Morgan wrote him, "If we have done anything wrong, send your man up to my man and they can fix it up."[42] The free enterprise system produced,

with governmental aid, financial trusts devoted to their own enrichment and indifferent to the needs and demands of the public. This Robber Baron achievement was a model for Al Capone, the National Crime Syndicate, and the aspiration of many a movie gangster.

This Robber Baron legacy of financial control is re-echoed in **The Little Giant.** Bugs Ahearn decides he wants a legitimate racket and is asked to join the board of directors of a bank who say they can use a man with his experience. Bugs is pleased and tells them, "Well, thanks, well, I, I, hardly know what to say. I, I, I want to thank all you gentlemen for letting me in on this. I appreciate your sacrifice, and at the same time I ain't overlookin' that it's a great chance for me! I wanna thank you for all that you've done on my behalf. I'll guarantee you plenty of service." By 1904 Woodrow Wilson noted a new machine disrupting America's garden of innocence:

Most men are individuals no longer as far as their business, its activities or its moralities, is concerned. They are not units but fractions; with their individuality and independence of choice in matters of business they have lost their individual choice within the field of morals. They must do what they are told to do or lose their connection with modern affairs. They are not at liberty to ask whether what they are told to do is right or wrong. They cannot get at the men who ordered it—have no access to them. They have no voice of counsel or protest. They are mere cogs in a machine which has men for its parts. And yet there are men with whom the whole choice lies. These are men who use it with an imperial freedom of design, whose power and whose individuality overtop whole communities. There is more individual power than ever, but those who exercise it are few and formidable and the mass of men are mere pawns in the game.[43]

"The Rising of the Ursurpers and the Sinking of the People"

The Robber Baron view of corporate responsibility to the public was most clearly expressed by Vanderbilt when he shouted, "The public be damned!" The gangster's "no" to the "yes" of American optimism was also rooted in the angry public's reaction to the Robber Barons: "the famous optimism of the pioneers tended to subside slowly and heavily while it was reported in the western press everywhere along the lines of Huntington, Gould or Villard that 'nothing is heard but one continuous murmur of complaint.' "[44]

Some of the Robber Barons displayed their power and wealth lavishly. Vanderbilt's mansions rivaled those of European aristocracy in their ornateness. Jim Fisk drunkenly threw his money around, wore flashy clothes, and had the most ornate carriage and opera house in New York. He liked to parade his clothes, car, and women on Fifth Avenue or Broadway as the crowds gaped.[45] Not all the Robber Barons were given to gaudy displays. Some were modest and religious. One of Fisk's partners, Jay Gould, led a puritanical private life and "disapproved of his partner's lavish style. . . ." The other partner, Daniel Drew, who held "the honest people of the world to be a pack of fools," sped to church to pray after completing "unusually lucky" deals, or gave churches money "to ease his conscience."[46] Religious respectability was to become a front for Prohibition gangsters and publicity-shy syndicate men who had kept their lives as modest-appearing as possible. The movie gangsters followed a flashier mode. In **Scarface** Tony Camonte shows his newly furnished apartment and new clothes to the girl he wants to impress. He asks her, "How do you like it?" "Kind of gaudy," she answers. "Ain't it, though!" replies the pleased gangster.

Jim Fisk and Tony Camonte enjoyed life more than most movie gangsters or Robber Barons, for whom the monomaniacal pursuit of power and wealth assumed a compulsive, repressed, and joyless tone. Banker James Stillman "confessed that he knew not how to enjoy himself. 'I have never in all my life done anything I wanted,' he said, 'and cannot now.' "[47] For Rockefeller, life was "work by day and worry by night, week in and week out, month after month." And Cornelius Vanderbilt "was a victim of insomnia and indigestion. The jockey anxiety rode him with whip and spur. He was in constant peril of apoplexy. He could not take needful exercise by walking in the park for fear of being accosted by tramps or insulted by socialist philosophers."[48]

Robber Barons and movie gangsters had glimpses of insight into how competitive individualism could function as an obstacle to the realization of human potential and a life of real meaning and satisfaction. Andrew Carnegie wrote in his diary, "to continue much longer overwhelmed by business cares and with most of my thoughts wholly upon the way to make more money in the shortest time, must degrade me beyond hope of permanent recovery."[49] In **The Little Giant,** Bugs Ahearn (played by Edward G. Robinson) wanted to quit the rackets:

"Say, you think I like to sweat and worry 24 hours a day; scheme, connive, play both ends against the middle, live on the edge of a volcano that's liable to blow up any minute?

"I suppose you think it's fun to spend your life waiting for some mug to spray you with a machine gun. Why, I can't go anywhere without a bodyguard. I'm always tense, coiled up like a spring, ready to duck the moment anybody flashes a rod. Everytime that I step into my car, get near a window, walk around the block, everytime somebody opens the door, I'm hunching in my shoulders waiting for that thunder. That's how I lived for the last ten years, and believe me, sister, I've had a bellyful!"

The movie gangster's Robber Baron ancestors embodied some basic qualities required by a society dominated by corporate industrial capital. Their personal qualities and methods of operation were mythically amplified by the movie gangsters during the Great Depression, when the society which the Robber Barons helped define began to appear criminally unjust to larger numbers of people. "Rico's career had been like a sky-rocket. Starting from the gutter and returning there," reads the final title in **Little Caesar.** Jim Fisk, like most of the Robber Barons, was still on top and even a popular figure when he was shot down by a man who had cheated him in love and business. His burial was one that would have pleased any movie gangster: "The funeral was splendid; the Ninth Regiment, followed by a great crowd, paraded in honor of the dead Robin Hood. A meteor of the financial skies had passed off into the darkness beyond."[50]

Jim Fisk's funeral

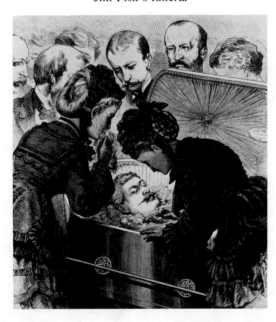

2

THE MYTH OF SUCCESS

Look at me! I got plenty. I got a house. I got a automobile. I got me a nice-a girl. (Burp) I got a-stomach trouble too! (Laughter)

Big Louie Costello in **Scarface**

The ladder of fortune

The legacy that the Robber Barons passed on through popular culture to the movie gangsters was embedded in a heritage that gave capitalism in America its rationale and mythology. The Gospel of Wealth and the Myth of Success which made up this heritage functioned as an apologia for private property and acquisitiveness, and as a badly kept promise of social mobility. The habits of thinking that shaped the heritage became a virtual creed that was broadcast by the economic, religious, political, and educational institutions of America in the late nineteenth century and was widely trumpeted by the organs of popular culture. Pre-eminent until the Great Depression, the creed of exalting wealth and success dominated the popular culture of industrial urban America and gave the gangster film plot its basic shape.

Deeply embedded in American culture, the roots of the Gospel of Wealth go back to the Puritan expressions of the Protestant Ethic. As Cotton Mather phrased it: "There are TWO CALLINGS to be minded by ALL CHRISTIANS. Every Christian has a General CALLING, which is, to Serve the Lord Jesus Christ, and save his own Soul, in the Services of RELIGION that are incumbent on all the Children of men. . . . But then, every Christian hath also a PERSONAL CALLING; or a *particular Employment* by which his usefulness, in his Neighborhood, is distinguished. . . . The CASE therefore now before us, is: WHAT IS THAT GOOD ACCOUNT, THAT A CHRISTIAN SHOULD BE ABLE TO GIVE OF HIS OCCUPATION? Or, How should a Christian be occupied in the Business of his PERSONAL CALLING, that he may give a good Account of it? A Christian should be able to give this Account, That he hath an occupation. . . . A Christian should be able to give a Good Account, not only, What is his occupation but also, What he is in his Occupation."

A Christian had to be engaged in steady gainful work "so he may glorify God by doing of good for others and getting of good for himself." The doctrine of calling gave worldly pursuits a religious significance. Since the Puritan doctrine of predestination made it impossible to know for certain if one was to be saved by God, the Calvinist tried to mitigate his anxiety by emphasizing worldly success as a sign of possible salvation. According to sociologist Max Weber, the Calvinist emphasis on industry, thrift, and sobriety led to an emphasis on acquisition as the best possible sign of God's grace. An ethos of acquisitiveness, maintains Weber, is the most important characteristic element of modern capitalism, in which "man is dominated by the making of money by acquisition as the ultimate purpose of his life."[1]

The Quakers, too, underscored the importance of a person's calling. "Business success could be regarded as a visible sign that one was indeed living 'in the light,' " William Penn told his children, "Diligence is a Virtue useful and laudable among Men: It is a discreet and understanding Application of one's Self to Business. . . . It is the Way to Wealth." Neither Puritan nor Quaker would have bluntly urged people to become wealthy as an end in itself, nor would they conclude that people were good because they were rich. Instead, the spirit of capitalism in America became manifest in a value structure which at once made a virtue of acquisition and emphasized those qualities particularly suitable to the making and keeping of money.[2]

Benjamin Franklin, whose business training was under the Quaker merchant Thomas Denham in Philadelphia, exemplified and amplified a secular version of the Protestant Ethic. In the 1757 article "The Way to Wealth," Franklin compiled the sayings of

Cotton Mather

Ben Franklin

Poor Richard that pertained to acquiring property through self-sufficiency, diligence, frugality, and remembering to ask heaven's blessing. The goal with which Franklin concluded *Advice to a Young Tradesman* was clear: "He that gets all he can honestly, and saves all he gets (necessary Expenses excepted) will certainly become RICH: if that Being who governs the World, to whom all should look for a Blessing on their honest Endeavors, doth not in his wise Providence otherwise determine."[3]

By the late nineteenth century, wealth became an end in itself. In the industrial age dominated by the movie gangsters' Robber Baron ancestors, the maniacal pursuit of wealth was creating an industrial society whose visible class distinctions raised some questions and doubts about democracy in

America. Although most of the industrial chieftains bothered to justify themselves only before investigating congressional committees, Andrew Carnegie felt compelled to combat adverse criticism in America and Europe, particularly after his corporation's bitter and murderous suppression of the Homestead Steel strike. Through such books as *Triumphant Democracy, The Gospel of Wealth,* and the *Empire of Business,* Carnegie sought to define democracy in terms of capitalism, explain away the exceedingly undemocratic distribution of wealth, and reconcile his material life of rampant acquisition with his religious upbringing and reform-minded Scottish ancestors. His motives are similar to those of other triumphant conservatives in the late nineteenth century who spread the Gospel of Wealth in boys' books,

Andrew Carnegie

sermons, and college classes to assuage poorer citizens' growing doubts and to justify industrial capitalism when faced with criticism, protests, and strikes by farmers and workers.

College presidents rushed to join in the defense and, as responsible Christian spokesmen, defined private property in terms of divine law.[4] According to Princeton's president, James McCosh, "God has bestowed upon us certain powers and gifts which no one is at liberty to take from us or to interfere with. All attempts to deprive us of them is theft. Under the same head may be placed all purposes to deprive us of the right to earn property or to use it as we see fit."[5] The God-given duty to acquire and defend property was to be sanctioned by governments. In fact, "Governments exist very largely—in the view of many, they exist solely—for the purpose of rendering this Service."[6] And if students missed these words from their college presidents, they got the same party line in their ethics classes. " 'By the proper use of wealth,' wrote D.S. Gregory, author of a textbook on ethics used during the 1880's in many American colleges, 'man may greatly elevate and extend his moral work. It is therefore his duty to seek to secure wealth for this high end, and to make a diligent use of what the Moral Governor may bestow upon him for the same end. . . . The moral Governor has placed the power of acquisitiveness in man for a good and noble purpose. . . .' "[7] The acquisition of private property was represented as a moral imperative. According to an 1868 treatise on ethics written by the president of Williams College,

"The Right to Property reveals itself through an original desire. The affirmation of it is early and universally made, and becomes a controlling element in civil society. . . . Without this society could not exist. . . . There could be no industry and no progress. It will be found too, historically, that the general well-being and progress of society has been in proportion to the freedom of every man to gain property in all legitimate ways, and to security in its possession. . . . The acquisition of property is required by love, because it is a powerful means of benefitting others. . . ."[8] Robber Barons were not ungrateful for this spirited academic defense of the sanctity of private property. " 'The Good Lord gave me my money,' said the faithful Baptist, John D. Rockefeller, to the first graduating class of the university which he had founded, 'and how could I withhold it from the University of Chicago?' "[9]

The pulpit also provided a useful forum for spreading the Gospel of Wealth. One of the most popular sermons of the Age of Enterprise was "Acres of Diamonds" by Philadelphia Baptist minister Russel H. Conwell. Six thousand times Conwell piously intoned: "to secure wealth is a honorable ambition, and is one great test of a person's usefulness to others. Money is power. Every good man and woman ought to strive for power, to do good with it when obtained. Tens of thousands of men and women get rich honestly. But they are often accused by an envious lazy crowd of unsuccessful persons of being dishonest and oppressive. I say, Get rich, get rich!"[10] Morality was reconciled with the hot-eyed pursuit of money through the concept of the Stewardship of Wealth.

Carnegie explained the moral obligation that his millions incurred: "This then is held to be the duty of the man of Wealth: First, to set an example of modest, unostentatious living, shunning display or extravagence; to provide moderately for the legitimate wants of those dependent upon him; and after doing so to consider all surplus revenues which come to him simply as trust funds, which he is called upon to administer, and strictly bound as a matter of duty to administer in the manner which, in his judgment, is best calculated to produce the most beneficial results for the community—the man of wealth thus becoming the mere agent and trustee for his poorer brethren, bringing to their service his superior wisdom, experience, and ability to administer, doing for them better than they would or could do for themselves." Carnegie regarded the Stewardship of Wealth as "the true antidote for the temporary unequal distribution of wealth, the reconciliation of the rich and the poor—a reign of harmony, another ideal differing, indeed, from that of the Communist in requiring only the further evolution of existing conditions, not the total overthrow of our civilization."[11]

During the Gilded Age, the Protestant Ethic was transformed into a Gospel of Wealth, which buttressed optimism with a morality rooted in private property and sanctioned by God. From the giddy heights of this Gilded Age, Bishop Lawrence of Massachusetts proclaimed, "In the long run, it is only to the man of morality that wealth comes. . . . Godliness is in league with riches. Material prosperity is helping to make the national character sweeter, more joyous, more unselfish, more Christlike. That is my answer to the question as to the relation of material prosperity to morality."[12]

The Gospel of Wealth was supported by a Social Darwinist litany that exalted the rugged individual in his battle to survive and gain riches. Herbert Spencer translated Darwin's theory of natural selection into a theory of social evolution that defined life as "a struggle for existence" in which "the survival of the fittest" would guarantee improvement of the race. Yale professor William Graham Sumner, characterized by Upton Sinclair as "a prime minister in the empire of plutocratic education," was the most influential advocate of this scientific justification of cutthroat business competition and corrupt politics. According to Sumner, evolutionary science—like God— was in league with riches:

The millionaires are a product of natural selection, acting on the whole body of men to pick out those who can meet the requirement of certain work to be done. . . . It is because they are thus selected that wealth—both their own and that entrusted to them—aggregates under their hands. . . . They may fairly be regarded as the naturally selected agents of society for certain work. They get high wages and live in luxury, but the bargain is a good one for society. There is the intensest competition for their place and occupation. This assures us that all who are competent for this function will be employed in it so that the cost of it will be reduced to the lowest terms.[13]

Carnegie eagerly embraced this "Law of Competition" and self-righteously stated that "whether the law be benign or not, we must say of it . . . it is here; we cannot evade it; no substitutes for it have been found; and while the law may sometimes be hard on the individual it is best for the race, because it ensures the survival of the fittest in every department. We accept and welcome, therefore, as conditions to which we must accommodate ourselves, great inequality of environment; the concentration of business, industrial and commercial, in the hands of the few; and the law of competition between these, as being not only beneficial, but essential to the future progress of the race."[14]

Another and even more pervasive gospel of capitalism was the Myth of Success. The promise of a rags-to-riches climb from obscure poverty to esteemed wealth was a myth that defined America as a democracy of economic equality. In such a society the individual was ultimately responsible for his or her economic condition, and the myth of success was the cultural road map for those destined for wealth, respectability, and status. Those who triumphed were awarded the distinction of being known as "self-made men."

The basic gangster film plot was patterned on the success myth. The movie gangster's social origins are depicted as working-class. Tom Powers in **Public Enemy** grows up in a working-class neighborhood and finds a job as a truck driver. Bugs Raymond in **Quick Millions** was also a truck driver and started his career as a paper boy. The success myth traditionally demanded that its heroes begin their careers humbly. Ben Franklin, "Having emerged from poverty and obscurity in which [he] was born and bred to a state of affluence and some degree of reputation in the world," wrote his autobiography for following generations who might find his success story "suitable to their own situations, and therefore fit to be imitated."[15] Orphans, bootblacks, newsboys, and other children of the street became success-story heroes as early as the 1830's, and the typical hero of the Horatio Alger novels is a newsboy, as in *Ragged Dick,* or a bootblack, as in *Mark the Matchboy.* In Alger's *Struggling Upward,* the hero begins his "boyhood of privation" as a janitor. "I was one of those sweepers myself," Carnegie told a college class in Pittsburgh. "I congratulate poor young men upon being born to that ancient and honorable degree which renders it necessary that they should devote themselves to hard work. . . . The partners' sons will not trouble you much, but look out that some

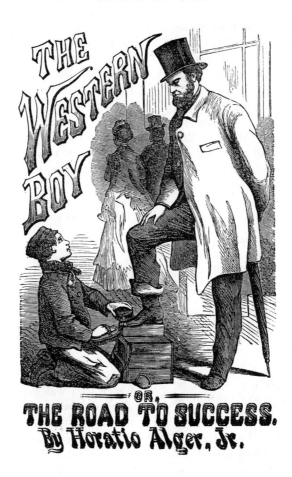

boys poorer, much poorer than yourselves, whose parents cannot afford to give them the advantages of a course in this institute, advantages which should give you a decided lead in the race—look out that such boys do not challenge you at the post and pass you at the grandstand. Look out for the boy who has to plunge into work direct from the common school and who begins by sweeping out the office. He is probably the dark horse that you had better watch.''[16]

The movie gangsters are constantly looking for opportunities ''to get up in the world''; as men on the make, they ceaselessly size up their employers. ''Aim high,'' advised Carnegie. ''I would not give a fig for the young man who does not already see himself the partner or the head of an important firm. Do not rest content as head clerk, or foreman, or general manager in any concern, no matter how extensive. Say to yourself 'my place is at the top.' *Be King in your dreams.*''[17] In **Scarface,** Tony Camonte seems to have followed this advice. He tells his pal Gino: ''This business is just waitin' for some guy to come and run it right, and I got ideas." "We're working' for Lovo, ain't we?" replies Gino. Tony fills him in: "Lovo! Who's Lovo? . . . just some guy that's a little bit smarter than Big Louie, that's all. Hey, that guy's soft. I could see it in his face. He gotta set-up, that's all, and we just gotta wait. Some day I'm gonna run the whole works!" In **Little Caesar,** Rico also sets his sights for the top. "Diamond Pete ain't so tough," Rico tells Otero; and, after taking over Diamond Pete's territory, he confides to Otero that even the Big Boy won't be number one much longer.

Starting poor and aiming high in a fiercely competitive environment was a success theme that characterized the lives of Robber Barons, movie gangsters, Prohibition racketeers, and the movie moguls who ran the studios. Harry "King" Cohn, who steered Columbia studios from "Poverty Row" to the big time, was described after his death as a "successful pirate" who "was very active as a young man, very ambitious; obviously he was going to get someplace."[18] Cohn started his success story as a delivery boy for a shoe store. Al Capone, according to a

On the road to success?

Chicago Internal Revenue collector, who figured the gangster could cash in for twenty million dollars, was another good success story candidate: "If he had only been honest, what a hero he would have made for a Horatio Alger tale!"[19] Capone's 1930 biography is suitably subtitled "The Biography of a Self-Made Man." In accordance with the Gospel of Wealth, it was very important to rise "from rags to riches."

One student of the self-made man in America argues that the typical Alger drama is basically a story of "rags to respectability."[20] The Horatio Alger success that most people associate exclusively with wealth is actually a popular simplification of a hero whose qualities make him an ideal employee rather than a millionaire executive. The typical Alger hero's rise is from working class to middle class rather than to the financial heights of millionaires. The movie moguls and gangsters were more ambitious than Alger's newsboys, but they also viewed respectability as an important ingredient in their formulas of success. One of the most important iconographic scenes in the gangster genre is the one in which the gangster is fitted for new clothes or is trying on a "monkey suit." The significance of this scene is the same as in an Alger story. "The most crucial event in the hero's life is his acquisition of a good suit. The good suit, which is usually presented to the hero by his patron, marks the initial step in his advancement, his escape from the dirty and ragged classes and his entry upon respectability."[21] "You could never picture me in overalls now, could you!?" Bugs Raymond asks his pal in **Quick Millions** as they admire their tuxedoed images in the mirror on their way to the opera.

Culture was another sign of respectability. Although book shelves could be a front for a revolving home bar in gangster movies, they could also contain books. Bugs Ahearn in **The Little Giant** goes so far as to read Plato, just as Alger heroes learned French or Latin. Bugs hums operatic arias, and lectures his girl friend and sidekick on the use of perspective in a modern painting he has just bought. His pal thinks the painting is a better example of a cocaine hallucination than art, while Bugs's girl thinks he's gone crazy. Undaunted, Bugs chases society people in Santa Barbara like any awe-struck Alger hero because "they're so cultured, so refined," until they prove to be crooked snobs.

Another respectable rung on the success ladder was to acquire a society woman through marriage. "If you have been promoted two or three times, you will form another partnership with the loveliest of her sex," advises Carnegie.[22] As Bugs Raymond, after successfully promoting himself several times, explains his interest in a debutante, "You know, goin' around with her gives me a lot of pres-tidge." "What?" asks his pal. "Front, you half-wit—Front!" Gangsters on the way up are constantly sloughing off girl friends who aren't respectable enough. When the gangster genre achieved its ultimate respectability with the censors by turning James Cagney into a G-man, the hero's final mark of social acceptance is to fall for a nurse who at first finds him vulgar, instead of a nightclub dancer who is his friend.

The success formula included fame along with respectability and wealth. In the gangster genre, another definitive scene is the success banquet in which a gangster is "honored by his friends." Little Caesar's ambition flares into a fiery determination to head for the big time after he reads about a banquet where "the Underworld pays its

respect to Diamond Pete Montana.'' All the gangsters wear evening clothes; testimonial speeches are given; the mobs are seated at long tables. The scene is pictorially identical with still photographs of corporation banquets, of East Coast society dinners, or of Colorado silver mine owners taken in the late nineteenth century. The scene is a celebration of the gangster's arrival in the world of wealth, prominence, and respectability, and the speeches refer to the social distances traveled. At one such testimonial dinner in **Quick Millions,** the gangster tells a full, cigar-puffing crowd:

''Why, this is one of the happiest moments in my life, havin' so many of our prominent citizens comin' here tonight: The honorable T.J. Hammond. Why I've know Tom since he was a walkin' delegate of the bricklayers union. (Laughter)

''And do I know Peter J. Madigan? Do I know 'im? Why, Pete gave me my first black eye. (Laughter)

''Larkin. Larkin over here. Why Ol' Cap Larkin used to help himself to the apples in front of my first produce market.

''Why, I used to spend all my nickels in Judge Albert's father's saloon, bless his soul!'' (Murmurs and laughter)

At Little Caesar's banquet, Flaherty the cop crashes the party to sarcastically tell Rico that he "likes to see you young fellas get up in the world." After the sour cop leaves, newspaper photographers ask if they can take a picture of the mobster on the rise. "Tell 'em to come on up," says Rico. "I want people to see this!" he tells another gangster, who warns him that it's a bad idea to attract too much attention. Newspaper notoriety was important in every gangster's rise. Rico runs out the next day to buy all the papers on the stand with an article and picture of his testimonial dinner. Golf, building dedications, top hats, and ornate interior decoration complete the image of success in gangster films. And charitable donations are a tip of the top hat to the stewardship of wealth; Bugs Raymond, following in the charitable footsteps of Capone and Carnegie, gives money to the newsboys' fund.

The ladder of success, from rags to riches and respectability, functioned as a promise of economic democracy that mythically defined America as an open, classless society. McGuffey's schoolbooks began the process of indoctrination early. Nearly all of American school-children were told by McGuffey's *Newly Revised Eclectic Second Reader:*

> Once or twice though you should fail,
>   Try, try Again;
> If you would, at last, prevail,
>   Try, try Again;

Immigrant children learning about America.

If we strive, it's no disgrace,
Though we may not win the race,
What should you do in that case?
    Try, try Again;
Time will bring you your reward,
    Try, try Again;
All that other folks can do,
Why, with patience, should not you:
Only keep this rule in view,
    Try, try Again.[23]

When they could read a little better, young readers were urged on in Horatio Alger books with such titles as *Strive and Succeed*

and *Struggling Upward*. If Alger's stories implicitly narrowed the horizons of mobility from lower to middle class by emphasizing the character traits of good employees and the importance of luck, respectability, and modest riches, other voices urged success-hungry readers to "aim high." College classes philosophized about millionaires, and popular magazines with titles such as *Success* kept on reminding readers of the goal. The myth of individual mobility in a fiercely competitive open society disguised the late nineteenth century industrial reality of an increasingly closed, stratified, and economically unequal society in which success required organization and cooperation of capitalists or workers. Even John D. Rockefeller admitted that individualism was becoming outmoded. How realistic was a poor boy's ambition to ascend to the top of America's corporate industry?

Economic historian William Miller questioned the usual image of American business leaders since the Civil War that emerged from history books. "That description is virtually always of the 'poor immigrant' or 'poor farm boy' who, barely entering his teens, first found work in the meanest of jobs, and 'fired by a passionate will to succeed,' rose from 'obscure origins' and 'from poverty to riches' mainly by dint of unflagging industry and resourcefulness.' In my analysis of 190 of the topmost American business leaders in the first decade of the twentieth century, however, poor immigrant and poor farm boys together are shown to have made up no more that three per cent of this group."[24] The other 97 per cent were white Anglo-Saxon Protestant men who came from high-status families. The mythical rags-to-riches success story that dominated American popular culture and education was a distinct exception to the rule of entrenched wealth that dominated the socioeconomic realities of corporate finance and industry in America at the time the first gangster film was made.

If the Alger success formula couldn't always point out the way to wealth, the story papers and dime novels suggested other possibilities. Factory workers and young readers were more likely to read this cheap and widely available literature than Carnegie's books. "As the robber-heroes are mostly grand-looking fellows, and all the ladies have white hands and splendid attire," worried the Reverend Jonathan B. Harrison,

after finding out what New England factory workers were reading in 1880, "it may be that some of the readers find hard work more distasteful because of their acquaintance with the gorgeous idlers and thieves, who, in these fictions, are always so much more fortunate than the people who are honest and industrious . . . and that people resort to it and feel a necessity for it in much the same way that others feel they must have whisky or opium."[25] In New York, where most of the dime novels were published, the crusader Anthony Comstock, who established the New York Society for the Suppression of Vice, attacked this popular literature in his book *Traps for the Young:* "The leading character in many, if not in the vast majority of these stories is some boy or girl who possesses usually some extraordinary beauty of countenance, the most superb clothing, abundant wealth, the strength of a giant, the agility of a squirrel, the cunning of a fox, the brazen effrontery of the most daring villain, and who is utterly destitute of any regard for the laws of God or man. Such a one is foremost among desperadoes, the companion and beau-ideal of maidens, and the high favorite of some rich person, who by his patronage and indorsement lifts the young villain into lofty positions in society, and provides liberally of his wealth to secure him immunity for his crimes. These stories link the pure maiden with the most foul and loathsome criminals."[26]

The most alarming threat of dime novel crime was an implicit recognition that the way to wealth did not follow the Alger mold. "What young man will serve an apprenticeship, working early and late, if his mind is filled with the idea that sudden wealth may be acquired by following the hero of the story? In real life, to begin at the foot of the ladder and work up, step by step, is the rule; but in these stories, inexperienced youth, with no moral character, take the foremost positions, and by trick and device, knife and revolver, bribery and corruption, carry everything before them, lifting themselves in a few short weeks to positions of ease and affluence."[27]

Although most middle-class spokesmen for the Gospel of Wealth and Myth of Success emphasized the importance of moral behavior in the pursuit of riches, the Robber Baron realities that dominated nineteenth century corporate industrial capitalism and the lurid promises of dime novel crime suggested that Henry James's "bitch-goddess success" was more a whore than a virgin.

The Gospel of Wealth and Myth of Success permeated American culture and virtually became a religion in Hollywood. "Our town worships success, the bitch goddess whose smile hides a taste for blood," wrote priestess/columnist Hedda Hopper. The gangster films were to become the passion plays that offered up abundant success in the plots and at the box office, and enough blood to keep the goddess happy.

Dime novel cover

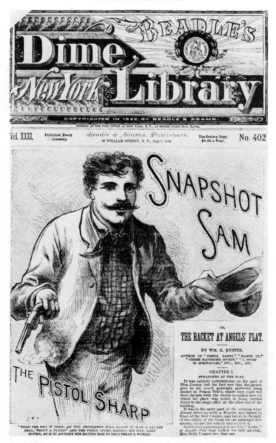

3

THE MAN OF THE CITY

The gangster is the man of the city, with the city's language and knowledge, with its queer and dishonest skills and its terrible daring, carrying his life in his hands like a placard, like a club. For everyone else, there is at least the theoretical possibility of another world—in that happier American culture which the gangster denies, the city does not really exist; it is only a more crowded and more brightly lit country—but for the gangster there is only the city; he must inhabit it in order to personify it: not the real city, but the dangerous and sad city of the imagination which is so much more important, which is the modern world.

Robert Warshow

The Naked City

The title card that begins **The Musketeers of Pig Alley** tells the audience that the story will take place in "New York's Other Side." From this very first title of its first significant film, the gangster genre went on to express the quality of life in urban America. The sights, sounds, smells, and language of the city define the texture of gangster films; the rapid pace of the genre's development and the action within each film reflect the bristling energy that is at the core of America's urban experience.

The city was the actual setting for the people who shaped the movie industry and who produced the gangster genre. The period of the gangster genre's rise and fall is one in which American culture experienced and recognized the growing pains of urbanization.

In the eyes of small-town and rural America the city was, in the words of William Jennings Bryan, "The enemy's country." Eastern city bankers fashioned their "cross of gold" to crucify America's yeoman farmers; the country men and women were lured into evil ways by the city's bright lights, big money, and easy virtue. These brick, steel, and glass marketplaces, which seemed to be inhabited mostly by foreigners, bankers, and thieves, housed a civilization that directly threatened the identity of America as a garden republic. Bryan warned urban financiers not to tamper with agrarian America: "Burn down your cities and leave our farms, and your cities will spring up again as if by magic, but destroy our farms and the grass will grow on the streets of every city in the country."[1]

Why was the city so threatening? According to Josiah Strong, a Protestant clergyman alarmed by "the possible future and present crisis of our country" in 1885.

It is the city where wealth is massed; and here are the tangible evidences of it piled many stories high. Here the sway of mammon is widest and his worship, the most constant and eager. Here are luxuries gathered—everything that dazzles the eye, or tempts the appetite; here is the most extravagant expenditure. Here, alas, is the *congestion* of wealth. The severest Dives and Lazarus are brought face to face; here in sharp contrast, are the ennui of surfeit and the desperation of starvation, the rich are richer and the poor are poorer, in the city than elsewhere; and, as a rule, the greater the city the greater are the riches of the rich and the poverty of the poor. Not only does the proportion of the poor increase with the growth of the city, but their condition becomes more wretched. . . . Is it strange that such conditions arouse a blind and bitter hatred of our social system?[2]

Economic inequality shaped city space into verticals of high and low, rich and poor. Up and down went the buildings; up and down went the stock market; up and down went the story of the gangster genre.

The Snapper Kid, the first movie gangster (in **Musketeers of Pig Alley**), never got above street level, but Thomas Ince's **The Gangster and the Girl,** made two years later (1914), choreographs the action up and down fire escapes and stairways and across rooftops. The naked steel beams of neighboring skyscrapers in construction draw strong vertical lines that soar on upward, past the robberies and shootouts between gangsters and cops, toward the gangster's penthouse future.

The gangster genre emerged at the same time as the city of towers in the history of American architecture. Preceded by the Flatiron Building in 1901 and the Singer Tower in 1907, The Woolworth Building in 1913 gave New York and America "The first effective tower form skyscraper."[3]

The movies pictured the mythic gangster's career as a struggle to get to the top of these urban towers. The gangster in **Public Enemy** begins his career on the street in front of a saloon. As a boy, he gets as high as the

The Flatiron Building

Wall Street

second floor of a department store, only to be chased back down to the street by a cop. When Rico first joins Sam Vettori's gang in **Little Caesar,** he finds the gang hanging out a little higher up, above the cheap restaurant/nightclub which is their front. At the height of his success, Bugs Raymond in top hat attends the dedication of a skyscraper, the construction of which he has successfully turned into a racket. The image is the highest vantage point the genre offers from the point of view of the gangster. Bugs realizes that the top floors of office buildings are exclusive places. After he has installed himself in a swank office in the top floor of the John Stone Building Corporation, Bugs tells the gang he will now act as their respectable front, and loftily informs his lieutenant, "Oh, Nails, I wouldn't bring the boys up to my office anymore if I were you. I'll drop down and see you fellas sometime."

The more popular the genre became, the

Broadway

Immigrants arrive

higher up the characters went. In **Underworld,** the first major gangster film of the 1920's, the gangster's hideout is up a few flights in a tenement building. In **Scarface,** when the genre was at the height of its popularity, a similar hideout is in a taller, more respectable building, from which we can look down on the surrounding city.

As the Western hero knows every tree and landscape of his domain, the gangster knows the alleyways and byways of the underworld. His familiarity with the bars, restaurants, shoeshine stands, pool halls, bowling alleys, and garages defines his mastery of the city. He knows which fruit store or flower shop is a front, and what the criminal reality is behind the facade. The gangster knows the urban landscape so well because he grew up there.

The city that the gangster came to represent was the ''enemy's country'' to rural Americans in large part because it was populated by ''foreigners.'' At the time of the first gangster film, 75 per cent of New

Orchard Street

York's population was first- or second-generation immigrants, and the waves of immigration from the 1880's to the mid-1920's appeared to native Americans to be alarmingly different from the predominantly German, Irish, and Scandinavian peoples who preceded them. Hordes of Italians and Jews from Eastern Europe assaulted America's white Anglo-Saxon Protestant self-image.[4] Henry James complained that he felt "a sense of dispossession of the luxury of such close and sweet and whole national consciousness as that of the Switzer and the Scots . . ." when, after twenty years, he returned to New York, "with its hodge podge of racial ingredients."[5]

The gangster genre began appropriately in the Lower East Side of New York, where it was filmed on location and previewed for a local audience. Although the main characters are not immigrants, Pig Alley itself teems with Russian Jews as much as any *stetl* (ghetto) within the Russian Pale. Gangster films since have remained thoroughly permeated with the flavor of immigrant life.

The movie gangsters were pictured mainly as second-generation immigrants, with names like Tony Camonte, Caesar Enrico Bandello, Sam Vettori, Nails Nathan, Matt Doyle, Tommy Doyle, Dan Quigley, Louie Ricarno, Ricca, Palmera, Greener Kaufman, Maxey Campo, Joe Forziati, and Dominic Valetti. Irish, Jewish, and primarily Italian characters who are usually short and/or dark-complected fill out the casts. European accents are unsystematically sprinkled throughout the dialogue of gangster films, and occasionally characters speak in Italian or Yiddish, as in *Mayor of Hell* (1933) or *Taxi* (1932).

The first meal that Rico eats in **Little Caesar** is spaghetti. "That's-a-nice," comments Tony Camonte when he inhales the aroma of the same dish served to him in his favorite restaurant; the last food that Louie Ricarno eats before he's killed in **The Doorway to Hell** is an order of "Delicatessen stuff."

The warm-hearted immigrant mother with a thick accent and a strong moral fiber is the central character in the gangster's family. She serves up the cabbage with her good cheer and faithful assurances to the neighbors that "my Tommy's a good boy" in **Public Enemy;** in **Scarface,** Mama serves spaghetti with anxious advice to the gangster's sister, Francesca, to stay away from him "because he's-a no good." Or, in **Little Caesar,** there is a highly emotional scene in which a worried mother reminds her soon-to-be killed gangster son of his religious upbringing as a choir boy. When a church does appear in a gangster film, it is Catholic—not Protestant—and the priests are always Irish. There are other colorful vignettes that accent the cinematic flavor of urban immigrant life,

such as the organ grinder and monkey in **Scarface** and "Tony Maggio's Fresh Vegetables" stand in *The Widow From Chicago* (1930).

A tone of nostalgic familiarity permeates the portrayal of immigrant life in gangster films. The tone is appropriate because the origins of the movie industry, organized crime, and the gangster genre are intimately interwoven in this urban immigrant experience. Families of movie moguls and the syndicate racketeers came from the ghettos of Grodno, Warsaw, Minsk and Kiev, and were molded by their experiences in the ghettos of American cities.

In the early 1930's, while a Russian Jew from Grodno (Meyer Lansky) was organizing the biggest crime syndicate in American history with other immigrants of Italian and Jewish descent, a Polish Jew from Krasnashiltz (Jack Warner) was producing gangster films in which an Irish movie star (James Cagney) was acting before cameras operated by Italian immigrants (Sol Polito and Tony Gaudio).

In 1883 Ben Warner, the shoemaker father of the Warner brothers, had left Poland when he received a letter that advised him: "You must come to Baltimore. Everyone wear shoes here. This is the land of riches and the streets are running with gold." Upon arriving, Warner found that his friend was doing piecework in a basement cellar below streets running with mud, not gold; but the wages of two dollars a week were "Better than Krasnashiltz," so he got a skid row room, opened a small shoe repair shop, and hung out his sign: "SHOES REPAIRED WHILE YOU WAIT."[6] He sent for the rest of the family; the two girls worked at home, and Harry and Albert worked in the shoe shop, sold newspapers, and shined shoes on neighborhood street corners.

Twenty-seven years after the Warner

family arrived, Max and Yetta Suchowljan-sky fled Russia from persecution and seized the opportunities for modest improvement that America represented. At Ellis Island the impatient immigration officers shortened the name to Lansky and assigned their son Meyer an arbitrary birthdate of July Fourth.[7]

The children of these immigrant families patriotically adopted their new culture, and like the young William Fox, another immigrant, they were consumed with "the desperate urgency to get ahead, to climb out on top." Strive-and-succeed careers followed a blueprint defined by the Gospel of Wealth and the Myth of Success, which they absorbed directly in the streets or read in manuals that offered greenhorn immigrants advice on how to survive in America:

Hold fast, this is most necessary in America. Forget your past, your customs, and your ideals. Select a goal and pursue it with all your might. No matter what happens to you, hold on. You will experience a bad time but sooner or later you will achieve your goal. If you are neglectful, beware for the wheel of fortune turns quickly. You will lose your grip and be lost. A bit of advice for you:

Playground

Bandit's Roost

Do not take a moment's rest. Run, do, work and keep your own good in mind. . . . A final virtue if needed in America—called cheek. . . . Do not say ''I cannot; I do not know.''[8]

Hard work, long hours, and a variety of jobs were the reality of the lives of immigrant children in American cities. Little Will Fox left school at the age of eleven, and began working in a clothing factory to help his parents and to save half his young brothers and sisters from the death which took the other half. He peddled ''stove-blacking, 'lozengers,' umbrellas, sandwiches and pretzles, buffalo pans, and Weber and Fields jokes'' on his way to building a studio that was taken away from him by bankers in 1933.[9] The stakes were as high as the lives of one's family for these tenement entrepreneurs, and the competition was fierce.

Part of the nostalgia for the immigrant milieu in gangster films is the yearning for a sense of community that large, close-knit families could provide in the city. ''Despite all its loneliness and primitive equipment the Warner home was a happy one. All the children went to work as soon as they were old enough—selling papers, shining shoes, running errands, weeding gardens, doing anything that would earn a dollar or two. My father worked sixteen to eighteen hours a day and, like the rest of us, he put his earnings into a common family fund. . . . Yet with all our poverty, there was laughter for the young ones and music and togetherness.''[10]

Stale beer dive below Bandit's Roost

The togetherness of New York's Lower East Side was also a question of high population density—in 1890 as high as 336,429, and 522 persons per acre in the most heavily crowded tenth, eleventh, and thirteenth wards of New York.[11] Waves of immigration pushed the population density even higher during the next thirty years. Henry James remarked that "the scene hummed with a human presence beyond any I had every faced."[12] The poorest and most dense wards were also the haunts of criminals, where police kept them concentrated to watch them and keep them away from the rich. Jacob Riis was alarmed by the way in which crime seemed to be woven into the very fabric of tenement life, but this association of crime and poverty was simply the most visible one.

The shame of the cities, according to Lincoln Steffens, was that from top to bottom, cities were in fact governed according to an ethic of criminality that obscured the difference between right and wrong. At the bottom, immigrant voters in the most dense wards provided Tammany politicians with a power base which they used to dispense necessary services, award permits, extend bail and pardons, control pesky building and health inspectors, and make millions in graft. The machine politicians used and demanded liberal bribes to maintain their power, along with occasional help from gangs of thugs. A Russian Jewish immigrant who had been forced into a system of bribery by Tsarist officials, enforced by Cossacks, found the same system at work in American cities. "To the peddler the first lesson in Americanism was to placate 'the brass button' whenever possible, 'to come to Limerick,' and 'five dollars protection money for the policeman' was the recognized business fee."[13] One Tammany leader, George Washington Plunkett, frankly proclaimed in 1905 that his business was a matter of:

"An honest graft, and I'm an example of how it works. I might sum up the whole thing by sayin': I seen my opportunities and I took 'em.

Just let me explain by examples. My party's in power in the city, and it's goin' to undertake a lot of public improvements. Well, I'm tipped off, say, that they're going to lay out a new park at a certain place. I see my opportunity and I take it. I go to that place and I buy up all the land I can in the neighborhood. Then the board of this or that makes its plan public, and there is a rush to get my land, which nobody cared particular for before. Ain't it perfectly honest to charge a good price and make a profit on my investment and foresight? Of course it is. Well, that's honest graft."[14]

When "William Fox, at the age of ten foreshadowing the great captain of industry, tried to send out a group of younger lozenge peddlers through Central Park they were arrested and warned by the judge to 'Go home and keep out of the parks'. . . . Little Will went home and after that he kept out of the parks—when the police were looking."[15] Later on, in his fight with trusts, Fox learned how to work with Tammany politicians, who controlled not only the parks but also the police and municipal regulations pertaining to the exhibition of movies.

Kids like Lucky Luciano, Meyer Lansky, Jack Warner, or Harry Cohn could not hope to enter Irish-controlled politics or the hauling, manufacturing, and large-scale commerce controlled by other longer-established immigrants. So they looked for other niches. They found that crime and show business were available avenues to success. Sometimes the future movie moguls became young criminals. Harry Cohn sold "hot" furs and hustled pool and bowling. He and young Will Fox, dodging the cops in the park, were fair game for what Plunkett described as "dishonest graft—blackmailing gamblers, saloonkeepers, disorderly people, etc."[16] For many young immigrants, the only way to avoid harassment by the police or other practitioners of "dishonest graft" was to join a gang—hopefully, one with Tammany connections.

There were large street gangs in New York as early as the 1830's, with names like Roach Guards, Plug Uglies, Bowery Boys, and Dead Rabbits, who stormed out of Bowery and Five Points saloons to battle each other and whoever else could be persuaded to fight. They led the anti-draft riots of 1863 to murder blacks and battle troops, who had to use artillery to re-take the city after a week. By 1885, it was estimated that the metropolis contained at least 30,000 men who owed allegiance to the gang leaders and through them to the political leaders of Tammany Hall.[17]

The gangs made their living by smashing ballot boxes, fighting, murder, robbery, and

Headquarters of the Whyo Gang

Some famous members of the Whyo gang (*left to right*): Red Rocks Farrell, Googy Corcoran, Slops Connolly, Piker Ryan, Bull Hurley, Dorsey Doyle, Mike Lloyd, Big Josh Hines, Baboon Connolly

looting. They were numerically strongest around 1900, when the Five Points gang and the Eastmans could each muster about 1,200 fighters, if necessary, but their criminal activities were limited, and they were tightly controlled by Tammany.[18]

Gangster films with a sociological conscience have shown how slum kids were quick to become gang members. As depicted in **Public Enemy,** the boys hang out at the Red Oaks Social Club, circa 1909. They gamble, listen to bawdy songs, and fence stolen goods. In *Mayor of Hell,* the gang works a protection racket in parked cars, knocks over a candy store, and pitches pennies to pass the time; later they're arrested for assaulting a storekeeper. In the gangster films of the late 1930's—**Angels With Dirty Faces, Dead End,** and **Angels Wash Their Faces** (1939)—the youth gangs move into the foreground of the genre, and films starring the East Side Kids or Dead End Kids formed a veritable sub-genre with its comic counterpart in the Our Gang comedies.

There was nothing funny about youth gangs as far as Jacob Riis was concerned. In a 1902 sequel to *How the Other Half Lives* entitled *The Battle With the Slum,* he devotes a chapter to "The Genesis of the Gang" in an effort to describe how gangs were an obvious product of the slum environment of the city. A typical gang member "was born in a tenement in that section where the Gilder Tenement House commission found 324,000 living out of sight and reach of a green spot of any kind, and where sometimes the buildings—front, middle, and rear, took up ninety-three percent of all the space in the block."[19]

For a slum boy, the traditional social forces of family, school, church, and playground were replaced by a street environment that "taught him gambling as its first lesson, and stealing as the next. The two are never far apart. From shooting craps behind the 'cops' back to filching from the grocer's stock or plundering a defenseless peddler is only a step. There is in both the spice of law-breaking that appeals to the shallow ambition of the street as heroic." The youngster "came naturally to accept as his neutral horizon the headlines in his penny paper and the literature of the dare-devil-dan-the-death-dealing-monster-of-dakota order, which comprise the ordinary aesthetic equip-

The Montgovery Guards

ment of the slum.''[20] Riis notes that, as the gang grows, ''There arises in the lawless crowd a leader, who rules with his stronger fists and his readier wit. Around him the gang crystallizes and what he is it becomes. He may be a thief, like David Meyer, a report of whose doings I have before me. He was just a bully, and, being the biggest in his gang, made others steal for him and share the 'swag' or take a licking. But that was unusual. Ordinarily the risk and the swag are distributed on a more democratic principle.''[21]

The equal division of loot and risk gave street gangs the democratic camaraderie that characterized movie gangs as the genre developed. Gangs came to represent a brotherhood that every other aspect of urban existence seemed to deny. And the gang tradition was one experience that a movie mogul could point to with pride. Jack Warner reflected that ''when Warner Brothers pioneered the gangster picture in the early thirties and thereafter made a fortune regularly bumping off Humphrey Bogart, Paul Muni, Edward G. Robinson, and James Cagney, some of the critics subtly suggested that perhaps I had once been a mobster myself. As a matter of fact I was. . . . I don't think my father ever knew that I was a member of the Westlake Crossing Gang in Youngstown, a teen-age mob led by a junior Dillinger whose name was Toughy McElvey. I survived a couple of rumbles with a rival gang in which we belted one another with our fists or threw stones that never hit anyone. Toughy eventually vanished from the scene—perhaps he turned into a Hollywood agent—and the gang broke up.''[22]

The experience of the street gang was for the head of Warner Brothers studio the equivalent of a politician's log cabin childhood in the mythology of America.

The Short Tail Gang

4

THE BIRTH OF THE GENRE

In my mind I was satisfied that the system then in operation was wrong, and that the proper social system of the world should be socialistic. I despised both capital and capitalists . . . then came the beginning of my savings, and finally in my penny bank I found myself one day the possessor of $10. in change, with which I opened my bank account. . . . I knew that if I had $10. the proper thing for me to do was not to hide it in the bank but to divide it with my friends. Instead I kept adding to this account, until I had $100. in the bank—and to me that $100. looked like a large percentage of the capital of the world. Afterward I couldn't make as fine an address from the soapbox. The things that I used to say from this soapbox were contrary to what I was practicing and the larger my savings grew the further I was getting away from my Socialistic principles.

William Fox

The movie industry's humble origins

The first twenty-five years of the movie industry were the beginnings of a success story worthy of any gangster film. Early business prosperity was followed by fierce and violent competition leading to an attempt to monopolize production and distribution, the beginnings of a dependence on bankers, and new efforts toward monopolization. The plots and tone of gangster movies were infused with the history of the industry that produced them.

Movies offered a few people the possibility of a rise from rags to riches and respectability. The spirit of Horatio Alger permeated the industry. Douglas Fairbanks "got a job as an order clerk on Wall Street with the idea of becoming a king of finance."[1] Adolph Zukor wrote of Mary Pickford: "There is no doubt about her tremendous drive for success and the cash-register nature of a segment of her brain. I am convinced that Mary could have risen to the top in United States Steel, if she had decided to be a Carnegie instead of a movie star."[2]

By 1918 little Mary was raking in a million dollars a year. Zukor himself rose "from a penny arcade to a skyscraper in Times Square." According to one historian of the film industry, the immigrant rags-to-riches stories were colorful, but.

The truth about Zukor is far more interesting—and significant, as a lesson in the ways of our civilization—than the far-fetched legends concerning him. The decade in which Zukor was learning what makes the wheels go round was the famous "trust era" and trusts were the most popular subject of contemporary discussion. Trust busting politicians raged at Rockefeller, Duke, Ryan, Havemeyer, Harriman, and other "malefactors of great wealth," calling on the Federal government to send them to prison. The muckraking magazines and the newspapers regularly attacked and exposed the iniquitous monopolies of illegal combinations. The government responded with a series of anti-trust lawsuits that acquired the popularity of sporting events, but a mind much less keen than Zukor's could not fail to observe that the prosecutions invariably came slowly to a common termination in the courts; the trusts were torn apart, "the eggs were unscrambled," "the octopus was cut to pieces," but no "malefactor of great wealth" ever got near a jail door.[3]

The origins of the movie industry were modest. Viewers paid a penny for a private "peep show" in a Kinetoscope cabinet that ran fifty-foot novelty films produced and patented by Edison and which were sold to penny arcade owners for prices ranging from ten to twenty-five dollars. Competition began when the Biograph Company quickly patented a camera that used a film and a cabinet viewer they called the Mutascope. Peep shows proliferated and remained the principal way by which moving pictures were viewed until 1900. These penny arcade origins were as humble as one could hope for in an American success story.[4]

Until 1902 projected movies were featured by vaudeville houses only when owners used them to break a performers' strike. The movies proved popular in themselves, and "before long the vaudeville trust declared the motion picture to be its surest weapon against 'the dissolution, bankruptcy and humiliation' engendered by the strike."[5] When the strike was over, vaudeville owners sold their projectors to penny arcade owners, who had found peep shows so lucrative that they were anxious to try projecting films. In 1902 an arcade owner, Thomas J. Tally, made money when he turned his Los Angeles arcade into an auditorium and showed movies exclusively; he charged ten cents and advertised his theater in the Los Angeles *Times* as "The Electric Theater. For Up-To-Date High Class Motion Picture Entertainment Especially for Ladies and Children."

Automatic one-cent vaudeville, interior.

Another promoter, George Hale, built a theater in a train coach and showed pictures of landscapes taken from the rear platform of trains. After a successful opening as a side show at the St. Louis Exposition, Hales Tours traveled the country, earning Mr. Hale two million dollars in two years. The movie business was taking off by the end of 1903, as audiences clamored for more pictures, and entrepreneurs began to realize that the movies represented a good opportunity for a fast buck.

Every branch of the fledgling industry seemed to promise profits. Take distribution, for example. In 1902 exhibitors bought their films directly from manufacturers or from independent jobbers who carried the films and catalogues around. Film distribution began in America when two ''Photografters and Mug Artists,'' as the Miles brothers called themselves, realized they could rent films to exhibitors at one-fourth to one-half the purchase price, and also pay manufacturers higher prices for a large variety of pictures. The manufacturers could concentrate on production instead of marketing, produce more films, and ask higher prices. Exhibitors were happy to pay lower prices and show more pictures to growing audiences. Other exchanges quickly sprang up, so that by 1907 one hundred exchanges distributed films in thirty-five key cities.[6]

The snowball of success rolled on. The exchanges further stimulated exhibition, and entrepreneurs tried to match increased earnings with more impressive surroundings designed to attract even larger crowds. In 1905, John P. Harris and Harry Davis outfitted an empty store in Pittsburgh with discarded opera furnishings and added piano accompaniment to the pictures. They called this impressive venture the "nickelodeon." By 1908, 8,000 to 10,000 nickelodeons were raking in nickels across the country and running from morning until midnight. The nickelodeons were situated in working-class

Nickelodeon

First-run theater

neighborhoods and the poorer shopping areas in the cities; the moving pictures were as yet unacceptable to the middle and upper classes.[7] To attract wealthier audiences, exhibitors began to build houses that were more fashionable, comfortable, and above all, much larger. The nickelodeons seated 100 to 200 persons per show and were often stuffy, noisy, and uncomfortable. The new theaters were built with two floors and richer furnishings, and exhibitors began to take greater care in selecting the music and films. These "first-run" theaters, as they came to be known, seated from 1,800 to 3,000 customers, who paid higher prices than in the neighborhood nickelodeons. They soon dominated the industry with "selected pictures for selected audiences."[8]

Profits were reinvested as production costs soared. The Kalem Film Company, for example, began manufacturing pictures with only $600 in 1905, and within three years the small company was making a profit of $5,000 per week, with production costs running at $200 per picture. According to Zukor, one-reel pictures cost from a few hundred to a

Vitagraph Studios: Filming three stories at once

thousand dollars when he made the first five-reel feature film in America, for an estimated budget of $40,000 to $50,000. Production of features soon leveled off at $10,000 to $20,000 per picture.[9] Such large financial demands sent the movie moguls to the banks for additional capital. Zukor went to Kuhn, Loeb and Company to request a loan of $10 million: "My associates held that the request for so large a sum was preposterous. I pointed out that if we got it, motion pictures would be regarded as an important industry. A request for only five million dollars, I argued, might be rejected by Kuhn, Loeb and Company on the ground that the firm dealt only in larger sums."[10] The bankers were suitably impressed with the profits, ranging from $40,000 to $60,000 per feature picture; Kuhn, Loeb and Company loaned Zukor the money and entered the movie business.

By 1918 the production, distribution, and exhibition of motion pictures was a successful enough industry to attract a number of bankers. The whole industry, according to one participant, represented investments of several hundred million dollars and gave employment to 100,000 people, but the era of bank domination lay in the future.[11]

Success in the movie industry demanded that entrepreneurs develop a mentality common to that of Robber Barons and gangsters. "Lewis Selznick used to say that each fellow was 'smarter' than the others, and he describes his own victories as triumphs in 'outsmarting' his competitors. It was a time of clever, cunning, daring operations. The plain undecorated truth about Zukor is that he persistently 'outsmarted' all other players of the game."[12]

According to a 1931 biography of movie mogul Carl Laemmle, the movie game at the time of the first gangster film was such that "one had to be hardy, alert, shrewd, to stand the racket at all."[13] Terry Ramsaye described the situation as "The Lawless Film Frontier" in the first comprehensive history of American movies: "The progressing outposts of the screen have often been established by enterprising gentry operating in splendid swashbuckling disregard of established codes in other business. . . . In the newly discovered world of the screen there was no law."[14]

The situation didn't change when laws were passed. Films were frequently "duped," or copied by exchanges and then distributed as original productions. In 1907 the *Moving Picture World* warned that "the number of copied films which are being offered for sale as originals is increasing." Exchanges further cheated exhibitors by sending badly damaged or wrong prints. One exchange advertised its honesty by reminding exhibitors: "If you are held up in the streets you lose your purse, but if you are held up by misleading methods of advertising, inexperienced shipping clerks, poor selections of films and songslides, you will lose your entire business."[15]

Exhibitors, in turn, found ways of cheating the exchanges through such practices as bicycling prints from one theater to another for different showings while paying for a showing only in one theater. As in other industries, the largest concerns used these conditions as a pretext to fashion a monopoly.

Jeremiah Kennedy, who ran the Biograph Studios, led the move to form a trust. Kennedy was a man of the Robber Baron mold. Like Jay Gould, Kennedy began his career as a surveyor. He learned the ropes working for a railroad, and he rose to success as an engineer and an executive whose skill lay in re-organizing corporations, among them one of Jay Gould's railroads. He was also adept at liquidating failing businesses for banking interests. Kennedy entered the movie industry as a collect-or-liquidate man for the Empire Trust Company, which was quite worried about a long overdue interest payment of $200,000 on a loan to the Biograph Film Company. Kennedy took over Biograph, and instead of liquidating he re-organized the company and began implementing a scheme to form a movie trust. After a year of negotiations and frustrating dickering with the other largest film companies, Kennedy delivered the first of a number of ultimatums that became the trust's characteristic style. "Say!" he roared at an Edison lawyer the day before the trust agreement was signed, "if that agreement does not go through, just the way it is, without the change of one word in it, Biograph is going to bust this business wide open. . . . If we can't get together and control this business we will make a first class wreck of it—and we'll have it now!"[16]

Over 100 small film companies challenged the giants of the industry when in 1908 the 9 largest film manufacturers and the largest importer of films pooled their patent claims and banded together. They announced the formation of the Motion Picture Patents Company, January 1, 1909.[17]

The trust proclaimed that only the 9 companies it licensed had the right to manufacture pictures; to back up the claim, the trust convinced the Eastman Kodak Company, which monopolized the production of raw film stock, to sell only to licensed members of the trust. The product was standardized to one-reel films, and the trust attempted to control exhibition by classifying theaters and charging them according to their category. The dates and selections of showings could not be changed once they were booked. And a tax of two dollars a reel was levied for the use of licensed equipment and the right to rent pictures from the trust. One West Coast exhibitor sent in his money

with a letter asking about the tax. He concluded, "If it is graft it is all right. We're used to it out here."[18]

If theater owners bought any films from unlicensed manufacturers, the trust revoked their licenses, cut off their supply of films, and tried to seize equipment. In the final attempt at vertical and horizontal integration, the trust forced fifty-seven of the fifty-eight major licensed film exchanges into a national distribution monopoly under the title of the General Film Company. William Fox recalled how the trust's representatives sent for him and said:

We have been very kind to you. We have allowed you to make a large profit for the last two years by leaving you to the last. Now we have to get you out of the way—how much do you want for your plant? I told them I wanted $750,000. They asked me if I thought that that was what I was going to get. I told them yes. They told me to think it over and come back later. I came back the next day and still quoted $750,000. They they told me they had decided to cancel my license. The next day there came a cancellation of my license in the mail. . . . I went back and suggested that they tell me how much they would give me for my establishment. They said $75,000.[19]

When economic pressure failed, the trust initiated legal actions. Laemmle's biographer described the trust's legal attitude:

Injunction suits—let there be injunction suits in large numbers, let them flock in from all quarters, let the federal courts and the state courts buzz with them. Scour the country for infringements; set spies on to every independent camera, projecting machine, reel of film, that could be found. Let actions breed and multiply, spread them over the widest possible area, drag them over the longest possible periods. Argue, temporize, postpone, appeal—let these be the terms of their constant thought. The lawyers were charmed. Seldom had a roving commission been so liberally given. They were to experience all the delights and rewards of sailing under the Jolly Roger, and none of its risks.[20]

The trust's lawyers brought 289 suits against Laemmle alone within three years. Zukor discovered that "in the eyes of the 'trust' I was an outlaw."[21] All the independent manufacturers, distributors, and exhibitors of motion pictures became outlaws. "As outlaws, we were fair game for the snoopers and raiders of the 'trust'," wrote Zukor. "[Edwin S.] Porter [cameraman] had, I believe, a Pathé camera. Even if in the clear on it, some of the other equipment might be debatable in court action. And by the time we had finished battling half a dozen injunctions, our heads might be too far under water for us ever to emerge. The studio was therefore closely guarded."[22] This secrecy was not unnecessarily paranoid. Kennedy "operated an intelligence system that would have done credit to Bismarck. By ingenious and obscure channels he kept advised of every movement among the independents. He had daily, almost hourly, reports on their affairs. He was informed by his espionage machine of everything. He knew most of their secrets. He was informed of even what

Arson: Ince's burned-out editing room

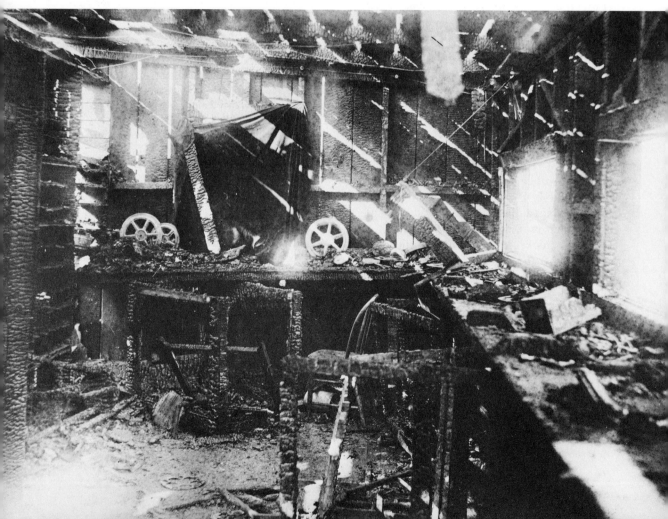

they ate and drank and who they drank it with and what was said. He had figures on their business, what they spent for film and where they got it, and to whom they sold and rented film and for how much."[23]

Gangs of thugs were employed, along with industrial espionage and legal muscle. According to one account, when the outlaws were discovered, "The Trust had no scruples about molestation. Laemmle's people, his directors and players and officials, could not move to and from the New York studios with safety. That is to say, they would not have been able to do so had not Laemmle employed more and better auxiliaries of his own. They worked, as it were, on commission. For every Trust auxiliary who was induced to get the hell out of this, the rate was five dollars. Sometimes the Patents gang got into the studios as workers. When they were detected by their opposite numbers in the Laemmle service, battles would ensue that were fought across the city into Hell's Kitchen."[24] At the same time Biograph produced **The Musketeers of Pig Alley,** the trust was sending gangs of sluggers after independents. In one typical instance of a gang raid, the police records of June 28, 1912, relate a riot and the arrest of two men said to have been employed by Universal; neither of them otherwise figures in screen history. "But from that day on a battalion of gunmen and sluggers was employed to protect the premises. . . . The raid would have been more successful if some of the mercenaries of the attacking army had not discovered that they belonged to the same gang as the defenders."[25]

The situation became too hot in New York, so that the outlaw producers made their films clandestinely or on the run. When the Eastman Kodak Company cut off the supply of film, "the result was an underground traffic in Eastman stock. Shipments ordered from Rochester for export were waylaid at steamship docks from Vancouver to New York, the cases opened and looted. Film was stolen, pirated and smuggled with all of the ingenuity now evident in the devious ways of the rum runners."[26] The outlaws searched for better and safer locations for production. After trying various possibilities, such as Florida, Cuba, the New Jersey woods, and abandoned Philadelphia studios, the independents gathered in Hollywood, where the sunshine, a variety of locations and—above all—the safety of the Mexican border proved ideal. Before long, these "outlaws" turned Hollywood into the movie capital of the world.

Two years before he made **The Gangsters and the Girl** (1914), Thomas Ince "found himself invested with the responsibilities of a general as well as director in charge." An old Civil War cannon was mounted to command the studio enclosure, loaded to the muzzle with scrap iron, and guards with sawed-off shotguns patrolled the gates. "Ince grew a corn on his hip carrying the largest obtainable size of Colt's frontier model forty-five revolver. A clash of arms was avoided or the canyon of Santa Monica would have been running deep with gore."[27]

The actual gangsters employed by the various studios were probably cast as the gang members in **Musketeers of Pig Alley,** made during the hottest period of the trust war, and in **The Gangsters and the Girl,** which appeared as the "outlaws" emerged victorious. Some of the "outlaws" rose from the criminal underworld to become movie entrepreneurs in their own right.

William Swanson, one of the key exchangemen who organized others to fight the trust, began by operating a moving picture tent for a carnival. In his spare time he taught the yokels the laws of chance with a pair of dice. Adam Kessel and Charles Bauman,

Charles Bauman

who formed one of the first outlaw compa-nies, Bison Films Corporation, were book-makers who entered the business when Kessel went to collect a loan that was invested in a film exchange. He collected the exchange instead and went to his friend Bauman, who was "operating a racing tip service and doing well selling 'selections for today' and 'best bets' to racing fans. 'Charlie, this is the bunk—these moving pictures are the new graft, come on in!' "[28]

Motion pictures emerged in America's urban immigrant communities as a readily accessible culture—a pictographic presenta-tion of values, myths, language, and feelings that transcended the different pasts of the audiences to provide them with an orienta-tion to present and future America. Film became a cultural cornerstone of the melting pot, and the new medium proved to have a powerful effect on audiences. When Zukor wanted to test his idea that the public would appreciate films longer than the standard one reel, he imported a three-reel version of the *Passion Play*. He recalled: "The scene was one of the most remarkable I have ever witnessed. Many women viewed the picture with religious awe. Some fell to their knees. I was struck by the moral potentialities of the screen."[29]

Another early indication of the "moral potentialities of the screen" was that nicke-lodeons enticed people away from saloons. Motion pictures challenged drink in making the lives of working people more palatable. William Fox concluded: "The workingman's wage was not large enough to buy tickets to the theater for himself and his family, so he found his recreation in drinking his glass of beer against the bar. But when the motion picture theater came he could buy a ticket for five cents. They could be entertained anywhere from two and a half to three hours, and the man found he was getting more than from his drink at the bar. I have always contended that if we had never had Prohibition, the motion pictures would have wiped out the saloon."[30] In the first book of American film criticism, the poet Vachel Lindsay devoted an entire chapter to the battle between saloon and nickelodeon. "Why do men prefer the photoplay to the drinking place?" he wondered:

For no pious reason, surely. Now they have fire pouring into their eyes instead of into their bellies. Blood is drawn from the guts to the brain. Though the picture be the veriest mess the light and movement cause the beholder to do a little reptilian thinking. After a day's work a street sweeper enters the place, heavy as king log. A ditch digger goes in sick and surly. It is the state of the body when many men drink themselves into insensibility. But here the light is as strong in the eyes as the whisky in the throat. Along with the flare, shadow and mystery, they face the existence of people, places, costumes, utterly novel. Immigrants are prodded by these swords of darkness and light to guess at the meaning of the catch-phrases and headlines that punctuate the play. They strain to hear their neighbors whisper or spell them out.[31]

Workers in the fledgling motion picture industry began to notice that beyond the pleasing power of entertainment lay a profound socializing function. These flickering images that could pull customers out of saloons could also educate them. Billy Bitzer, the gangster genre's first cameraman, sometimes went to different nickelodeons with director D.W. Griffith to test audience reactions. "At the nickelodeon in the lower East Side of New York we noticed that immigrants learned English by reading the titles aloud."[32] Immigrants learned more than the American spoken and written language. The nickelodeons were oracles of the language of America culture, where a new world was interpreted and its goals, values, and mores were presented with humor, action, or melodrama. Frank Woods, a photoplay writer who worked with D.W. Griffith and who was one of the earliest film critics, wrote that the motion picture was widely popular for the very reason that "it has supplied a new and universal language for telling stories and recording events."[33]

Traditional religious leaders were quick to notice the medium's powers of attraction. An envious Philadelphia preacher suggested to his flock, "Let us raise ten, twelve, fifteen thousand dollars that our Church may be so enlarged and reconstructed . . . whereby . . . we could have motion pictures . . . on a Saturday night when our streets, playhouses, and saloons are crowded, to be conducted with gospel services of a practical sort. . . ."[34] Since the content of most of the photoplays leaned closer to lurid sensationalism than religious piety, debates raged, first in the pages of religious journals and then in the organs of secular respectability as to the movies' effects on the "lower classes." The liberal "custodians of culture" suggested that photoplays could have an educational impact on American workers.[35] Conservative opposition, beginning in 1909, demanded censorship by government control.[36] The film industry responded with its own philosophical defenses in the pages of the trade papers, and by turning away from the relatively amoral naturalism of the first photoplays toward a didactic trumpeting of the moral traditions of nineteenth-century America.

Motion pictures at the time of the first gangster film gave audiences educational

The Great Bank Robbery

melodramas of good versus evil, infused with an overriding optimism, patriotism, and faith in divine justice. The success myth was preached in films like *A Self Made Hero* or *From Cabin Boy to King* (both 1910), while audiences in the Progressive era were instructed to avoid drink and embrace marriage, family life, work, honesty, and patience. It is interesting that the Western hero, as Broncho Billy Anderson and later William S. Hart, rode onto the screen as if blown by this wind of moral fervor, and that workers and immigrants were educated by a patriotic iconography of America's past in films that "always ended with a close-up of Old Glory billowing proudly in the breeze, 'inspiring the beholder with a pride for his adopted land.' "[37] Early films (1903–1909) had portrayed a sympathy for poor people, as in *The Eviction*, and a critical look at the evils of capitalism in pictures like *The Crooked Banker*, *The Politician*, or *The Grafters*. By 1912, movies tried to inspire audiences with a dislike of organized labor and attributed labor unrest to drink, lazy workers, or workers who were unjustly envious of their sympathetically portrayed bosses, (*Strike, The Loafer, Lazy Bill and the Strikers, The Iconoclast*). In films such as *Capital vs. Labor*, or *The Two Sides*, the Church is depicted as the workers' only true friend.[38]

Although photoplays were generally reactionary in their attitude toward labor, they were occasionally influenced by the reform impulse of the Progressive era. Child labor was attacked in films such as *Why?*, and films investigated slum conditions and convict labor. "The New Woman" was also sometimes treated sympathetically in films such as *The Factory Girl* and *Female Reporter*. By 1912 muckraking was an important function of the Progressive movement, and some films reflected this determination to document the social ills of American society and frankly discuss what was wrong with America.

High on the list of visible social problems were the street gangs of American cities, which Riis and Lewis Hine documented so effectively in their books and photographs. It is in the context of Progressive documentary realism that the first gangster film appeared. Crime films had been popular with American audiences from the very beginning of story films. One of the first lessons film makers learned was that crime paid very well in the movies. Films like the *The Great Train Robbery* (1902) and *The Great Bank Robbery* (1903) quickly fulfilled the action potential of crime films. Other early crime films such as *The Bandit King* (1904) or *Burglar Bill* (1904) went on to portray outlaws sympathetically as men of courage who were capable of loyalty and Robin Hood qualities. These early films were romantic portrayals of bandits very different in mood from the documentary flavor of **The Musketeers of Pig Alley,** the first gangster film.

The Musketeers of Pig Alley established several basic characteristics of the genre. Like the films of the twenties and thirties, it sprang from newspaper stories. Lillian Gish recalled that D.W. Griffith got the idea for **Musketeers** from a newspaper article.[39]

In 1912 there was a series of gangster killings and vice scandals that implicated the police. The newspapers headlined these events, and the climax came with the shooting of a gambler named Herman Rosenthal. The social realism of stories and situations based on newspaper reports that we have come to associate with the gangster genre began when the Biograph Company capitalized on these headlines and the subsequent cries for reform.[40]

Griffith shot the film on location and cast actual gangsters like "Kid" Brood and

"Harlem Tom" Evans to play in the rival gangs. According to the *Biograph Bulletin* of October 31, 1912, "this picture production, which does not run very strong as to plot, is simply intended to show vividly the doings of the gangster type of people."[41]

The episodic plot begins in "New York's other side," where a "poor musician goes off to improve his fortune." On the way home, he shows his earnings to a friend in the street. The Snapper Kid, Chief of the Musketeers, sees the full wallet, follows the musician, hits him over the head, and takes the money. After recovering, the musician goes out to find his money, leaving the little lady, his girl friend, worrying about his safety and the rent. A friend comes to cheer up the little lady and takes her to a dance—the gangster's ball. A respectable-looking gangster invites the little lady for a drink and slips a drug into it. The Snapper Kid watches the scene and stops the little lady before she downs the drink, thus provoking a gang war. During the shootout, the musician sees the gangster and grabs his money back during the confusion of the battle. The police break up the fight and arrest everyone but the Snapper Kid. He escapes to the little lady's flat, reminds her that he saved her from being drugged, and invites her out. She refuses and says she'll

Griffith, Bitzer, and the Biograph business agents

stay with her husband. The gangster shrugs it off, thinking she must be crazy to prefer the musician, and leaves. A cop nabs him and begins to arrest him for taking part in the gun battle, but the Snapper Kid says he has an alibi—he was visiting his friends. The little lady and the musician back up the Kid's story because, as the title card reads, "One good turn deserves another." The Kid makes a gesture of friendship with his hands and goes out. After a title, "Links in the system," a mysterious hand slides into the picture from out of frame and gives the Snapper Kid some money. The couple embrace, and the film ends.

Griffith pictured the Snapper Kid sympa-

Elmer Booth as the Snapper Kid (with Harry Carey)

thetically. Elmer Booth portrays a likeable, tough, coarse thief and killer. Lillian Gish has said that Elmer Booth was a distinct precursor of James Cagney.[42] Like gangsters played by Cagney, the Snapper Kid is short, powerful, explosive, and expressive with his body, face, and gestures. He is violent and quick to act in movements that snap out like his name. He is good-natured about the little lady's rejection, sly enough to avoid going to jail, wise enough not to fight in the Big Boss's place, and constantly putting plans into action to get what he wants. He exudes a healthy self-confidence and is proud of the snappy way he dresses. Griffith's mixing of a firm sense of realistic detail and a romantic bias have shaded the Chief of the Musketeers as more chivalrous than the movie gangsters who followed, but the Snapper Kid launched the central character of the genre—a sympathetic gangster—and the movie gangsters who followed shared many of his traits.

The Lower East Side locations in **Musketeers** provide an appropriate setting for the birth of the genre. "New York's other side," as a title describes the setting, is comprised of dingy rooms and hallways, saloons, narrow streets teeming with immigrants, and

Street scene (Lillian Gish at right)

Alleyway

Saloon

The rival gang

underworld alleyways filled with garbage cans, dust, and debris. City textures and dark places predominate. The action takes place around the bottoms of buildings, and we never see the sky. There are no country or uptown alternatives for the Snapper Kid— no penthouse aspirations. The gangster genre began in the slums, and the people who lived there appreciated the film. Billy Bitzer, who was Griffith's cameraman regularly and who shot **Musketeers,** recalled an early preview of the film:

Another way we learned was through tryouts. Tryouts were usually in remote theaters, and it was to our advantage to be there. One memorable tryout was held in a converted store in the lower East Side Jewish section of Manhattan. It was in 1912 for the *Musketeers of Pig Alley,* an early gangster film with Elmer Booth, much of which was filmed in that locale. We got very strong and favorable reactions—it was one of the first "realistic" films, one of our best.[43]

The criminal world depicted in **Musketeers** is one of rival gangs, armed robbery, dodging the police, saloons, drugs, dances, and alleyways peopled with underworld characters. Besides an underworld milieu, a gangster protagonist and a pictorially realistic urban setting, **Musketeers** contributed several other basic elements to the genre.

The gang, of course, is an essential element of gangster films. The Snapper Kid's gang includes seven armed henchmen, sporting scars, derby hats, broken noses, and a cocky willingness to mix it up. And, as in most gangster films that followed, there is one gang member who is the protagonist's sidekick, played by Harry Carey in **Musketeers.** He is the main character's constant companion until the end of the film; his function is to back up the gangster in times of trouble and generally to amplify the protagonist's personality and actions. When the Snapper Kid swaggers, Harry Carey hitches up his pants and echoes the gesture. As the genre developed, the sidekick was used to exaggerate certain qualities of the gangster's character, as Otero underscores Rico's ruth-

"THE MUSKETEERS OF PIG ALLEY"

LATER

THE LITTLE LADY MEETS
"SNAPPER KID"
THE CHIEF OF THE
MUSKETEERS

"THE MUSKETEERS OF PIG ALLEY"

THE LITTLE LADY AT THE
GANGSTER'S BALL

lessness in *Little Caesar* or Little Boy comically exaggerates Tony Camonte in *Scarface.*

Another of the gangster's defining characteristics is that he takes what he wants, whether it's money, an occupied chair at the Gangster's Ball, or a woman. In **Musketeers,** after a title that reads, "The Little Lady meets the Snapper Kid," the gangster sees the girl come out of her room and grabs her by the arm to demand a kiss. But the little lady is tougher than most of her sisters who followed in the genre. She energetically slaps him hard in the face, thereby winning the first round in the battle of interpersonal violence that was to characterize relations between men and women in the genre. This fiery outburst further intrigues the Kid, who pursues the little lady throughout the film until she tells him she already has a man. Movie gangsters in the twenties and thirties were more persistent and sadistic, and less chivalrous, but their approach was to be basically the same. And they were to find women who appreciated their blunt demands more than the little lady. In **Public Enemy,** Jean Harlow tells Cagney that she likes him precisely because he takes what he wants.

Griffith also established the iconographic tradition of the Gangster's Ball in **Musketeers.** The sign outside reads: "Grand Dance of the Jolly Three. Admission 25cts." Inside, the hall is filled with animated couples dancing to some lively music. The dancers project a happy and comfortable sensuality that is infectious, and the friend who brought the little lady is swept into the dancing crowd as soon as they arrive. The dance hall has an adjoining saloon where other dancers are refreshing themselves, and both rooms are ruled over by a gangster known as "the Big Boss," who is feared by the other gangsters, including the Snapper Kid. The scene typically ends in a fight over a woman. This scene, appropriately entitled "The Little Lady at the Gangster's Ball," has appeared in nearly every gangster film to follow **Musketeers.** Although the nightclubs or speakeasies were to become gaudier, the dancers more drunk and lustful, and the music characteristic of the Roaring Twenties—so that we usually associate this scene with the Jazz Age—the basic elements are present in the first gangster film. The Gangster's Ball lightens the violent, competitive, and hostile tones that dominate gangster dramas, and it defines the gangster milieu in terms of city night life.

Another essential iconographic scene that appears in **Musketeers,** one that is shared with other action genres, is the shootout. Titled "The Gangsters' Feudal War," the first gangster shootout begins with the Snapper Kid and his gangster rival rounding up their gangs. The Snapper Kid spins the barrel of his revolver to make sure that it's fully loaded, shoves it into his pocket, and leads his gang to the fight. The gangs stalk each other through saloons and alleyways ducking around corners and fences and hiding behind garbage cans. The not-so-innocent bystanders who realize what is going to happen run for cover. When the gangs run into each other in a litter-strewn alleyway, there is a short and explosive gunfight. Billows of gunsmoke obscure the fighting gangsters, parting occasionally to reveal some wounded gunman staggering and falling or others aggressively moving forward and blasting away with their revolvers. This deafening battle ends when squads of police come rushing in to haul the survivors off to jail. The ritualistic weapons check, the deadly certain stalking, the explosive gun battle recur again and again, with a number of variations in the gangster films that followed. As in **Musketeers,** the shootout scene has usually been presented as the climax of the

"THE MUSKETEERS OF PIG ALLEY"

LINKS IN THE SYSTEM

movie, and audiences expect it to be the most violent and terrible moment of the film.

Musketeers launched the genre with an episodic slice of pictorial realism, characteristic of the social realism of the Progressive era, muckraking, instead of a strong melodramatic plot. Griffith began the genre with a sympathetic gangster and several characteristics that were to become basic to gangster films. By 1912, the gangster film was securely rooted in American film history. The success story, the negative tone, the slangy dialogue, and the gangster's heroic popularity lay in the future.

Two years later, Thomas Ince made **The Gangsters and the Girl.** Jim Tracy, the gangster, is the heroine's boy friend when the picture begins. He helps her raise money to get her father out of jail and engineers her escape when she is wrongly convicted as a

Thomas Ince

pickpocket. The gangster is moderately sympathetic in this picture, but when a handsome detective enters the scene and joins the gang as an undercover agent, there is little doubt as to who will wind up with the girl.

The Gangsters and the Girl gave the genre the characteristic scene of dividing the take, including a fight over the division of the loot, after which one gang member becomes a stool pigeon. There is also an interesting shootout on the rooftops of New York, which offers a dramatic cityscape of steel girders of tall buildings under construction. But the film lacks the realistic emphasis that the normally romantic and sentimental Griffith gave to **Musketeers.**

Griffith went on to use gangsters and the gangster milieu melodramatically in the "Modern Story" of *Intolerance*. Gangsters, gambling dens, prostitutes, and crooked orphanages represented the evils of the modern world. By 1916, rushing trains and speeding cars were associated with gangsters as symbolic expressions in movies of this modern world. The gangster character and the primitive gangster films remained in a melodramatic mold until they were drastically altered by the events of the Roaring Twenties.

Intolerance

Evil vs. Good in early Ince production

PART II

THE ROARING TWENTIES: THE RISE OF THE GANGSTER MOVIE

5

OUR CHANGING MORALS— THE BUSINESS OF AMERICA

Bolshevism is knocking at our gates. We can't afford to let it in. We have got to organize ourselves against it, and put our shoulders together and hold fast. We must keep America whole and safe and unspoiled. We must keep the worker away from red literature and red ruses; we must see that his mind remains healthy.   Al Capone

Lon Chaney as ''The Buzzard'' in *The Penalty*

When the "lawless decade" began, movie criminals were bizarre and twisted embodiments of evil. Lon Chaney as "The Buzzard" in *The Penalty* (1921) was typical. The picture begins with the erroneous amputation of a ten-year-old traffic victim's legs. The bitter boy grows up to be "The Buzzard," lord and master of the city's underworld, whose slaves are "the underground powers of the reds." "When Satan fell from heaven he looked for power in Hell," The Buzzard tells his daughter in explaining why he has become a criminal. His depraved plan is to loot the city with "thousands of disgruntled foreign workers." This image of an evil criminal was also typical of the last burst of patriotic posturing that had stimu-Scare that launched the decade was a continuation of various illegal, immoral and unconstitutional activities against anti-war and radical groups.

The Russian Revolution, a series of anarchist bombings, the Seattle general strike, the Boston police strike, and the steel strike of 1919 gave right-wingers and anti-laborites a pretext they used to attack those who advocated socialism or who tried to organize labor. Thousands of suspects were rounded up and thrown into jail, or run out of the country; I.W.W. organizers were lynched and castrated in the Northwest; in Indiana a jury quickly acquitted a man who murdered another for shouting, "To hell with the United States." The era in which gangsters were to become cultural heroes began with a burst "of lawless and disorderly defense of law and order, of unconstitutional defense of the Constitution, of suspicion and civil conflict—in a very literal sense a reign of terror."[1] In Chicago and in the South, blacks were terrorized and murdered when black veterans dared to enjoy the democracy they had helped to save the world for. America was "cleansed" by the removal of thousands of radicals, as The Buzzard was reformed when a blood clot was removed from his brain.

Lon Chaney went on to play the same

The Penalty

Wall Street bombed, 1920

twisted criminal in *Outside the Law* (1921) and *The Unholy Three* (1921). In most of the crime films in the early twenties, the criminal was pitted against the hero who represented Good; in many of these films the criminal was reformed, as in *While the Devil Laughs* (1921), *Play Square* (1921), or *Beating the Game* (1921). By 1923, this particular plot was so recognizable that a reviewer for the *Film Daily* wrote of *The Soul Harvest*, "you have the conventional crook situation in which there is a band, a master mind at the head of it, and the usual hero and heroine crooks who want to reform. Then comes the healer who brings about the regeneration of the whole band."[2]

A few years later, this simple Manichaean depiction of criminals was considered old-

The thrill of the underworld in *Gang War*

fashioned. It was replaced by a tolerant and admiring view of gangsters that was based on several cultural attitudes that typified the Roaring Twenties.

"The business of America is business," proclaimed President Calvin Coolidge, voicing a glorification and justification of profiteering that was trumpeted throughout the prosperity decade. Al Capone joined the chorus by announcing, "Everybody calls me a racketeer; I call myself a businessman."[3]

The rapid development of service and consumer industries during the twenties provided gangsters with another rationalization. In the 1920's, gangsters, like businessmen, could reasonably argue that they were performing a service. And the public heartily agreed. According to Andrew Sinclair:

The concept of the honest bootlegger making a living out of their trade just as other people did, was a common rationalization of respectable men to excuse their patronage of criminals. This attitude even extended to their children, who voted in one survey that the bootlegger took first place in community activities.[4]

The glorification of business was proclaimed with an almost religious fervor. In one best selling book of the mid-twenties, Jesus was portrayed as the world's greatest businessman: "He picked up twelve men from the bottom ranks of business and forged them into an organization that conquered the world."[5]

By the mid-twenties, Jesus himself would have needed a corporation to do business in America. The mass production and consumption on which twenties "prosperity" depended was accomplished through further oligopolistic concentration of control and profits. Mergers led to ever larger corporations, and "efficiency" became the catchword in the American business outlook.[6] The efficient and well-organized racketeers of the Prohibition era found the prevailing attitudes toward business quite amenable:

The fact of making a living was more sacred to many Americans than life itself. The whole of American society was too close to the violence of the frontier and the city jungle to worry unduly over the vendettas of gangsters. Where the law was inefficient and graft-ridden (no legal punishment was given for even one of the 130 gang murders in Chicago between 1926 and 1927), respectable people were content to let

Eddie Quinlan in *Big Money*

Robert Armstrong and Carole Lombard in *The Racketeer*

criminals slay their own. In the belief in rough justice rather than the rotten enforcement of the law, in the dislike of informing on men who were fulfilling a public service in the eyes of most city dwellers, the prohibition racketeers flourished unchecked. . . .[7]

A craving to consume accompanied the reverence of business. "The steady secularization of Sunday has made it more than ever before in this country an occasion for spending money,"[8] reported the President's Research Committee on Recent Social Trends.

The "consumption habit" that emerged in the twenties constituted a fundamental and pervasive threat to traditional morality. The strong urge to buy things overwhelmed the spirit of abstinence and the economic philosophy of rigorous saving and cash payment that was so important in the traditional American outlook. The reluctance to buy goods on credit evaporated during the twenties.[9] American attitudes reflected a shift away from religious goals toward a frame of reference in which secular and material happiness assumed transcendent importance.[10] The movies were a powerful ally of advertising in promoting the consumption habit. As one Hollywood executive proudly expressed it, "American mass production . . . the American assembly line received its momentum and reached full speed in very large degree from the selling power of the Hollywood film."[11] On movie screens across the country,

The mockery of ethics of the old "inner goodness" of the film heroes and heroines was paralleled by the new regard for material things. A burning ambition to be identified with the rich, a deep reverence for material goods, characterized American attitudes. Silk stockings, silk underwear, furs, automobiles, phonographs, elaborate furniture, servants, apartment houses, electrically equipped kitchens, hotels, night clubs, country clubs, resorts, sports, colleges—these were paraded across the screen in exaggerated splendor.[12]

Lon Chaney and Virginia Pearson in *The Big City*

Stylish gangsters in the newspapers and the movies became fashion models in the tantalizing display of worldly goods.

By the mid-twenties, movie criminals were no longer portrayed in the simple and obvious role of the villian. In *The Law and the Lady* (1924), Dapper Dan Hollins is a likeable leader of a gang of thieves. In *Grit* (1924), the protagonist crook is a sympathetic gangster who wants to quit the gang. Criminals could also be aristocratic; the patrician gangleader in *Jim the Penman,* a 1921 crime melodrama involving forgery and bank swindles, is a baron.

Movie gangsters remained suave and debonair even after some began to appear more and more like their real-life immigrant counterparts. In *Dressed to Kill* (1928), "Mileaway Barry" is a handsome, chivalrous gangster who helps a girl get her innocent lover out of jail at the cost of his own life. And Malone Keene in *The Racketeer* (1929) is "a suave racketeer" who helps the heroine regenerate a down-and-out violin player.

Gangsters fascinated society people. In *Come Across* (1929), society girls became nightclub dancers or found some other way to enter the alluring underworld. In *Danger Street* (1928), a depressed socialite flits into the underworld in the middle of a gang war in an attempt to kill himself. Instead, he finds the love of a chorus girl, who gives him a reason to live.

"Americans in the 1920's," according to William Leuchtenburg, "became obsessed with the subject of sex."[13] It is hard to know if Americans moved any closer toward a genuine healthy sexuality during the twenties. Freud was popularized and invoked to show that civilization was repressive, and that America needed to loosen up. Americans seemed to unbend whether they read Freud or not. Women who by the twenties had moved a little toward economic emancipation seemed to become more independent-minded and more determined to enjoy themselves as much as men. But whether people had more joyful orgasms during the twenties than before or after is a subject historians have not yet researched.

Most of all, sex was used to sell things—cars, soap, mouthwash, shows, victrolas, tabloids—and particularly movies. "The screen was invaded by hordes of 'hot mammas,' bathing beauties, and Volstead violators, as each movie tried to outdo its predecessors in daring licentiousness."[14] In the movies, emancipated women, particularly society ladies, found gangsters very attractive. In *The Exciters* (1923), for example, a rich young girl marries a member of a gang because he's "a real man." When he turns out to be a police agent, she's disappointed. In several films, like *While the City Sleeps* (1928), **Alibi,** or *Ladies Love Brutes* (1930), respectable young women found gangsters irresistible; this fascination was widespread in the popular culture of the twenties. After interviewing Al Capone, Mrs. Eleanor "Cissy" Patterson, the society editor of the Washington *Herald,* wrote: "It has been said, with truth, that women have a special kind of sympathy for gangsters. If you don't understand why, consult Dr. Freud."[15]

The crimes in these early films were usually robbery, preferably of jewels, second-story work, safe cracking, extortion, murder, kidnapping, blackmail, or white slavery. Occasionally, as in *There Are No Villians* (1921), drugs were involved.

Prohibition of the manufacture, distribution, and sale of intoxicating liquors went into effect in 1920. Bootleggers to supply illicit liquor appeared on the screen as early as 1922 in *The Bootlegger's Daughter,* a melodrama about the heroine's battle for respectability. By 1924, crooks were often

Carole Lombard, Robert Armstrong, Roland Drew, Jeanette Coff in *The Racketeer*

Joan Crawford and Louis Natheaux in *Four Walls*

George Bancroft and Fay Wray in
Thunderbolt

Edmund Lowe and Mary Astor in
Dressed To Kill

John Gilbert and Joan Crawford in
Four Walls

Safecrackers: Edmund Lowe, Paul Page, William Harrigan in *Born Reckless*

bootleggers, as in *Poison, Grit, Contraband,* or *Those Who Dance.* And bootlegging was central to the gangster's growing popularity.

Actual and movie gangsters flourished in the twenties because they were pleasure sellers in a hedonistic age. As Al Capone expressed it: "I make my money by supplying a public demand. If I break the law, my customers, who number hundreds of the best people in Chicago, are as guilty as I am. The only difference between us is that I sell and they buy."[16]

As the first movie bootleggers appeared, Capone began his selling career as a bouncer and a pimp who was called to Chicago to help his friend Johnny Torrio run the family business under Uncle Jim Colissimo, who died shortly after Capone arrived. Four years later, Capone was known to be making $4 million a year from twenty-five road houses in and around Chicago, which offered the pleasures of drinking, gambling, and sex.[17] Two years later, the revenue from Capone's territory, Chicago's South Side,

The Bootlegger's Daughter

Romance of the Underworld

was estimated at $22 million.[18] By the end of the decade, the Brooklyn bouncer, who had arrived virtually penniless in Chicago in 1920, was making $60 million per year, according to what the Internal Revenue Service was able to estimate.[19] Capone was simply the most spectacular and newsworthy racketeer, and his territory was only a portion of Chicago. Syndicates in New York, Boston, New Jersey, Detroit, Cleveland, Philadelphia, and New Orleans were also making millions selling the suckers what they wanted. They were to create economic empires and use trade union and political power on a scale that dwarfed Capone's activities.

The bootleggers supplied a thrilling sense of getting away with a crime while supplying liquor to customers. And the law-breaking buyers were often treated to swashbuckling action on the part of the gangsters. In battles with the Prohibition agents, "Millions of Americans sided with the lawbreakers. On one occasion, thousands of bathers at Coney Island watched an encounter between Coast Guard cutters and rumrunners: they cheered the rumrunner as it opened a lead on the pursuing government boats."[20]

Prohibition overburdened the nation's po-

Hold of rum-runner

Harry Daugherty (1860–1941), U.S. Attorney General during the Harding administration, photographed at the time of his trial (1927)

Albert Fall

lice and legal framework. No serious attempt was made to enforce the unpopular law, with the result that reasonable law enforcement agents were considerably demoralized; the most obvious lesson was that crime paid very well.[21] Prohibition turned the profits of the liquor and beer trade over to gangsters and provided them with enough capital to expand their other activities, to secure legal and political protection, and to buy a certain amount of respectability.[22]

The demoralization and helplessness of enforcement officials, the prosperity of the gangsters, and the open flaunting of the Volstead Act generated a pervasive disrespect for law. As one A.F. of L. president later complained to the Wickersham Con-

gressional Committee: "There is a feeling of corruption, of everything being corrupt, and it is bringing itself into the trade unions. They feel if a judge can be bought for liquor, he can be bought for anything else; if a police officer can be quieted by a little money for liquor, he can be quieted for something else."[23]

The pervasive feeling of corruption wasn't simply a result of successful bootlegging, no matter how securely Al Capone had Chicago Mayor Big Bill Thompson stuffed in his hip pocket. The gangsters were small-timers compared to some politicians who acted like gangsters.

No events set the cynical tone and mood of immorality for the gangsters' popularity

Al Capone

better than the Harding Administration scandals, which were completely investigated only in the early thirties, as the gangster genre's popularity was reaching its peak.

The Harding scandals had all the elements of a Roaring Twenties gangster melodrama. President Warren Harding made his old pal Harry Daugherty the Attorney General of the United States. Daugherty, a Columbus, Ohio, corporation lawyer, had run Harding's campaign and "had an unsavory reputation as a lobbyist and a fixer." The Attorney General, along with some cronies known as the "Ohio Gang," set up two road houses of their own, the "Little Green House" at 1625 K Street, which was a center of bootlegging, gambling, prostitution, and dope peddling,

and the "House on H Street," where the President could relax with his mistress, Nan Britton. When Harding proclaimed a "return to normalcy" after World War I, he meant business as usual. To the Ohio Gang, normalcy meant about $2 billion in graft and government waste. Most of their rackets involved bribes and fixing of government contracts and trials, such as building veterans' hospitals at four times the cost or selling the rights to peddle narcotics to inmates of federal prisons. Their most spectacular racket was the "Teapot Dome" oil deal, in which Harding's Secretary of the Interior, Albert Fall, arranged secret oil leases of naval reserves to two of his pals, Edward Doheny and Harry Sinclair, each of whom

Will Hays

hoped to clear $100 million in the deal. The grateful Sinclair contributed $260,000 to the Republican Party campaign fund as part of the required bribe. When the news of the oil racket leaked out and the Senate Committee on Public Lands and Surveys tried to investigate Fall, he invoked national security in contemptuously refusing to answer questions. It took more than a decade to put the whole story together, through a series of trials and investigations in which congressmen and witnesses were bribed, threatened, and harassed. Harding died somewhat mysteriously. Some Ohio Gang members "committed suicide." The ringleaders were rich when they died of old age, having fled the country or beaten the rap at home. "The most striking feature of this corruption in government, the worst in at least half a century, was the public response to it. Instead of public indignation, there was a barrage of abuse at the men who brought the corruption to light."[24]

Goals that seemed to matter most in the twenties were those that gangsters exemplified. Gangsters broke laws and long-established moral codes and got what they—and seemingly everybody else—wanted in the Roaring Twenties: wealth and recognition. Who was to deny them their heroic place in the movies? Certainly not the former Postmaster General in Harding's cabinet, Will Hays. Hays was head of the Motion Picture Producers and Distributors Association, which was established by the film industry to regulate the moral content of pictures as well as curb the most flagrant abuses of the larger corporations' monopolization of the film industry. Will Hays, who was known as the "czar" of movie morals, had been the man who accepted Sinclair's $260,000 bribe to the Republican campaign funds. Appropriately, "all the Hays Office succeeded in doing in the 1920's was to add hypocrisy to sex by insisting on false moralizations and the 'moral' ending."[25]

6

RESTLESS AMERICA: THE GANGSTER AMPLIFIED

Yeah, there's money in the big town, all right. And the women! Good times. Somethin' doin' all the time. Excitin' things, you know. Gee, the clothes I could wear!

Joe Massara in **Little Caesar**

Rural backlash: KKK initiation, 1924

"This is a story of Main Street and Broadway—a story that could have been taken out of last night's newspapers," says the prologue of the first all-talking picture, *The Lights of New York* (1928). The film's theme of country innocence versus city decadence was central to the cultural climate that nurtured the mythic gangster. The first shot is of a small-town Main Street, which is dominated by the church. "Main Street," says the title card, "Forty-five minutes from Broadway—but a *thousand* miles away." The audience is introduced to the city with the title, "Broadway—Forty-five minutes from Main Street, but a *million* miles away." The lively urban atmosphere is sketched in with shots of Chinatown, street vendors hawking their wares, a girl speaking to her boy friend in a thick Brooklyn accent, and a drunk asking a cop how to cross the street.

This film, like dozens of others throughout the twenties, expressed a profound ambivalence toward the rapidly growing cities, which were at the same time proof of the nation's progress and a threat to traditional America. By 1920, America was demographically an urban nation. Throughout the decade, country people were drawn to the cities—often for compelling reasons. The Prosperity Decade just meant hard times for farm people. During the twenties the farmers' percentage of the national income slid from 16 per cent to 9 per cent, and farm acreage decreased for the first time in American history.[1] Small-town and rural people, who found the bright lights and big-city action too exciting to resist, left the country. Many of those who remained felt threatened by the cities, and anti-urban sentiments coalesced into the Prohibition Movement, the Fundamentalist Crusade, and the Ku Klux Klan. These groups blamed the cities for letting loose a flow of liquor, new habits, and new ideas on the rest of the country. But in their efforts to stop the historical momen-

tum of urbanization, the drys, the fundamentalists, and the Klan were fighting a losing battle. Their failure was most evident in the cities themselves, where the gangsters were in the victorious ranks of the conquering culture. "In wet cities, like New York and San Francisco, a stranger could most easily locate a 'speakeasy'—a saloon operating on the sly—by asking an obliging policeman."[2] City newspapers, particularly in New York, Chicago, and San Francisco, strongly opposed Prohibition in their editorial policy and so heavily publicized the breaking of dry laws that in the period 1919–1929 the evasion of Prohibition occupied more newspaper columns than any other issue.[3]

A common belief shared by Klansmen, drys, and fundamentalists was that immigration had to be stopped. There had been a tremendous post-war burst of immigrants who came mostly from Southern and Eastern Europe. The strains and inequities of industrialization and urbanization destroyed American confidence in the nation's ability to absorb an unlimited number of strangers, and a nativist backlash culminated in the 1924 congressional act that drastically restricted immigration further.

The most notorious actual gangsters in the twenties were immigrants. Al Capone, Meyer Lansky, Dutch Shultz, Dion O'Banion, Lucky Luciano, and others were carving out their own versions of the success myth, and many immigrants found nothing wrong with the rapid rise of gangsters.

The wealthy racketeer and bootlegger was, in the eyes of the Italian or Slavic community, the American dream come true. The recent immigrants had come to America in pursuit of a golden mirage, and those among them who made fortunes by violating antipathetic laws were their first heroes and helpers.[4]

Movie gangsters became identified as immigrants in the late twenties and early

Ethnic dance hall. Clara Bow in *Grit*

thirties. Until that time, crime pictures had only sporadically depicted criminals as immigrants or foreigners. American poor and ethnic neighborhoods, like Hell's Kitchen in *Fools First* (1922) or San Francisco's Chinatown and international settlement in *The Penalty* (1921), could be typical settings for crime stories, but only occasionally did films appear that were completely about the underworld in American immigrant communities, such as *Fair Lady* (1922), an underworld melodrama that was a Sicilian Black Hand revenge story.

Until the late twenties, criminals for the most part had names like "The Scarab" (*Broad Daylight*, 1922), "Fancy Charlie" (*Beating the Game*, 1921), "Black Mike" (*Outside the Law*, 1921), "The Peacock" (*Souls in Bondage*, 1923), "Dapper Dan Hollins" (*The Law and the Lady*, 1924), or "The Hawk" (*The Penalty*, 1921). As they

became popular in the late twenties, movie gangsters began to have foreign-sounding names with increasing frequency. Although some gangster protagonists continued to have names like "Bull Weed" (**Underworld**), "Bull Savage" (*Crooks Can't Win*, 1928), or Black Jack Connel (*Gang War*, 1928), gangsters began to appear in films with names like Bennie Horowitz (*Four Walls*, 1928), Nick Scarsi (**The Racket**), or Nick Verdis (**Broadway**). By the time Edward G. Robinson appeared as Caesar Enrico Bandello (**Little Caesar**), gangsters were clearly identifiable as immigrants: Tony Garotta (*Night Ride*, 1930), Louis Berretti (**Born Reckless**), Joe Forziati (*Ladies Love Brutes*, 1930), Nickey Solomon (*Playing Around*, 1930), Fingers O'Dell (*Outside the Law*, 1930), and Louis Ricarno (**The Doorway to Hell**).

The gangsters were associated with the

money, sex, booze, gambling, style, and high living that made the cities such sinful and attractive places in the popular imagination. As an immigrant or suave sophisticate associated with the evils and excitements of the city, the movie gangster in the twenties evolved as a mythic representation of America's urbanization.

The gangster also mythically expressed American industrial culture, particularly in his relationship with automobiles. The movie gangster's life and success was intimately associated with autos. **Underworld** begins with Bull Weed's getaway car waiting for him as he "closes out another bank account." Bull Weed runs out of a bank with the loot, jumps into his car, and roars off. **Little Caesar** begins with a car driving up to a gas station at night; shots are fired; the cash register rings and is rifled; Rico speeds off into the night with Joe Massera. After using the trucking industry to work his way up, Bugs Moran in **Quick Millions** rides around in a chauffeur-driven limousine, as does Louis Ricarno in **The Doorway to Hell.** In **Public Enemy,** Tom Powers, who also begins his criminal career in the twenties as a truck driver, marks his success with cars as well as clothes, as every gangster should. Gary Cooper, as the Kid, begins his career as a truck-driving bootlegger in **City Streets,** who gleefully shows off his new car to his girl friend when he cashes in.

The gangster had to be as skillful with his car as a cowboy with his horse, and the inability to handle a car could mean death for the incompetent. When Tony has trouble with the getaway car in **Little Caesar,** the gang begins to realize he's started to turn yellow—he's lost his mechanical manhood. The gang shoots him down from a speeding car.

The car itself could be a useful weapon and an extension of the movie gangster's aggressive nature. In **Quick Millions,** Bugs Moran rams a limousine with his truck to show the

Sabbath prayers. Carmel Myers, Vera Gordon, John Gilbert in
Four Walls

Immigrants in *Kid Gloves* and *Those Who Dance*

chauffeurs "who runs this town." In **City Streets,** the Kid crashes through a roadblock of hijackers on his first job, and the climax of the film comes when the Kid is at the wheel of a car full of gangsters who are trying to take him for a ride. He threatens to kill them all by narrowly beating a train at a crossing and by zooming around mountain curves at 70 miles per hour until the terrified gangsters give up. In **Scarface,** Tony Camonte furiously runs a carload of would-be assassins off a road by ramming their car until both cars go over a cliff. The images of the gangster using his car as a weapon, of

gangsters speeding through the streets as they blast away at enemies or the cops, or of a car screeching around a corner as a body is flung out are basic iconographic elements of the genre—reflections of the rapid and violently aggressive nature of American industrialization.

In the unrestrained gang warfare of the twenties, cars and trucks were used as armor in pitched battles, as when Bugs Moran attacked Capone's hideout with a squad of twenty-two cars which cruised by in single file, blasting away with shotguns and submachine guns—an incident that appeared in

Scarface (and much later in **The St. Valentine's Day Massacre**). Al Capone's own car was an armor-plated limousine, a veritable tank.[5]

Cars and gangsters rose to prominence in American culture together. Economically, the automobile industry was broadly responsible for the booming conditions of the twenties. The actual production of cars absorbed a tremendous amount of capital and directly involved several related industries, such as rubber, steel, and glass. The petroleum industry thrived, roads were built, and various related services prospered because of the new cars. Gangsters were associated with automobiles in several ways. According to one researcher of organized crime, Hank Messick:

The automobile . . . helped revolutionize crime. It was essential to the transportation of bootleg booze and permitted gangsters to range farther and farther while making hits and pulling jobs. Moreover, the sucker had greater mobility as well. No longer was it necessary to have a brothel

Lon Chaney in *While the City Sleeps*

Ford factory

or gambling joint in each neighborhood within walking distance of the customers. Joints became fewer and plusher. In time, in many cities, the joints were moved where protection was cheaper and more reliable. Later, as the airplane came into more general use, and better cars and roads were built, a system of regional vice centers developed in the United States.[6]

The newsreels of Al Capone usually show him leaping out of cars (on the way to quash indictments) and climbing back into them (having successfully done so). In New York, Meyer Lansky began his successful career in organized crime as an auto mechanic, "a master of the model T," who worked his way up by providing fleets of souped-up cars and trucks to various gangs, and then by taking over the transportation of liquor.[7]

Chase

and crash in *The Racket*

Since they were first used in movies, automobiles could provide a lot of action, as they did in the gangster films. In the Roaring Twenties they also evoked a distinctly sinister dimension of urban industrial America. According to one historian, "the armor-plated cars with windows of bullet-proof glass, the murders implicit in Hymie Weiss's phrase 'to take for a ride,' the sedans of tommy-gunners spraying the streets of gangland, all created a satanic mythology of the automobile that bid fair to rival the demonism of the saloon."[8]

Death was at the core of this "satanic mythology" of cars and gangsters. The first dialogue spoken by movie gangsters (in *The Lights of New York,* 1928) includes the instructions "take him for a ride." **Quick Millions,** four years later, ends when Bugs's own gang takes him for a ride. The gangster's death in dozens of films is preceded by cop cars streaming out of headquarters for final

Angelo Genna's funeral in Chicago

shootouts. The metaphorical equation of gangsters and cars equaling death was a concrete reality in the auto industry, where Henry Ford hired Detroit mobsters to stop efforts to organize auto workers.

The gangster's final ride was his funeral. The stylized movie versions were modeled after the twenties gang funerals in Chicago, particularly those of Dion O'Bannion and Angelo Genna, in which a funeral procession of slow-moving limousines, flanked by tuxedoed gangsters bearing flowers, followed the coffin through the city streets.

Actual gangsters and film gangsters mastered a machine that symbolized modern life—a machine that, like so many others, was helping to shatter the myth of the garden. The gangster figure was quite at home and in control in the modern mechanized world. He used cars, trucks, telephones, machine guns, airplanes, radios, and wire services to gain power in the criminal world and prestige in popular culture. In *The Great Train Robbery,* outlaws stopped the machine in the garden; the gangster who emerged as a popular and heroic figure in the twenties was a mythic power in the driver's seat of American technology.

The growing urban industrialized society stimulated a process which Walter Lippmann described as "a vast dissolution of ancient habits."[9] The almost ritualized hysteria of Valentino's funeral or Lindbergh's flight and triumphant return are indications that Americans desperately needed new cultural heroes and a new mythology. The need for heroes was certainly not new to the twenties; what was new was the dramatic amplification of popular culture by radio, the movies, and the newspapers.

The impact was even greater because of the declining importance of the family's economic and educational functions.[10] During the twenties, the common function of the family more overtly became the development of the child's personality through the teaching of attitudes that would facilitate social adjustment rather than the molding of character based on well-known moral ideals.[11] This change in the role of the family, reflected in psychologist John B. Watson's behaviorist notions of child rearing, helped shift the burden of defining values and ends of life to institutions and the communications media of the growing urban society.[12]

The most important social role of mass communications, according to several scholars, has become relating the individual to his or her social environment.[13] This social function includes the process of social typing and the articulation of explicit or implicit cultural values. According to one movie executive, "As Hollywood successfully sells American production, it also successfully sells the concepts of our democracy without deliberate intent, without an effort to sell anybody anything."[14]

IMP

Mass media began to define a national popular culture with startling rapidity. Radios appeared in every household that could afford one, movie attendance climbed throughout the country, newspaper circulation expanded, and a whole new tabloid industry appeared. The mass media reached out to America from the cities, and they shaped American culture with an urban point of view. As Sherwood Anderson wrote in 1932, "Now the players do not come to the towns. They are in Los Angeles. We see but the shadows of players. We listen to the shadows of voices. Even the politicians do not come to us now. They stay in the city and talk to us on the radio."[15]

City values, city voices, and city music dominated the radio waves in the twenties. And radio played a key role in making heroes and heroines of sports figures, daredevils, and aviators like Lindbergh. A mania for

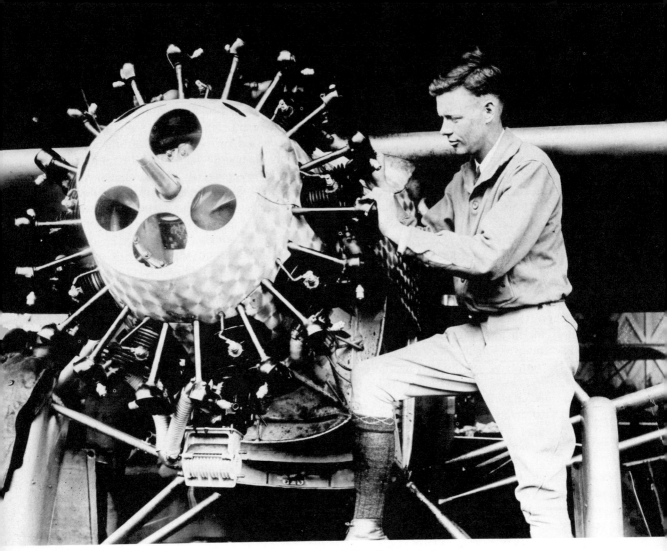

New age hero: Lindbergh and airplane

sports swept the country in the twenties; football, baseball, golf, long-distance swimming, boxing, and auto racing became absorbing rituals of national scope. Heroes and heroines re-affirmed competition, aggression, being the first, the fastest, the biggest, and number one. In this process, movie stars became more god-like than ever.

The tabloids and newspapers played the key role in making gangsters popular. They heavily publicized real gangsters as noteworthy cultural figures and laid the mythological foundations for the heroic gangster.

Newspaper circulation in the United States, steadily rising before World War I, received a boost from the coverage of the war.[16] The increasing circulation attracted more advertisers, and, since advertising gave the publisher three-quarters of his income, methods of maintaining high circulation were at a premium.[17] To replace the excitement of the war and the Red Scare, newspapers utilized the "big play" story, which usually emphasized crime and sex.[18] The gangster murders in the twenties and early thirties figured prominently in these stories.[19]

The heyday of the tabloids, 1925–1929 (which coincides roughly with the emergence of the gangster to heroic status), further demonstrated the rewards of sensationalism to the more respectable daily papers. The publishers and financial backers, whose outlook was that of big business, preferred the emphasis on the "safe" issues of crime and sex to a concern with political controversy.[20]

The competitive trends in circulation made gangsters valuable copy, and reporters founded the gangster mythology by garnishing their reportage with fictional elaboration. The best example is the assignment of nicknames to gangsters. "We don't give ourselves names," reported one gangster, "it's the newspapers."[21]

The newspapers' role in assigning gangsters their nicknames was important in creating the gangster as a mythic hero. "In all

Radio reaches out

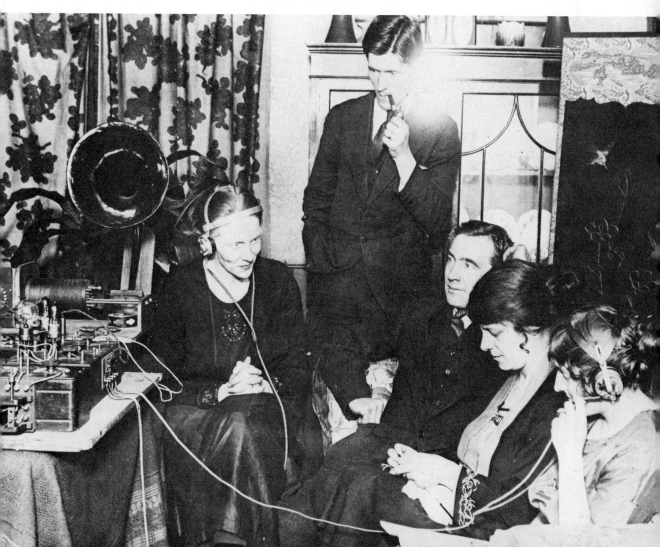

mythical cosmogonies, as far back as they can be traced, the supreme position of the word is found,'' wrote Ernst Cassirer.[22] In a mythic frame of reference, as contrasted with a rational or scientific one, the word or name is not simply symbolic of the object; it is inseparable from the object. To utter the name of a spirit or deity is to actually call him into being.[23] The journalists, who acted as modern interpreters of reality, like ancient priests, assigned names to gangsters and thereby took the first step in establishing the gangsters as modern mythic heroes.

It is significant that the screenwriters of some of the most important gangster films—Ben Hecht, John Bright, Kubic Glasman, and Bartlett Cormack—traced their ideas about gangsters directly to their experiences as newspaper reporters. They were able to amplify the mythic foundations in movies which they had earlier helped formulate in print.

Newsstand

Little Caesar reads about the big time. Douglas Fairbanks and Edward G. Robinson in *Little Caesar*

The importance of the newspapers was explicitly acknowledged in the gangster films themselves. In **Underworld,** for example, the gangsters' cafe has a bulletin board for relevant newspaper articles where Bull Weed reads an account of a bank robbery he has committed. **The Doorway to Hell** begins with presses rolling, and the film title and credit sequence are presented in a front-page format. In **Little Caesar,** Rico must continually check the newspapers for recognition of his rise within the gangster world, and it is insulting, unfavorable newspaper publicity that finally lures him into a police trap. One of the genre's familiar sub-plots involves crusading newspapermen, or curious ones who somehow become involved with gangsters.

Like Little Caesar, real-life gangsters were damned by bad publicity. After the 1929 St. Valentine's Day killings and the gangland murder of Chicago *Tribune* reporter Jake Lingel, the newspapers declared war on the gangsters.[24] After the twenties, gangsters and racketeers were extremely careful and insistent about avoiding publicity.[25] They felt that Al Capone had attracted too much public attention for his own good, or theirs.

Most newspaper writers expressed a point of view that reflected the values of urban industrial society. Few of those who became novelists and screenwriters were as successful as Ben Hecht, who wrote the screenplays for **Underworld** and **Scarface,** two of the most important films in defining the genre.

In 1910 Hecht fled college and headed for Chicago, where at age sixteen he became a reporter for the Chicago *Journal*. Drawn into the excitement of the city, the young reporter "haunted streets, studios, whore houses, police stations, courtrooms, theater stages, jails, saloons, slums, mad houses,

Bull Weed reads

fires, murders, riots, banquet halls, and workshops."[26] His fervent admiration of H.L. Mencken's cynical wit (if not his sustaining bitterness) and his participation in the Chicago literary world from 1916 to 1924 placed Hecht at the center of the "revolution in morals."[27] He felt no compunctions about enjoying sex or drink and was contemptuous of repressive hypocritical morality. "Bawdiness, in fact, had been a natural atmosphere since boyhood."[28]

Hecht held no righteously indignant attitude toward the Chicago criminals he saw as a young journalist. He recalled that his sympathies for the culprit had roots in two general attitudes toward criminals that also facilitated America's acceptance of the gangster as a hero.

First of all, criminals and gangsters were to Hecht, as they had been to Lincoln Steffens, a natural part of the urban environment and were not automatically evil be-

Writers Ben Hecht and Arthur Rossen

cause of their criminal activities. They were creatures of circumstance. Hecht appreciated the fact that to the middle and upper classes of urban society in the twenties, the gangster performed a service and gained respectability. To the lower classes, the world of crime was a frontier that kept alive the promise of American life.[29]

The immigrant relatives whom Hecht fondly recalls in his autobiography certainly shared his concern with success and a reverence for millionaires, but Hecht, in his memoirs at least, does not explicitly glorify gangsters as Alger figures.[30] If the success aspect of the Alger tradition made real gangsters heroes in the immigrant communities and enviable figures generally in society, the gangster that Hecht projected to heroic proportions in **Underworld** was born of a more romantic outlook.

A concern for individual expression and self-fulfillment is a consistent theme running through Hecht's autobiography.[31] His attraction to colorful characters and his ability as a novelist and screenwriter to create them was a result of a boyhood spent in a rooming house that his parents shared with retired circus performers; an early interest in imaginative literature; his life as a reporter; and his participation in the determinedly iconoclastic literary and art worlds of Chicago and New York. Hecht found gangsters interesting because they had "glamorous occupations" in a society that increasingly demanded conformity and routine.[32] And he thought of them as romantic figures because they faced danger. "Crooks and hopheads toting machine guns became the national

idols," Hecht wrote, "for all such hooligans had one honorable thing in common. They risked their own lives in their bid for power."[33]

When Hecht went to Hollywood, he knew that the public agreed with him. "As a newspaperman I had learned that nice people—the audience—loved criminals, doted on reading about their love problems as well as their sadism. My movie grounded on this simple truth was produced with the title **Underworld**."[34]

The public's appreciation of gangsters, however, had to meet the internal standards of censorship that the industry had established with the Hays Office in 1922. The movies' post-1919 assault on traditional morality and the widely publicized Hollywood sex scandals in 1920 and 1921 provoked a stern reaction from women's magazines and religious groups. As Will Hays later remarked, "None could deny that the lusty infant which was the movies had by 1922 transgressed some of the religious, ethical and social mores upon which our society was built."[35] When Hecht arrived in Hollywood, he was told by his friend and fellow screenwriter, Herman Mankiewicz, that the hero had to remain pure but the villain could "have as much fun as he wants" as long as he got his just deserts in the end. Considering the audiences' preferences and Hollywood's demands, Hecht quickly decided that "the thing to do was to skip the heroes and heroines to write a movie containing only villians and bawds. I would not have to tell any lies then."[36]

7

SUCCESS: THE MOVIE INDUSTRY AND MOVIE GANGSTERS

The outlook of the world today is for the greatest era of commercial expansion in history. The rest of the world will become better customers.

President Herbert Hoover
July 27, 1928

As Joe and me walked to the door, Nucky said somethin' that made me feel pretty good. "Charlie," he said, "I like the way you handle yourself. Most of all, I like the way you dress. You're starting to look like a real corporation executive!" Comin' from a guy who practically ran a whole state, I really appreciated that.

Charles Lucania (Lucky Luciano)

Bull Weed. George Bancroft in *Underworld*

In 1926, the movie gangster was on the verge of success. A need to acknowledge the brutal, ruthless exploitation for profit in urban industrial society through a mythic figure, the development of mass media capable of amplifying heroes, and the notoriety of actual gangsters prepared the right climate. Films about criminals appeared throughout the decade, and prohibition racketeers put in sporadic appearances on America's movie screens. When Paramount released **Underworld,** the gangster genre began to move into the foreground.

Underworld, often referred to as the first gangster film, was a critical and financial success. According to some accounts (probably apocryphal), the film ran all night when it opened in New York, as crowds lined the sidewalk waiting to get in. The film tells the story of a powerful and attractive gangster named Bull Weed who robs banks and jewelry stores. Bull Weed helps out an alcoholic lawyer, Rolls Royce, who subsequently falls in love with Bull's girl friend, Feathers McCoy. Bull kills a rival gangster (Buck Mulligan), for which he is sent to prison and condemned to death. Feathers and Rolls Royce, though in love, remain loyal and try to help Bull escape, but their plans are foiled by the police. When the newspapers play up a love affair between Feather and Rolls Royce, Bull thinks he has been betrayed. He escapes by himself and starts hunting for his former lover and friend. The police surround Bull in his apartment hideout, and Rolls Royce comes to rescue him through a secret escape passage. When Bull sees that Rolls Royce and Feathers had remained loyal to him, he doesn't mind that they are in love. He tells them to escape and then remains behind to surrender to the police.

Bull Weed is a gangster of heroic proportions. He's big, and he's strong enough to bend a silver dollar in half. He has a hearty and jovial manner and is well liked by other

Bull and Feathers. George Bancroft and Evelyn Brent in *Underworld*

Bull's rival—Buck Mulligan. Fred Kohler in *Underworld*

Bull bends coin for Rolls Royce. George Bancroft and Clive Brook in *Underworld*

Bull gives Rolls money. Clive Brook, George Bancroft, and Evelyn Brent in *Underworld*

Bull's hideout. Evelyn Brent and George Bancroft in *Underworld*

gangsters (except Buck Mulligan) and the police. Bull Weed is generous enough to delight in giving gifts of jewels or wads of money, and he has enough character to recognize that true friendship is worth more to him than anything else in his life, a theme that was to become part of the genre.

With **Underworld** the gangster had definitely won the sympathies of the movie-going public. As one fan letter expressed it:

Underworld next brought to me
Crooks and gats and bullets binging.

As I wept, I prayed to see
Bull Weed, Killer, saved from swinging. . . .[1]

Underworld takes place in a number of locations that grew to typify the genre: the city at night, beginning with the financial district, where Bull Weed robs a bank; the below-street-level underworld cafe, Dreamland, run by a character named Paloma; midtown city streets crowded with shoppers, where Bull Weed holds up a jewelry shop; the crowded residential neighborhood of brownstone buildings, stoop-sitters and fruit vendors where Bull Weed has his hideout; the ballroom where "the underworld's annual armistice" dance is held; the courtroom where Bull Weed is convicted and sentenced; the prison where he is to be executed and from which he escapes. Director Josef von Sternberg photographed these locations in such a characteristically strong and well-lit way that **Underworld** seems to define many elements of the genre.[2] In fact, these locales

The gangsters' ball in *Underworld*

were used over and over throughout the decade; they congealed in the gangster films of the late twenties. The box office success of **Underworld** simply focused the attention of producers and moviegoers as well as film historians on the genre. As a reviewer for *Motion Picture Classic* noted in an article that sounded like a toast from an underworld banquet, "Here's to crime. Ever since **Underworld** came through with flying colors, most every producer including its particular sponsor, Paramount, has been trying to duplicate it. . . ."[3] By the end of the twenties, gangster films had presented a milieu that through constant reiteration became so thoroughly familiar to film viewers that a reviewer could feel that he or she already had a quite firm grasp of what the underworld was like. According to New York *Daily News* reviewer Irene Thirer, *Tenderloin* (1928) had an "underworld atmosphere of the most convincing sort. Lights, shadows, crooks, police, secret dives. . . ."[4]

The movie gangster's success was reflected in his surroundings. The gang's hideouts, since the beginnings of the genre before the war, generally had the same dark and dingy quality, ranging from the baroque, as in *The Penalty,* to the very simple, as in *Badge 444,* a twenties' serial about gangsters and police. Criminal haunts early in the decade had been pictured in poor and immigrant neighborhoods, as in *Fair Lady* (1921) or *Fools First* (1922). Toward the end of the twenties, gangsters' hideouts became increasingly well-decorated offices, usually in the back of a nightclub.

Nightclubs themselves became more elaborate, particularly after the introduction of sound. In the early twenties, as in *Chicago Sal* (1922), the gangsters have their meeting place in a "low dance hall." The Dreamland Cafe in **Underworld** was more of a dance hall than a nightclub, but by the end of the decade the night clubs, as in **Alibi,** had become fancy Art Deco palaces with awning-covered entrances attended by uniformed doormen, long hallways, and large, lively ballrooms filled with society people.

Often in the gangster films of 1928 and 1929 the nightclub locale became the main setting for the story, as in the Paradise Club in **Broadway** or the Sphinx Club in *Come Across* (1929). These nightclubs were also appropriate locations for staging bootlegging operations.

When sound was introduced, nightclub sequences gave film makers the opportunity to include music and dancing sequences as an integral part of the film. Beginning with *The Lights of New York* (1928), nightclub acts with chorus lines and a song or two by the female lead became a firm part of the genre. And, as in most actual road houses, the music was New Orleans or Chicago jazz.

During the late twenties the theater played an important role in helping to catalyze the mythic gangster's rise from the front page to fame on the silver screen. A gangster play craze that began with *Broadway* in 1926 brought some of the best stories, actors, and dialogue to Hollywood. This vogue for gangster material occurred just at the time the movie industry was looking to the stage for writers, actors, and material suitable for sound movies. James Cagney and Joan Blondell began their Hollywood careers in *Sinners' Holiday* (1930), which was a movie version of the play they were starring in on Broadway. Edward G. Robinson's role as the gangster Nick Scarsi in **the Racket** brought him considerable attention around the country—particularly in Los Angeles. Paul Muni, who was to play the title role in **Scarface,** was a star of New York Yiddish

Hideout exterior in *Voices of the City*

Hideout interior in *The Mighty*

Penthouse heights. Joan Crawford and John Gilbert in *Four Walls*

theater and had played the gangster Bennie Horowitz in the play *Four Walls* (which was made into a film without Muni).

The late twenties plays *Broadway, Crime, Nightstick, Pardon My Glove, Me Gangster, The Squealer, A Handful of Clouds,* and, above all, *The Racket* gave the already popular gangster figure further dramatic impetus in a form Hollywood could easily convert into movies.

The Racket was one of the most important gangster films to appear in the late twenties.

In several ways it is a film that exemplifies the rapid development of the genre in the last two years of the decade from the appearance of **Underworld** to the films of 1930. The film was based on a popular play written by Bartlett Cormack, a Chicago *Daily News* society reporter who was a friend of Ben Hecht. Howard Hughes bought the screen rights and produced the film, which was directed by Lewis Milestone and distributed by Paramount. The play and the movie had a realistic tone that was quite different from that of the romantic **Underworld.** The city is meant to be Chicago; the gangster, Nick Scarsi, was modeled after Al Capone;[5] the crooked mayor resembled Big Bill Thompson; and the story was written by a journalist who, like other Chicago newspapermen, had cashed in on firsthand observations of the gang wars and gangsters that raged through the Windy City. The connections between gangsters, cops, and politicians were pre-sented in a straight-forward way with the cynical overtones characteristic of the twenties' attitudes toward political corrup-tion. The play had been so realistic that it was banned in Chicago. Mayor Big Bill Thompson didn't regard art imitating life as flattery. Bartlett Cormack gave a reason why the play was banned and the film so heavily censored:

I suppose the suggestion that the district attorney

Lon Chaney, Marceline Day, James Murray in *The Big City*

Nightclub in *Fools First*

Nightclub in *Four Walls*

Nightclub in *Midnight Life*

Nightclub in *Broadway*

could be in league with an underworld baron too much for a politician to let the public see.

Consider some of the titles cut, and then form your own opinion. For instance, there is the one where the district attorney tells Scarsi, "We can't carry you and this election both;" or where the racketeer defies the district attorney: "Do you imagine I'd let any lousy politician who'd knock his own mother over the head for a vote tell me what to do?" And the newspaper reporter's explanation of why the district attorney's assistant finally shot Scarsi when the latter threatened

to spill the works: "So the government of the professionals by the professionals, and for the professionals shall not perish from this earth. . . ." Can you think of any but political reasons for the cutting of such titles?[6]

The New York Motion Picture Commission demanded that scenes showing Scarsi bribing police and a state official phoning to have a gangster released from jail be deleted. The delineation of political corruption which was to become characteristic of the so-called

Joan Blondell and James Cagney in *Sinner's Holiday*

Edward G. Robinson in the play *The Racket*

Bribe in the play *The Racket*

''social realism'' of the thirties was introduced in the late twenties; it offended the
censors in New York, Chicago, Dallas, and
Portland. According to one Portland newspaper, ''this was apparently a political deci-
sion, the chief reason offered being that the
film showed city officials as crooks. Pure-
minded Portland must never see an official
on the screen who was not honest. It might
begin suspecting the home folks.''[7]

Tuned Up in 1924 had shown that crooks
were in league with a bank president, while
City Gone Wild (1927) had also shown
connections between gangsters and capitalists. What had uniformly offended the censors in 1928 was that **The Racket** came too
close to giving a clear picture of how the
liaison between gangsters and politicians
worked: how gangsters traded votes (or
campaign contributions) for protection from
the law that politicians could offer, and how

bribing cops and Prohibition agents was
simply part of the business. Films that were
more heavily censored for violence, such as
The Mighty, did not provoke the kind of
letters and anger that reached the censors
over **The Racket.** The President of the P.T.A.
of the Public Schools of Far Rockaway
complained to the New York censors, ''A
film such as this can only serve to create in
the minds of our youth contempt for our
courts and judicial officers and prosecutors
and disgust for and disappointment in a
government where crime and criminals can
run rampant: in open defiance of law and
order.''[8] *Protection,* made a year later,
picked up the theme with a story of a
muckraking reporter whose story is killed
when he exposes the method used by high
city officials to protect bootleggers.

Studio publicity emphasized the realism of
The Racket: ''[Director] Milestone felt that

Bribe in the movie *The Racketeer*

Filming *While the City Sleeps* on location in Los Angeles, 1928

he could add an extra touch of pepper if he were to engage some originals to help him with incidental details . . . so he went into conference with a bootlegger friend, and eight genuine Chicago racketeers who for various good reasons were 'on the lam' and temporarily going straight in Los Angeles were rounded up and induced to work in this crook melodrama."[9] The ads for *Dressed to Kill* urged, "Go with Edmund Lowe, Mary Astor, and Ben Bond behind the scenes of the underworld! See real newspaper headline stuff in the making! Get the thrill of your lifetime breathlessly watching the outcome of the heart stopping gun battle in the dark between the 'brains' of the gang and his henchmen—with Mary Astor the prize at stake."[10]

While some films were shot on location, the most genuinely realistic quality that stamped the genre was the diaglogue. "The breezy talk of Broadway," as an advertisement for *Speakeasy* (1929) expressed it, was one of the first and most important things audiences and critics began to associate with gangster films from the moment in *The Lights of New York* when a girl in the street trumpets her Brooklyn accent. By 1929, gangster pictures were praised or criticized harshly for their realistic use of sound.[11] A reviewer complained that "Dolores Costello said 'cahn't' with too broad an 'A' for the Tenderloin district and Conrad Nagel's voice was too blasting, country, evangelistic. . . ."[12]

By 1930, the sound of gangster films had established a realistic tone as one of the genre's qualities. Gangster films began to have a characteristic sound—a mixture of the American idiomatic language of the streets, gun shots, automobile sounds, jazz, and more. By 1929 a reviewer of **Alibi** found that the gangster genre had added artistry to realism in the genre's use of sound:

This picture has the speed and the sinister staccato sound quality of a machine gun. Every sequence is staccato . . . from the very beginning when your ears are assailed by the sinister shuffle of the convicts' feet, until the end when Chick falls to his death from a bungalow on top of a skyscraper nightclub. Roland West and Chester Morris have taken sound and so dramatized it that an almost perfect talking picture has resulted.[13]

The characteristic action sequences of the genre took shape by the end of the twenties. If the staging of action sequences became more fluid, sophisticated, and explosive in the thirties, the basics were the same: gun battles and car chases between police and gangsters or between rival gangsters. Shootouts involved mostly handguns, with machine guns becoming a requisite part of the action in the late twenties. In **Underworld,** Bull Weed shoots it out with the cops as they stage an elaborate assault on his hideout. In dozens of other films, such as *Gang War* or *City Gone Wild* (both 1927), gun battles were staged with complicated car chases. Occasionally such shootouts were too specific or frightening in their violence for the censors. The New York Motion Picture Commission demanded that close-ups of gunfire be eliminated—particularly when police were the victims, or when, as in *Tenderloin* (1928), gangsters pointed their weapons directly at the camera.

The genre had fleshed out considerably by the end of the decade. Most of the basic characteristics were clearly defined, and the genre was already a springboard for takeoffs and comedies. Paramount, for example, produced one comedy, *The Carnation Kid* (1929), in which a typewriter salesman accidentally changes clothes with a gangster. All the studios were familiar with the genre by 1929. Paramount had led the parade, but M.G.M., Fox, Warner Brothers, De Mille Pictures, Columbia, and Universal had also produced gangster films. And studio person-

Bull Weed shoots it out with the cops. George Bancroft in *Underworld*

nel were familiar with gangster films by 1930. Cameramen like Tony Gaudio, directors like William Wellman, writers like Ben Hecht, and workers in all studio departments were well versed in the successful new genre.

The popularity of gangster films was a suitable reflection of the business realities and growth of the movie industry as well as a metaphor of boomtime America. Like twenties Prohibition racketeers and screen gangsters, the film industry continued its saga of success. By 1926 weekly movie attendance at 20,000 cinemas was reported to range from 60 million to 100 million. According to *Variety,* $2,000,000,000 were invested in the film industry, and the industry did an annual business of $1,250,000,000 to $2,000,000,000.[14]

Success in the movie industry, moreover, was achieved in roughly the same way that the bootleggers built and were to continue to build their empires.

The movie moguls who had been "out-laws" in their battles against the trust became in their turn the Robber Barons. The industry began the decade with a fierce battle for control over the exhibition of motion pictures. The men who ran the studios realized that if they controlled the production, distribution, and exhibition, they could eliminate some of the vicissitudes of a business based on popular tastes. This realization had led to the system of block-booking, by which a studio with enough of the most popular stars would, in effect, say to distributors and exhibitors, "If you want the pictures with our stars, you have to play all the other films that we produce." The more independent the exhibitors remained, the freer they were to choose from other producers and exhibitors. The best possible way to guarantee a studio's profit was to control as many theaters as possible, particularly the big, first-run houses that set the trend for other exhibitors and the chains of theaters in different parts of the country. The ultimate goal was to achieve a complete monopoly through eliminating the competition by denying them outlets for their product. The basic methods of unrestricted capitalist competition were applied, ultimately employing intimidation and violence. Gangsters were using the exact same strategy and methods to control the speakeasy outlets for their booze. Two years before Johnny Torrio and Al Capone were fighting it out with the O'Bannionites, Bugs Moran's gang, and the terrible Gennas for the control of the liquor industry in Chicago, Adolph Zukor of Paramount was moving against First National and Metro for control of the most strategically important movie theaters in the country.

Zukor bought controlling interest in various distribution and exhibition circuits and even bought into corporations controlled by his First National rivals. In New England and the South, Zukor's companies were particularly aggressive. S.A. Lynch, in charge of the Southern strategy, sent his salesmen, who were soon known as the "dynamite gang" or the "wrecking crew," to force exhibitors to show Paramount pictures or go out of business. Lynch's reputation was soon fearsome enough so that he only had to buy a neighboring theater and exhibitors would close their doors.[15]

As with other industries during the 1920's, the ultimate decisions in this economic warfare were made by bankers. For example, when Lynch moved into Texas to attack the big First National chain, $1 million was deposited in the account of his corporation, Southern Enterprises of Texas. The manager of the well-established First National outlets, named Hulsey, had re-invested his fortune, and borrowed hundreds of thousands of dollars from his bank to build new theaters. When Hulsey's banker heard of his rival's deposit, he called in Hulsey and demanded that he sell out to Lynch.[16]

Prior to the 1920's, it had generally been the practice of the industry to finance itself by re-investing profits and by finding private investment. But from 1914 to 1924, the average cost of producing a feature film rose from $20,000 to $300,000.[17] As productions became more extravagant and production costs rose, movie moguls looked to Wall Street for public financing through issuing stock. Zukor at Paramount led the way into this new era of finance, and soon he was followed by every other large corporation involved in the film industry. Most of the Wall Street firms with whom the film makers allied themselves re-invested profits gleaned from war industries.[18]

Investment bankers facilitated the concentration of the film industry into only the largest enterprises. Companies in the film and bootlegging industries shared a similar

Paramount Studios before . . .

. . . and after success.

business experience; an enterprise either had to merge with a larger firm or go broke. Financial interests refused to invest in or quickly abandoned independent producers and distributors. By the end of the decade, Wall Street firms had accomplished what the Motion Picture Patents Company and General Film Trust had been unable to achieve a decade earlier.

As with other industries, ownership was divorced from management, and emphasis was placed on production efficiency. Furthermore, management meant corporate management—not the rule of an individual, no matter how powerful and charismatic he might be. The old Robber Baron was giving way to a new gang—the corporation. By the end of the decade, ''Carl Laemmle, . . . the sole survivor of pioneer days, remained as the only movie magnate owning the majority stock of a general producing and distributing corporation.''[19] The situation was similar to

''Take him for a ride.''
Tom Dugan, Tom McGuire, and Wheeler Oakman in *Lights of New York*

Talkie success: *Lights of New York* premiere.

what was beginning to take place during the twenties in organized crime. In the Mafia the older generation of gangsters, contemptuously referred to as "Mustache Petes" by the youngers gangsters, believed in a strict patriarchy headed by one boss of all the bosses. Gang wars were often fought for revenge or along strict lines of ethnic origin. The younger gangsters, such as Lucky Luciano and Meyer Lansky, saw the melting pot as a pot of gold and wanted to set up a multiethnic crime syndicate more on the lines of a corporation, with efficiency and profit the sole guiding lines for management.[20]

Concentration of control in the movie industry was increased by the financial demands of the introduction of sound. At first, the major companies regarded sound as a fad that would quickly pass—no more likely to revolutionize the movies than color or 3-D. Sam Warner of Warner Brothers felt differently.

By 1925, Warner Brothers Studio was getting pushed to the wall by the five major companies that dominated the industry. Warner productions were no longer reaching first-run theaters. Quarterly reports had become losses instead of profits, and Warner stock was sinking on the exchanges.[21] Warner Brothers gambled on sound out of sheer and total desperation—and hit the jackpot. They produced shorts of vaudeville acts with synchronous sound and feature films with musical accompaniment. With *The Lights of New York* (1928), Warners came out with the first all-talkie. The majority of moviegoers flocked to theaters wired for sound. Fox, which quickly followed with Movietone, and Warners couldn't supply the demand for talkies fast enough. A year later, all major companies were committed to sound movies, which drove the silents from the screen. Movie attendance shot upward. The film companies found themselves even more dependent on investment bankers to supply the capital required to wire thousands of theaters for sound and to produce the talkies to fill them. Like speakeasies, the talkies were still pulling in moviegoers after the stock market collapsed in 1929. By the end of the decade, investment bankers "considered pictures a 'depression-proof industry' and advised investors to place selected film shares on their most preferred lists. In 1909 motion picture investment was scorned;

in 1919 it was a doubtful speculation; in 1929 it had become a favorite of conservative bankers and economists!"[22]

Like gangsters, the movie industry marked its financial success with a gaudy display. Movie houses, once the lowly nickelodeons, became incredible "picture palaces" which in the large cities could seat over 5,000 customers. In the largest picture palaces, like New York City's Roxy or Capitol, the films were preceded by a prologue which consisted of an elaborate stage show involving chorus lines and orchestras.

By the end of the decade the most successful and powerful corporation in the film industry was Paramount, the studio that produced the most successful gangster films of the decade.

The commercial warfare of the movie industry and the prosperity decade provided a suitable background for the rise of the gangster genre. The genre's full development a few years later would take place in the general context of the Depression, when the monopolists of the movie industry closed in for the kill.

Picture palace: the Roxy interior

PART III

THE DEPRESSION: FROM GANGSTER TO G-MAN

8

THE MOVIE RACKET

A racket is best described, I believe, as something that is not what it seems to the majority of people. Only a small "inside" group knows what it is about. It is conducted for the benefit of the very few, at the expense of the very many.

Gen. Smedley Butler
War Is a Racket

It's not a business; it's a racket.

Harry Cohn
President, Columbia Studios

Takeover in *Little Caesar*

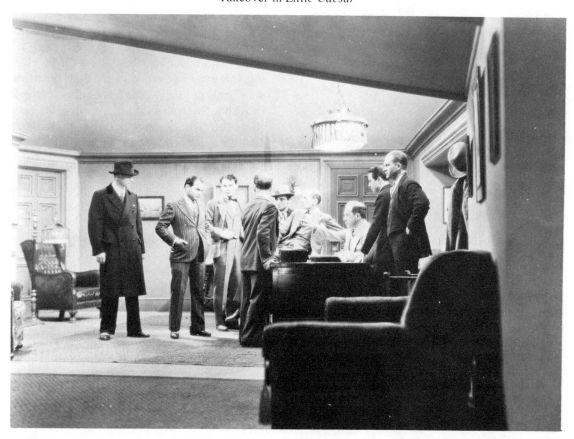

A group of men stride purposefully up the stairs to an underworld meeting at the First Ward Social Club. One of them picks up a spittoon and hurls it through the marbled glass window in the door which bears the name of the club president, whom they have just assassinated. Tony Camonte, alias Scarface, introduces a new president, Johnny Lovo, who tells the assembled gangsters:

"All right, you guys. I'm making a speech. Here it is: Big Louie got soft. He let you run beer into the South Side . . . you can still stay in but from now on you're operatin' the way I say."

A gangster in the crowd:

"You askin' us or are you telling us?"

Johnny Lovo:

"I'm tellin' ya! We're goin' to get organized and I'm gonna handle the works! It's goin' to mean twice as much dough for everybody and half as much trouble."

Another gangster in the crowd:

"You got something figured, Johnny?"

Johnny Lovo:

"Everything. Running beer ain't a nickel game anymore. It's a business and I'm goin' to run it like a business!"

Third gangster in the crowd:

"Swell, we've been cuttin' each others' throats long enough."

In **The Doorway to Hell,** Louie Ricarno tells a similar meeting:

"Now we're all in one racket or another and lately there's been a lot of double crossing—one mob crashing into another mob's territory. We're in big business. The only thing wrong with it is that it needs organizing and it needs a boss. I'm taking over both jobs. I'm gonna lay this town out in zones—I'll give each mob what I think is comin' to 'em and not one inch more. Get that! Each gang'll kick into me and I'll take care of everything. . . ."

The takeover scene has become one of the most characteristic scenes of the genre. When the scene was introduced, it echoed the economic realities of the movie industry in the early days of the Depression.

In 1930, movie executives and investment bankers thought they were in a Depression-proof industry. Weekly movie attendance, which had skyrocketed from about 57 million in 1927 to an estimated 80 to 90 million in 1929, continued at that level in 1930.[1] But two years later, as dozens of movie gangsters died in the gutters, attendance had dropped to 50 million. In mid-1933, as one-fourth to one-third of the population went jobless, 5,000 of the country's 20,000 movie theaters shut down. The film industry was floundering, and the banks moved in for the kill. Paramount, which had towered over all others and which had led the way in developing the gangster genre in the late twenties, was bankrupt in 1933. The banking interests in Kuhn, Loeb and Company, allegedly gave the control of Paramount over to Lehman Brothers, which, with the Atlas Corporation (both Morgan banking interests), reorganized Paramount in 1935. The Chase National Bank, a Rockefeller interest, took control of the Fox Film Corporation and Twentieth Century Films, which merged in 1935 as Twentieth-Century Fox. R.K.O. went bankrupt in 1934 and was reorganized when the Rockefeller-owned parent company, R.C.A., passed controlling interest over to Lehman Brothers and the Atlas Corporation. Chase National Bank and Dillon Read and Company bought into Loew's, Inc., and Universal Chain Theaters Corporation went bankrupt and re-emerged in 1936 as Universal Pictures in the hands of the Standard Capital Corporation.[2]

Takeover in *Homicide Squad*

Takeover in *Doorway to Hell*

Takeover in *City Streets*

Warner Brothers Studio, 1931

The motion picture industry had gone into debt to banking interests in the twenties in order to acquire theaters and to produce and exhibit talkies. Millions of dollars were poured into theater construction, and the maintenance of theaters saddled the industry with fixed costs. As long as movie attendance kept rising, along with the stock of the various firms in the industry, the debt could be paid back easily. When the Depression caught up with the movie business, the banking interests bought cheap, extended their control, and began to exert an even more direct influence over the industry.[3] Four of the five major film corporations were controlled by either the Rockefeller group (Twentieth-Century Fox and Loew's) or the Morgan banking interests (R.K.O. and Paramount).

Warner Brothers had retained its independence by means of a fortunate fast financial shuffling of debts and stocks through the family's personal holding company, Renraw. When Warner Brothers originally incorporated, the company owned 300,000 of the 350,000 shares of stock that were issued. They sold the stocks for the cash necessary to finance the acquisition of theaters and their sound gamble. By 1928, the family company held only 60,000 shares of stock and was in about $10 million worth of debt. But the rising price of Warners' common stock from $39 to $139 per share in 1928 gave the company the money necessary to reap large profits quickly from its sound gamble. When the market crashed and Warners' stock plummeted toward $0.50 per share, the family holding company bought back 265,000 shares with the profits from its sound gamble and retained control of the company while the banks were reorganizing the other majors.[4]

When the banks concentrated and solidified their control of the industry, starting in 1933, the five major firms—Paramount, Loew's, R.K.O., Warner Brothers, and Twentieth-Century Fox—and the minors—Columbia, Universal, and United Artists—virtually controlled the industry. At this time the National Recovery Act was passed, setting up industry self-regulation through the Code of Fair Competition for the Motion Picture Industry. In submitting the Code to President Franklin D. Roosevelt for approval, Hugh Johnson, N.R.A. administrator, introduced the Code with the acknowledgment that "the industry assumes a position of universal importance because of its far-reaching influence upon social and economic standards and conduct throughout the world."[5] The Motion Picture Code gave the corporations that were already in control of the movies the legal muscle to enforce the marketing pattern they had established during the twenties by gaining control of the first-run theaters. "The code for this industry," wrote Johnson, "was formulated by representative industrial groups, because there is in this industry no trade or industrial association fairly representative of the industry."[6] The N.R.A. gave the controlling interests in the industry the opportunity to combine openly through writing the Code and controlling the zoning and grievance procedures. This de facto syndicate legitimized the way in which they had already divided the territories and profits of the industry. This cooperation continued after the N.R.A. Code came to an end in 1935. In 1938 anti-trust proceedings were started against a combination of the five major and three minor firms, charging them with "con-spiring to restrain trade unreasonably and to monopolize the production, distribution, and exhibition of motion pictures."[7] The grievances were, specifically, that the combination had been "1. conditioning licenses to theaters of their co-conspirators or receiving similar preferences for their own theaters, 2. excluding independently produced films from their theaters, 3. excluding independent exhibitors from first and other runs in which defendants operated theaters, 4. using first and early runs in affiliated theaters to control the supply of films, runs, clearances, and admission prices of competing unaffiliated theaters, 5. pooling profits in cities where two or more defendants operated theaters, and 6. effecting a division of territories in the entire United States."[8] At the depths of the Depression the N.R.A. had allowed the motion picture industry to accomplish openly that which had been forbidden by anti-trust laws. As Bugs Ahearn told his gang in **Quick Millions,** "That's the dream of every racketeer, boys—to have a legitimate racket!"

Five months after Roosevelt signed the Motion Pictures Code, which sanctioned the combination's control of the industry, the largest corporations in another industry held a national conference in New York's Waldorf Astoria Hotel to organize a similar combination. A national crime syndicate was also designed to effect "a division of territories in the entire United States," in organized crime's post-bootleg era of expansion and diversification. Representatives gathered from syndicates in New York, Chicago, Cleveland, Minneapolis-St. Paul, Boston, Philadelphia, Miami, New Orleans, and New Jersey. An attorney, "Aaron Sapiro, 500 Fifth Avenue, drew upon his experiences in and out of government to propose that the national organization be created along the lines of the National Recovery Act. . . .

Filming *Public Enemy* (with real bullets)

Public Enemy

Regional boards would be set up to control all activities and there would be an overall commission to hear appeals and make final judgments. The larger cities would be divided along industry lines—gambling, prostitution, liquor, the garment business and labor racketeering in general; there would be no president but regional bosses would sit together as needed in an association of equals. Territories would be allocated and no poaching permitted. Joint ventures would be encouraged in undeveloped cities, but no one would have to participate."[9]

Gangster films became popular at the same time organized crime and the movie industry were sharing an identical economic process involving the combination of the largest enterprises to monopolize the business. But actual gangsters and the movie industry shared more than parallel economic growth. Organized crime moved directly in on the movie industry in several ways.

Following the Wall Street crash, gangsters found that loan-sharking became even more profitable than before. With banks failing or unwilling to loan money, some desperate businessmen turned to the bootleg barons, who had large amounts of cash readily available. The process of infiltrating legitimate businesses, which was to become increasingly the direction of organized crime, quickened during this period. Some movie moguls turned to gangsters in desperate attempts to retain control of their studios or to avoid being gobbled up by larger corporations.

In 1932, Harry Cohn was locked in a fierce and bitter battle with his brother Jack over the control of Columbia Pictures. When the third partner, Joe Brandt, decided to sell his share of the company, Harry Cohn was able to borrow money from gangsters through a man named Johnny Roselli, who was associated with the syndicate's wire service in Hollywood. Brother Jack failed to raise the capital from legitimate sources, so Harry triumphantly took over the management of the studio as President. William Fox had also turned to underworld sources in his unsuccessful effort to retain control of his company.

The most successful penetration of the movie industry, however, was through labor racketeering.[10] In 1933 film industry unions were striking to improve wages and working conditions. The Motion Picture Producers and Directors Association, headed by Will Hays, hired gangsters to break the union strikes. At the same time that the czar of the nation's movie morals wrote in his annual President's report that "the insistent message 'crime does not pay' as flashed from the screen is the most forceful proof of the success of self-regulation in the motion picture industry," he hired Johnny Roselli as "labor conciliator."[11] Roselli told the Kefauver congressional committee that his previous employment in Hollywood had been "as an extra in pictures and at various odds and ends."[12] The odds and ends included his association with "Antonio Cornero Stralla, known to the underworld as 'Tony Cornero, King of the Western Rumrunners,' "[13] as well as his piece of the wire service. Roselli recalled for the Kefauver Committee how he did the job:

"At that time, to go back, I didn't have much money. They had a strike in the industry and the unions—that is, the studios—were in difficulty. The unions were trying to get on to this—I don't know whether it was a demand for higher wages or recognition or what it was. I have forgotten just what it was at the time. There was a little rough play around and the studios naturally didn't want it. They didn't want their workers hurt. They needed some cameramen to go back to work, and they had been threatened through some people. They had asked if I could help. I said: "The only

Harry Cohn

way to help is to fight fire with fire. You don't have to knock anybody on the head doing it, but you can just get them enough protection for these fellows so no one will approach them with any rough play.''

''So I think at that time they asked me how much I would charge for this performance of duties. I said: ''I don't want anything but I would like to get a job. You just pay the men that I will get out and hire to protect these people going to work in the studios, and later on you can give me a job as a negotiator or assistant or something.''

''He gave me some expenses. Within one week it was all over.''[14]

Strike-breaking had been a usual service that gangsters had provided for industrial-

ists, but there were other golden opportunities. The newly formed syndicate, whose representative in Hollywood was Bugsy Siegel, had learned of a labor racket that had begun earlier in Chicago when two gangsters named Bioff and Browne shook down movie theater owners Katz and Balaban for money to run soup kitchens for unemployed projectionists. The take was $20,000, $4,000 of which went to a lawyer and $5 of which went for two cases of soup.[15] Such a lucrative racket did not go unnoticed. Browne and Bioff were called to a meeting of the Chicago syndicate, where the two gangsters were told that their business had just been taken over and was about to expand.[16]

Shortly thereafter, the national convention of the International Alliance of Theatrical Stage Employees and Moving Picture Operators of the United States and Canada took place in Louisville, Kentucky. Along with the representatives of IATSE locals were an assortment of prostitutes and particularly tough goons led by "Joe Arcadia, alias Joe Batters" (later known as Tony Arcardo), whose job it was to get Browne elected president, which they easily accomplished. After a nationwide shakedown of theater owners in which IATSE threatened to strike to place two projectionists in the booth unless they got money for the union's unemployment relief fund, the syndicate was ready to take on the studios in Hollywood as representatives of the union. In 1935, as the gangster was becoming a G-man on the screen, gangster-controlled IATSE forced producers to recognize them as the bargaining agent for studio workers in Hollywood.

Labor racketeering in Hollywood was just one part of a profitable diversification into gambling, prostitution, loan-sharking and dope dealing. The proximity to the Mexican border was as appealing to the crime syndicate as it had been to the early outlaws of the motion picture industry.

On the screens across America, gangsters were taking over territories, forming syndicates, and capitalizing on those made helpless by the Depression in much the same way as the monopolists of the motion picture industry and the organized criminals who were beginning to prey on it.

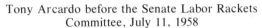

Tony Arcardo before the Senate Labor Rackets Committee, July 11, 1958

9

THE DEPRESSION
AND THE MOVIE GANGSTER

The sympathetic roles are those of criminals. . . . We are surrounding the gang leader with so much legend and tradition that fifty years from now, people will look back on this era of gang rule as being as romantic as the day of robber barons.

Edward Woods (actor at Warner Brothers)

Gangsters are really the invention of capitalists. My first job was breaking a strike, at twenty bucks a day; and all I had to have was a gun. I was over on one strike in Pennsylvania and saw a lot of my countrymen working there and living like animals; so I decided I was on the wrong side of the fence, and became a labor leader and later an underworld power.

Louie Ricarno to reporter in
Rowland Browne's original script
for **The Doorway to Hell**
("A Handful of Clouds")

Breadline, 1931

New York, 1933. The scene is the front of a relief office on a cold, rainy night. A man rushes by the camera; he pulls his threadbare coat around him to keep warm and tugs the brim of his hat over his face to keep out the rain. Inside, a crowded office is filled with soaked and wretched people looking for help. A young woman is being grilled by a priggish relief worker. In another part of the city, her mother is dying of pneumonia in the storeroom of a grocery where they have sought shelter after having been evicted. Kindly neighbors bring in a little food. The woman tells the relief worker that she can't find work and that she quit her last job because the boss "wouldn't leave her alone." The bureaucrat gives her a runaround and curtly dismisses her by saying, "Anyway you have a roof over your heads and you're not starving—there are hundreds that are. Next, please!" **Blondie Johnson,** a 1933 gangster film by Warner Brothers, begins at the emotional depths of the Depression. People are starving to death; a pretty young woman, who is faced with the choice of becoming the boss's mistress to keep her job or going on relief, is turned down by the self-righteous bureaucrat whom she begs to help save her dying mother. Blondie's mother dies, and, when the young woman seeks retribution and help, an oily lawyer tells her that it takes a lot of money to fight the city or the landlord, while a priest solemnly urges her to look for work, which he admits is not there. Blondie turns to crime and as a gangster overcomes the despair and degradation that caught her at every other turn.

Such frank depictions of the Depression were rare in Hollywood films. Much of the power of gangster films was based on their explicit and implicit acknowledgment that the American economy and society were in deep trouble.

After 1929, the economy slid into a decade of stagnation that could be changed only by the massive economic stimulation of the Second World War. The *official* unemployment statistics never dropped below 15 per cent during the decade and admitted to 25 per cent at the time Blondie was in the movie relief office. Unofficial estimates placed unemployment at 33 per cent, and even these estimates were on the conservative side.[1] Other economic statistics, such as capacity utilization and capital investment, also indicate the economy's fundamental stagnation throughout the decade. Americans didn't need numbers to know that the country was going broke. Starving people waited in lines for food; families were evicted from rented apartments and mortgaged homes and farms; Hoovervilles sprang up in every major city; families were broken up as people began wandering from place to place.

There was a reluctance to admit that conditions were disastrous. Radicals and some intellectuals were ready to conclude with Edmund Wilson that "Karl Marx's predictions are in the process of coming true. The money-making period of American history has definitely come to an end. Capitalism has run its course and we shall have to look for other ideals than the ones that capitalism has encouraged."[2] The willingness to confront the deteriorating conditions was retarded by such official optimistic assertions as "Prosperity is just around the corner" and dozens of hope-ridden rituals, like hanging an effigy of "Old Man Depression" at the 1931 opening of the New York City subway.[3] As people died of starvation or illnesses associated with malnutrition, President Herbert Hoover told the country, "Nobody is actually starving. The hoboes, for example, are better fed than they have ever been."[4]

The media followed the government's ex-

Unemployed

ample. Radio news programs conducted "a blackout on current problems," and newspapers almost unanimously followed the government's ostrich-like posture in refusing to acknowledge the Depression.[5] In Middletown, for example, "the local press . . . became a conscious and unconscious suppressor of unpleasant evidence. Hopeful statements by local bankers and industrialists . . . tended to make the front page, while shrinkages in plant forces and related unhappy news commanded small space on inside pages or were omitted entirely."[6]

According to the Protestant *Christian Century,* a liberal magazine, the American press across the country was out of touch with its readers, and during the Depression it seemed and acted like "a rich man's property, conducted to curry to the rich man's favor to spread the rich man's prejudices, to impose the rich man's will on the nation."[7]

The film industry played a similar role in pushing the Depression off the front pages of America's consciousness. Movies were meant to make people forget the Depression by entertaining them while they were unemployed or worried about losing jobs and about wage cuts. Will Hays expressed the industry's viewpoint in the 1934 President's Report to the Motion Picture Producers and Distributors Association: "No medium has contributed more greatly than the film to the maintenance of the national morale during a period featured by revolution, riot and political turmoil in other countries. It has been the mission of the screen, without ignoring the serious social problems of the day, to reflect aspiration, optimism, and kindly humor in its entertainment."[8] For the most part, those in the industry shared this viewpoint. As Busby Berkeley put it, "I tried to give them entertainment to take them away from all that."[9] In an interview James Cagney said, "I find this compensation in being an actor—

that for an hour, here and there, we are able to make sufferers forget their own particular brands of suffering. We lift the load for a few feet of film."[10]

Grateful fan mail, aided and abetted by fan magazines, indicated that for many people in the audience the movies were doing just what the industry workers and spokesmen said they were doing. "Movies have helped us forget," wrote Floyd Casebolt from Waxahachie, Texas. "It is a delight to move up the economic ladder. But it is trying indeed to have to descend, so mankind has sought relief from trouble and worry. In most cases though funds for respite from harassing care have been quite limited. Thank God for the movies—they have provided the sanity-saving diversion, often the inspiration that

James Cagney and Jean Harlow in *Public Enemy*

mankind can afford and has so sorely needed in the most trying days within the recollection of people living today."[11] Movies, it seemed, could help supplement relief for the unemployed; lines leading to the box office were spiritual and emotional breadlines: "Downhearted and discouraged from lack of employment these months past, I stood back from the curb out of a dreary drizzling rain yesterday. Suddenly I decided to go inside a movie house nearby and pass the time away, despite my lack of money. . . . I came out whistling."[12] The movies could also bring relief to those who anxiously clung to their jobs. "A faithful *Movie Mirror* reader" from New York wrote that "as a poor working girl, most of my time is spent in a factory. My ears have become attuned to the noise of power machines, sighs of regret and complaints here, there, everywhere. . . . The

Barton MacLane in *Big Town Czar*

Lew Ayers in *Doorway to Hell*

movies make me forget that I'm tired. I forget the factory—noise, complaints and everything unpleasant. Nothing matters but this world of make believe—the house of cards that will fall when the curtain comes down—the movies are my rose colored glasses and I love them and am thankful for them."[13]

Motion pictures played a role that was more important than that of a simple diversion. Fans wrote of being dependent on movies as "a necessary stimulant," a prop to the optimism necessary to somehow keep the world from collapsing. "We like to see dramatized the lives of ordinary people who have problems like ours and are able to work out a happy solution to them. Please don't take away the happy endings. We *need* to believe in them."[14] Some in the audience even clung to the pictures as a reality more

genuine than existence outside the cinemas: "To me the motion picture is life," wrote M.T. Rucker, Jr., from San Angelo, Texas. "We are senseless puppets in a crazy distorted condition if the motion picture is not life. . . ."[15]

"The movies in America," wrote Gilbert Seldes in 1933, "may take the place of a religion as 'opiate for the people'; but they represent definite aspirations and unconscious desires, and in the depression three or four types have been most effective; the sentimental (as always); the smart comedy of infidelity among the rich; the gangster epic (rude manners, brutality, and action—contempt of authority, the theme of the bowl of cherries and the raspberry; and the desire for work); and the exotic melodrama (savagery and escape)."[16]

What aspirations and desires did the

James Cagney in *Public Enemy*

gangster films—with their theme of a "bowl of cherries and a raspberry" represent? Gangster films were popular with many moviegoers because they expressed a hard-boiled, courageous approach that was as tough in tone as the Depression was in reality. The audiences got the feeling that "we will be better able to gather up our worries and thrash them soundly; to line up our cares against the wall, shoot them one by one and glory in it just as we saw the hero do."[17] Gangsters on the screen projected a self-confident, defiant determination to withstand the most adverse circumstances, and they energetically attacked obstacles that confronted them. Movie gangsters couldn't be pushed around. They pushed others. When Bugs Raymond (played by Spencer Tracy) is chewed out by a cop in the opening scene of **Quick Millions,** he tells the cop, "If you take that badge off, you muzzler, I'll make you eat it." When the cop removes the badge, Bugs leaps on top of him, fists flying. Later he tells his girl, "A guy can't let a cop push him around, can he?" Cagney knew that he expressed a determination to fight back and fight against the psychological effects of the country's economic miseries. He told one interviewer, "The thing I'm most afraid of is the *slave complex*. There is

such a thing. I've watched it growing. Fellows who once had salt in their blood and steel in their nerves, who were four square on their feet and as independent as all hell, have gone cringy and fearful. Fearful of losing their jobs. Cringy to their bosses and to those in power."[18] The ability to project a fighting stance in the face of the Depression was, according to one fan magazine editorial, the very basis of stardom:

Local insiders recall that when the great blight fell on American business, and all over the land the consequent retrenchment made theaters begin to flatten like uncorked champagne, it looked as if a

Spencer Tracy jumps a cop in *Quick Millions*

very bad time had set in for the motion picture industry. But just to show you that there is something, after all, in that ancient adage about a silver lining to every cloud and the sun shining tomorrow—at least two of the major companies can directly trace their biggest money-making bets to the general low state of national feelings! For with everyone feeling a bit down, we all have flocked to those pictures in which appear people who are cocky, confident, thoroughly assured and evidently masters of every situation in which they find themselves, forcing the breaks to come their way. Warner Brothers, beyond all their competitors, have been the shrewdest and most active in capitalizing on this increasing tendency on the part of theater-goers—to their own financial betterment and the raised good spirits of the country at large. They appreciated that a picture in which

Wisconsin farmers spill milk on the road in a desperate attempt to raise prices.

Unemployed demonstrate

a fighter—a man or woman with a "sock," to use the town's phrase—appeared, was something of a national high ball. And that is why through their pictures you see the gay parade of Cagney, Robinson, Blondell, George Brent, Douglas Fairbanks, Jr., Warren William, Ann Dvorak, Bette Davis, Frank McHugh, and Aline MacMahon. Each one of whom constantly and completely demonstrates that he has everything under control at all times. And now they have Paul Muni to add to their roster.[19]

When the national mood was characterized by apathy, defeat, disorientation, and insecurity, movie gangsters were active; they knew what they wanted and they knew how to get it; they were self-reliant and unafraid in pursuit of their goals; and they projected a quality of forthrightness that stood in contrast to the hypocrisies of the Hoover regime and the media's coverage of the Depression. As one fan wrote, "It's the decisive smartness gangsters evince in crime cinemas that incites patrons to admire them, even though they abhor crime in itself. The gangster makes no hypocritical 'bones' about what he wants and acts; [he goes] about methodically to get it. This practicality appeals to the common sense of the audiences."[20]

The common sense of audiences in the Depression told them that conditions were terrible, that there was something fundamentally wrong with the way the country was being run, and that they were being lied to in a thousand subtle and not-so-subtle ways. The gangster films represented a certain truthfulness of desires, hopes, and moods. If gangster films, as Robert Warshow wrote, were the "no" to the optimistic "yes" of American culture, the "no" in the Depression was a refusal to be lied to, to be made a sucker of, to be rendered helpless by conditions seemingly beyond an individual's control, and to accept blandly the injustices and inequalities that existed. There was something unjust about the way oranges were burned and milk spilled on the roads as people went hungry. It was wrong that people starved when there was surplus food. It was wrong that banks failed and people who couldn't pay their mortgages were evicted. It was wrong that a man's house was sold when he couldn't pay his taxes because the city he worked for owed him six months' back wages. Although the dominant mood in the country was helpless apathy, there were many incidents of spontaneous rebellion. Groups of people descended on stores and simply walked out with food without paying. Armed farmers prevented evictions and blocked roads. Unemployed councils and self-help groups sprang up to find alternative distribution schemes for food. Unemployed miners began bootlegging millions of tons of

Unemployed fight police

Gangster as neighborhood hero. George Bancroft in *Ladies Love Brutes*

coal. Under these conditions, traditional heroes of American culture were inadequate. "What is a girl to do?" wrote a movie reviewer:

It's all very confusing, that's what it is. Time was when a girl knew a hero when she saw him. He wore his shirt open at the throat and he had wavy hair and one of those profiles. You know—Greek. He was the big outdoor type and he usually wore a cowboy hat and chaps. Maybe he had one of those little mustaches. . . . But now everything is different. You can't tell the hero from the heavy, to

save you . . . they get riddled with machine gun bullets or hanged or electrocuted or taken for a ride—all the nice ones. . . . what Hollywood needs desperately at this moment is a good up to date first class improved, 1931 model hero. Our old heroes have grown sadly shopworn and we haven't, as yet, any very satisfactory substitutes.[21]

The movie gangster began to appear more heroic because he was, in part, seen as a Robin Hood character. The movie gangster was attractive as a proto-revolutionary bandit who expressed a longing for justice and a more equitable distribution of wealth. According to one fan, "there is usually the satisfying human side to the gangster who cares for a crippled brother or pays off the mortgage."[22] The gangsters on the screen shared the outlaw status of folk heroes like Pretty Boy Floyd, who was praised for burning all the mortgages when he robbed a bank. And when the gangster, like nearly all Robin Hoods, is shot down, his "horrible end gains for him only sympathy because of his 'big hearted' portrayal,"[23] and "frequently we gulp a tear in his behalf and long to punch a perfectly worthy judge in the jaw."[24]

Even Al Capone had been cast in the Robin Hood tradition when he set up soup kitchens in Chicago. Hollywood gossip held that big Al would play "a Robin Hood character" in a movie.[25] The Robin Hood angle caught the eyes of publicity depart-

Al Capone's soup kitchen

Blondie makes it to the top. Chester Morris and Joan Blondell in
Blondie Johnson

ments. *Born to the Racket,* according to an ad, featured "A Robin Hood Racketeer in the Fantastic Tapestry of New York's Underworld!"[26]

There were very few full-blown Robin Hood characters in the movies, and when they did appear the setting was never that of Depression America. Warner Brother's *Robin Hood* (1938) took on the dimensions of the international situation. *Viva Villa* (1934), which was set in Mexico, could "jerk us out of our complacency, to squeeze our hearts and make our throats ache for the little peoples of the earth—the workers who go on toiling dumbly for generations under a yoke, to go suddenly mad with rebellion against the whip. . . ."[27] Movie gangsters struck back for those in the audience who were faced with actual adversity or the anxiety of facing economic ruin. Blondie Johnson became a

gangster after having been pushed around once too often. Like all folk hero bandits in the Robin Hood tradition, she is pushed into banditry by conditions beyond her control. Although Blondie doesn't share her wealth with the poor and downtrodden she has left behind in the relief office, she does remain loyal and honest in her dealings with the gang she ultimately takes over.

Gangsters inevitably punished those who wronged them, and their revenge was usually presented as justifiable. In **Little Caesar, Public Enemy, Scarface,** and **City Streets,** the protagonists all overcome assassination attempts and either run their adversaries out of town or righteously kill them off.

Usually gangsters shared their wealth with family or friends; Tom Powers is continually pressing money into his mother's hands in **Public Enemy.**

In rare cases, gangsters specifically took from the rich and gave to the poor. In **The Little Giant,** Bugs Ahearn applies his "Chicago Plan" to return money to hundreds of small investors who have been bilked out of their money by a bank. When the bankers also trick the gangster into assuming control of the bank (when he tries to buy his way into the investment fraternity), Bugs calls his boys together and explains the situation. The gang forces the members of the board of directors to buy back all the worthless paper they had sold. "We're just selling you what you sold to a lot of other chumps!" they tell one banker. "If they put us in the can for selling 'em to you, they'll put you in the can for selling 'em in the first place!" they tell another. Bugs gets back all the money for the small investors, and the film ends happily.

In *Mayor of Hell* (1933) a gangster casually

Gangster as Robin Hood. Cagney stops whipping in *Mayor of Hell*

Gangster as reformer, helping poor kids learn democracy.

visits a reform school which is part of his political booty. The wretched conditions of the young inmates who grew up in the same neighborhood as the gangster makes him furious, especially when one boy is whipped on the barbed wire that he gets caught on while trying to escape. The racketeer, played by Cagney, takes over the school when he tells his political boss to "Go to the governor. Go to the President if you have to! I want the job of running that joint, and I'm gonna run it my way . . . and if I don't get it I'll take my votes and peddle 'em elsewhere." The gangster gets the job and, with the help of an upper-middle-class nurse and a high school textbook, turns the reform school into a "model democracy," teaching respect for law, order, and the dollar. The kids are happy with improved conditions;

they become less rebellious and take an interest in their self-government. But when the gangster has to lay low for murdering a double-crosser, the old warden takes over the reform school. He returns conditions to their previous state and kills one of the gang. The kids revolt, raid the arsenal, burn down the prison, and kill the warden—who, it turns out, has been making a large profit from running the school.

The Robin Hood facet of the movie gangster shared some affinities with the American left, which was again beginning to grow stronger in the early thirties. The socialist and communist critiques of the disasters of the American economic system were more accurate than the bland optimism of the government and the media. The concern for social welfare and human needs

Gangsters as truckdrivers. James Cagney and Edward Woods in *Public Enemy*

expressed by Socialist party and Communist party platforms in 1932 was officially ignored by Republicans and Democrats but later became the basis for the successes of the New Deal. The predictions of class conflict and warfare appeared to be coming true in Toledo, San Francisco, Washington, D.C., and elsewhere. If the left was unable to organize in an effective electoral way,[28] and

if by 1940 factional disputes seriously damaged its effectiveness, it did play a role in the dialogue about national priorities.

Gangster characters had working-class or poverty-line origins. Louie Ricarno's younger brother tried to remember his past for a friend. ''I only know there seemed to be lots of trouble in our house. And lots of times there wasn't much to eat either!'' In an interview entitled, "Little Caesar tosses some verbal bombs," Edward G. Robinson revealed where his sympathies lay:

I was a Socialist for a time. I believed . . . in a more just and even distribution of wealth. I still believe in that, and I still believe that eventually some state of affairs will come to pass. I hate the horrible contrasts one is faced with daily—one man riding in upholstered luxury; another man, half a mile away, breaking his heart because he can't pay his meagre rent and give his children decent educations. I hate the though there are so many men who cannot have the necessities of life and enough of the comforts to make life more than a bearable thing.[29]

The gangster character in the early thirties was only partially a Robin Hood character expressing a call for justice and a more equitable distribution of wealth. The gangster was *at the same time* a Robber Baron figure identified with exploitation and individualism instead of economic democracy and cooperation. Whereas there was some envy of the Robber Baron's success, the identification was primarily a negative

Selling beer

James Cagney, Edward Woods,
Douglas Gerrard in *Public Enemy*

George Stone and Edward G.
Robinson in *Little Caesar*

Spencer Tracy and Warner Richmond
in *Quick Millions*

Gangster's new car.

Lew Ayres, James Cagney, Dorothy Mathews in *Doorway to Hell*

Edward G. Robinson in *Little Giant*

Clark Gable and Norma Shearer in *A Free Soul*

one. The Robber Baron aspects of movie gangsters were the more prevalent ones within the genre, and they were more expressive of the forces that ruled the economy of the nation and the movie industry. As the gangster in *Gunsmoke* (1931) explained it to his gang, "We're capitalists. . . . It's a great country. Columbus discovered it. George Washington founded it. And a hundred and twenty million suckers worked for it, and when they got it all done—we took it! (Laughter)."

The success story plot of gangster films was central to the Robber Baron aspect of the genre, and in the Depression it replaced the various melodramatic and romantic plots of the twenties' gangster films. The protagonists of the most popular films start at the bottom of society as workers or small-time crooks and fight and scheme their way up into the silk hat crowd of bankers and industrialists. Starting off poor but ambitious, the protagonists of films like **The Doorway to Hell, Little Caesar, Quick Mil-**

lions, Public Enemy, Scarface, Blondie Johnson, or **City Streets** join up with gangs or organize them and move into various rackets, including beer, robbery, protection, confidence, extortion, and gambling. As they grow increasingly prosperous, the gangsters are outfitted in suitably sumptuous clothes, cars, and apartments. They begin to attend theater, opera, and cocktail parties, and they become patrons of the arts; they romance the daughters of the rich. The success story in the context of the early Depression was plausible because the successful were criminals. Although success was still desirable, gangster films offered a creeping recognition that success was more dependent on selfish and criminal behavior than on work or even luck.

The identification of success with criminality was an attitude extended to bankers, who had been revered during the twenties. A select Senate Committee, with Ferdinand Pecora as counsel, revealed the dishonest maneuverings of the most respected bankers of Wall Street. Investment moguls were cast as shysters and bandits. Senator Burton Wheeler of Montana suggested that "the best way to restore confidence in the banks would be to take these crooked presidents out of the banks and treat them the same way we treated Al Capone when he failed to pay his income tax."[30]

The success myth in gangster films of the thirties was tinged with nostalgia as well as criminality. The Robber Baron moguls in the worlds of finance, crime, and the movies were already becoming relics of an early stage of capitalism. Economic empires were ruled by corporations, not individuals, and the corporations and banks were consolidat-ing and expanding their control, as in the movie industry.

The Robber Baron quality of movie gangsters also expressed the fascist trends that thrived in American society during the thirties.

Big business and banking interests, alarmed by President Franklin D. Roosevelt's populist leanings, began to study the fascist dictatorships in Italy and Germany with growing interest and approval. According to *Barrons* financial journal in 1933, as F.D.R. was about to take office, "of course we all realize that dictatorships and even semi-dictatorships in peace time are quite contrary to the spirit of American institu-

Success in *Little Caesar*

tions and all that. . . . And yet—well, a genial and lighthearted dictator might be a relief from the pompous futility of such a Congress as we have recently had. . . . So we return repeatedly to the thought that a mild species of dictatorship will help us over the roughest spots on the road ahead."[31] *Fortune* magazine devoted an entire journal to praising fascism in Italy. The issue's editor concluded that "the good journalist must recognize in Fascism certain ancient virtues of the race, whether or not they happen to be momentarily fashionable in his own country. Among these are Discipline, Duty, Courage, Glory, Sacrifice. . . . Fascism is achieving in a few years or decades such a conquest of the spirit of man as Christianity achieved only in ten centuries."[32]

Organized fascism in America appeared in various forms throughout the decade as the American Liberty League, the Silver Shirts, or the German American Bund; and they followed a number of demagogues, such as Huey Long, Gerald L.K. Smith, Father Coughlin, and William Dudley Pelley. In 1934, as the gangster became a G-man in the movies, the American Liberty League was reported to be organizing a fascist coup in which they hoped to raise an army of discontented veterans, led by former Marine general and war hero Smedley Butler, which would march on Washington with arms supplied by the DuPont Corporation. This army would pressure Roosevelt into accepting an "assistant president" who would actually run the government according to policies dictated by the backers of the Liberty League—the Morgan and Rockefeller interests, the DuPonts, General Motors, and several other oil and financial conglomerates. The plot failed to materialize because Butler refused to go along with the plot and exposed it to the McClellan-Dickstein Committee on Un-American Activities.

The newspapers at first ridiculed Butler, and when his testimony was verified they relegated news of the plot to the back pages.

The movie gangster was more of a Robber Baron than a Robin Hood, and if gangster films can be used as a political barometer, the genre indicates that fascism was stronger than socialism in America during the Depression. Certainly the gangster character fits in with Upton Sinclair's succinct 1934 definition of fascism as "capitalism plus murder." The gangster's success story is a road littered with corpses—so much so that violence has at times seemed to be the very content of the genre.[33] "I'm what the newspapers call a gang leader, Miss Varney," explains one gangster. "My business is murder. . . . there isn't any law where I work. There's only me."[34]

The violence of gangster films was typical of a fascist character who must control those around him. The authoritarian movie gangster rules over a pecking order that demands obedience unto death and which is characterized by the sado-masochistic nature of the gangster figure's personal relations with both men and women. The gangster's sadism dominates the sexuality of the genre. There are very few tender or sensual moments and almost none that promise the kind of joyful pleasure that occurs in Mae West films. Violence constitutes the orgiastic release in gangster films, and it is the most strongly felt physical moment in the gangster's relations with women. Most women in gangster films were objectified as sexual punching bags to be smacked with grapefruit, hands, or feet and dragged around by the hair. The Depression conditions put a tremendous strain on masculine identities rooted in men's roles as bread winners and the frustration bred an agression that was expressed in this violent behavior toward women.

The culmination of the fascist direction the

Mae Clark and James Cagney in
Public Enemy

Mae Clark and James Cagney in *Lady Killer*

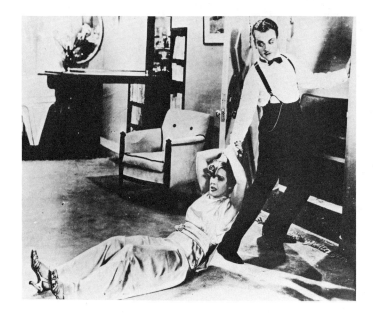

Gangster's battered moll in *Sing and Like It*.

gangster represented was war. And war was the only thing that pulled the American economy out of the Depression. As Louie Ricarno in **The Doorway to Hell** told the head of a military school where he has sent his younger brother,[35] "ah, . . . but war is a grand racket. . . . Er, ah don't misunderstand me. I mean of course that war is a big business." Smedley Butler, the Marine general who refused to lead a fascist coup in 1934, also saw war as a racket:

I spent 33 years . . . being a high-class muscle man for Big Business, for Wall Street and the bankers. In short, I was a racketeer for capitalism.

I helped purify Nicaragua for the international banking house of Brown Brothers in 1909–1912. I helped make Mexico and especially Tampico safe for American oil interests in 1916. I brought light to the Dominican Republic for American sugar interests in 1916. I helped make Haiti and Cuba a decent place for the National City Bank boys to collect revenue in. I helped in the rape of half a dozen Central American republics for the benefit of Wall Street. . . . In China in 1927 I helped see to it that Standard Oil went its way unmolested. . . . I had . . . a swell racket. I was rewarded with honors, medals, promotions. . . . I

THE DEPRESSION AND THE MOVIE GANGSTER

might have given Al Capone a few hints. The best he could do was to operate a racket in three cities. The Marines operated on three continents.[36]

Gangster films were poised between two alternatives that confronted America's crumbling economic system: socialism and fascism. The gangster as a figure of both Robin Hood and Robber Baron dimensions symbolically resolved these contradictory elements by becoming a G-man as the New Deal temporarily resolved the dilemma between fascism and socialism. The genre endures as long as the fundamental dilemma remains.

10

THE GANGSTER GENRE
IN ITS PRIME

Gangsters . . . gunmen . . . gamblers . . . hoodlums . . . heist guys . . . hold-ups . . . "baby faced killers" . . . bandits . . . bullets . . . murders . . . morgues . . . molls. Hollywood is going at the pace that "kills" at the box office! Of all the theme picture epidemics none has equaled the intense rush of gangsters to the box-office. . . . So great is the public demand for this type of picture that gangster yarns are being booked into "key" theaters before the ink is dry on the scenario.

Dorothy Manners, **Motion Picture Classic**
June, 1931

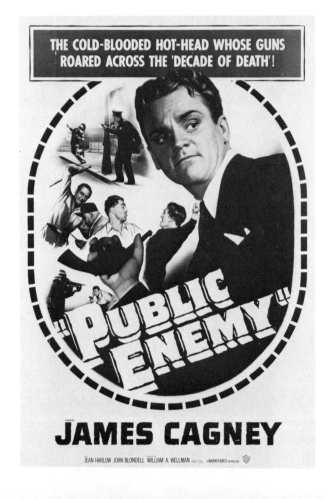

The movie industry from 1930 to 1935 developed the full range of conventions that formed the gangster genre and have basically been copied with few real changes down to the present day. Those conventions of the genre that had been developed by the end of the twenties were completely articulated, refined, polished, and reiterated to the point of predictability.

The dominant image of the movie gangster was formed primarily by the stars who played the gangster character so successfully—James Cagney and Edward G. Robinson. Nearly every major star of the thirties played a gangster. Clark Gable, Gary Cooper, Spencer Tracy, Humphrey Bogart, and Paul Muni all played interesting gangster characters, but Cagney and Robinson early became most closely identified with the role. It was a typecasting that both actors had to fight against throughout their careers. Robinson told one writer that "everywhere he goes people think of him as Al Capone."[1] By 1934, Cagney was also fed up with being typecast:

I'm sick of walking, talking, gesticulating like a tough. . . . Now I don't mean that the tough guy hasn't been successful. The public has liked me tough, but I'm looking ahead. The day of the gangster, the mug, the guy who slaps his women down is through. . . . But I'm having a devil of a time to get my studio to see it, for audiences don't realize it themselves. Not long ago the studios announced that they were going to clean up Jimmy Cagney's parts—and what happened? Thousands of people wrote in and said, "Don't. We like him as he is. Besides, we doubt if he could be a gentleman!"[2]

Both Robinson and Cagney entered the movies via gangster roles in the theater, but their best preparation for the movie gangster roles was life itself. Both stars grew up in working-class immigrant environments and achieved success. Robinson's fan magazine

life story begins, "A small boy stood at the rail of a large ship which was nearing America's shores. . . ." and it concludes with, "America kept her promise to Eddie Robinson."[3] Cagney's story, entitled "Up From the East Side," was a battle through a number of jobs (errand boy, department store bundle wrapper, Wall Street runner) to vaudeville, the theater and Hollywood.[4] Both Robinson and Cagney lived the immigrant's dream of success, and they had survived in tough neighborhoods along with acquaintances who later became gangsters. They knew the experience of being poor and becoming rich, and the language and attitudes of America's city streets.

By 1933 Cagney was making $1,000 per week, and if he understood the success and wealth that defined the Robber Baron dimension of movie gangsters, he was also able to project a Robin Hood attitude because he felt a genuine outrage at the inequalities of American life which the Depression emphasized:

People have asked me if it hasn't sort of calloused me, coated me over, taken the sting out of the memories of growing up poor since I've been in movies, making money, enjoying comfort and ease. No—a thousand No's. I can't enjoy them. Having them has made it worse. It has made me more acutely aware of the bitter contrasts there are in life and lives. If I meet some fellow from 'way back—from my old hoofing days, perhaps— some fellow who hasn't made the grade and who can't seem, any longer, to meet me on the old common ground, it hurts like hell. It makes the appalling fact that *sixty per cent of the wealth of this country is controlled by one per cent of the people* a personally painful, personally shameful matter. A shame that is going to lead us—well, it isn't so good. It makes me ache to know that on one street there are houses where good food and comforts and servants are the order of the day and on the next street there are houses and fore-closure notices and undernourished children and

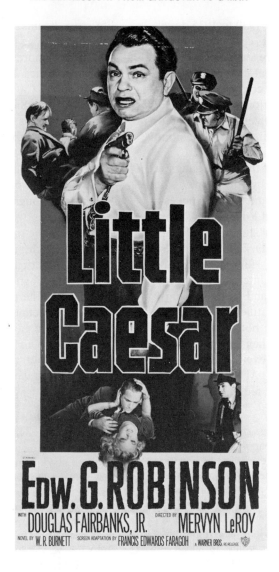

empty larders and heart break. Stiff, isn't it, that we fortunate ones can and *do* eat hearty dinners and lie down in warm beds while our neighbors go hungry and hopeless and cold? . . . That is why the troubles of the past few years have hit me right between the eyes. The neon lights haven't given me astigmatism.[5]

People in the audience appreciated the way in which Cagney projected these egalitarian sentiments into the gangster and shyster roles that he played. "He's the best bet on the screen," wrote one fan from Crawfordsville, Arkansas. "After all, what we need now is a well-placed sock from the one and only Cagney to lift us out of this mental depression and replace the old smile and cheerio on the face of millions."[6]

Critics also responded warmly to Cagney.

The New York *Herald-Tribune* reviewer wrote that Cagney "plays with a simple, relentless honesty." And the National Board of Review critic saw that "the real power of the **Public Enemy**—and it has a certain power, of the hit-you-between-the-eyes kind—lies in its vigorous and brutal assault upon the nerves, and in the stunning—stunning in its literal sense—acting of James Cagney."[7] Lincoln Kirsten most precisely pinned down Cagney's contribution:

Cagney has an inspired sense of timing, an arrogant style, a pride in the control of his body, and a conviction and lack of self-consciousness that are unique in the deserts of the American screen. . . . No one expresses more clearly in terms of pictorial action the delights of violence, the overtones of a semi-conscious sadism, the tendency toward destruction, toward anarchy which is the basis of American sex appeal.[8]

Both Robinson and Cagney gave the gangster character a nearly demoniacal energy and forcefulness through a rapid delivery of dialogue and a constantly moving physical style which could also be exceptionally graceful. Robinson added a strutting dimension to the successful Caesar. Both actors were short: "You could chin yourself on a curbstone," says Alice White to Edward G. Robinson in his first role as a

Edward G. Robinson in *Little Caesar*

James Cagney in *Public Enemy*

gangster.[9] Cagney went on to play the same tough type, whether he played a con man, taxi driver, race car driver, or boxer. He developed mannerisms over several films that were associated with the gangster character. He recalled that "there is a piece of business where I punch the other characters as a gesture of friendliness or affection. . . . this punching mannerism came about because of a conviction on my part that this bird would not embrace or kiss his mother. His idea of affection would be to take a light punch at her. We did it once and it was effective, so whenever you do it once and it's

good you do it again. . . . Well, don't you know that for the next four pictures I was asked to do that very same thing?"[10]

By 1932 gangsters were nearly always immigrants, and quite different from previous American heroic types. As Lincoln Kirsten noted:

The strong silent man is the heir of the American pioneer, the brother of Daniel Boone whom James Fenimore Cooper immortalized as the American type for Europe. . . . The strong silent man has been a trapper, a cowboy, a miner, a railroad man, a soldier, a sailor, a U.S. Marine. . . . He is more American than Uncle Sam, and now, he's a gangster. . . . The origin of the lean, shrewd, lantern-jawed, slow voiced, rangy blond American pioneer was in the New England adventurer of the West. The type has become a short, red-headed Irishman, quick to wrath, humorous, articulate in anger, representing not a minority in action but the action of the American majority—the semi-literate lower middle class. . . . Cagney in a way creates his own type. After the creation we can put it in its proper niche in the Hall of Fame of our folk legends. Cagney is mick Irish. . . . He is the first definitely metropolitan figure to become national.[11]

The most reliably consistent trait of movie gangsters was their sartorial progression from dark and wrinkled nondescript clothing to flashy double-breasted, custom-tailored striped suits with silk ties and suitable jewelry. Snap brim hats became fancy fedoras or derby hats; and spats were added to shoes as gangsters became successful. The pinnacle of a movie gangster's success was always celebrated in a tuxedo and an occasional top hat, for mingling with high society. The gangster was always armed, and the

William Powell and gang in *Street of Chance*

weapon was sometimes selected to match his outfit, as when George Raft selects a pearl-handled pistol to match his elegant outfit on the way to the opera in **Quick Millions.**

The supporting roles were more fully developed in the early thirties and played a larger role in defining the genre. The gang was given more attention. In some films, like **Little Caesar,** the gang was presented to both the audience and Rico, who has just joined them. Sam Vettori takes Rico into the back room to introduce him to the gang:

Aw, they're a hunnert per cent all right, every one of 'em.'' (The camera swish-pans to a close-up of each face as Sam describes the gang members.)

"There's Tony Passa, he can drive a car better than any mug in the town. . . . Otero. He's little but he's the goods, all right. . . . Bat Carrillo. . . . Killer Pepe. . . . Kid Bean. . . . And this one here. Scabby. What a smart guy he is. . . . Boys! Come on, Tony. Wake up. I want you to meet a new guy what's gonna be wid us. This is, ah, ah, . . .''

RICO: "Caesar Enrico Bandello."
SAM: "Oh, Little Caesar, huh!"
RICO: "Yeah . . . sure. . . .''

The gang in **The Doorway to Hell** has simi-

Edward G. Robinson and gang in *Little Caesar*

Pals. Paul Muni and George Raft in *Scarface*

larly picturesque names and faces—Midget, Hymie, Rocco, Big Man, Mileaway, Nigger Mike, and Gimpy. The gangs in **Scarface, Quick Millions,** and **The Little Giant** are composed of big, beefy types, whose jobs are mainly to protect the protagonist and take part in the gang war action.

Within the gang there are only two or three characters who are developed or prominent throughout the picture. One gang member is the protagonist's pal, a character that George Raft played well in **Scarface** as Guino and in **Quick Millions** as Jimmy, or as played by Douglas Fairbanks, Jr., in **Little Caesar.** The nature of the relationship between the gangster and his primary pal could range from a latent homosexuality (as in *The Little Giant*) through genuine friendship (as in **Public Enemy**) to simple business partners (as in *The Ruling Voice*) (1931). Often there was one ambitious member of the gang who hoped for, or plotted, the protagonist's downfall, like Rocco in **The Doorway to Hell** or Nails in **Quick Millions.**

The women in gangster films were usually limited to being molls or mammas, with the notable exception of Blondie Johnson. As molls, women were either sex or success objects to keep the gangsters entertained or help them move into the golden circles of high society. As mistresses, the women in gangster films were usually slim, blonde, and sensual—as in **Public Enemy, Quick Millions, Scarface, The Doorway to Hell,** or **The Little Giant.** As a gangster moved up the social ladder, his mistresses were paid off and discarded; in **The Little Giant,** Bugs gives his mistress a $25,000 brush-off gift

Jean Harlow in *Public Enemy*

with the line, "Thanks, you've been a great gal, honey." In **Quick Millions** the gangster gives his loyal mistress a trip to Europe to get rid of her so that he can woo the debutante daughter of his industrialist partner. Wealthier and "more respectable" women were brunettes; they spoke in what was meant to be a more refined manner, and they played the piano. A gangster would rarely get married; when Louie Ricarno marries his mistress in **The Doorway to Hell,** she is quickly unfaithful to him and has an affair with his best friend and chief henchman. With the exception of the light-hearted **The Little Giant,** gangsters never managed to marry the society ladies they pursued. The gangster in **Quick Millions** is taken for a final ride by his own gang when he wants to "hijack the bride" of a society wedding he felt should have been his.

If the gangster's background or family life was depicted, his warm-hearted immigrant mother had a strongly typed role. In *Sinner's Holiday* (1930), Cagney uncharacteristically weeps in his mother's arms and begs her to help him out of a jam. In **Public Enemy,** Tom Powers gives his Irish mother money but refuses to tell what he does; she turns a deaf ear to his brother's explanations of his illegal activities and insists, "he's a good boy." Tony Camonte's mother knows her son is a rat and warns her daughter that "your brother, he's-a no good; he's gonna hurt you like he hurt everybody." The mothers usually had thick accents; they dressed in simple peasant clothes and were normally to be found in the kitchen preparing food. Occasionally a gangster would have a sister whose role was a bit more interestingly developed, as in **Scarface.** Cesca Camonte is a vivacious, fun-loving girl who fights against the domination of her brother, whom she both fears and loves. By the end of the film, her love for Guido has helped her to understand how

destructive and cowardly her brother is without somebody to dominate.

The genre also encompassed upper-echelon gangsters like Nails Nathan in **Public Enemy** or the Big Boy in **Little Caesar;** high-society types who were usually wealthy industrialists or bankers and their families; white-haired, stern and honest judges; fast-talking, paper-shuffling lawyers; and cynical newspaper reporters and editors who knew the score and how to write it up, as in **Scarface,** or who played some larger role in the plot, as in *Road House Nights* (1930) *The Finger Points* (1931), or **The Secret Six.** When cops did play a role, it was more often that of the older detective who knew the gangster from boyhood and had a friendly fatherly relationship with him, as in **Quick Millions** or **The Doorway to Hell.** Other cops, like Flaherty the Bull in **Little Caesar** or O'Hara in **Scarface,** wanted nothing more than to put the cuffs on the gangster hero.

The city settings of gangster films defined the strong urban flavor of the genre as much as the protagonist and supporting players. Gangster films could begin in a small city or on the road, as with **Little Caesar,** or end in the country, as in the atypical **City Streets,** but the settings of gangster films were rarely outside the city. When the story line did take the gangster beyond the city limits, it was for the purpose of hijacking or bootlegging liquor, as in *Road House Nights;* or when the gangster tries to retire, as in **The Doorway to Hell** or **The Little Giant,** in which cases the gangster seems quite out of place. By the end of 1934 these city settings of the genre had been completely established, and except for changes in style they continued to provide the basic loci for gangster stories.

When the gangster's boyhood neighborhood was shown, it was primarily an immigrant community near an industrial area. **Public Enemy** begins with a series of high-

From beer . . .

angle establishing long shots that pan across factories, railroad yards, and stockyards. A factory whistle shrieks mournfully as shots move closer to the crowded streets and saloon where the audience first sees the gangster as a boy. Louie Ricarno in **The Doorway to Hell** was born on the fifth floor of a tenement.

Dozens of city streets sets defined the genre. They ranged from crowded streets in shopping areas—where one might find Little Caesar buying papers with his picture or

street gangs working a fledgling protection racket on parked cars, as in *Mayor of Hell* (1933)—to empty alleyways in warehouse districts, where fur stores or breweries were robbed or gangsters were shot down.

As gangsters began to work their way up in life, settings included stockyards (**The Secret Six**), trucking company offices (**Quick Millions**), car and truck garages (**The Doorway to Hell, G-Men, Scarface**), construction sites (*Ladies Love Brutes* (1930), **Quick Millions, The Ruling Voice** [1931]), and a series of

. . . to champagne

locations associated with brewing and bottling beer (**The Secret Six, City Streets, Public Enemy,** *Those Who Dance* [1930], *Road House Nights* [1930]). There was considerable variety in speakeasies, ranging from the simplest walk-in joint (**Scarface** or **Public Enemy**) to the more complicated, like the Pal Social Club, a restaurant dance hall in front connected to a back room bar by a telephone booth, in *Those Who Dance.*

Cafes and restaurants, such as the Club Palermo in **Little Caesar,** the Steakhouse Cafe in **The Secret Six,** or the Crescent Moon Cafe in *The Widow from Chicago* (1930), were often the fronts for the gangsters' offices and the usual locations for success banquets. When the gangs weren't hanging out in these locations, they could be found in poolrooms, as in **The Doorway to Hell,** or hangouts like the First Ward Social Club in **Scarface,** with its card and pool tables. Gangsters could also be found sprucing up in barber shops (**Scarface**) or in tailor shops being measured for new and even flashier clothes (**Public Enemy,** *Ladies Love Brutes*).

Nightclubs, which were in every gangster

George Bancroft and Ferike Boros in
Ladies Love Brutes

William Collier Jr. and Ferike Boros
in *Little Caesar*

The Big Boy's place.
Sidney Blackmer and Edward G. Robinson in *Little Caesar*

film, became in the early thirties even more crowded and elaborate than those of the twenties, with larger stage shows and full jazz orchestras. Nightclubs could on occasion be the front for gambling joints (**Little Caesar,** *Czar of Broadway* [1930]).

A variety of apartments amplified the gangster's rise and fall and became the locations for developing the gangster's stunted love life. The gangster began living in a small, one-bedroom flat, as in **Quick Millions,** and moved to gaudy penthouses, as in **Little Caesar,** *The Ruling Voice,* or **The Little Giant.** On the way down, the gangster could wind up in a grimy flat with cracked walls and torn window shades (**The Doorway to Hell**) or in a flophouse for winos (**Little Caesar**).

At the top, the gangsters' offices became ornate, replete with large desks and secretar-

Lawyer springs gangster.
Walter Huston, Jean Hersholt, Tully Marshall, and Robert Homans in *Beast of the City*.

ies (**Blondie Johnson, Quick Millions**). Parties with socialites or visits to their houses were also in suitably ornate surroundings (**Quick Millions,** *Ladies Love Brutes, The Ruling Voice*).

Other prominent locations were newspaper offices and press rooms, banks, theaters, racetracks, flower shops, and bowling alleys. Courtrooms and prisons also became standard locations.

Gangster stories rarely used different or highly imaginative sets in the early thirties. Occasionally a shooting gallery (**City Streets**), penny arcade (*Sinners' Holiday* [1930]), or auto court (**G-Men**) would add some variety to the genre, but for the most part, a consistent picture of the gangster's milieu emerged from the films of the early thirties and has changed very little. Gangster films were not blockbuster productions until recently. Sets of gangster films were straightforward and relatively inexpensive, and the best work of art directors was saved for more lavish and exotic productions. Talented workers like Anton Grot at Warner Brothers did their most impressive work on films like the pirate epic *Captain Blood*.

No gangster film was nominated for an Academy Award for photography in the early thirties. The cinematography of the

Editor and reporter in *Czar of Broadway*

Gangster threatens reporter in *Night Ride*

Guarino the cop makes an arrest.
George Raft and C. Henry Gordon in
Scarface

Cops confront gangsters in *Beast of
the City*

Set in *Little Caesar*

Spaghetti dinner in *Scarface*

Brewery in *What! No Beer?*

genre was not spectacular or elaborate. Rather, it has been characterized by photography that was straightforward and utilitarian, with reference to presenting the story and the action. The characteristic energy and pace of gangster films were more a matter of the vitality of the stars and the dialogue, the editing and the sheer amount of activity on the screen.

The photographic moods of the genre continued in two directions which were marked out by the gangster film's first

cameraman, Billy Bitzer: 1. a documentary directness in camera movement, placement, and pictorial composition, and 2. a dramatic use of lighting.

The almost documentary quality of **Musketeers** continued to by typical of the genre in the thirties. For the most part, camera setups were simple; there were few moving shots, and the camera angle was normally at eye level. There were few subjective photographic moments—as in the soft focus extreme close-ups of Rico when he decides he can't kill his old pal Joe Massara. Tne introduction of sound demanded a relatively static use of the camera, and the gangster films actually seemed quite fluid compared to other contemporary films—but in comparison with the films of the late thirties and after, these classic gangster films appear photographically stiff.

Occasionally camera angles were effectively used—as in the opening shot of **Blondie Johnson,** in which the camera is at gutter level shooting up at the front of the relief office, or in *Love Is a Racket* (1932),

where the downward camera angle gives a penthouse view of the street below. The genre is not characterized by elaborate camera movements, but there are dozens of different camera movements in gangster films which are discreetly utilitarian. In **Quick Millions** the camera dollies back from a medium long shot of a trucking company's docks below to include Bugs and Nails in a medium shot in the foreground; they are talking business in an office above the loading docks, which remain in the background. Traveling shots from trains and cars

Skyscraper office in *High Pressure*

were also typical, as in the opening shot of **Quick Millions** or the shot from the top of an omnibus going down Fifth Avenue in *The Widow from Chicago*. Pans and tilts were usually used in action sequences when required and occasionally for their effect, as when, in **Quick Millions,** the camera tilts up from two newsreel soundmen in a truck to the top of a skyscraper, the dedication of which they are recording; or the swish pans from one face to another when the gang is having a meeting in **Blondie Johnson** or when the gang is introduced in **Little Caesar.**

The lighting in gangster films was more important than a roving camera in defining the genre, particularly the low key lighting and stark black and white contrasts of many of the scenes. The lighting was expressive of the dark and sinister side of American culture and city life. Appropriately, many scenes in gangster films are at night, and thus, the low key lighting was a good complement to the screams and gunfire.

The cameraman who pioneered the gangster-genre is also credited with being the first to use artificial lighting dramatically.[12] It is fitting that another pioneer and artist of artificial illumination photographed the two most beautifully lit gangster films of the early thirties—**City Streets** and **Scarface.** Lee Garmes had photographed an entire film with artificial light by 1927, and had already become one of the most respected cameramen of the silent era when he filmed these gangster movies.

City Streets moves from one remarkably lit scene to another, as faces are suddenly illuminated by flaring matches or flashlights, or in restaurant windows at night. There are close-up portraits—such as that of Sylvia Sidney's eyeball when she takes aim in a shooting gallery, or of Gary Cooper wearing his fancy new clothes—that are as strong as the best portrait work of still photographers

at the time. A moonlit beach, a huge nightclub ballroom, or a mechanized brewery are lighting challenges that are effectively met by Garmes, as is the final burst of backlit birds flying into the sky that concludes this rather operatic film. **Scarface** is also effectively lit, especially in the opening and closing scenes, the barber shop, Poppy's bedroom, and some of the nighttime action sequences. The shooting of a killer's shadow, which is effectively used in the opening sequence and in the St. Valentine's Day massacre re-creation, is one of the most familiar photographic conventions of the genre.

Most of the camerawork in gangster films was simple and craftsmanlike. (The fast pace of the Warner Brothers films left the viewer or the cinematographer little time to develop dramatic camera movements.) Sol Polito, Tony Gaudio, Dev Jennings, and Barney McGill provided the careful, straightforward photography that allowed the action and story to move forward as directly as possible. The focus is always suitably sharp, there is a full black and white tonal range when required (thanks to the introduction of panchromatic film), and camera movements are pressed into the service of the story.

Camerawork rarely involved process shots in the gangster films. On occasion, such shots were used, as in **Quick Millions,** when a high-angle cityscape is combined in a matte shot with a shot of the actors in the foreground dedicating a skyscraper.

The gangster films of the early thirties were also edited in a straightforward fashion designed to keep the story as fast-paced as possible. In general, this meant match-cutting within scenes to preserve the smoothness of action and the use of fade-ins and outs or dissolves between scenes. Dialogue scenes were, for the most part, edited according to the shot-reverse-shot method in which they were filmed cutting on the last

Efficient and dramatic lighting in *G-Men*

Frozen moment of montage action sequence: the nightclub holdup in *Little Caesar*

word. The film editing that was most characteristic of the genre was the creation of montage action sequences. The nightclub in **Little Caesar** or the crime wave sequence in **G-Men** are typical. They are composed of a series of shots dissolved one into the other with accompanying gunfire, screeching tires, screams, crashes, and an occasional line of dialogue. The technique appeared in the late twenties when the optical printer made special effects more widely available. Montage sequences were used in **Alibi** in 1929, but the tight compression of action and the imaginative use of sound made the thirties sequences quite effective. They were often accompanied by superimposed newspapers that zoomed out at the audience with such headlines as "CRIME WAVE SWEEPS MIDWEST" or "GANGSTERS THREATEN NATION'S FOOD SUPPLY."

The genre also became distinguished by its sound—an overall noise of blasting and crashing, machine gun fire, and other action noises, "a magnificent clamor of guns and broken glass," as one reviewer wrote, combined with urban-accented dialogue and jazz music.

There were occasionally brilliant uses of sound—particularly in **City Streets,** directed by Rouben Mamoulian. The film has a variety of sounds unsurpassed by films of the thirties. These range from the gurgling of a large vat of beer, which subtly dissolves into the sound of a river, to the tinkling of thousands of beer bottles in a brewery. And sound is used imaginatively, not simply to accompany the picture, as in the shooting gallery scene which begins with a momentary silent close-up of Sylvia Sidney's eye as she takes aim. Bang! goes her shot, and the camera pulls back as penny arcade music, barkers, and crowd noise fade up to define the environment. **City Streets** also has the first sound flashback to be used in talkies, when Sylvia Sidney lies in jail remembering her conversation with her lover, who has just told her during a visit that he has joined the gang. Her fear and worry about his safety are expressed in repeated fragments of the conversation, which become increasingly loud and jarring as the girl becomes more frightened.

The dialogue of gangster films contributed to the genre as a type of noise as well as spoken drama. The improvements in talkie technique were manifested in the clarity, ease, and speed of dialogue delivery. The slang had a realistic quality that was strong, direct, refreshing, and emotionally suitable to the characters. For some in the audience, like Robert H. Quinn of Mechanicsville, New York, the dialogue was simply offensive: "A few of the reasons I no longer attend the movies: 'Oh Yeah?', 'Well, get a load of this!', 'What am I suppose to do, cut out cryin?', 'Says you! Says me!', 'Ya double-crossin skirt—Bam!' "[13] The dia-

logue could range from the briefly efficient "Scram!" to the poetic "handful of clouds—the kind that comes out of a .38 automatic," depending on whether it was written by a journalist or a playwright.

By the time **G-Men** appeared, the basic conventions that defined the genre had crystallized. The movie industry had evolved a symbolic language of gangster sights, sounds, and events that the subsequent introduction of color, additional settings, and different emphases in the plot have done little to change.

Of the gangster movies of the early thirties that defined and crystallized the genre's characteristic elements, **Scarface** is the most elaborate, powerful, and disturbing. The film is structured on the criminal career of Al Capone (which Ben Hecht denied when visited by Capone's emissaries). According to director Howard Hawks and actor George Raft, Capone was flattered by the film, despite the fact that nobody dared call Big Al "Scarface" to his face. (He was known as "Snorky" to his pals.) The picture used actual gangland incidents associated with Capone's rise to power: e.g., the murder of Big Jim Colissimo, the St. Valentine's Day massacre, and the machine-gunning of Capone's headquarters.

Howard Hughes was determined to produce the gangster film to end all gangster films, so **Scarface** is easily the most lavish of the thirties gangster pictures. A team of writers labored over the script, led by Ben Hecht, who wrote **Underworld,** and W.R. Burnett, who wrote **Little Caesar.** Hawks was reluctant to do a gangster picture at first, but Hughes and Hecht convinced him by comparing the story of Scarface to the history of the Borgias, with their elaborate, murderous scheming and incestual relationships. Hughes made sure that the picture

Big Louie's last meal. Harry J. Vejar
in *Scarface*

Tony "Scarface" Camonte. Paul
Muni in *Scarface*

Scarface gets out of jail on a "writ of hocus pocus."
Edwin Maxwell, Bert Starkey, C. Henry Gordon, Paul Muni, George Raft in *Scarface*

Money to mother. Paul Muni and Inez Palange in *Scarface*

Tony sees Poppy. Paul Muni, Karen
Morley, and Osgood Perkins in
Scarface

"Poppy"
Karen Morley in *Scarface*

Silk shirt success.
Paul Muni and Karen Morley in
Scarface

Tony takes over.
Osgood Perkins, Vince Barnet, Paul
Muni, Karen Morley, George Raft in
Scarface

Tony and gang.
Osgood Perkins, Vince Barnet, Paul
Muni, Maurice Black, *et al.* in
Scarface

Tony moves in on his last rival

The heights:
Tony and gang arrive at nightclub

wreaked more cinematic destruction and death than any of the preceding gangster pictures, and, as a result, the film caused a greater sensation and generated more opposition than other gangster stories when it was released. The picture was banned outright in several areas and could not be shown in New York until the subtitle "Shame of the Nation" was added and some of the more disturbing footage cut out. Over Hawks's objections, a scene of a citizens group demanding the elimination of gangsters was added, and it was directed by someone else.

The film displays all the basic elements that had formed the genre up to 1932. Paul Muni's Tony Camonte is the most powerful and energetic gangster of the early thirties (and possibly throughout the genre). He is thoroughly ambitious, totally ruthless, and absolutely fearless until the end, when he surrenders to the police a quivering coward. He has a bravado and a sense of humor that often make him likeable and a spaghetti-savoring ethnicity that generates nostalgia for the immigrant experience, just as **The Godfather** films would do forty years later.

The plot of **Scarface** is a pure expression of the gangster's rise and fall, a career littered with the corpses of rivals or friends as well as the baubles of success. Tony Camonte starts as a bodyguard for bootlegger Johnny Lovo. He helps Lovo take over the liquor racket by knocking off old-style kingpin Big Louie Costello, organizing the South Side liquor racket under the control of one boss, and battering North Side saloon keepers into buying Lovo's beer. As he rises, Camonte acquires a taste for fancy clothes, going to the theater (*Rain*), and Johnny Lovo's girl friend Poppy, whom he ceaselessly tries to impress. He takes over the gang, and, when Lovo tries to have him assassinated, he kills his former boss and picks up Poppy as a prize. From her apartment, he wryly appreciates the neon sign of an investment bank proclaiming, "The World Is Yours." Finally, Camonte eliminates his remaining rival, Gaffney, and goes off on a trip to Miami. During his absence, Guido Rinaldo (Tony's best friend and right-hand man) and sister Cesca Camonte fall in love and get married. When Tony returns and finds out that Cesca is living with a man, he goes over to her apartment, gun in hand. He shoots Guido in a jealous rage and staggers crazily to his hideout, followed by Cesca, who intends to kill him in revenge. His gang is arrested or shot, so Tony is left to shoot it out with the police, being accompanied by a distraught Cesca, who changes her mind and decides to help her brother. She dies murmuring Guido's name, and Tony becomes terrified of being left alone. He surrenders to the police, and when he tries to break away he is shot down in the gutter. The camera pans up from his bullet-riddled body to the neon sign that mockingly flashes, "The World Is Yours."

All the iconographic elements are there: the trappings of success, the gang, the rivals, the pal, the moll, the cops, the newspaper people, the scenes of the takeover of the gang (two of them), the quick release from jail thanks to a shyster lawyer, the gangsters' ball in a snazzy nightclub, and various ritualized killings and well-staged car chases.

Muni's demonic energy seems to light up certain scenes with the intensity of his performance, as when he fires a machine gun for the first time or sells booze to reluctant speakeasy owners. His energetic performance is nicely balanced by that of George Raft, whose cool, coin-flipping character carved out a different dimension of the gangster character's soul—a smoldering volcano tradition that DeNiro and Pacino were to use effectively in the **Godfather** films.

Scarface summed up what was so attractive and disturbing about the gangster movies in the early thirties. It has remained the classic film of the genre and retains its impact on the viewer. Appropriately enough, the picture is rarely seen, as its producer, Howard Hughes, has hidden the film from the public eye as a rare and precious commodity. **Scarface** is the high-water mark of the genre's expressive power in the early thirties.

Tony dead in the gutter

11

FROM GANGSTER TO G-MAN

There is a sentimentalism in some people which makes popular heroes out of criminals, which needs replacement by a sentimentalism that makes a popular hero of the policeman for the courage and devotion he shows in protection of our citizens.

Herbert Hoover

Gangsters on the run in *G-Men*

Gasping the words, "Mother of mercy, can this be the end of Rico?" Little Caesar clutched his heart, rolled his eyes, and died in the alleyway mud. In **Scarface** the police gun down Tony Camonte under a neon sign that flashes "The World Is Yours" in relentless mockery. The mummified corpse of Tom Powers in **Public Enemy** is delivered to his mother's house after a rival gang kidnaps him from the hospital. A rival gang also guns down Louie Ricarno at the end of **The Doorway to Hell. Quick Millions** ends when Bugs Raymond's own mob takes him for a ride. These endings were typical of the majority of gangster films; gangsters were spared only in the more offbeat films. Blondie Johnson goes to prison for five years, after which, the audience is led to believe, she and her gangster boy friend will get married and go straight. Bugs Ahearn, who tries to go straight throughout the gangster comedy **The Little Giant,** finally succeeds and even marries an impoverished society lady. In **City Streets,** Gary Cooper avoids the final ride his gang plans for him and winds up heading into the sunset with his girl friend and his favorite car.

In general, movie gangsters had to die according to the censorship codes that prevailed. The glorification of some actual criminals and movie gangsters was a disturbing trend for many citizens. "I was amazed one day while in a newsreel theater," said Rudy Vallee, "to hear some people actually applaud a picture of Dillinger . . . I can understand people admiring and applauding great artists, athletes and statesmen. But to applaud a deadly criminal—it's beyond me!"[1] National circulation magazines objected to the "Romantic halo of bravery and adventure" which had turned gangster films into a "kindergarten of crime."[2] "There's quite a controversy over the three boys who robbed a bank in Berlin, Connecticut," wrote one fan:

The prosecuting attorney claims that the pictures were to blame. I sincerely agree with him. We've had a great many gangster pictures lately. I have two nephews—fourteen and fifteen. They are nice, sensible lads, but whenever they are allowed to go to the pictures they are so changed and affected on their return home that we don't know them. They play hold up and go through all the motions that they have seen on the screen.[3]

Convicts and wardens were reported to agree that gangster pictures incited crime because, according to one Sing Sing inmate:

The picture producer creates thrills by making the hero a handsome devil-may-care kind of gangster loyal to his mob and poison to his enemies—in whom there is no fear. Or they make him a hard ruthless type, with courage of a kind, who reveals a sudden unexplained strain of tender heartedness. In short, they create mythical types and situations that strongly appeal to certain kinds of minds by stimulating their imaginations.[4]

A growing concern about the harmful effects of motion pictures on youthful minds led a group called the Motion Picture Research Council to commission a series of studies financed by the Payne Fund and headed by W.W. Charters, Professor of Educational Research at Ohio State University. The first of ten books published by the Payne Fund set the overall tone of concern: *Movies, Delinquency and Crime* concluded that movies indirectly encourage criminal behavior by stimulating fantasies and daydreaming.[5] Groups calling for censorship didn't need scientific proof of the movies' immoral influence; they had already been convinced for a decade of the need to muzzle the movies.

In response to outcries over the "new immorality" of films in the twenties, the Motion Picture Producers and Distributors As-

Little Caesar's last shot. Edward G.
Robinson in *Little Caesar*

King of the *Roaring Twenties*

Paul Muni in *Scarface*

sociation issued eleven "don'ts" in 1927 for movie producers which concentrated on nudity, lewdity, drug traffic, and miscegenation.[6] Three years later, the Hays Office issued a new code partially in reaction to the burgeoning popularity of gangster films. The code was oriented to the violent disregard of the law, and it began with an attack on what was seen as a general tone of lawlessness, and on depicting specific criminal methods.

(I) Crime Against The Law. These shall never be presented in such a way as to throw sympathy with the crime as against law and justice or to inspire others with a desire for imitation.

(1) Murder
  (a) The technique of murder must be presented in a way that will not inspire imitation.
  (b) Brutal killings are not to be presented in detail.
  (c) Revenge in modern times shall not be justified.
(2) Methods of crime should not be explicitly presented.
  (a) Theft, robbery, safecracking, and dynamiting of trains, mines, buildings, etc. should not be detailed in method.
  (b) Arson must be subject to the same safeguards.

Odds Against Tomorrow

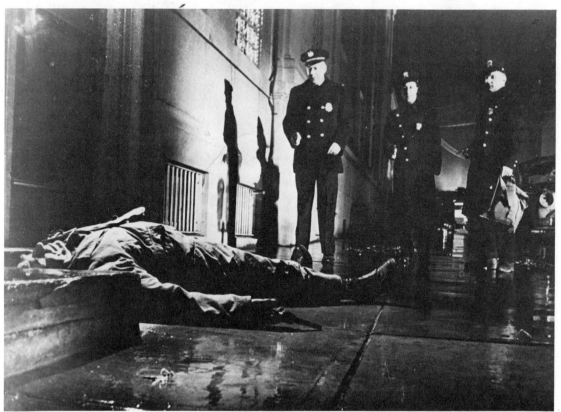

"He used to be a big shot."
James Cagney and Gladys George in *Roaring Twenties*

(c) The use of firearms should be restricted to essentials.

(d) Methods of smuggling should not be presented.[7]

As more gangster films were produced, the cuts relating to breaches of the law which were ordered by censorship boards also increased. Half of the censored material ordered by the Illinois censorship board in 1930–1931 pertained to "glorification of the gangster or outlaw" and "showing disrespect for law enforcement."[8] Gangster films, however, were simply too popular for the studios to pay much attention to a code that, after all, the industry itself administered. In order to mollify some of the criticism, the studios tacked on prologues, added scenes with concerned and angry citizens groups, and had Will Hays assure everybody that these gangster films flashed "the insistent message 'Crime Does Not Pay.'"[9] The Warner Brothers publicity department warned exhibitors of **Little Caesar,** "Do not in any way attempt to glorify the gangster or racketeer. In fact, it would be well to stress the helplessness of gangland to the law. Follow the ad copy and illustrations in this press sheet to the letter and you will be on the safe side."[10]

The gangster died in each gangster film so that the studios could be on the safe side in rationalizing the gangster films as deterrants. "Isn't it more logical," concluded one fan, as he was meant to, "that the children who see these crime and crook pictures have the desire to follow in the footsteps of the heroes of these pictures—the cops and the detectives—and not the criminal who is either brought to justice or killed in every gangster film? Every boy . . . knows that the crook gets killed in the end and that it is the hero of the story who does the killing."[11]

The movie gangster also died because in some ways the character was a scapegoat for the miseries and anger bred by Depression conditions. John Spivak, a reporter investigating anti-Semitic and anti-communist activities for the *New Masses,* concluded that the Depression mood was ripe for scapegoats:

People can be told for just so long that unemployment and hunger are the results of a temporary depression, that we have gotten out of other depressions, that ever lowering wage scales are temporary measures. Eventually they must be told that their misery is due to definite causes or in their growing bitterness the people may turn against the economic system; hence capitalism needs a scapegoat on which to blame the economic conditions of the country. This need is not always the result of a clearly defined perception; often it is an instinctive grasping at any explanation which avoids the logical consideration of economic causes that would lead to the realization that capitalism has now fulfilled its historic function and is disintegrating because of its inherent contradictions.[12]

A standard scene of the early genre was one in which a citizens group meets or a reformer speaks to discuss the threat that gangsters pose to American civilization. The scene provided a rationale for the gangster's death, and it functioned as the industry's genuflection to the moral code. "Fellow suckers," says a radio reformer to his audience in **Quick Millions,** "since we are all permitting the racketeer and the gangster, who you all know is a direct by-product of the bootlegger. They are threatening our safety, menacing our government, raising our rent, increasing the price of everything from the vegetables we eat to the milk our children drink." When a citizens group meets to discuss the problem and draw up a plan of action, a society lady tells the group, "Another twenty years at this rate, gentlemen, and we'll no longer have a republic. We'll have a gangster-governed kingdom. *Why*!? Why can't we do something? We've got the laws and we've got the officials sworn to enforce them."

The District Attorney admits he's ashamed at his inability to get more indictments and convictions, but he blames the businessmen who shield the racketeers for being greedy or "becoming yellow—and yellow is an ugly word. . . . You're guilty and being taken for a ride, and you sit there trying to think out wisecracks," he tells the leading citizens of the city:

Why, no later than last night at dinner, my daughter said to me, we have the best judges that money can buy. That, ladies and gentlemen, is the attitude of the younger generation. . . . We're becoming hoodlum-minded. We're becoming a race of underdogs tearing at the entrails of society, a society based upon wealth instead of intellectual attainment and . . ., but that's another matter. The facts are that we have had dishonest, or let us say weak, judges [turning to judge] but they have been in the minority. Now all crime is

"Irate citizens" in *Special Agent*

based on money, and money must be banked; and, in one of our recent bank disasters it was found that they were financing crime, making it big business, hiding their profits under assumed names in safety deposit boxes so that these millionaire racketeers could defeat the income tax. And one of our largest cities lately went broke because it couldn't collect its taxes. . . . ha!

Making the gangster a scapegoat may have included an implicit recognition that individual success at the expense of others was no longer desirable. Mrs. Franklin D. Roosevelt pointed out that "fundamentally it was a spirit of cooperation that pulled us through

the depression."[13] The individual who had grown rugged exploiting others was not lauded as such or as readily tolerated in 1932 as in the twenties. Success was still desirable, but exploiters were not, as the attitude of the Pecora Commission on banking revealed.

As an immigrant, the gangster was even more readily a scapegoat. Most of the citizens-group scenes were tinged with a xenophobic call to action that had characterized the Palmer raids and the exclusion of immigrants in 1924. When President Hoover began to acknowledge the seriousness of the

Depression by fixing the blame abroad, he told a radio audience that "the depression has been deepened by events from abroad which are beyond the control either of our citizens or our government."[14] Like the Depression, gangsters were foreign to America. In *Star Witness* (1931), an old Civil War veteran tells a judge that "Abraham Lincoln would have rose up and flung them plumb in the ocean. It's time we was doin' the same thing, because I'll tell you, a danged furriner can crowd an American jest so fur . . . jest so fur. . . . We put the old flag up there for you and you can keep her up there or haul it down because you're skeered of a lot of back-stabbin', yeller-bellied furriners. . . ." A newspaper owner in the **Scarface** citizens-group meeting suggests, "Put teeth in the Deportation Act. These gangsters don't belong in this country. Half of 'em aren't even citizens."

Italian community leader: "Dat's-a true. They bring nothing but disgrace to my people."

Newspaper owner: "All right, I'll tell you what to do. Make laws and see that they're obeyed. If we have to have martial law to do it! . . . The army will help, so will the

"A danged furriner can push an American jest so far!" Charles Sale and Ralph Ince in *Star Witness*

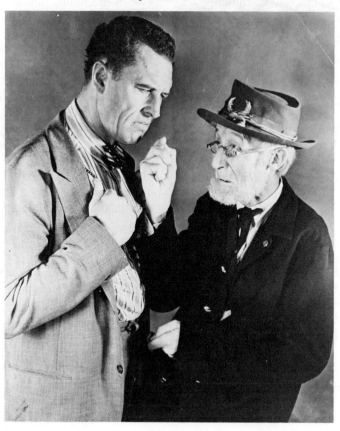

American Legion. They offered their services over two years ago, and nobody ever called on 'em. Let's get wise to ourselves, we're fighting organized murder.''

The citizens-group denunciations, the killing off of the gangster at the end, and the prologues were insufficient to quiet the fears of the censors. Moreover, the industry often ignored censorship boards and put pressure on the boards to eliminate certain scenes. For example, the records of the New York Motion Picture Commission show that they sent a letter to First National Picture Distribution Corporation on October 14, 1930, which asked the company to "eliminate details of holdups," of "Rico shooting McLure, . . . All views of Rico with stolen money . . . all views of gangsters' funerals." On December 8, a second letter went out saying, "kindly disregard the letter of October 14."[15]

The Production Code of 1930 was simply not being enforced. According to one 1933 study of the film industry, "It is not likely that anybody, whether within the industry or outside, has any idea that this code would be sufficiently effective to cause those responsible for production to rid pictures of the characteristics which render them unsatisfactory. . . . It is difficult to believe that directors have always even attempted to comply with its provisions."[16] Outraged moviegoers began to write letters "protesting the vulgarity and coarseness of current productions," and in 1932 Senator Smith Wildman Brookhart from Iowa introduced a resolution to investigate the film industry because, among other things, "Mr. Hays has done nothing toward improving the moral tone of the movies . . . the truth is that Hays was employed primarily as a 'fixer' to protect the industry against any sort of reform or regulation through public action."[17] In 1934, Representative Wright Patman tried to form

a Federal Motion Picture Commission. He maintained that he spoke for 2,000 civic, social, and religious organizations that were demanding federal censorship.[18]

Periodically, representatives of the industry would meet to display their concern for the social responsibilities of motion pictures, but their actions, such as their refusal to place the Production Code under N.R.A. jurisdiction (and legal enforcement) spoke more loudly of their intentions.

In April, 1934, the Legion of Decency went on the march. Catholic groups had worked with the Hays Office, and a Jesuit had written the 1930 Code; the Legion said it was dismayed by the criminal and libidinal cinematic outbursts of the early thirties (when the failing film industry turned to the reliable sex-and-crime formula to bring moviegoers back into the theaters). The Legion of Decency campaign was an organized boycott of "vile and unwholesome" motion pictures conducted by the Episcopal Committee of the Catholic hierarchy. Catholics were asked to sign a pledge that was concerned mostly with sex and "immorality" in pictures. With regard to gangster films, the signer of the pledge swore that "I shall do all that I can to arouse public opinion against the portrayal of vice as a normal condition of affairs and against depicting criminals of any class as heroes and heroines, presenting their filthy philosophy of life as something acceptable to decent men and women."[19] The Legion reached out to other denominational groups and to like-minded fraternal and civic organizations. A propaganda campaign was launched through speaker's bureaus, radio programs, and extensive national press coverage. Lists of condemned films were circulated, some theaters were picketed, and parochial school children were sent marching with banners such as "An Admission to an Indecent Movie Is a Ticket to Hell."[20]

The producers capitulated in 1934 before the campaign picked up full steam. They agreed not to release or distribute a picture that did not have a certificate of approval, which was to be issued according to the 1930 Code and administered by a revamped Hays Office, which promised to be more serious about censorship. Finally, a $25,000 penalty was to be charged for producing, distributing, or exhibiting a picture without the certificate of approval.

The movie industry finally consented to take self-regulation seriously. Although the industry managed to avoid governmental regulation and even after 1934 continued to evade the Code whenever profitable (there is no record of the $25,000 fine having been levied), future gangster films would have to be made with more care for the censors' point of view.

Not everybody wanted censorship. **Scarface** was one of the gangster pictures that raised the loudest outcry from various censorship boards. In an effort to please the censors, the subtitle "Shame of a Nation" was added, along with a different ending in which Tony Camonte was hanged by the state—being shot down in the gutter by the police was evidently not instructive enough. The citizens-group meeting was added over the objections of Howard Hawks, who directed the picture. "Why couldn't we see that great picture **Scarface**, as it was produced?" demanded one New York fan, "Wasn't every scene in it something which actually occurred right here in our own country?"[21] In a letter he titled "Unpopular Censors," J.W. Smith from Fort Stanton, New Mexico, was more bitter:

The latest stupidity of these self-appointed guardians of public morals was the barring of Howard Hughes's crime picture, "Scarface," later renamed "Shame of a Nation" . . . . The stupid censors made Howard Hughes change the title, cut the picture and dress it up in lace drawers, so that it would be dainty enough for an old woman's sewing circle, or lukewarm enough for a fourth rate policeman . . . the censors have a racket and they are making suckers out of all of us. They tell us one hundred twenty million Americans what we can and cannot see at the cinema. But no matter how stupid the censors are, we the theater goers are ten times more stupid for tolerating them.[22]

The best way to exploit the genre's immense popularity and to satisfy the censors at the same time was to turn the gangster character into a cop. As early as 1931, the front page of the New York *Times* carried the headline: "HOOVER CONDEMNS GLORIFYING OF THUGS INSTEAD OF POLICE." The article reported Hoover's address to a convention of police chiefs. "Instead of the 'glorification of the cowardly gangster,' the President said, 'the country needs the glorification of policemen who do their duty, and give their lives in public protection.' "[23]

Some of the many gangster films produced between 1930 and 1934 were sympathetic to the police. *Beast of the City,* for example, a hysterically violent film about gangsters and crooked cops, portrayed a crusading cop whose brother becomes involved with the mob. It was the kind of film the Legion of Decency was looking for. The Legion's radio program, "Endorsed Motion Pictures," warmly proclaimed:

Good Evening, Friends of the Radio Audience: There is a high note of good news this week! The motion picture industry is *not an ailing institution.* . . . To a great many people the title *Beast of the City* will mean many harsh things. We are glad to be able to tell you this is a story of a captain in the police department who through conscientious work is rewarded by the appointment to police inspector. His aim is to bring justice to those who are brought before him. It is a counteractant story to gangster heroics. . . .[24]

Beast of the City

Another gangster film, **The Secret Six,** endorsed vigilante death squads as a means of dealing with the gangsters. But for the most part, in 1930–1933, gangsters were heroes, and even though they died as scapegoats, their Robin Hood qualities kept them more attractive than cops in the deeply depressed years before the New Deal.

By 1934 the time was ripe for the re-incarnation of the gangster as a G-man. The mood of the country was different than that which had fostered gangster popularity earlier. The New Deal demanded optimism, cooperation, a resurgence of national feeling, and a faith in federal authority such as that which had mobilized the country in World War I. The wartime experience was the basis for the National Recovery Administration's blue eagle ballyhoo and the similarity of it's organization to the War Industries Boards of 1918. The gangster hero was drafted into this war on the Depression; the motion picture industry did its part by turning the gangster into a G-man. Moreover, the studios had glutted the gangster film market, so movie gangsters were no longer the guaranteed money makers that they had been two years earlier; and censors were ready to pounce on gangster movies.

The transition was not particularly painful for the gangster character or the film industry. The first re-incarnated gangster appeared in Warner Brothers **G-Men.** The film exploited every characteristic that had made gangster films popular, except a gangster protagonist who was part Robin Hood. The hero, played by Cagney, grew up in the slums but has avoided a life of crime because a benevolent older gangster has sent him to law school to "make something of himself."

At first, Cagney has a tough time as a poor but honest lawyer. The picture opens with Cagney punching a local ward heeler who wants the young lawyer to become a mouthpiece for criminals. A close friend who had joined the F.B.I. drops by to recruit Cagney, but at first he wants no part of the federal government. When his unarmed friend is shot to death by gangsters during an attempted arrest, Cagney decides to enlist to get revenge. He says goodbye to his gangster "angel" and a nightclub dancer who has a crush on him, and goes to Washington, D.C. After he learns the techniques of criminology

Advertisement for *G-Men*

James Cagney in *G-Men*

James Cagney in *G-Men*

Special Agent

and proves that he already knows how to shoot and fight, Cagney leads in the hunt of the gang that has killed his friend as well as other agents. He falls in love with a nurse who is the sister of one of his fellow agents and who is an appropriately respectable mate for a G-man. The film has all the characters, locations, and techniques of sound and cinematography that had defined the genre. There is even more action than in most gangster films, with several deafening shootouts and fast-paced holdup montages and chase scenes.

Like **G-Men,** *Special Agents* (1935) was also released in 1935 by Warners and di-

rected by William Keighley. The film opens in Washington, D.C., with a meeting of G-men who decide to use the income tax laws to crack down on gangsters in order "to prove the cleverest racketeer isn't smart enough to outsmart the federal government." The familiar nightclub setting is used as the basis for a story about an undercover agent who pins the tax rap on the gangsters. The swank nightclub is a front for a number of rackets, ranging from a gambling den where the rich are cheated to a candy story racket of taking nickels from school children. The gangsters are strong enough to beat local murder indictments, but according to the

FBI files

J. Edgar Hoover and Bureau employee

movie, the public should not worry because "Uncle Sam won't stand for it."

The transformation of the movie gangster into a G-man was partially the movie industry's contribution to propaganda for a strong federal government involving the imaginative resources of a film form of proven popularity. The G-man films also placed greater emphasis on the gangster figure as a scapegoat.

The gangster turned G-man on the screen, as the new F.B.I., headed by publicity-hungry J. Edgar Hoover, was riding the crest of a media-produced crime wave which was creating what one commentator saw in 1935 as "The Myth of the G-Man."

Beneath the enthusiasm for the war on crime lay, after four years of national panic, the public's desperate need for a bogeyman. This is an old and inveterate failing of society beset by economic straits. In most of present-day Europe, the bogeyman is a political or religious minority; in this country he has taken the form of a moral minority—the criminal.[25]

Both **G-Men** and *Special Agent* asserted a belief in the authority of the federal government and maintained that this authority depended ultimately on firepower. "Arm your agents!" a Justice Department spokesman exhorts a Congressional Committee in **G-Men:**

". . . and not just with revolvers. If these gangsters want to use machine guns then give your special agents machine guns, shot guns, tear gas—everything else. This is war!

"Now understand, I don't want to make them a

group of quick trigger men. But I do want the underworld to know that when a federal agent draws his gun, he's ready and equipped to shoot to kill with the least possible waste of bullets!''

The gangster turned G-man can kill more dirty rats than ever, and in return for asserting federal authority, he is allowed to live at the end of the picture, to fall in love, get married, and become respectable—a gun-toting Horatio Alger. Will Hays lauded **G-Men** in his annual *President's Report* for placing ''a healthy and helpful emphasis on law enforcement.''[26] The exhibitors duly played up this ''patriotic'' line. As one theater owner in Lamar, Missouri, told *Time* magazine, ''We honestly believe every theater should play this for the reason that it leaves a lot of people thinking our government is okay.''[27]

Turning the gangster character into a federal employee temporarily resolved the contradictory qualities of Robin Hood and Robber Baron. However, the rosy crime-fighting affirmation that the G-man was supposed to represent was infused with an ominous spirit of fascism. ''It is the spirit that seeks order at the expense of justice,'' wrote Milton Meyer. ''It advocates 'treating em rough,' whether 'em' are laborers on strike, Communists at talk, or criminals in flight. It embraces the creation of a police army to fight crime, with the general view that police armies may be put to a number of uses.''[28]

Pulp cover

PART IV

THE GANGSTER GENRE
1935-1976

12

CLOSE-UP: THE MOVIE GANGSTER

The studios have a big investment, tremendous theater exchanges, and they must pay—so if anything has sold once at a great profit, they must sell it again. That is understandable and that is generally the reason why actors are kept to the kind of thing that they have been successful at. When the studios spend a million dollars, they want to get it back and then some. If something has been successful once or twice it will be again.

James Cagney

The impact of gangster movies on the public, the number of pictures produced per year, and the importance of gangster pictures compared to other types of stories had reached its peak in the film cycle that ended in 1934, when gangsters were turned into G-men. The genre was fully formed in the early thirties, and the films that followed went on to repeat and embellish the movie conventions that had been articulated in this early period. From time to time after 1934, studios tried unsuccessfully to revive the full-fledged popularity of the early years of the genre. But the novelty of movie gangsters had been exhausted, and the crisis mood of despair and bewilderment that gripped the country in the early days of the Depression did not return. Gangster pictures have become technically more polished and different conventions of the genre have been emphasized at one time or another, but the gangster genre's basic form has not changed. The genre's continuity of convention is revealed in a closer look at the gangster protagonist as portrayed since 1935.

THE GANGSTER PROTAGONIST

A gangster as the main character has remained the basic—though not exclusive—convention in defining the genre. There are surprisingly few gangster films that have remained rigidly true to this central convention of the genre, and they have erratically moved in and out of the treacherous mainstream of movie popularity.

During the late thirties, in an environment

James Cagney and gang in *Roaring Twenties*

Humphrey Bogart in *High Sierra*

defined by open class warfare on the labor front, the returning Depression, a rise in fascism at home and abroad, and the impending Second World War, gangster protagonists came roaring right back. Warner Brothers studios again led the way with taut and glossy pictures like **Angels With Dirty Faces** and **The Roaring Twenties.**

With few exceptions, such as **High Sierra,** gangster protagonists waned in the forties as *film noir* thrillers, starting with **The Maltese Falcon** (1941) fused the gangster character with the detective. In several B movies gangsters joined forces with the Nazis but the gangster protagonist was also drafted for the war effort to battle Nazi agents in **All Through The Night** and **Lucky Jordan** (1943).

By the end of 1945, films like **The Last Gangster** seemed to be heralding the end of gangster protagonists, when two low-budget gangster pictures appeared that began a trend of gangster biographies that was to emerge fully fifteen years later. **Roger Touhy, Gangster!** (1945) and **Dillinger** kept the gangster hero afloat. There were numerous post-war crime thrillers and gangster-filled dramas in which all the other conventions of the genre except a gangster protagonist were fully exploited. With rare exceptions like **The Gangster** or **Force of Evil,** the main characters were tough drifters, as in **Key Largo,** or the already familiar G-man reincarnation, as in *Undercover Man* (1949). (Even in an extraordinarily powerful gangster drama like

Edward G. Robinson in *The Last Gangster*

Gangsters fight Nazis: 1943 marquee

John Garfield in *East of the River*

White Heat, the protagonist is an undercover agent. Most of the film time is devoted to the police attempt to hunt down the gangster, although Cagney's portrayal of Cody Jarrett completely overwhelms the G-man character.)

Psychotic gangsters and a movie mania for law and order were appropriate to the reactionary post-war period dominated by Senator Joseph McCarthy and America's slide into yet another war. Some gangster protagonists were drafted to fight in the back alleys of the Cold War, as in **Pickup on South Street** or *A Bullet for Joey* (1955), in which gangsters are patriotically pitted against Communists in spite of their mercenary inclinations.

For the most part, the gangster films of the fifties were dominated by a concern for crime syndicates. When gangster pictures did have gangsters in the central role, their stories were based on their struggles with the syndicate, as in **Underworld USA,** *New York Confidential* (1955), or **The Brothers Rico.** Cops and detectives formed in the gangster mold also appeared in numerous films throughout the fifties, of which **The Big Heat** and *My Gun Is Quick* (1958) are perhaps the best examples.

As the syndicate craze culminated in films like **Murder Inc.** and *Pay or Die* (1960), the gangster protagonist returned to the center of the genre in a spate of gangster biographies which served to revive the gangster protagonist's ailing career.

The gangster protagonist again faded into

James Cagney in *White Heat*

Kirk Douglas in *The Brotherhood*

the background during the sixties, appearing only rarely in nostalgic revelries like **The St. Valentine's Day Massacre,** a Mafia drama, **The Brotherhood,** a sub-genre outlaw idyl like **Bonnie and Clyde,** or a complex updated gangster drama like **Point Blank.**

As the idealism of the early sixties dissolved into the social tensions engendered by a vicious, unpopular war and by the intimations of a corrupt government that climaxed in the Watergate revelations, the ground was prepared for a reflowering of the gangster genre. Once again, the gangster protagonist was at the center of the resurgence of a rich variety of gangster pictures. Gangster biographies came back with yet another *Capone* (1976), **Lepke,** and **Dillinger.** Mafia nostalgia returned with *The Don Is Dead* (1973), **The Valachi Papers,** and *Honor Thy Father* (1973). There were sleazy gangster dramas

with small-time protagonists, like **The Friends of Eddie Coyle,** *The Killing of a Chinese Bookie* (1976), and *Mean Streets* (1975). Black gangster movies like **Superfly** and **Black Caesar** extended the genre to the black audiences. And the gangster protagonist moved firmly into the forefront of movie popularity with **The Godfather** and **The Godfather, Part II**—a position he had not enjoyed since the early thirties. Although the **Godfather** films conferred blockbuster status on the gangster genre they were consciously, carefully, and expensively built on a foundation of gangster protagonists that had been reiterated in popular culture for over four decades.

THE ACTORS

The durability of the movie gangster's image in American popular culture is due in part to the fact that nearly every American movie actor has played the role at one time or another in his career. Some of those are: Edward G. Robinson, James Cagney, Humphrey Bogart, Paul Muni, John Garfield, Charles Bronson, Lee Marvin, Clark Gable, Alan Ladd, Richard Conte, Charlton Heston, Mickey Rooney, Lew Ayres, George Bancroft, Gary Cooper, Marlon Brando, George Raft, Robert Taylor, Broderick Crawford, Ray Danton, George Siegel, Al Pacino, Robert De Niro, Akim Tamiroff, Keenan Wynn, David Janssen, Spencer Tracy, Preston Foster, Anthony Quinn, Victor McLaglen, Lon Chaney, Glenn Ford, Karl Malden, Sterling Hayden,

Tony Curtis, Richard Barthelmess, Fred MacMurray, Barry Sullivan, Richard Widmark, Dick Powell, John Cassavetes, Burt Lancaster, Peter Lorre, Paul Lukas, Ricardo Montalban, Dane Clark, Sidney Greenstreet, Buster Crabbe, Stuart Whitman, Peter Falk, Lee J. Cobb, Ray Milland, Dan Duryea, William Bendix, Charles Bickford, Wallace Beery, Steve Cochran, Franchot Tone, Paul Newman, John Derek, John Payne, Edward Arnold, Robert Montgomery, Kirk Douglas, John Barrymore, Gene Kelly, James Mason, Jason Robards, Rod Steiger . . . the list of every actor who played a gangster is by no means complete.

The movie gangster was fully articulated in

Charles Bronson in *Machine Gun Kelly*

Tony Curtis in *Lepke*

Robert Mitchum in *The Friends of Eddie Coyle*

Moses Gunn in *Shaft's Big Score*

particular by having four movie stars play powerful gangster roles throughout their careers. Edward G. Robinson, James Cagney, Humphrey Bogart, and George Raft played young gangsters on their way up, old gangsters on the way down, and dying gangsters on their way out. Each actor imparted a flavor to gangster characters based on his own personality, so that the four have played a key role in shaping the image of a gangster.

Edward G. Robinson refined his gangster character in over twenty-five different movies and hundreds of theatrical performances. Following his energetically vicious and ambitious portrayal of Caesar Enrico Bandello, his gangster characters grew more quietly menacing, thoughtful, and substantial in oozing power from every pore. Robinson

also took the gangster character through the cycle to G-man. In **Bullets or Ballots,** Robinson went from G-man to gangster and back again. He played a tough New York cop who must join a gang in order to break it up and find out who ultimately controls crime in the city. In order to accomplish his task, he has to take over the gang in classic Little Caesar fashion. In **The Last Gangster,** a glossy gangster drama for MGM, Robinson grows wise as a vengeful gangster who must battle his old gang and a changed world after his release from prison. Warner Brothers' imaginative gangster comedy **Brother Orchid** presented Robinson as a gangster who returns from his European culture binge to find that he has lost control of his gang. He survives a one-way ride and winds up in a monastery, where the monks earn money for the poor by

Marlon Brando in *The Godfather*

Al Pacino in *The Godfather Part II*

Publicity artwork for *Angels with Dirty Faces*

growing flowers. The gangster begins to enjoy his recovery in the peaceful pastoral cloister when his former life catches up with him; he then has to battle his old enemies, who plan to move in on the monastery's flower business. Robinson took the gangster character through a wide range of parts. In films like **The Little Giant, A Slight Case of Murder, Brother Orchid,** *Larceny Inc.* (1942), *Robin and the Seven Hoods* (1964),

Edward G. Robinson in *Key Largo*

Edward G. Robinson in *Key Largo*

Edward G. Robinson and Raquel Welch in *The Biggest Bundle of Them All*

James Cagney in *G-Men*

James Cagney in *Never Steal Anything Small*

or *The Biggest Bundle of Them All* (1960), Robinson also burlesqued the character that he had grown so familiar with. In straight gangster roles later in his career, Robinson emphasized the ruthless and arrogant qualities of the movie gangster in powerful portrayals with good scripts, as in **Key Largo,** or routine crime pictures like *Black Tuesday* (1954). Robinson gave the movie gangster a dramatic credibility that was based on his forty years of familiarity with the role and on the long audience identification of Robinson with gangster parts since he exploded on the screen in **Little Caesar.** In 1971 Robinson wrote:

LITTLE CAESAR, many say, is the most imitated screen character in all medias. "All right, you guys, I'm boss here, See!" has been the stock and trade.

I've been parodied so many times and so broadly, that when I get to play the type of character that I've been known for, it is necessary that I do so with greater emphasis, otherwise I fall short of my imitators.[1]

Like Robinson, James Cagney resented the tendency of studios and audiences to identify him exclusively with gangster roles. Yet Cagney also portrayed gangsters over a forty-year period in seventeen films. He gave the character a restless, driving, staccato quality and a number of mannerisms that also spilled over into his other roles, such as hitching up his pants. The aggressive posture of potential menace in which he squared his shoulders and took a fighter's stance, the malevolent gleam in his eye, and the energetic physicality that Cagney gave the role were maintained down to his last gangster part.

In *Never Steal Anything Small* (1959), at age fifty-five, Cagney played a dockworker/racketeer who rises from the docks to the executive office of a union he takes over Cagney imbued the movie gangster's face, with expressions ranging from righteous anger to sadistic glee, courageous determination, friendship, and fear. In **Angels With Dirty Faces, White Heat,** and **Love Me or Leave Me,** Cagney gave the gangster an emotional depth rarely equaled in American movies, particularly in stories about men. **White Heat** is the emotional high-water mark of the genre. Cagney's Cody Jarrett is a man whose psychotic criminality is bursting out of his skull. Cagney also gave the gangster character's love for his mother a depth that began in his first film, *Sinner's Holiday* (1931), and climaxed in **White Heat,** in which his final words, "Top of the world, Ma!" are the last shriek of an extraordinary portrayal of Oedipal love.

Humphrey Bogart began his contribution to the gangster character with a minor role as the "mug" in *Three On a Match* (1932) and in a slightly larger role as the gangster Garboni in Universal's *Midnight* before he appeared as Duke Mantee in **The Petrified Forest.** Except in **The Roaring Twenties** and **Bullets or Ballots,** Bogart's gangsters lacked the single-minded success mania so typical of the gangster's character. Instead, Bogart strengthened the gangster's tough-guy foundation in his many late-thirties roles such as Rocks Valentine in *The Amazing Dr. Clitterhouse* (1938), Joe "Red" Kennedy in *San Quentin* (1937), "Baby Face" Martin in **Dead End,** "Czar" Martin in **Racket Busters,** Joe Gurney in *The King of the Underworld* (1939), Chuck Martin in **Invisible Stripes,** and George Hally in **The Roaring Twenties.** As Raymond Chandler described Bogart, "Bogart is so much better than any other tough-guy actor. He can be tough *without* a gun. Also he has a sense of humor that contains the grating undertone of contempt.''[2] Bogart broadened this tough-guy foundation into more interesting and sympathetic gangster roles in **High Sierra** and **The Big Shot** and in the *film noir* detective dramas *The Maltese Falcon* (1941) and *The Big Sleep* (1946). In the tough-guy roles he developed in the forties, the good/bad guy emerged as a more complicated and ironically detached character with a cynical understanding of the realities of power that was combined with a romantic sentimentality that refused to give up loyalty and love in a cold and ruthless world. Bogart's more straightforward gangster roles emphasized the gangster's malevolent snarl and the cold determination of a killer. Whether his gangster roles were symbolic distillations of the character, as in **The Petrified Forest,** or more realistic portrayals, as in **High Sierra,** Bogart infused them with a potent individualism that has always been at

Humphrey Bogart, Bette Davis, Leslie Howard in *The Petrified Forest*

Humphrey Bogart and Alan Jenkins in *Dead End*

Humphrey Bogart in *The Desperate Hours*

Humphrey Bogart in *The Maltese Falcon*

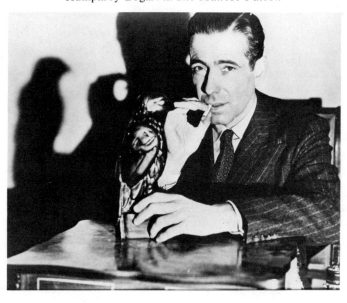

George Raft

George Raft and Sylvia Sidney in *You and Me*

the core of the gangster's character. Bogart wound up his twenty-five years of gangster characters in 1955 as another gangster-on-the-run in *The Desperate Hours.*

George Raft also played gangster roles over a span of forty years. Starting with **Quick Millions,** *Palmy Days* (1931), and **Scarface,** Raft gave his gangster roles an understated authenticity that was based on a lifelong intimacy with and acceptance of underworld figures:

In my time I knew or met them all. Al Capone, Joe Adonis, Frank Costello, Vito Genovese, Dutch Schultz, Machinegun Jack McGurn, Lucky Luciano, Vinnie Coll—most of them were around when I was a young guy. I'll tell you the truth: I admired them. They became names, top people in the country. And when you talked with them as I did you learned a lot. The really big guys—not the punks—were interesting company. Over dinner at a good restaurant or club they were more fun and laughs than any business man or studio head I met. What they did in their work was their business, not mine.

Sure, I admired Owney Madden. He was a big hero in our neighborhood. He ran things in New York and even the mayor and the governor of New York liked him.

The worst thing I ever did for Owney was help his boys move some booze from one place to another. In those days no one saw that as crime. It was a service. The main crimes I committed were on the silver screen.[3]

Raft gave the movie gangster a sexual presence of sensual self-assurance that he had developed as a Broadway dancer and gigolo during the Roaring Twenties. Raft's gangster roles also ran the gamut from vicious villains, as in *Rogue Cop* (1954), to a sympathetic, loyal character, as in *Race Streets* (1948); from ex-cons, as in *You and Me* (1938) or *Invisible Stripes* (1939), to gangster-turned-G-man, as in *Johnny Allegro* (1949). Raft also gave the movie gangster a cool, suave demeanor and coated a gambler's hardness with silky sophistication. Raft brought a fashion fanatic's love of clothes to his work,

George Raft and Humphrey Bogart

Edward G. Robinson and Humphrey Bogart in *Brother Orchid*

so with him the normally fashion-conscious gangster had a particular elegance. By the end of his movie career, Raft burlesqued his own movie role in several different films (**Some Like it Hot,** *Oceans Eleven* [1960] and *Skidoo* [1968]), while he moved into the real world of crime as a front man for gambling operations in Cuba and London. Like Bogart, Robinson, and Cagney, Raft became identified by the public with his gangster's role because he played it so long. He was able to give his gangster characters an easy verisimilitude because Raft consistently portrayed himself and because he was also frequently associated with gangsters in the pub-

lic mind through frequent exposure in the news media.

The fact that all four actors played gangsters throughout their careers helped define the movie gangster in a more realistic way and strengthened the genre over the years. Like the characters in the comic strip "Gasoline Alley," the movie gangsters aged right along with their movie audiences. The movie gangster's durability through the decades owed much to the appearances of these four stars in nearly one hundred films during four decades. In some films, like **The Roaring Twenties, Bullets or Ballots,** and *A Bullet for Joey* (1955), the stars acted together in the same film and gave the gangster genre the strength of their combined presences.

GANGSTER BIOGRAPHIES

Gangster biographies have also played an important role in building up and defining the gangster protagonist since the thirties.

Al Capone was the earliest, most frequent, and most durable subject of gangster biographies. Gangster characters in **The Racket, Little Caesar,** and **Scarface** were supposedly patterned on Capone, and rumors spread throughout Hollywood that the gangster would play himself in a movie. In 1947

Undercover Man was concerned with the I.R.S. trapping of Al Capone. In 1959 Rod Steiger starred as Big Al in **Al Capone.** Neville Brand also played the gangster in *The Scarface Mob* (1962) and *The George Raft Story* (1961). Jason Robards played the famous gangster in **The St. Valentine's Day Massacre,** and finally Ben Gazzara starred in another version of *Capone* (1976).

At first, gangster films were fictional treatments of gangsters. Then, starting with *Roger Touhy, Gangster!* (1945) and **Dillinger,** films began to appear that professed to be true stories of actual criminals. *Roger Touhy, Gangster!* had little to do with the

Rod Steiger in *Al Capone*

Warren Oates in *Dillinger*

facts of Touhy's real life. Rather, it exploits the well-established conventions of the genre to tell a story of how this Capone rival was framed by a crooked banker on a kidnapping charge and how he breaks out of prison to seek revenge. The biography of the outlaw Dillinger was produced in 1945 by Monogram as a low-budget exploitation of what the producers claimed was the real story of the folk hero. **Dillinger** also used the conventions of the gangster genre, as well as actual stock footage from earlier films, including the robbery sequence from *You Only Live Once* (1937). Another more powerful B version of **Dillinger** appeared two decades later. The later treatment offered a much more factual account and a more carefully crafted film, with loving attention paid to costuming and locations. Yet another low-budget homage to Dillinger was produced

with the title *Young Dillinger* (1965). And the character of Dillinger appeared in **Baby Face Nelson.**

In the late fifties a cluster of gangster biographies appeared, probably spurred on by the success of *The Untouchables* television series. This burst of biographies began with **Baby Face Nelson,** directed by Don Siegel and featuring Mickey Rooney in a powerful performance as the pint-sized psychopath who becomes progressively more insane. Roger Corman's **Machine Gun Kelly,** starring Charles Bronson, was quickly followed by *Pretty Boy Floyd,* (1959), *The Bonnie Parker Story* (1958), **The Rise and Fall of Legs Diamond, Portrait of a Mobster** (Dutch Schultz), **Al Capone,** *King of the Roaring Twenties* (1960) (Arnold Rothstein), and *Mad Dog Coll,* 1961. These movies painstakingly recreated the 1930's gangster

Mad Dog Coll

Karen Steele and Ray Danton in *The Rise and Fall of Legs Diamond*

character and milieu in nostalgic, self-conscious fashion. Yet another wave of gangster biographies appeared in the mid seventies, with the theatrical release of **Dillinger,** *Al Capone* (1960), *Lucky Luciano* (Italian, 1975), **The Valachi Papers** and **Crazy Joe** (Joey Gallo), and the television film of *Pretty Boy Floyd* (1960) and *The Virginia Hill Story* (Bugsy Siegel, 1976).

THE GANGSTER'S CHARACTER

Gangster protagonists have been ascribed the same character traits whether or not they were based on fact or fiction. Rico Angelo begins a classic testimonial dinner in the film *Party Girl* (1959) with a speech about one of his oldest lieutenants, a man who has recently double-crossed him. The eulogy turns from praise to vituperative ranting, climaxed by Rico bashing in the man's head with a solid silver pool cue intended as a trophy. The shocking graphic violence of the scene, based on an incident in which Al Capone beat two of his henchmen to death with a baseball bat at a dinner, typifies the movie gangster's extremely violent nature. From **The Musketeers of Pig Alley** through *The Godfather,* the movie gangster's character

has remained firmly rooted in violence. Over the years, the gangster genre has defined the protagonist's world as one of every kind of violence: punching, kicking, scratching, biting, slicing, chopping, whipping, beating, stabbing, impaling, burning, shooting, and exploding. Fights, rapes, tortures, murders, and massacres have filled the genre with so much vicious mayhem that the gangster has an aura of accumulated violence that defines his character whether he is a protagonist or not in whatever type of film he appears.

Violence and terror have remained the sources of the movie gangster's power. Whether he needs to control his own gang or eliminate competitors and obstacles, the movie gangster ultimately relies on violence. In the **St. Valentine's Day Massacre** the motivations of Al Capone and Bugs Moran are reduced to killing each other off. As Robert Warshow pointed out, the movie gangster's implicit business is killing people. This observation has become more valid as murder has explicitly become the gangster's main business. Since the thirties, the movie gangster's penchant for murder has become formalized and businesslike, so that in some films, like **The Enforcer,** *Murder Inc.,* or *The Mechanic* (1972), the gangster's business has in fact been reduced simply to murder of a cold, impersonal nature.

At the same time, the movie gangster's violence has also continually had a sadistic quality. Sadistic violence, particularly after wars, has grown increasingly brutal and painful for the victims and pleasurable for the sadists since the thirties. Extremely sadistic gangsters have regularly appeared in the genre's history who, like Tony Camonte in **Scarface,** "liked to hurt people." Eli Wallach's Dancer in *The Lineup* (1958), Richard Widmark's giggling killer, Tom Udo, in **The Kiss of Death,** William Bendix in *The Glass Key* (1943) and *Dark Corner*

(1946), or Dan Duryea in *Criss Cross* (1949) and *Larceny* (1943) are characters whose main activity and only pleasure is hurting people. The most sadistic gangster characters have usually been too aberrant to be the main characters. Rather, they amplify this characteristic quality and express it in such a powerful way that it seems to permeate the entire genre.

The gangster character passed a legacy of sadism on to various cop and detective characters, as in *The Maltese Falcon* (1941), **Dirty Harry,** *My Gun Is Quick* (1958), and *The French Connection* (1971). Sadism particularly governs the movie gangster's attitude toward women. Since the thirties, the misogynist trait of the movie gangster's character has continued to grow more violent and terrible. The rape in *Johnny Belinda* (1948), the disfiguration of Gloria Grahame's face with boiling coffee in **The Big Heat,** the beatings that accompany the marital battles in **The Godfather,** or the slave barn and gang rape in *Prime Cut* (1975) are grotesquely typical of the movie gangster's need to dominate and humiliate women. This compelling need to control women completely and violently is rooted in the movie gangster's continued inner fear and mistrust of women. Little Caesar won't go near women; Tom Powers in **Public Enemy** beats up a woman the morning after she has (improbably) seduced him while he was helpless in a drunken stupor. In *Street With No Name* (1948), Alec Stiles (Richard Widmark) gives this misogynist attitude its most direct expression when he warns another gangster, "Don't ever trust dames".

Since Louie Ricarno's wife cheated on him with his best friend in **The Doorway to Hell,** gangster movies have continued to present women as basically unworthy of trust. During the next few decades, women were increasingly depicted as deceitful in various

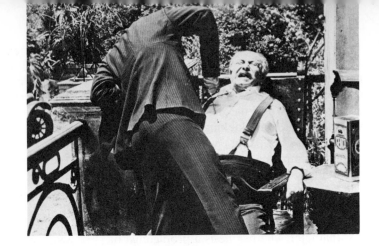

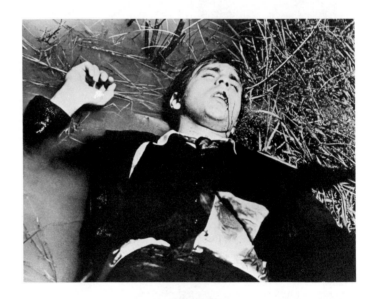

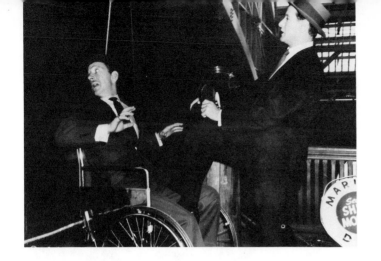

Lee Marvin throws boiling coffee in Gloria Grahame's face in *The Big Heat*

dramas. Men leaving their women to go to war in the forties, the general Cold War paranoia of the fifties, and increasing sexual and economic liberation of women during the sixties and seventies augmented this distrust of women in movies. Double-crossing beautiful women with hidden motivations became central to gangster dramas like **The Killers,** *Criss Cross* (1949), and *Out of the Past* (1947). These films expressed a fear of women being able sexually to control or destroy men. Whether the fear was overtly sexual, as in **Gun Crazy** (also titled **Deadly Is the Female**), or subdued, this mistrust and fear motivates the gangster's sadistic approach to women. **Love Me Or Leave Me**

focuses on an aging gangster's attempt to completely control a nightclub singer. **Point Blank** begins with a man being double-crossed by his wife and best friend, an act of betrayal that is used to justify his violent actions and attitude throughout the rest of the movie. In *Hell Up in Harlem* (1973) and *Slaughter* (1972), the molls' betrayals also take on racial overtones. Throughout the genre, a sense of mistrust and a feeling of betrayal have consistently been used to justify movie gangsters' sadistic treatment of women.

"You can dish it out but you can't take it," repeats Little Caesar throughout his rise. The gangster character, from **Brother Orchid** through *Dead Reckoning* (1947), *He Walked By Night* (1949), **Point Blank,** and **The Godfather,** has also had to endure brutal violence as part of his character. In some films, like **The Roaring Twenties** or *Slaughter,* war has provided the fiery baptism required for the gangster's murderous education.

Throughout the history of the genre, the gangster's violent nature has also defined his movie persona as a man of action. Scarface's motto, "Do it first, do it yourself, and keep on doing it," is still the movie gangster's first commandment. This active quality is central to the aggressive posture a movie gangster must maintain. From Cagney's Eddie Bartlett in **The Roaring Twenties** through Charles Bronson's Machine Gun Kelly in the fifties and Lee Marvin's Walker in **Point Blank** in the sixties, to Robert Mitchum's Eddie Coyle and Robert De Niro's Vito Corleone in the seventies, the gangster character has been portrayed as a man who knows what has to be done and takes the required initiative through aggressive, violent action. When the gangster fails to be true to this

Lee J. Cobb and Marlon Brando in *On the Waterfront*

James Cagney in *Roaring Twenties*

character trait (because of moral scruples or some other reason) and fails to act in a violently decisive manner, it leads to his downfall and death. The plot of **The Gangster,** for example, is concerned with a hoodlum who has become rich by running an extortion racket, and who, because of his desire to become respectable, fails to react to a clear territorial challenge by another gang. By the time he realizes the danger, it's too late; his flawed character (for a gangster) dooms him to humiliation and death. Above all, the gangster's violent actions provide the visual excitement that has remained central to the genre's popularity.

As in the early thirties, the movie gangster's gun continued to represent a number of things, from a symbolic macho wand of sexual power to a simple tool of the trade. In **Point Blank** a door flies open. A man in slow motion wildly bursts into his ex-wife's bedroom and fires a .357 Magnum revolver at the bed, aiming to kill a man who has betrayed him. The exploding bullet leaves a gaping hole in the mattress, and the revolver's recoil in slow motion makes the gun seem to throb as it spurts flame and lead. Some time later in the same film, a pipe-smoking assassin in a tweed jacket calmly unscrews a high-powered rifle after he has shot a man he doesn't know through the heart at a distance of 500 yards. In *The Lineup* (1958) the hired killer, Dancer (Eli Wallach), carries his gun and silencer in a brief case.

In **Public Enemy** the young gang members get their first guns in a scene that is presented practically as a hallowed moment—a communion with the world of death. When Scarface first fires a machine gun, his face beams with exhilaration. Gangster films have opened with a close-up image of a gun (**The**

Big Heat) and have begun and ended with the sound of gunfire (**The Doorway to Hell**), and they have continued to present attitudes of ritual adulation toward all kinds of guns, mostly .38-caliber revolvers, .45 automatic pistols, shotguns, and Thompson sub-machine guns. Gangster movie advertisements have shown women stroking the gangster's gun. In some movies, like **Gun Crazy,** gun consciousness takes over the plot and characters as well as the title.

Some changes in movie gangster weaponry have taken place. Gangsters' guns have increasingly become equipped with silencers, which have given gunfire a sinister new sound. Movie cops, however, are still allowed the big bang. In **Dirty Harry,** the cop is fond of pointing his long-barreled .44 Magnum revolver at crooks' heads and intoning, "This is the most powerful handgun in the world . . . it can blow your head off!" In *McQ* (1974), John Wayne as the cop gets his hands on the latest weapon, a machine pistol equipped with a silencer that fires 200 shots per minute. The weapons fetish goes off on an extreme tangent in the

Lee Marvin in *Point Blank*

Maurice Black, Paul Muni, Karen Morely, George Raft in *Scarface*

James Cagney and Edward Woods in *Public Enemy*

James Cagney and Edward Woods in *Public Enemy*

Eli Wallach in *The Lineup*

Warren Beatty and Faye Dunaway in *Bonnie and Clyde*

The Purple Gang

Andy Robinson in *Dirty Harry*

Richard Roundtree in *Shaft in Africa*

Richard Roundtree in *Shaft's Big Score*

Richard Roundtree in *Shaft's Big Score*

James Cagney with the Dead End Kids in *Angels with Dirty Faces*

James Bond films, but the iconography remains the same as in the gangster films.

Weapon iconography symbolizes the movie gangster's adaptability to the latest technology in general. Movie gangsters have updated their technological sophistication through increased use of telephones, radios, airplanes, helicopters, and electronic spying equipment. The technological advantage, however has remained with the police.

Since the thirties, the movie gangster has remained a schizoid Robin Hood and Robber Baron figure in whose heart beats the myth

of success. In **Dead End** and **Angels With Dirty Faces,** gangsters are idolized by teenage gang members in their old neighborhoods. As the priest tells Rocky in **Angels With Dirty Faces,** "You know, with them its kind of a hero worship." The Dead End Kids worship the gangsters for their money, clothes, self-assurance, and helpful advice on how to succeed in various competitive and illegal activities. As one of the gang members hopefully expresses it, "You ought to be able to loin us somethin', Rocky!" From these films to **The Godfather,** the saga of success has remained the most important narrative theme to motivate a movie gangster. Even when a picture's story was not directly about his rise and fall, an aura of success in the past or in the future constantly surrounds the movie gangster. The gangster's goal is implicitly clear, whether the plot directly embraced the success theme or not. Like the gangster protagonist, the success plot moved in and out of the foreground of the genre's history, but the icons of success remained the same. In **The Rise and Fall of Legs Diamond, Portrait of a Mobster, Al Capone,** or **Lepke,** the rituals of being measured and outfitted in personally tailored clothes are carefully re-created. In **Superfly** or *Shaft* (1971) the costuming becomes a virtual fashion show. As ever, the acquisition of more expensive cars continues to mark the gangster's rise, ranging in taste from Superfly's and Willy Dynamite's gaudy pimp specials to the Corleones' conservative Cadillacs in **The Godfather.**

The movie gangster still acquires women

Humphrey Bogart with the Dead End Kids in *Dead End*

Frank Campanella in *The Gang That Couldn't Shoot Straight*

Ron O'Neal in *Superfly*

according to the rules of success. As Dutch Schultz says to one girl in **Portrait of a Mobster,** "I knew you was *real* class!" "Class" for Dutch Schultz, Legs Diamond, or Michael Corleone has remained white Anglo-Saxon Protestant and conservatively stylish. Above all, "classy" dames denoted respectability—the final essential ingredient in the success formula.

Respectability has become increasingly important in the movie gangster's ambitions. Charlie Lupo in *New York Confidential* (1957) and Shabunka in **The Gangster** become so obsessed with respectability that their judgment is warped. In **The Godfather** the pursuit of respectability motivates much of what the Corleone clan undertakes, from moving to the suburbs to attempting to avoid international drug traffic. (The Corleones' blackmail of a Senator is undertaken with the certain knowledge that power must wear the

mask of respectability to remain entrenched.)

In their unbridled pursuit of success and the goal of legitimizing their criminal activities, movie gangsters have remained true to their Robber Baron roots. Throughout the genre, the gangster has emerged more distinctly as a businessman. In **The Killers** the criminal mastermind is a businessman (played by Ronald Reagan, who later represented large business interests as governor of California). In **Force of Evil** a bookkeeper refuses a racketeer's request for information because he doesn't want anything to do with gangsters. The questioning gangster is offended. "What do you mean gangsters? This is business." **Force of Evil** is one of the stronger portrayals of the basic business mentality of gangsters. The story concerns a former bootlegger who hires a Wall Street lawyer to help him take over the numbers racket, using the same methods as the "Big Boys" on Wall Street. Gangsters are presented as only a slightly more lurid type of capitalist. The definition of the gangster as a businessman has grown increasingly sharper since the late thirties, when, in **Bullets or Ballots,** bankers were revealed as the ultimate bosses of criminal activity in the city. The syndicate films of the fifties, and films like **Point Blank** and **The Godfather** in the last two decades, have continued to emphasize this viewpoint.

There has been, however, a major shift in the gangster's horizon of success. The old Robber Baron dream of being number one, of being the individual on top, as in **The Boss,** has become rare. The Robber Baron gangster has had to be content with a place on the governing board of directors of a corporate crime syndicate.

A clear perception of a crime syndicate developed in the films of the late thirties. One advertisement for **Bullets or Ballots** described the picture as "the first big drama

The wedding in *The Godfather*

Ronald Reagan in *The Killers*

of the Secret Syndicate of crime that supplants the Public Enemies as the Nation's Number One Menace." Other films, like *Big Town Czar* (1939) or *Smashing the Rackets* (1938), reiterated the syndicate theme and emphasized that well-organized crime had legitimate connections. The films of the fifties amplified the syndicate qualities of movie gangsters, following Senator Estes Kefauver's assertion in *Crime In America:* "A nationwide crime syndicate does exist in the United States despite the protestations of a strangely assorted company of criminals, self-serving politicians, plain blind fools, and others who may be honestly misguided that there is no such combine."

The change of emphasis from the individualistic Robber Baron gangster to the syndicate and Mafia movies has provided an adequate mythic expression of the shift of the American economy toward ever-increasing domination by multinational corporations. From the syndicate films of the fifties to **The Godfather** in the seventies, gangster pictures have presented the crime syndicate as a group much like the modern corporation, which, according to one writer, "is a clustering of animal jealousies, status displays, hunting bonds, tribal assemblies and tribal rituals."[4]

Whether syndicate man or Robber Baron, the movie gangster has remained unremit-

John Garfield in *The Force of Evil*

The big boys in *Bullets or Ballots*

Board meeting in *New York Confidential*

Syndicate meeting in *The Brotherhood*

tingly anti-labor, as depicted in films like *The Garment Jungle* (1957) or **On the Waterfront.**

To a lesser extent, the movie gangster has also retained a Robin Hood persona. The Robin Hood tradition of sharing loot with poor people was upheld only rarely in gangster movies, most clearly in the outlaw branch of the gangster genre, in films like *Pretty Boy Floyd* (1960), **Dillinger,** and **Bonnie and Clyde.** Gangster characters in the late thirties acted out of a sense of social justice, brotherhood, or generous impulse in films

such as **Brother Orchid, High Sierra,** or *Mr. Lucky* (1943). In **Dead End** or **Angels With Dirty Faces,** gangsters give money to kids in the neighborhood because it makes them feel as though they are appreciated by the community.

During World War II the gangster as Robin Hood was drafted to support the Allied cause. Humphrey Bogart in **All Through the Night** And Alan Ladd in *Lucky Jordan* (1943) battle ruthless Nazi agents. Ladd, who had just vaulted to stardom in *This Gun For Hire*

(1942) as a cold killer, is motivated to fight the Nazis after they beat up an old woman who had helped him. As in Westerns, vengeance provides a basic plot that bestows Robin Hood qualities on the movie gangster.

Revenge for some particularly unjust killing has continued to motivate gangster dramas, and, as in **The Godfather,** revenge has justified movie gangster violence in the eyes of the audience. Over the years, re-venge has provided the genre with another basic plot. Just as for the poorest prisoner, revenge could be the gangster's final recourse for honor. After the Second World War, revenge often motivated the movie gangster's Robin Hood behavior. Movie gangsters of the fifties sought revenge for the murder of relatives or loved ones in films like **Underworld USA** or *Gang War USA* (1958).

Although there have rarely been altruistic

Labor under the gun in *Slaughter on 10th Avenue*

Lee Marvin in *Point Blank*

The Asphalt Jungle
Gangster's mortgaged family farm.

Steven Keats, Robert Mitchum, Peter
Boyle in *The Friends of Eddie Coyle*

Black Robin Hood gangster:
Jim Watkins in *The Cool Breeze*

Ron O'Neal samples cocaine in
Superfly

actions, such as Al Capone giving away 10,000 Christmas dinners in *The Scarface Mob* (1962), the Robin Hood dimension of the movie gangster has usually been represented by an assertion of individual rights and worth that are increasingly threatened in an expanding corporate and bureaucratic society. Bogart, in particular, expressed the qualities of moral toughness and individual worth in the tough guy and detective roles that he went on to play in the forties and fifties (like **Key Largo**) that were built on his earlier gangster roles. In **Point Blank** the protagonist, Walker, has to crash through layers of corporate anonymity to get his money and revenge. The story concerns the progressive unmasking of and seeking retribution from one crime executive after another in a series of elaborate double-crosses. *The Outfit* (1973) similarly pits two free-lance bank robbers against a criminal organization.

Noble or selfless goals motivated various criminals in heist movies that the gangster genre spawned. In **The Asphalt Jungle,** Dix Handly intends to buy back his family's foreclosed Kentucky farm. **The Friends of Eddie Coyle** is a story of a small-time, middle-aged underworld figure whose predicament stems from his unwillingness to allow his family to go on welfare.

The gangster's Robin Hood qualities of the early thirties were fostered by Depression conditions, which for black people in America have remained chronic. Although there was at least one known black gangster film, *Underworld* (1935), made by the remarkable independent film maker Oscar Michaud, few of the early films made exclusively for black audiences have survived. There was a black gangster vogue of Jim Crow pictures during the thirties that dominated the ghetto market. *Moon Over Harlem* (1937), about a protection racket, *Straight from Heaven* (1939), about a racket involving rotten canned food, and *Gang War* (1940), about gangsters battling over control of jukeboxes often presented gangsters as Robber Baron exploiters. Recently, gangster films made primarily for black audiences have emphasized the gangster's Robin Hood side. Starting with *Sweet Sweetback's Baadasssss Song* (1971), a series of black outlaw films in the early seventies presented tough black heroes faced with crime as the only road available. The system of overwhelming economic injustice that calls forth Robin Hoods has been coupled with centuries of slavery and institutionalized racism. In *Cool Breeze* (1972), a black gang undertakes a jewel robbery for the purpose of establishing a people's bank, but as in the genre in general, such avowedly revolutionary actions are rare. More often, the black gangsters symbolized black power and self-respect based on a sensibility that blacks could be bad as well as beautiful. Black gangsters fought back in the same proto-revolutionary fashion as Depression-era movie gangsters, and at one level they represented a refusal to accept racial and economic oppression.

The gang warfare in the black gangster films took on racial overtones as white gangs and crooked police usually symbolized the oppressors and black gangsters the liberators, as in *Across 110th Street* (1973), *Hell Up in Harlem* (1973), and **Black Caesar.**

Like the Prohibition-era gangsters, Superfly was a type of bootlegger; he supplied cocaine instead of liquor. His audiences shared his outlaw status, often in the same theater where the film played. The hypocrisy of a self-righteous campaign against dope users and smugglers was suggested by portraying the police commissioner as the city's biggest drug dealer.

Superfly wanted to make one last deal and then quit. He earned the audience's sympathy by supplying the drug as well as their respect by wanting to escape from the corrupt world he had mastered. Along with a few other exceptional gangsters, he broke the genre's rule, which states that a gangster can never quit the gang and the world of crime.

The black crime and gangster films were called "blaxploitation" movies in the trade press because they quickly exploited a black movie market for sex and violence. Most of all, they exploited the profound frustrations and yearning for justice of their audiences in the same manner as the gangster films did for Depression audiences in the early thirties.

Gangster pictures have continued to reflect a chronic criminality and the particular mythic contradictions of capitalist culture in America's urban industrial society.

13

MEAN STREETS:
THE MOVIE GANGSTER'S WORLD

We would like to recommend, in passing, that you be less emphatic, throughout, in the photographing of this script, in showing the contrast between conditions of the poor in tenements and those of the rich in apartment houses. Specifically, we recommend you do not show, at any time or at least that you do not emphasize, the presence of filth, or smelly garbage cans, or garbage floating in the river, into which the boys jump for a swim. This recommendation is made under the general heading of good and welfare because our reaction is that such scenes are likely to give offense.

Quoted in a letter from Joseph Breen to Samuel Goldwyn concerning the screenplay for **Dead End**

Humphrey Bogart and gang in *Racket Busters*

The mean streets down which gangsters must go also define the genre. The mythic dimensions and significance of gangster movies are expressed by the settings, supporting players, and technical styles, as well as by gangster protagonists and the conventional stories of success and vengeance. Through reiteration, refinement, and constant addition of new material to the basic framework of the early thirties, the genre has evolved a complete and resilient register of conventions and icons. The genre has remained resilient because it has retained a quality established in the early thirties of being nostalgic and contemporary at the same time.

Basically the settings, scenes, and icons of the gangster genre have remained the same. They have also dominated nearly all the cop, detective, and heist sub-genres that have appeared since the thirties.

Gangster pictures have continued to be peopled with the same cast of supporting characters. The gang is still composed of hired hoodlums who provide the necessary army to enforce the gangster's will. And in the gang there is still usually a sidekick or trusted lieutenant, like Nick Magellan (Richard Conte) in *New York Confidential* (1955), and some other scheming subaltern, like the disloyal Tessio in **The Godfather.** Generally, as in **Little Caesar,** each gang member also has a particular skill required by a professional group. The driver, muscle man, hit man (enforcer, mechanic, button man, gunsel, torpedo, etc.), doctor, burglar, safecracker, and lawyer are all specialists who conventionally make up the model gang of the genre. In the heist or caper films, which can be considered a sub-genre (or a separate genre), the interaction of these specialists becomes central to the drama. Although the origins of heist films can ultimately be traced back to *The Great Train Robbery* (1903) and

the jewel robbery films of the twenties, the balletic teamwork, precision, and underworld settings that are characteristic of films like **The Asphalt Jungle** or *The Killing* (1956) are first clearly discernible in gangster movies, as in the montage sequence in **Little Caesar,** in which the gang holds up The Bronze Peacock.

Supporting characters who have continued to populate gangster films have been developed with more detail and have occasionally become protagonists. The standard warmhearted immigrant mother of **Public Enemy** rejects her gangster son with a sharp slap in **Dead End** for becoming a gangster. In **The Brothers Rico** or **The Godfather,** the character reverts back to her classic role of the stoic immigrant who accepts the vicissitudes of life and new-found wealth that her offspring bring as proof of America's promise. If Mama Rico and Mama Corleone kept up the traditional roles, other mothers aided and abetted their son's careers in crime. In **White Heat,** Margaret Wycherly's Ma Jarett is as shrewd a schemer as her son, and *Queen of the Mob* (1940), *Ma Barker,* and *Ma Barker's Killer Brood* (1960) presented the gangster's mother in the starring role (while drawing on the rural bandit tradition of Ma Barker).

With few exceptions, like **Blondie Johnston, Lady Scarface** (1941), or *Lady Gangster* (1942), nearly all the women in gangster films have remained in the familiar roles of mothers or molls. Furthermore, there are very few gangster movies in which women have substantial roles, as in **Marked Women** or **Love Me Or Leave Me,** the latter actually the biography of torch singer Ruth Etting. The portrayal of women has followed the same overall pattern of reverence to rape that has characterized American movies in general, as Molly Haskell has noted. The melodramatic heroines, like the Little Lady in **The Musketeers of Pig Alley** or "Molly, a

Edward G. Robinson and gang in *Key Largo*

Peter Boyle and gang in *Crazy Joe*

The gang in *Hell up in Harlem*

Humphrey Bogart and Marjorie Main
in *Dead End*

James Cagney and Margaret Wicherly
in *White Heat*

Bette Davis and sisters in struggle in
Marked Woman

Doris Day in *Love Me or Leave Me*

Rita Hayworth in *Gilda*

Marilyn Monroe in *Some Like It Hot*

Ava Gardner in *The Killers* (1946)

Gloria Grahame in *The Big Heat*

Tony Curtis signs out of jail in *City
Across the River*

Legal advice:
Luther Adler and John Russel in
Hoodlum Empire

Consiglieri:
Robert Duvall in *The Godfather*

girl of the slums'' in **The Gangsters and The Girl,** became flappers like Feathers (**Underworld**), gold diggers like Jean Harlow's Gwen Allen in **Public Enemy,** or aging drunken mistresses, like Gloria Graham in **The Big Heat** or Claire Trevor's Gaye Dawn in **Key Largo.** Expensive prostitutes and society girls have continued to be objectified as status symbols who mark the movie gangster's rise to riches and respectability. And from **Scarface** through *New York Confidential* to **The Godfather,** daughters and sisters amplify the movie gangster's concern for respectability.

According to the lawyer in **The Asphalt Jungle,** ''Crime is only a left-handed form of human endeavor.'' The lawyers, who have always had an important place in the gangster genre, emerged early as protago-

nists in films like *The Mouthpiece* (1932). Sometimes the mouthpieces became involved in love stories, as in *Party Girl* (1959), but most often they retained the same professional status as Robert Duvall's *consiglieri* role in **The Godfather.** Occasionally the mouthpieces were presented as more dishonest than the gangsters they represented, as in **Angels With Dirty Faces.**

When cops didn't become protagonists in the various off-shoots of the G-man tradition, they remained ineffectively in the background, as in **The St. Valentine's Day Massacre,** or else they greedily joined forces with the crooks, as in **The Asphalt Jungle** or **The Godfather.**

Reporters for various news media have also remained a consistent element in the genre. They have helped give gangster

City editor

The gangster goes on television in *A Face in the Crowd*

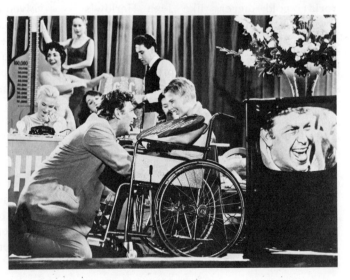

Coffee shop scene of shootout in *Al Capone*

City street in *Naked City*

Factory locale in *Ma Barker's Killer Brood*

stories a surface topicality and represent a self-conscious acknowledgment of the media's mythologizing function. The media have continued to have a narrative function of moving the plot forward by providing information for both the audience and the characters in the film. Newsreels fulfilled this function, along with newspapers and radio in **Bullets or Ballots** and **The Rise and Fall of Legs Diamond,** and television fulfilled the same role in *Party Girl* and *The Garment Jungle* (1957). And, since *The Finger Points* (1931), which was based on the murder of Chicago reporter Jake Lingel, there have

been crooked reporters, like Martin Balsam's Marc Keely in **Al Capone,** and reforming reporter protagonists who became involved with gangsters, as in **Each Dawn I Die.**

Whether or not they occasionally became protagonists, the same supporting characters welded the genre together over the years. Formidable gangster rivals, the gangs, the sidekicks, the Big Boys, the police, the mouthpieces, politicians, molls, society girls, mothers, families (rarely with fathers), newspaper reporters and editors, reformers, boxers and club owners, prison inmates,

Produce market in *Racket Busters*

On the Waterfront

Flower shop in *Al Capone*

Skyscraper office

Casino in *Angels with Dirty Faces*

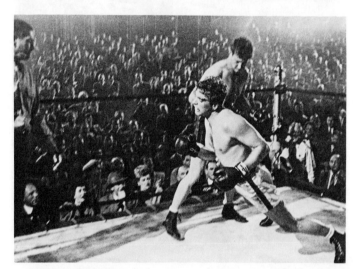

Ringside in *The Killers*

Airport locale in *Bullitt*

wardens and guards, and a variety of other occasional free-lance underworld grifters have continued to people the genre. Street crowds and passersby have also inhabited the genre since **The Musketeers of Pig Alley.** Shopkeepers, beat cops, and paper boys have wandered in and out of gangster movies, along with smaller crowds of people who watched funeral processions, appeared in nightclub audiences, sports events, and the occasional depictions of places of production and work. The use of large crowds of extras, as in the blockbuster **The Godfather,**

Part II has been rare in the gangster genre, which for the most part is made up of films that have been low-budget productions.

Similarly, gangster settings have rarely been as elaborate as in **The Godfather.** The genre's conventional settings have upheld the traditions of the thirties. City locations still predominate and shape the gangster's world: city streets and alleyways, immigrant neighborhoods, warehouse districts, flophouses, dives and penthouses, gutters and skyscrapers, poolhalls, bars, offices, subways, piers, boxing clubs, churches, night-

Dead End waterfront set

Puerto Rican neighborhood in *Cry Tough*

clubs, jails, mansions, funeral parlors, garages, casinos, newspaper offices, politician's offices, penny arcades, barber shops, flower shops, and more recently, airports, carwashes, and auto junkyards. The major cities of New York, Chicago, Detroit, Los Angeles, St. Louis, San Francisco, Phoenix, Miami, and San Diego have all been used as locations for gangster pictures, as well as several smaller fictional cities.

The city settings have been used to present an implicit environmental theory of the causes of criminality since **Public Enemy** and *Mayor of Hell* (1933). This trait was emphasized in the gangster films of the late thirties (**Angels With Dirty Faces, Dead End,** and *Crime School* [1938]) and the black gangster films of the early seventies. The rather mild view that poor neighborhoods breed crime helped support the Robin Hood facets of the

gangster genre and sometimes verged on admitting the existence of a class system in America, much to the dismay of censors like Breen.

Gangster films have proven themselves adaptable in keeping up with the evolution of American cities. Immigrant neighborhoods, while for the most part remaining Italian (as in *Mean Streets,* 1975), have also become Puerto Rican (*Cry Tough,* 1959) and black (*Hell Up in Harlem,* 1973) when appropriate. Instead of simply moving up to penthouses, successful gangsters like Johnny Lupo in *New York Confidential* or the Corleone clan in **The Godfather** have moved into suburban mansions and underworld compounds in wealthy neighborhoods outside the city.

The city sets have slowly become more numerous and elaborate, beginning with those in the late thirties, as in **Dead End** and

The Roaring Twenties, through the nostalgic re-creations in films like **The Rise and Fall of Legs Diamond** and **Al Capone,** to **The Godfather** and **The Godfather, Part II.** The underworld milieu has rarely been as well depicted as in Lyle Wheeler and Chester Gore's sets for William Keighley's *Street With No Name* (1948), with its flophouses and cheap rooms near the bus depot, the penny arcade and boxing gym, the gang's warehouse hideout and hidden arsenal, the cops' office, and the nightclub. As is com-

mon with feature films in general, larger-budget films had more elaborate sets.

City locations did change according to two radically different stylistic tendencies that characterized gangster films of the forties and fifties. The gangster genre has been flexible enough to include a surrealist disposition, as in the *film noir* pictures that began to appear in the forties, and a vogue of "documentary realism" that appeared in the films that immediately followed the Second World War—although both trends are al-

Suburban splendor in *7-11 Ocean Drive*

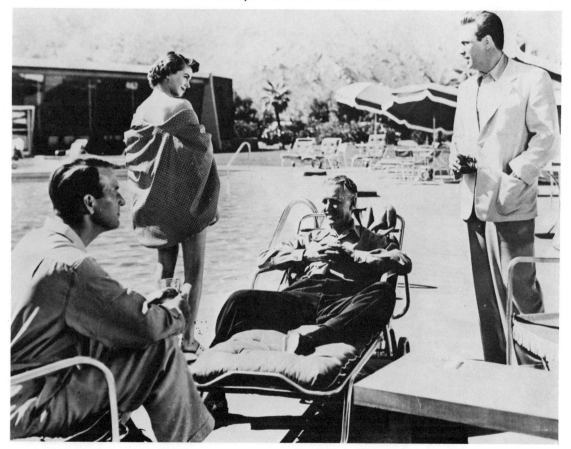

ready discernible in the photographic styles
and in some locations of the films of the early
thirties.

The dark and sinister tone of a number of
post-thirties' crime dramas led to their being
characterized as *films noir* by some French
critics, who noticed that the films projected
stark pessimism, hard-boiled cynicism, and a
sense of overwhelming personal and social
corruption. The negative mood of these films
is traceable to the early thirties' gangster
movies, but it was augmented by the work of
several European refugees from fascism—

Fritz Lang, Robert Siodmak, Billy Wilder—
who had experienced the social consequences in countries taken over by groups
devoted to values expressed in gangster
films. Like gangster movies, *films noir* were
rooted in a pulp imagination nourished by the
rise of fascism, the Second World War, and
the invention and use of the atomic bomb.

The low key lighting seen in the early
thirties continued to be suited to the negative
mood of these films. Usually set at night, the
films are dreamlike in their graphic starkness
and emotional power. *Marked Woman*

Henry Fonda and Sylvia Sidney in *You Only Live Once*

Marlon Brando and Eva Marie Sainte in *On the Waterfront*

(1937), for example, opens in front of the Club Intime at 3 A.M. The *film noir*'s titles indicate that the American dream factories were manufacturing nightmares: *Nocturne* (1947), *Night and the City* (1950), *They Live by Night* (1949), *Clash by Night* (1952), *So Dark the Night* (1946), *The Long Night* (1947), *Nightmare Alley* (1947). The nightmare quality was manifested in the photographic depiction of madness, as in the hallucinations in *The Lost Weekend* (1945) or *The Snake Pit* (1948). In gangster movies, radical camera angles and startling superimpositions emphasized a dream-like surreality in which a veneer of cheery middle-class optimism was punctured by a wild-eyed

perception of a grotesque underlying reality of a world gone mad with war and a preview of the possibilities of total nuclear destruction. Significantly, Freud became fashionable at the same time in Hollywood, bringing renewed interest in the power of unconscious fears and desires, along with a sense of the repressive effects of "civilization."

For the most part, the camera movements have remained relatively straightforward and utilitarian. The camera started moving more often in the glossier gangster movies of the late thirties. There were more tracking shots like the one that introduces the priest (Pat O'Brien) in **Angels With Dirty Faces,** in which the camera follows a sound truck

Neon (Robert Mitchum in *The Racket*)

and shadow (Edmund O'Brien in *D.O.A.*)

blaring jazz through a crowded ghetto street. The shot was similar in style and function to the opening shot of **Public Enemy,** in which the gangster is introduced as a boy in an immigrant neighborhood, circa 1909. Optical effects and lap-dissolved montage sequences were still used in the late thirties, as in **Marked Woman,** where the nightclub environment is quickly depicted with optically printed images of people drinking, dancing, smoking, and gambling. Such optical effects and montage sequences have for the most part become outmoded, and have rarely appeared in recent years. Perhaps the most notable development of this style has been in the multiple-screen bank holdup sequence in the heist film *The Thomas Crown Affair.* Slow-motion violence was made popular by

Filming *Naked City* on location

Naked City street scene

Bonnie and Clyde, although throughout the genre since the twenties, the manipulation of film speed has been used mostly for the purpose of fast-motion action and car-chase sequences. As yet, the gangster film has not lent itself to the more spectacular experiments of 3-D and Cinemascope. Color was also reserved for first experimentation in musicals and other more spectacular genres.

The use of color in films like *Party Girl* or **The Rise and Fall of Legs Diamond** was at first garish and occasionally symbolically expressive, although for the most part it has been simple and utilitarian. Red became an early and obvious favorite in bloody shootouts. There have also been rare uses of color motifs (red in *Party Girl* or orange in **The Godfather**). The color in gangster set direc-

tion and cinematography has become softer as a result of new film stocks and lab techniques, and its use more subtle and realistic in intent.

"Realism" through an impulse toward documentary approaches has also continued to grow in the gangster genre. The gangster films that followed the Second World War self-consciously displayed a new documentary approach that was inspired by newsreels and the documentary experience of movie industry personnel on the war-time propaganda films, like the *Why We Fight* series. Louis De Rochemont persuaded Darryl Zanuck to apply "March of Time" techniques to the spy feature *The House on 92nd Street* (1945). At first, the documentary approach was applied to crime detection films like

Street With No Name (1948), *T-Men* (1947), or *Naked City* (1948). With this trend, the mythic gangster became vulnerable to a new emerging mythology of a strong faith in the methods and results of science. This new faith was required by an increasingly technological society to uphold an optimism that the Western movie genre could no longer support.

Documentary realism, first of all, meant fidelity to actual locations. People and places should look on the screen as they do in life. Mark Hellinger was one producer who pushed for more realistic pictures. He told his agent on one of his first trips to Hollywood:

Pictures . . . should be a lot more realistic. I don't claim to be a genius, Johnny, but I think I know

the real from the unreal. Hell, if you picture a one armed beanery, it should look like it, with flies buzzing and dirty aprons and a busted electric fan and people who bend over their food and never smile. . . .[1]

Hellinger's point of view is discernible in **Naked City, Brute Force,** *Criss Cross* (1949), and **The Killers,** which favored location photography with natural light. Billy Daniels won the genre's first Academy Award for black and white cinematography on **Brute Force** by interpreting these prime tenets of photographic realism.

An increased number of actual locations, the setting of scenes at different times of day, and the use of natural light gave the narrative a stronger sense of verisimilitude by further extending the story into a world of space and

Cyd Charisse dancing to jazz

Al Capone

Some Like It Hot

Al Capone

The St. Valentine's Day Massacre

time closer to that shared by the audience. When the documentary techniques were combined with the sinister dark and dream-like dimensions of the *films noir,* as in **Naked City, The Kiss of Death,** or **White Heat,** the mélange can be exceedingly powerful.

Hellinger's intended realism led him to play the role of the narrator himself in **Naked City.** The use of narrators like Gayne Whitman in *T-Men* or Paul Frees in **The St. Valentine's Day Massacre** was another news and documentary technique that enjoyed a vogue of popularity in the genre and contributed to the genre's overall bias toward a tone of realism (that is, surface realism).

To enhance the dramatic impact of sound, the uses of effects and music have grown more sophisticated and subtle. Contemporary music has developed from the jazz used in **The Roaring Twenties** to the exactly appropriate dance music used in the wedding sequence of **The Godfather. The Godfather** also carries on a tradition of the imaginative use of sound established by such early gangster films as **Alibi** and **City Streets** in a much more complex and sophisticated way by employing naturally occurring noises at key emotional moments in the story. Subway roars, screeching brakes and tires, and ominous thunder are expressionist uses of sound with realistic sources that give the film a much stronger emotional impact.

A consistent use of the same stories,

Edward G. Robinson turns back the clock in *Little Caesar*

characters, and styles has re-inforced the genre's basic structure. Sometimes remakes duplicated early films, as with *Mayor of Hell* (1933) and *Crime School* (1938) or **White Heat** and *The Law Versus Gangsters* (1959). There are also a number of smaller iconographic elements that act to bind the genre together.

Various scenes have evolved that typify gangster films and that show the art of the genre in flower. The impressive choreography of speedier, more dangerous and destructive car chases, for example, can be traced through the chases in **Scarface, The Big Shot** (on ice!), *The Lineup* (1958), *Bullitt* (1968), and *The French Connection* (1971). It is significant that an accomplished gangster film director like Don Siegel began his film career by editing montage action sequences. Other scenes have also risen above the narratives of the individual films in which they appear to represent the overall genre.

The St. Valentine's Day Massacre has grown from an actual gangland assassination of six members of the Bugs Moran gang in Chicago by killers hired by Capone lieutenant "Machine Gun" Jack McGurn. The killers, masquerading as police, entered a garage hangout of the Moran gang, lined them up against the wall, and murdered them with machine guns and shotguns. The killings, of course, received spectacular press coverage. The infamous massacre was depicted in **Scarface,** *Al Capone* (1960), and the comedy **Some Like It Hot,** and was inflated into the subject of **The St. Valentine's Day Massacre.** The massacre has, for the most part, been faithfully reenacted and has come to represent the thorough and ruthless duplicity of urban gangster warfare. Its separate elements, like the police disguise, have appeared over and over again in other variations.

There are also dozens of smaller iconographic elements that constantly recur. Clocks and watches regularly introduce the gangster's mastery of time—an essential quality for a mythic hero of a technological society. Little Caesar's clever resetting of a clock in a diner to obscure the time of a hold-up, the passage of time from the mid-twenties to 1931, as marked by license plates in **Quick Millions,** or the superimposed machine gun firing over falling calendar leaves in **Scarface** strongly established this motif in the early thirties, and shots of clocks to mark the start of a robbery have continued throughout the genre. This recurring reference to the manipulation of time suggests the deeper mythic and emotional dimensions of gangster pictures. Emotional, narrative, or mythic time is marked by traumatic events rather than by hours and minutes. The Greeks called this concept of time *kairotic*

Dick Powell takes his time in *Johnny O'Clock*

(as opposed to chronological time). The movie gangster is so durable because he exists in the kairotic time marked by the dislocations of American society, rather than just in the twenties and thirties, with which the character is chronologically associated.

There is a poetry in gangster pictures suitable to the emotional depths of the mythology that gangsters represent in America. In *D.O.A.*, there is a chase through the city at night of gleaming streetcar tracks and flashing neon signs. A man turns a corner, and suddenly there are leather footsteps on steel stairs echoing in an abandoned factory, accompanied by the fluttering of birds' wings. The sights and sounds of the mean streets that make up the gangster's world make up a poetry of terror that fully contribute to defining the genre.

14

HOODLUM EMPIRES

Sure, I got a past—the gutter! But I got a future too! I'm going to take what I can get—until they get me!. . . . James Cagney as Rocky.
Advertisement for **Angels With Dirty Faces**

Congressional hearing in *Hoodlum Empire*

News cameras whir. Bulbs flash, and the faces of committee members register shocked and righteous surprise as a gangster describes the power and extent of a vast criminal network. The scene is from *Hoodlum Empire* (1952), a Republic production that sought to exploit the televised Kefauver hearings of the previous year. The sensational television coverage of the Senate Special Committee to Investigate Organized Crime in Interstate Commerce gave the genre another characteristic scene that symbolized a people's tribunal in which a gangster who represented a threat to public welfare would be dragged into the white light of glaring public exposure. The syndicate-oriented films that followed throughout the fifties—*The Captive City* (1951), *Chicago*

Joseph Valachi testifies before McClellan Senate sub-committee September 27, 1963

Gambling: a common theme in gangster movies
and in the growth of organized crime.

Confidential (1958), *The Big Combo* (1956), and *The Miami Story* (1954)—all adopted the same posture of searing exposé. These films augmented a theme that has characterized the gangster genre since the appearance of **The Musketeers of Pig Alley.** Gangster movies have always tantalized audiences, to some degree, with a promise to tell "the true story" of the world of crime. And just as the Biograph *Bulletin* described **Musketeers** in terms of its newspaper origins, countless publicity flacks have sent out a barrage of material that has played up the true-story angle and further contributed to the genre's investigative pretense.

Like the news media, gangster pictures have emphasized the picturesque and sensational aspects of crime. The genre has exploited some facts and documentary techniques to make fiction appear "realistic." But over the years, the gangster genre has not presented a thorough and accurate picture of the range and methods of underworld activities in America. The noted "realism" of the gangster genre is more apparent than real; it is a matter of style rather than of substance.

Several congressional investigations, a few determined state and federal attorneys general, some crusading district attorneys, a handful of serious investigative reporters, and crime experts have revealed a picture of crime in America that is more enormous, complicated, and persistent than that which is suggested by gangster movies.[1] By the early seventies, an estimated income of $50 billion makes organized crime twice the size of General Motors.

The national crime syndicate organized in the early thirties, as the movie gangster became a G-man, invested hundreds of millions of dollars derived from bootlegging, as well as the organizational skills required for interstate and international operations, in the growth and diversification of a gigantic crime industry.

Gambling was the first and easiest area for growth, with the building of gambling meccas in Hot Springs (Arkansas), Las Vegas, Miami, and Cuba. Slot machines, horse and dog races, bookie networks, wire services, and numbers rackets have provided a rapid and steady income that numbers in the billions. Labor racketeering came next—not only in the use of unions to extort money from both employers and workers but also in complex investment schemes, such as those involving the use of union funds to construct syndicate gambling facilities in Las Vegas, land development in Phoenix, Arizona, and the development of leisure-time resorts, like La Costa in San Diego.[2]

The diversification into prostitution; pornography; drugs; large-scale hijacking of all kinds of goods; fencing of stolen merchandise, ranging from cigarettes to jewelry to stocks and bonds; loan-sharking (''shylocking'') at enormous interest rates, often lead-ing to control of a debtor's legitimate business; arms dealing; extortion; and murder continue to provide an army of syndicate soldiers with livelihoods.[3]

The diversification of organized crime has also led to an emphasis on moving into legitimate business wherever possible. By 1971, according to an I.R.S. report, 85 per cent of the gangsters in America had investments in legitimate businesses.[4]

The efforts and occasional successes in the prosecution of criminal cases, as with Al Capone and Lucky Luciano, have taught syndicate gangsters the importance of achieving immunity from the law through complicated financial manipulations and political influence. Organized criminals have used increasingly sophisticated techniques in ''laundering'' money, leading ultimately to the control of banks. Despite the political origins of the earliest published definition of the word ''gangster'' and the implicit acknowledgment of the movie gangster's political connections, the genre has basically avoided the subject. A few films, like **The Racket** or **The Godfather,** have shown gangsters achieving control over politicians, but such films are exceptional. Actual gangsters have continued persistent efforts at political control of ever-higher levels of the federal government—from the Internal Revenue Service to the President of the United States.

One expert on the American underworld has predicted that ''organized crime will put a man in the White House someday, and he won't even know it until they hand him the bill.''[5] Significantly, Richard Nixon had numerous and complicated connections to organized crime. Mickey Cohen, the notorious Los Angles gambler, contributed $26,000 to Nixon's 1968 presidential campaign, but his contribution was insignificant compared to the Hughes Las Vegas casinos' $100,000,

President Richard Nixon, left, with friends C. G. Rebozo (c), and Robert Abplanalp, aboard Rebozo's houseboat at Key Biscayne, Fla. (11/3/73).

I.T.T.'s $400,000, and the many millions of dollars involved in the various activities of Bebe Rebozo and his underworld connections. Rebozo, who appeared on *Life*'s cover, was described in that magazine as "the only person Nixon really trusts." Nixon's closest friend started his success story as an unknown gas station operator who made a fortune during the Second World War as southern Florida's biggest tire recapper—a business regulated by the Office of Price Administration (OPA), for which

Nixon went to work when war broke out. Nixon's job was in the tire-rationing branch in a unit that handled interpretations for the legal section. Rebozo, who was closely connected to right-wing Cubans (some of whom were the Watergate burglars) and national crime syndicate members like Cleveland's "Big Al" Polizzi and Meyer Lansky, subsequently became a multimillionaire through complicated real estate and banking operations. Nixon's friendship with Rebozo and his alleged links to mobsters

Political clout in *The Racket*

Political activity in *Body and Soul*

Prostitutes in *Marked Woman*

and *Willy Dynamite*

Five Against the House

Making loaded dice in *Phenix City Story*

Marlon Brando rolls 'em in *Guys and Dolls*

date back to the then-Congressman's late forties' visits to Miami Beach, which at that time was characterized by Kefauver's investigation as the syndicate's unofficial center of bookkeeping and financial activities. Nixon's fondness for gambling led him to visit Cuba and the Bahamas in the company of his new Miami friends.

Thirty years later, as **The Godfather** was being filmed in the streets of New York, Nixon was relaxing regularly at the Presidential compound on Key Biscayne, a piece of real estate owned and developed by people and companies with mob connections. The President's associations with anti-Castro Cubans and businessmen linked to banks and corporations notorious for "laundering" organized crime income are yet another part of the Watergate scandals that needs to be fully investigated.[6]

Gangster films have only rarely attempted to detail the manner in which criminal organization has resulted in a steady flow of profit, as in the examination of the numbers racket in **Force of Evil.** Rather, armed robbery, the first pictorial action in American dramatic movies, has continued to be the most popular crime of the genre because it is the bluntest expression of gangster action and the easiest to understand. Profit from prostitution and gambling, for example, have been alluded to but never revealed through a serious and comprehensive treatment in gangster movies. Films like **Marked Woman** or *Willie Dynamite* (1975), which have ostensibly been about prostitution, have merely exploited the theme for the purposes of melodrama or titillation. *King of the Gamblers* (1937) is a murder mystery and *King of the Roaring Twenties* (1939), about gambler Arnold Rothstein, was a character study that showed very little about how gamblers operated. In these and other films, like *Las Vegas Story* (1952), the world of gambling is a

background which has grown increasingly elaborate without revealing how profits are generated.

The details of bootlegging have been bathed in a rosy, nostalgic light since the early thirties, but the scope of bootleg empires and the role that liquor played in the formation of a national crime syndicate has not been articulated in the gangster biographies or syndicate films of the fifties.

Labor racketeering has been used as a background for powerful personal dramas in **On the Waterfront** and the *Garment Jungle* (1957), but even when such films are emotionally pro-union, they don't clarify the nature and the methods of labor racketeering beyond depicting a climate of extortion and a vague warning that gangsters who intend to take over unions are a front for management control.

Since the mysterious hand at the end of **The Musketeers of Pig Alley** offered the Snapper Kid money with a title that reads, "Links in the System," the gangster genre has remained reluctant to show the origins and destinations of criminal revenue. The flow of money through the underworld has continued to be obscure. Despite a rare down-to-earth glimpse of loan-sharking, as in a film like *Killing of a Chinese Bookie* (1976), an over-all understanding of such activities or of the methods used to launder criminal income has not emerged from the genre. Yet, the movement of billions of dollars is central to the day-to-day reality of the underworld as well as a key to understanding how criminal empires operate.

J. Edgar Hoover refused to believe in the existence of the Mafia, an oversight that the movies have bent over backward to correct. The gangster genre has distorted a multi-ethnic businesslike national crime syndicate in favor of a picturesque Italian organization steeped in ritual and a baroque tradition. *The*

Labor racketeering in *On the Waterfront*

A ritual Mafia kiss in *The Brotherhood*

Crime-fighting newsreel in
Smashing the Rackets

Black Hand (1950), *Pay or Die* (1960), *Honor
Thy Father* (1973), *Inside the Mafia* (1959),
The Brotherhood, The Valachi Papers, *The
Brotherhood of Evil* (1971), and even **The
Godfather** (inadvertently) have helped reinforce the popular notion that the Mafia is
synonymous with organized crime. Actual
crime syndicate figures have enjoyed anonymity in part because of a smoke screen
that the movies and media have created out
of Mafia mythology.

Bullets or Ballots begins with two gangsters
going to see a crusading anti-crime newsreel,
"Syndicate of Crime." They have been sent
to make sure that the newsreel is not
revealing too much about their activities.
Shortly thereafter, the newspaper editor
responsible for the series is murdered for his
attempt to expose gangsters. The scene is
fairly typical of Hollywood flattering itself
with an allusion to a crime-fighting posture it
never really had. But gangster movies do
convey a certain truth about a pervasive
criminality in American society.

From Depression America to the America
of the Vietnam war and Watergate in the
seventies, gangster movies have mythically
manifested the large-scale tensions and dislocations of American economic and social
life, and a criminality more profound and
disturbing than that of organized crime. As a
character who is associated with death and
weapons and whose activities and attitudes
help diminish respect for life, the movie
gangster has remained a suitable representative of a society whose economy requires a
high, sustained military expenditure. The
successes of the American economy depend
on a spiraling arms race and a level of
planned military spending that is as high as
25 per cent of the Gross National Product.[7]
With or without a war, massive arms expenditures have staved off an otherwise chronic
depression since the First World War. Since
the Korean war, the American economy has
been on a permanent military footing.

Furthermore, the military spending has
resulted in an arsenal of destruction fully

deserving of the darkest dreams and the most nightmarish and negative dimensions of American culture that the gangster represents. If anything, the gangster is an inadequate representative of the threat to the human race symbolized by a gun-crazy economy with its products of total destruction—nuclear bombs, laser death rays, and germ and genetic warfare designed to inflict death to last 10,000 years.

Meanwhile, in films like **Superfly**, black gangsters blaze their way out of the ghetto. Even an economy propped up by military expenditures has not been able to employ everyone. In the bicentennial year, for example, an estimated 60 per cent of young black men in urban areas were unemployed. The popularity of black gangster films of the early seventies indicates that the gangster still represents an attitude that crime is the only route to success for impoverished minorities in America.

Murder Inc. was an appropriate film to begin a decade in which America was plagued by a continuous and ghastly spectacle of mysterious murder and criminality at the highest levels of government. The assassinations of President John F. Kennedy, his brother, Attorney General Robert Kennedy, and Martin Luther King have raised ques-

Robert Kennedy mortally wounded.

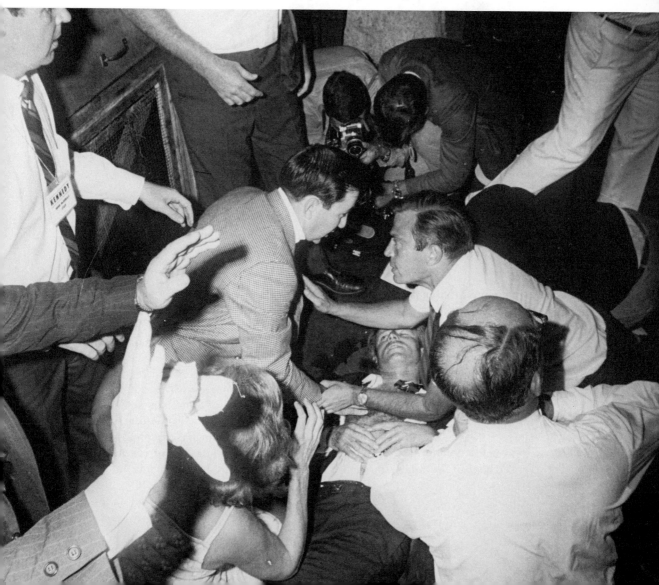

TV G-man—*The Untouchables* (Robert Stack as Elliot Ness)

tions and doubts more profoundly disturbing than the wildest paranoia of **Murder Inc.**

A parade of public criminality was particularly apparent during the Nixon years. The Watergate extravaganza, with its cast of burglars, bagmen, and "Big Boys," and a million-dollar cover-up climaxing in the most spectacular of all public congressional investigations, reinforced the dark vision presented in gangster films, which views all of society as thoroughly corrupt and corruptible. The deposed head of the largest union in

America simply vanishes one day without a trace. The mysterious disappearance of James Hoffa, a man pardoned by a President who was soon to be pardoned himself, is the most recent event in a parade of spectacular and sinister mysteries which are simply the glittering examples of a criminality woven into the fabric of American society.

As if society was trying to reassure itself, the movie G-man has become more prevalent than the gangster in recent years, particularly in the movies made for television and the various police series: *The Untouchables*, series, which played a key role in bringing gangster characters to television audiences, *Dirty Harry* (1971), *McQ,* (1974), *Madigan* (1968), *Brannigan* (1974), *Kojak, Police Story, Police Woman, Hawaii 5-O, Cotton Comes to Harlem,* (1970) *Swat,* etc. Recently, the cops who pass through worlds of infinite corruption are often at odds with their bosses and are left to their own devices in their resolute pursuit of justice and equality before the law—even though the society they represent does not always appreciate and support them.

Whether they are rugged individualists or professional elites, the latest G-men function as a cultural dike that will, hopefully, stem a tidal wave of perceived criminality in America that ranges from street gangs of killer children preying on old people to the Presidency.

But a gangsterish reality has even begun to overwhelm the public's image of the G-man.

In recent years, questions have slowly been raised in the media and in Congress about the F.B.I.'s hidden role in the assassination spectacles of the sixties, and in the systematic murders of black and native American militants. The entire intelligence community has been implicated in a range of secret and subversive activities against American citizens that have grown from the Hollywood Ten persecutions to the complex Cointelpro operations, complete with concentration camps.

The international operations conducted by the C.I.A. are more adequately represented by the movie gangster's ruthless and raw-edged capitalism than the G-man's dutiful idealism. According to the inside story of one disillusioned agent, the basic function of the C.I.A. has become the elimination of obstacles to the economic domination of multinational corporations, rather than the gathering of information to defend America's national integrity.[9]

The French Connection

John Roselli, 1975, when he told a U.S. Senate
subcommittee how the CIA recruited him in the
early sixties to assassinate Cuban premier Fidel
Castro

The worldwide perception of the actual G-man has changed from a heroic figure who emerged in the thirties and forties as a tough-guy individual agent who fought the Nazis to a member of a bureaucratic goon squad whose secret activities no longer represent the American people but rather the multinational conglomerates that also govern American society. The C.I.A. aided in the establishment of a fascist junta in Chile as a representative of I.T.T. and a copper syndicate, not the American people and the democratic principles that Americans would like to believe they are identified with. The actions of the C.I.A. in Vietnam have also revealed a gangster's soul in a G-man's body. The infamous Phoenix program was a genocidal plot that dwarfs all the publicized Mafia wars and syndicate killings since the turn of the century in cold cunning and murderous barbarity.[10] In Vietnam the C.I.A. also became involved in drug traffic that reached an estimated one-half of the American armed forces, as well as lucrative markets back in the United States.[11]

August 1976. A fifty-gallon oil drum floats up to the calm surface of Biscayne Bay off the Florida coast. The drum contains the waterlogged corpse of a key witness in an upcoming investigation into the connections between the C.I.A. and organized crime in the repeated assassination attempts against Cuba's Fidel Castro. Johnny Roselli, who used to bust unions for the motion picture bosses, had surfaced for the last time. Roselli and Sam Giancana had reportedly helped recruit syndicate assassins for the C.I.A. Both were mysteriously murdered immediately prior to testifying before congressional committees.[12]

While the James Bond and G-man images were popular, a type of gangsterism on an international scale was trying to overthrow democratic governments around the world, training torturers and assassins, aiding drug dealers, and working closely with gangsters. The implication of "former" C.I.A. agents in the Watergate scandal, along with CIA-trained anti-Castro Cubans, and the revelations of the agency's actual activities, have given further impetus to the idea that the genre's transformation of movie gangster into G-man has disguised a grim development in which America's actual G-men were behaving like gangsters.

The movie gangster has again grown popular as a mythological acknowledgment of the deepest doubts and darkest dreams in American culture, a culture beset by a general and overwhelming malaise. The Robin Hood aspect of the movie gangster persona that represents traditional American democratic principles of liberty, equality, and justice is being overwhelmed by a Robber Baron-cum-syndicate gangster who represents liberty to exploit, equality only among elites, and justice for the right price. This is not to say that those who make and distribute movies are consciously catering to the audience's need for a mythic acknowledgment of entrenched criminality. Rather, as Lévi-Straus suggests, myths signify the mind that produces them. In several crucial ways, the gangster genre's evolution denotes the social and cultural dimensions that define the outlook of the movie industry—perhaps more closely than that of the society at large. The movie industry has made films that also reflect the dislocations, power realities, and consequences of its own evolution within American society and economy.

For the characters in **Scarface** as well as those in **The Godfather,** the world is pictured as one governed by the same set of values. Characters are successes or failures, smart or stupid, exploiters or exploited, lucky or unlucky. The same values are central in the outlook of those who run and have run the movie industry, as well as the entertainment sector of the economy, of which motion picture production is a part. But Hollywood has changed in many ways, and the gangster genre has reflected a basic shift in the structure of the movie industry. **Scarface,** the most powerful early gangster film, is the rise-and-fall story of a powerful individual gangster whose world is uncomplicated by crime syndicates. The film was appropriately produced by Howard Hughes, the billionaire individualist whose quirky personal control of his empire is as legendary as the mysteries surrounding his death. Hughes himself opposed the syndicate both in Las Vegas and in Hollywood when underworld figures tried to engineer a takeover of the R.K.O. studios. In the gangster epic of the seventies, **The Godfather,** Don Corleone's success story takes place in an underworld environment that becomes dominated by a crime syndicate. Paramount, the studio that produced **The Godfather,** is today but a tiny component of the Gulf and Western multinational corporation, whose principal businesses are chemical, metal, and electrical products.

In the mid-fifties, as the syndicate craze was sweeping through the gangster genre, a relatively small company in Houston, Texas, was about to begin a corporate success story of phenomenal business expansion. Gulf and Western, like Vanderbilt, Meyer Lansky,

Howard Hughes

and many movie gangsters, began its rise in the transportation sector of the economy in 1957 by manufacturing and marketing automobile parts. Within a quick ten years the corporation had acquired eighty companies with operations in many parts of the world, and it grew in annual income from $6.5 million to $1.67 billion. Paramount Pictures accounted for a small 5.17 per cent of the total conglomerate income.[13] Warner Brothers, Universal, United Artists, Columbia, and Twentieth Century-Fox have all become parts of larger corporations devoted principally to operations other than the movies. The multinational corporations are infusing the motion picture business with an air of cold efficiency that had previously been confined to the New York financial offices. The tone is expressed in the conventional syndicate movie scene of a board

Gulf and Western Plaza

meeting, in which ruthless decisions are based on a bookkeeper's numbers and the simple philosophy that what's good for business is good for the mob, despite the human consequences.

The movie business, however, remains a risky undertaking that doesn't lend itself readily to an operation of predictable efficiency. As Darryl Zanuck is quoted as saying of motion pictures, "You've got to gamble. The movie industry isn't a slide rule business and never will be. It's the world's biggest crap game."[14]

The gambling theme that saturates the film industry has always been characteristic of gangster movies and studio tycoons. The movie moguls who dominated Hollywood in its heyday of the thirties and forties were inveterate gamblers. The depiction of the world as a wheel of fortune, presented in **Smart Money** or *King of the Gamblers* (1937), is one in which the movie tycoons fervently believed. As in gangster pictures, movie people gambled in small card games and in large casinos. There were cockfights in the Hollywood hills and gambling in the Colony Club casino down on Sunset Boulevard. Gambling debts could rise as high as Harry Cohn's reported $400,000 obligation, and the passion for gambling was intense enough to send David O. Selznick forty miles to a desert shack one night while on location to lose $10,000 on a roulette wheel he knew was rigged. George Raft, once reportedly described in a syndicate meeting as a former "stand-in crap shooter" at the Club Durant, went from his starring gangster roles to work for his friends in casinos in Cuba and London.[15]

The society page pictures of Raft and Betty Grable at horse races sold papers in the same way that pictures of Al Capone and his retinue at the race track in Chicago spiced up the newsreels of the twenties.

Race tracks have been a familiar setting in the gangster genre as well as for the operations of the crime syndicate. In **Quick Millions** the society girl whom Bugs has taken to the races is surprised to find out that racing is also a racket. Louis B. Mayer at the height of his career became involved in horse racing in order to relax from the cares of the movie business, on the advice of his doctor. Typically, he soon had the best racing stable in America. Harry Cohn gave Johnny Roselli $25,000 to invest in the Agua Caliente race track in Tijuana. Mervyn Leroy, who directed **Little Caesar,** became the president of the Hollywood Park Racing Association. Horse racing, movie gangsters, and studio ownership are as much a part of the new Hollywood as of the Hollywood managed by the moguls. The Leisure Time Division of Gulf and Western, which controls Paramount Pictures, Inc., also includes Chicago Thoroughbred Enterprises, which manages the Washington Park and Arlington Park race tracks. Horse racing, cable television, records, audio-tape, *The Untouchables* television series and movie production that make up the Leisure Time Division are all part of a gigantic corporation which considerably dwarfs the once-proud movie giant of the twenties ruled by Adolph Zukor that produced **Underworld.**

The nostalgia for ethnic movie moguls and Prohibition-era gangsters is also partially a wistful yearning for a less impersonal society characteristic of a market economy that has been replaced by a planned corporate economy in which egomaniacal individuals are less valuable and efficient in running corporate empires than those executives who possess the ability to cooperate and submerge their individuality for the good of the company. Photographs show Louis B. Mayer beaming in the company of presidents and royalty, in the winner's circles at race tracks, and dancing with beautiful stars and starlets in nightclubs. Like Al Capone, the boss of M.G.M. gloried in media coverage and was fiercely proud of the well-publicized fact that he earned the largest salary in America as head of production at the studio, a position to which he had literally risen from a scrap heap. The colorful and overbearing tycoon personalities were adequately expressed in the gangster genre during the thirties and the forties, but gangster movies proved adaptable in reflecting the changing pattern of movie industry ownership in which the new owners had become the silent and unseen power brokers of the giant corporations.

The movement of the multinational corporations into the movie business has prompted some scholars and critics to wonder and worry about the ultimate effects and purposes of conglomerate control over an industry whose greatest artistic achievements and few liberal political statements were made possible by executives willing to take chances. One long-time industry insider questions "whether the entry of these Big Business Goliaths may not prove to be the direct or indirect means of taking control of communications . . . ."[16] For corporations as well as for syndicate criminals and totalitarian governments, the control of communication is an important guarantor of immunity from a right of public scrutiny, which is at the heart of constitutional freedom of the press. If the multinational conglomerates do intend to limit freedom of expression, they will be following a precedent established by the studio moguls, who were careful to promulgate the views and politics of the ruling class in America.

William Fox and Louis B. Mayer learned from experience that political clout could have important consequences in their business battles. Mayer's assiduous cultivation

of Herbert Hoover and his staunch support for the Republican party helped him defeat Fox in a behind-the-scenes attempt to take over M.G.M. Political leverage is of even greater importance to the multinational corporations in their lobbying efforts for favorable legislation and in providing tax loopholes and investment benefits. In exchange for governmental benevolence, the movie industry has consistently acted in the interests of big business and in complicity with those who would control the movies as part of a larger effort to stifle dissent.

Mayer and his production chief, Irving Thalberg, leaped into action in controlling and distorting communication during their furious and vicious campaign to defeat Upton Sinclair in the 1934 California gubernatorial election, in which the M.G.M. bosses extorted Republican campaign money from their employees and produced a smear campaign of phony newsreels and dire threats to remove the film industry to Florida.

In 1947 the flashbulbs and whirring cameras ushered in another searing exposé, this time of the supposed threat that communism was posing to the film industry. There was a new twist to the scene in that an arrogant crook was asking the questions. The head of the committee, Parnell Thomas, was soon indicted and convicted for corruption, winding up in the same prison with those screenwriters who had somehow dared to express a concern for social welfare in the bosses' dream factory. The Hollywood Ten scandals were precipitated as a red-baiting attack on union organization in the movie industry. Its purpose was basically the same as when Will Hays hired Johnny Roselli to bust unions. The cold war patriotic righteousness which the Hollywood Ten trials spearheaded proved useful in the wars in Korea and Southeast Asia.

The manipulation of communication has

always been most evident during war-time: the Liberty Bond drives, which starred Charlie Chaplin, Douglas Fairbanks, and Mary Pickford, backed by a Sousa band; the *Why We Fight* series of World War II; the war adventure stories about Korea; and the ominous silence throughout the Vietnam war, broken only by the pro-war screech of the hawkish *Green Berets* (1974), indicate the obedient posture of uncritical acceptance that marks the motion picture industry's attitude toward government policies.

Whether by mogul or multinational corporation, the control of communication performs the same function through the less obvious but more pervasive presentation of a middle-class ideology designed to reinforce the status quo and to mute possibly effective criticism of the government and of the structure of ownership that controls the government.

Ben Hecht and Howard Hawks describe similar visits of gangster emissaries from Al Capone, who wanted to make sure that **Scarface** would not tarnish his reputation. Capone, according to George Raft, was satisfied with the results.[17] His concern about what image the movies were projecting was also typical of the old Hollywood tycoons, or of Little Caesar, or of the multinational corporations that control the new Hollywood.

Throughout the history of the gangster genre, actual gangsters have held as enduring a fascination for many movie people as they have held for movie audiences. Jack Warner's pride in his boyhood gang displayed the same type of attitude that led to his friendship with Bugsy Siegel, in retrospect, a friendship the boss of Warner Brothers studio says he wasn't sure he wanted:

I didn't want Bugsy Siegel in my house. I wasn't going to wake up some morning and see the front page saying "Movie Tycoon Machinegunned by Opposition Mob," and then I wouldn't be able to read the paper anyway. But he got in.[18]

Siegel came up the hard way to a Beverly Hills mansion and his dream of a legalized gambling mecca in Las Vegas that would be attractive to Hollywood high rollers. He began his career as part of the Bugs and Meyer (Lansky) mob that became Murder Inc. Lansky went on to become the reported "brains" of the national crime syndicate, and Siegel went to California to see what kind of syndicate business he could drum up in the movie capital.[19] Such Hollywood luminaries as George Raft and Jean Harlow helped introduce Siegel to Hollywood society, and Raft and Hellinger provided Siegel with references in a gambling trial as "a man of good moral character."[20] But the syndicate didn't share such faith in Siegel. With his old pal Lansky's approval, he was eliminated by the mob when he defied its authority during the construction of the Flamingo Hotel in Las Vegas. Raft was particularly saddened because Bugsy died owing the gangster movie star $100,000 dollars.[21]

Harry Cohn became such close friends with gangster Johnny Roselli that he proudly wore a matching star sapphire ring the mobster gave him as a token of their friendship.[22] "Why not befriend gangsters?" The movie people thought. The moguls shared and fulfilled the same dreams of success and early days of immigrant poverty, as well as many of the same attitudes toward life. Intimate knowledge of actual gangsters and friendships with them extended to stars, tycoons, writers, and producers in Hollywood and provided the gangster genre with a touchstone for reality. The gangster movies symbiotically fed off of the personalities of the mobsters who came to prey on it.

Mark Hellinger was a man somehow ideally suited to write and produce gangster

Benjamin Siegel and George Raft

movies. His stint as Broadway's favorite columnist during the twenties and early thirties put him in close proximity with the New York underworld. According to his close friend and biographer:

Hellinger cultivated the gangsters, racketeers and hoods of his time. He liked them. And they liked him. He knew Dutch Schultz and Legs Diamond and Owney Madden and Big Frenchy de Mange and many many others including Abner Zwillman. They liked him so well that, before Prohibition ended, they agreed to stop killing each other and named Mark Hellinger as personal arbiter of the underworld. Thus the columnist often settled disputes between them, substituting for the tommy guns they formerly used.[23]

Hellinger came to Hollywood and helped shape the genre by writing the original story of **The Roaring Twenties,** and producing such powerful gangster dramas as **High Sierra, Naked City,** and **Brute Force.** His overwhelming ambition was to be the boss of his own production company, a goal he was on the verge of reaching when he died from a heart attack. Hellinger cultivated the speech

Mark Hellinger and Jules Dassin on location
filming *Naked City*.

and mannerisms of gangsters. Dark blue shirts and white ties became his sartorial trademark; his wife, Gladys Glad, had been the most beautiful girl in the *Ziegfeld Follies* chorus line.

Movie people appreciated gangsters professionally as well as personally. The racketeers provided useful skills and services, as well as friendship. Eddie Mannix began his rise to the executive offices of M.G.M. as a bouncer for the Schenck brothers in their New Jersey amusement park. He was sent to Hollywood by the New York-based Schencks to keep an eye on Mayer, with whom he soon became fast friends. Mayer also appreciated the companionship of Frank Orsatti when the latter supplied him with liquor and women. Orsatti soon had a studio job and found lucrative work as an agent. For his strike-breaking work, Roselli was awarded an appropriate producer's job with the Warner Brothers B unit, and he married an aspiring actress, June Lang.[24] Sometimes the line between gangster and movie mogul dissolved. Joe Schenck was sent to prison for a year over a $100,000 extortion payoff. (According to one underworld expert, the incident was created by syndicate power-house Abner "Longie" Zwillman as an act of revenge.)

Gangsters who shared the same values, ambitions, and world view as many movie makers, and who provided useful skills and services, have clearly been more acceptable company than political radicals in Hollywood. As Hellinger's biographer expressed it during the cold war:

Mark Hellinger worked closely with both the Federal Bureau of Investigation and the California underworld. He knew the Bugsys and the Smileys as well as he knew Richard Hood of the Los Angeles FBI office. He helped to uncover Communists and tax dodgers for Uncle Sam while, at the same time, he helped to keep the mob men out of trouble.[25]

Hellinger was a flamboyant character whose style of life merged with the movie gangster world he helped create on the screen.

The gangster genre in the seventies continues to reflect the movie industry's fascination with and need for people with underworld connections. Individuals connected

Mr and Mrs. Mark Hellinger with Mr. and Mrs. Jack Warner.

with the movie world and underworld are natural products of the same social forces that make gangster films popular. They are admired by the public because given the conditions and values of American society they are more models of success than censure.

June 27, 1976. The New York *Times* describes a tall, trim, distinguished-looking man with graying hair who sits at his usual corner table with two phones in an expensive Beverly Hills restaurant, of which he is a part owner. Beautiful women come over to kiss him. He is a multimillionaire who owns a mansion in the exclusive Bel Air section of Los Angeles which has an elaborate security system, one of the finest wine cellars in the city, a fabulous art collection, and as many as eight of the most expensive automobiles at one time. " 'Sidney Korshak is probably the most important man socially out here,' said Joyce Haber, the Hollywood columnist. 'If you're not invited to his Christmas party, it's a disaster.' "[26] Lew Wasserman, the chief executive of the entertainment conglomerate M.C.A. Inc., "described Mr. Korshak as a 'very good personal friend' and one of the 40 or 50 people in Hollywood with influence. 'He's a very well respected lawyer,' Mr. Wasserman said in an interview. 'He's a man of his word and good company.' "[27] As a successful labor lawyer and an astute business adviser for major corporations, Korshak fulfills the old Hollywood prophecy, "Blessed are the deal makers, for they shall inherit the industry." In the new Hollywood run by the multinational conglomerates, the dealmakers have become more important than ever. There are fewer productions and higher budgets. The production level of the seventies is only one-fourth to one-third of what it was in the late forties. And the large corporations are even less willing to take risks than the moguls. Agents who can "package" stars and directors of proven popularity—i.e., "bankable"—have thus become more important than ever. And in the new Hollywood, Sidney Korshak is a consummate dealmaker. Cinema International Corporation, for example, was formed as a joint real estate and film-leasing venture through complex negotiations between Charles Bluhdorn of Gulf and Western, Lew Wasserman of M.C.A., and multimillionaire Kirk Kerkorian, who owns M.G.M., among other holdings. Bluhdorn recalled for the New York *Times* that Korshak was essential in concluding the complex deals " 'Mr. Korshak was very close to Wasserman and Kerkorian and played a key role as a go-between. . . . It was a very, very tough negotiation that would have broken down without him.' "[28] Korshak was introduced to the Gulf and Western chief by **Godfather** producer Robert Evans shortly after the conglomerate bought Paramount Pictures, Inc. "Mr. Bluhdorn recalled that during early casting for 'The Godfather,' one of the biggest successes at Paramount, his company's subsidiary, Mr. Korshak obtained for the production the services of Al Pacino, the actor then under contract to MGM."[29]

According to the *Times'* six-month-long investigation, Korshak's power and influence stemmed from his former underworld connections in Chicago. His immense influence and many connections make him an infinitely more powerful man than the **Godfather** movie character for which he arranged the right movie star. U.S. Department of Justice officials described Korshak to the *Times* as "the archetype of a new kind of intermediary who is able to deal simultaneously with organized crime and the highest echelons of legitimate business," and as " 'a senior intermediary for and senior advisor to' organized crime groups in California, Chicago, Las Vegas and New York. 'He directs their investments, their internal affairs, their high level decision-making. . . .' "[30] A 1968 Justice Department report "described him as perhaps 'the most significant link in the relationship between the crime syndicate, politics, labor and management.' "[31]

The powerful "wheeler-dealer" and "mystery man," as the Chicago newspapers circumspectly described Korshak, "began defending members of the Capone mob soon after his graduation from law school. . . . Many of the city's union were then dominated by the Capone mob, and Mr. Korshak quickly became involved in labor law."[32]

Willie Bioff testified in his 1943 Hollywood extortion trial that he was introduced to Korshak in a Chicago hotel in 1939 by Charles (Cherry Nose) Gioe, a Capone mobster, who said: "Sidney is our man, and I want you to do what he tells you. He is not just another lawyer, but knows our gang and figures our best interest. Pay attention to him and remember any message he may deliver to you is a message from us."[33]

In 1952 Korshak "served as general counsel for a group of investors who purchased control of R.K.O. Pictures Corporation for slightly more than $7 million. Shortly after the deal was announced, the *Wall Street Journal* published an exposé on R.K.O.'s new owners, in which it reported that some of them had known connections with mobsters and other questionable ties. Mr. Korshak was described as 'a sort of catalytic agent' in arranging the purchase. The

Sidney Korshak testifies

Michael V. Gazzo refuses to testify in *The Godfather Part II*

R.K.O. takeover was bruptly called off, and Mr. Korshak resigned as counsel."[34] The *Times* article concluded that "Though he began his career defending members of the Capone mob, Mr. Korshak has in recent years appeared in public as a widely respected attorney or consultant for large corporations involved in labor strife or negotiations."[35] Despite numerous legislative investigations, F.B.I. probes, and investigative newspaper articles, Korshak has not been indicted and convicted of any crimes. As he told one associate during a 1968 business meeting, " 'I've been investigated by more Congressional committees than anybody . . . but nobody's got anything on me.' "[36] Korshak's discreet and respectable posture is suitable to the film industry that has been taken over by the multinational corporations. It is consistently appropriate that a lawyer who used to represent the mob should be involved with the multinational corporation—and, in a small way, with the film itself—that made **The Godfather.** The third biggest money maker in the history of American movies is a film which, according to one leading critic, Pauline Kael, reflects a grim acknowledgment of a gangster mentality in American culture without the tone of certain retribution that had characterized the films of the early thirties.[37] After a decade of investigation, the doubts linger and cynicism grows. The Kefauver, Kennedy, and McClellan committees, investigating organized crime; the investigations of the assassinations of King and the Kennedys; of the My Lai massacre; of the operations of the C.I.A. in Chile; of oil price-fixing; and of Watergate have all created the right climate for the continued popularity of the movie gangster by failing to satisfy the American public's desire for truth and for justice.

Again a crowded room quiets down as a movie gangster faces a Senate investigative committee. But in **The Godfather** the gangster has a lawyer with him and the calm assurance of a person beyond the law. The scene, like the film, is permeated with an acceptance of the gangster's durability, as opposed to the strident certainty that public exposure automatically destroys gangsters that had characterized syndicate films like **Hoodlum Empire.** The syndicate movie gangster who grew from Robber Baron and Robin Hood roots rises with the tide of a pervasive criminality in America which is more profound than the presence of a few successful syndicate men. Despite its durability during this period of our history, the gangster genre—like the malignant mentality of systematic exploitation, destruction, and greed it represents—is ultimately Born To Lose.

NOTES

PART I

Introduction

1. W. Lloyd Warner, *American Life: Dream and Reality* (Chicago: University of Chicago Press, 1953), p. 210.

Chapter 1

1. *The 1935 Film Daily Yearbook of Motion Pictures* (New York: *The Film Daily,* 1934), p. 301.
2. Robert Warshow, "The Gangster as Tragic Hero," in *The Immediate Experience* (New York: Doubleday and Co., 1962), p. 90.
3. Interview with the author.
4. John G. Cawelti, *The Six Gun Mystique* (Bowling Green, Ohio: Bowling Green University Popular Press, 1968), pp. 35–46.
5. Kent L. Steckmesser, *The Western Hero in History and Legend* (Norman, Oklahoma: University of Oklahoma Press, 1965).
6. Homer Croy, *Jesse James Was My Neighbor* (New York: Duell. Sloan, & Pearce, 1960), pp. 12–13.
7. *The Badmen,* Columbia Records, LL10B, 1960.
8. Steckmesser, *The Western Hero.*
9. E.J. Hobsbawm, *Bandits* (London: Ebenezer Bayliss and Sons, Ltd., 1969), Chapter 1.
10. Jim Kitses, *Horizons West* (London: Thames and Hudson, Ltd., 1969), p. 11.
11. Cawelti, *The Six Gun Mystique.*
12. Joseph Campbell, *Hero With a Thousand Faces* (New York: World Publishing Co., 1956), p. 17.
13. Frederick Jackson Turner, *The Frontier in American History* (New York: Holt, Rinehart and Winston, 1920).
14. Henry Nash Smith, *Virgin Land* (New York, 1950).
15. André Bazin, "The Western or the American Film *par excellence,*" in Hugh Gray, ed. and trans., *What Is Cinema?,* Vol. II (Berkeley: University of California Press, Inc., 1967). Also, J.L. Rieupeyrout, *La Grande Aventure du Western (1894–1964)* (Paris: Paris Editions du Cerf, 1964).
16. Bazin, "The Western or the American Film par excellence," and Rieupeyrout, *La Grand Aventure.*
17. Cawelti, *Six Gun Mystique,* pp. 58–60.
18. There were some films in which the cowboy did hope to settle down and own land. In *Red River* the protagonist's ambition is to become a cattle baron.
19. Frank Waters, *Book of the Hopi* (New York: Viking Press, 1963), pp. 29, 137.
20. Quoted in Mathew Josephson, *The Robber Barons: The Great American Capitalists* (New York: Harcourt, Brace & Co., 1934).
21. Ibid., p. 151.
22. Ibid., p. 135.
23. Quoted in Ida M. Tarbell, *The History of Standard Oil* (New York: McClure Phillips & Co., 1904).
24. Anonymous, "The Vanderbilt Memorial," *The Nation,* LX (November 18, 1869).
25. Quoted in Leo Marx, *The Machine in the Garden* (New York: Oxford University Press, 1964), p. 13.
26. Hank Messick, *Lansky* (New York: G.P. Putnam's Sons, 1971), Chapter 17; Lowell Bergman and Jeff Gerth, "La Costa," *Penthouse* (March 1975), p. 47.

27. Tarbell, *History of Standard Oil,* p. 65.
28. Josephson, *The Robber Barons,* p. 274.
29. Ibid., p. 299.
30. Ibid., pp. 128, 139.
31. Ibid., p. 353.
32. Mathew Josephson, *The Politicos* (New York: Harcourt, Brace & Co., 1938), p. 118.
33. Thomas C. Cochran and William Miller, *The Age of Enterprise* (New York: The Macmillan Co., 1942), p. 157.
34. Josephson, *The Robber Barons,* p. 353.
35. Ibid., p. 228.
36. Quoted in Cochran and Miller, *The Age of Enterprise,* p. 160.
37. Records of Motion Picture Commission of the State of New York.
38. Ibid.
39. Henry May and Charles Sellers, *A Synopsis of American History* (Chicago: Rand McNally, 1960).
40. William Z. Ripley, "Main Street and Wall Street," quoted in Cochran and Miller, *The Age of Enterprise,* p. 193.
41. Josephson, *The Robber Barons,* p. 15.
42. Ibid., p. 157.
43. Ibid.
44. Leo Marx, *The Machine in the Garden.*
45. Josephson, *The Robber Barons,* p. 15.
46. Ibid., p. 336.
47. Ibid., pp. 105–106.
48. William A. Croffut, *The Vanderbilts and the Story of Their Fortune* (Chicago: Clarke and Co., 1886), p. 272.
49. Josephson, *The Robber Barons,* p. 270.
50. Ibid., p. 157.

Chapter 2

1. Ralph Gabriel, *The Course of American Democratic Thought,* 2nd ed. (New York: Ronald Press, 1956), p. 157.
2. Frederick Tolles, *Meeting House and Counting House* (Chapel Hill: University of North Carolina Press, 1948), p. 56.
3. Benjamin Franklin, *Autobiography and Other Writings,* ed. by L. Jesse Lemisch (New York: New America Library, 1961).
4. Gabriel, *The Course of American Democratic Thought,* p. 155.
5. Ibid.
6. Quoted in Gabriel, ibid., p. 157.
7. Ibid.
8. Ibid., p. 158.
9. Ibid.
10. Ibid.
11. Ibid., p. 160.
12. Ibid., p. 158.
13. Richard Hofstadter, *Social Darwinism in American Thought* (Boston: Beacon Press, 1964), p. 58.
14. Gabriel, *The Course of American Democratic Thought,* p. 159.
15. Benjamin Franklin, *Autobiography,* p. 1.
16. Quoted in Moses Rischin, *The American Gospel of Success* (New York: Quadrangle Books), p. 97.
17. Ibid., p. 92.
18. Bob Thomas, *King Cohn* (New York: G. P. Putnam's Sons, 1967), p. 8.
19. Fred Pasley, *Al Capone: The Biography of a Self-Made Man* (London: Faber and Faber, Ltd., 1931), p. 78.
20. John Cawelti, "From Rags to Respectability: Horatio Alger," in Lawrence Levine and Robert Middlekauff, *The National Temper* (New York: Harcourt, Brace and World, 1968), p. 118.
21. Ibid.
22. Rischin, *The Gospel of Wealth,* p. 21.
23. Ibid., p. 46.
24. William E. Miller, *Men in Business* (Cambridge: Harvard University Press, 1952), p. 148.
25. Quoted in Henry Nash Smith, *Popular Culture in Industrial America* (New York: New York University Press, 1967), p. 402.
26. Ibid., p. 424.
27. Ibid., p. 426.

Chapter 3

1. R. Butterfield, *The American Past* (New York: Simon and Schuster, 1947), p. 221.
2. Josiah Strong, "Perils—the City," in *Our Country, Its Possible Future and Its Present Crisis* (New York: The Baker & Taylor Co., 1885), pp. 128–144.
3. Christopher Tunnerd and Hope Reed, *American Skyline* (Boston: Houghton Mifflin Co., 1956), pp. 154–176.
4. Moses Rischin, *The Promised City* (Cambridge: Harvard University Press, 1962), p. 9.
5. Henry James, *The American Scene* (New York: Charles Scribner's Sons, 1964 ed.), pp. 85–86, 130–139, *passim.*
6. Jack Warner, *My First 100 Years in Hollywood* (New York: Random House, 1965), p. 18.
7. Upton Sinclair, *Upton Sinclair Presents William Fox* (Los Angeles: privately printed, 1933).
8. Quoted in Rischin, *The Promised City,* p. 75.

9. Sinclair, *Upton Sinclair Presents William Fox*, p. 50.
10. Warner, *My First 100 Years*, p. 54.
11. Jacob Riis, *How the Other Half Lives* (Cambridge: Belknap Press of Harvard University Press, 1972), p. 202.
12. James, *The American Scene*, p. 16.
13. Rischin, *The Promised City*, p. 222.
14. William L. Riordan, *Plunkett of Tammany Hall*, Introduction, Ray V. Peal (New York: Alfred A. Knopf, 1948).
15. Sinclair, *Upton Sinclair Presents William Fox*, p. 16.
16. Riordin, *Plunkett*, p. 3.
17. Herbert Asbury, *The Gangs of New York* (New York: Alfred A. Knopf, 1927).
18. Ibid., p. 168.
19. Jacob Riis, *Battle with the Slum* (New York: The Macmillan Co., 1902), p. 228.
20. Ibid., p. 231.
21. Ibid.
22. Warner, *My First 100 Years*, pp. 35–36.

Chapter 4

1. Zukor, *The Public Is Never Wrong* (New York: G.P. Putnam's Sons, 1953), p. 184.
2. Ibid., p. 27.
3. Benjamin Hampton, *A History of the American Film Industry* (New York: Dover Publications, 1970 ed.), pp. 183–184.
4. Lewis Jacobs, *The Rise of the American Film* (New York: Harcourt Brace and Co., 1939), Chapter 1.
5. Terry Ramsaye, *A Million and One Nights* (New York: Simon and Schuster, 1926), pp. 1–20.
6. Ibid., p. 427.
7. Ibid., p. 430.
8. Jacobs, *The Rise of the American Film*, Chapter 1.
9. Zukor, *The Public Is Never Wrong*, pp. 79–80.
10. Ibid., p. 181.
11. Hampton, *A History of the American Film*, p. 190.
12. Ibid., p. 185.
13. John Drinkwater, *The Life and Adventures of Carl Laemmle* (New York and London: G.P. Putnam's Sons, 1931).
14. Ramsaye, *A Million and One Nights*, p. 308.
15. *Moving Picture World*, July 6, 1907.
16. Ramsaye, *A Million and One Nights*, pp. 524, 573.
17. *Views and Film Index*, Oct. 12, 1907, p. 450.
18. Drinkwater, *The Life and Adventures*, p. 87.
19. Upton Sinclair, *Upton Sinclair Presents William Fox* (Los Angeles: privately printed, 1933).

20. Zukor, *The Public Is Never Wrong*, pp. 73–74.
21. Ramsaye, *A Million and One Nights*, p. 465.
22. Zukor, *The Public Is Never Wrong*, p. 77.
23. Georges Sadoul, *Histoire Generale du Cinema*, Vol. II, *Les Pionniers du Cinema* (Paris: Les Editions Denoel, 1947), p. 43.
24. Ramsaye, *A Million and One Nights*, p. 492.
25. Drinkwater, *The Life and Adventures*, p. 84.
26. Ramsaye, *A Million and One Nights*, p. 529.
27. Ibid., p. 528.
28. Zukor, *The Public Is Never Wrong*, p. 57.
29. Sinclair, *Upton Sinclair Presents William Fox*, pp. 36–37.
30. Vachel Lindsay, *The Art of the Moving Picture* (New York: 1915; Liveright ed., 1970).
31. G.W. Bitzer, *Billy Bitzer, His Story* (New York: Farrar, Straus, Giroux, 1973), p. 68.
32. Frank Woods, "Spectator's Comments," *Dramatic Mirror*, Oct. 23, 1909, p. 23.
33. *Views and Film Index*, Oct. 5, 1907, p. 65.
34. Henry F. May, *The End of American Innocence* (New York: Alfred A. Knopf, 1959), p. 31.
35. Ruth Inglis, *Freedom of the Movies* (Chicago: University of Chicago Press, 1947), Chapter 1.
36. Lewis Jacobs, *The Rise of the American Film* (New York: Harcourt, Brace and Co., 1939), p. 76.
37. Ibid., p. 150.
38. Lillian Gish, with Ann Pinchot, *The Movies, Mr. Griffith and Me* (Englewood Cliffs, N.J.: Prentice Hall, 1969), p. 74.
39. *Biograph Bulletin*, Oct. 31, 1912.
40. Ibid.
41. Ibid.
42. Lillian Gish on *The Dick Cavett Show*, Feb. 10, 1971, ABC Television Network.
43. G.W. Bitzer, *Billy Bitzer*, p. 87.

Chapter 5

1. William E. Leuchtenburg, *The Perils of Prosperity, 1914–1932* (New York: Harper and Row, 1962), p. 101.
2. *Film Daily*, April 15, 1923, p. 6.
3. Andrew Sinclair, *The Age of Excess* (New York: Harper and Row, 1964 ed.), pp. 18, 46.
4. Ibid., p. 227.
5. Bruce Barton, *The Man Nobody Knows* (Indianapolis: Bobbs Merrill, 1925).
6. George Soule, *Prosperity Decade* (New York: Rinehart and Co., 1947), pp. 138–147.
7. Sinclair, *The Age of Excess*, p. 220.
8. President's Research Committee on Recent Social

Trends, *Recent Social Trends in the United States* (Washington, D.C.: Government Printing Office, 1933), p. 866.

9. Ibid., pp. 218–268.

10. Ibid., Chapter VIII, "Changing Social Attitudes and Interests."

11. Eric Johnson, "Hollywood: America's Salesman," in R.D. MacCann, ed., *Film and Society* (New York: Charles Scribner's Sons, 1964).

12. Lewis Jacobs, *The Rise of the American Film* (New York: Harcourt, Brace & Co., 1939), p. 406.

13. Leuchtenburg, *The Perils of Prosperity,* p. 216.

14. Jacobs, *The Rise of the American Film,* p. 405.

15. John Kobler, *Al Capone* (New York: G.P. Putnam's Sons, 1971), p. 312.

16. Sinclair, *The Age of Excess,* p. 220.

17. Kobler, *Al Capone,* p. 312.

18. Ibid., p. 299.

19. Ibid.

20. Leuchtenburg, *The Perils of Prosperity,* p. 216.

21. Ibid., pp. 194, 205.

22. Ibid., pp. 286–287.

23. Ibid., p. 282.

24. Ibid., p. 94.

25. Ibid., p. 169.

Chapter 6

1. William E. Leuchtenburg, *The Perils of Prosperity, 1914–1932* (New York: Harper and Row, 1962), p. 101.

2. Ibid., p. 216.

3. Andrew Sinclair, *The Age of Excess* (New York: Harper and Row, 1964 ed.), p. 312.

4. Ibid., p. 226.

5. John Kobler, *Al Capone* (New York: G.P. Putnam's Sons, 1971), p. 312.

6. Hank Messick, *Lansky* (New York: G.P. Putnam's Sons, 1971), pp. 24–25.

7. Ibid.

8. Sinclair, *The Age of Excess,* p. 318.

9. Leuchtenburg, *The Perils of Prosperity,* p. 176.

10. President's Research Committee on Recent Social Trends, *Recent Social Trends in the United States* (Washington, D.C.: Government Printing Office, 1933), p. 667.

11. Ibid., p. 661.

12. I am accepting Daniel Bell's definition of mass society: "The conception of 'mass society' can be summarized as follows: The revolutions in transport and communications have brought men into closer contact with each other and bound them in new ways; the division of labor has made them more interdependent; tremors in one part of the society affect all others. Despite this greater interdependence, however, individuals have grown more estranged from one another. The old primary group ties of family and local community have been shattered; ancient parochial faiths are questioned; few unifying values have taken their place. Most important, the critical standards of an educated elite no longer shape opinion or taste. As a result, mores are morals are in constant flux, relations between individuals are tangential or compartmentalized rather than organic. At the same time greater mobility, spatial and social, has intensified concern over status. Instead of a fixed or known status symbolized by dress or titles, each person assumes a multiplicity of roles and constantly has to prove himself in a succession of new situations. Because of all this, the individual loses a coherent sense of self. His anxieties increase. There ensues a search for new faiths. The stage is thus set for the charismatic leader, the secular messiah who, by bestowing upon each person the semblance of necessary grace and fullness of personality, supplies a substitute for the older unifying belief that the mass society has destroyed." From "The Theory of Mass Society," *Commentary,* July 1956, pp. 75–83. Cf. C. Wright Mills, *The Power Elite* (New York: Oxford University Press, 1956), Chapter 13, "Mass Society."

13. See David Kretch and Richard Cruthfield, "Perceiving the World," in Wilbur Schramm, *The Process and Effects of Mass Communications* (Urbana: University of Illinois Press, 1954), pp. 116–138; David Riesman, "Socializing Functions of Print," and Raymond and Alice Bauer, "Mass Society and Mass Media of Communications," in Charles Sternberg, ed., *Mass Media and Communications* (New York: Hastings House, 1964).

14. Eric Johnson, "Hollywood: America's Salesman," in R.D. MacCann, ed., *Film and Society* (New York: Charles Scribner's Sons, 1964).

15. Quoted in Leuchtenburg, *The Perils of Prosperity,* p. 2.

16. Frank Luther Mott, *American Journalism,* (New York: The Macmillan Co., 1950), pp. 686–711.

17. Ibid., p. 632.

18. Ibid., p. 696.

19. Ibid., p. 704.

20. T.J. Kreps, "The Newspaper Industry," in N. Adams, ed., *The Structure of American Industry* (New York: The Macmillan Co., 1954).

21. R. Cauliez, *Le Film Criminel et le Film Policier* (Paris: Editions du Cerf, 1956), p. 7.
22. Ernst Cassirer, *Language and Myth* (New York: Dover Publications, 1946), p. 45.
23. Ibid., pp. 53–56.
24. Jake Lingel was a possible liaison between the underworld and publishing interests when newspaper owners used gangsters in circulation wars.
25. See Andrew Sinclair's epilogue to Pasley's *Al Capone: The Biography of a Self-Made Man* (London: Faber & Faber, Ltd., 1931).
26. Ben Hecht, *A Child of the Century* (New York: Simon and Schuster, 1954), pp. 113, 149.
27. Ibid., pp. 168–177.
28. Ibid., p. 377.
29. Sinclair, *The Age of Excess*, p. 219.
30. Hecht, *A Child of the Century*, pp. 85–109, 380–382.
31. Ibid., pp. 14–16, 362, 368.
32. Ibid., pp. 357–358, 486–487; C. Wright Mills, *The Power Elite;* David Riesman, *The Lonely Crowd* (Yale University Press, 1950).
33. Hecht, *A Child of the Century*, p. 383.
34. Ibid., p. 479.
35. Ruth Inglis, *Freedom of the Movies* (Chicago: University of Chicago Press, 1947), p. 64.
36. Hecht, *A Child of the Century*.

Chapter 7

1. Letter from Mrs. Clara Philippi Johnson, *Photoplay*, April 1928, p. 11.
2. Also, *Underworld* is the most widely distributed twenties gangster film, as of this writing.
3. Quoted in *Motion Picture Classic*, August 1928, p. 52.
4. Irene Thayer review, New York *Daily News*, Mar. 16, 1928.
5. Sidney Skolsky, "Putting Little Caesar on the Spot," *New Movie Magazine*, Dec. 4, 1931, pp. 37, 90.
6. Dunham Thorp, "Muffling the Racket," *Motion Picture Classic*, December 1928, pp. 63, 65.
7. Ibid., p. 63.
8. Records of New York State Motion Picture Commission, Letter from Abraham Kutz, Counselor at Law, Sept. 18, 1928.
9. *The Widow from Chicago*, Warner Brothers, 1930.
10. *Photoplay*, April 1928, p. 9.
11. "Current Pictures," *Motion Picture Magazine*, July 1929, p. 62.
12. Blan Johan, "The Talk of New York," New York State Motion Picture Commission Records, Mar. 16, 1928.
13. Rosa Reilly, "The New Technique of the Talkies," *Screenland*, July 1929, pp. 26–27.
14. Benjamin Hampton, *A History of the American Film Industry* (New York: Dover Publications, 1970 ed.), p. 362.
15. Ibid., p. 256.
16. Ibid.
17. Ibid., p. 313.
18. Ibid., p. 244.
19. Ibid., p. 411.
20. Hank Messick, *Lansky* (New York: G.P. Putnam's Sons, 1971).
21. Hampton, *A History of the American Film Industry*, p. 382.
22. Ibid., p. 409.

Chapter 8

1. James Conant, *Antitrust in the Motion Picture Industry* (Berkeley: University of California Press, 1965), p. 29; Lewis Jacobs, *The Rise of the American Film* (New York: Harcourt, Brace & Co., 1939).
2. Conant, *Antitrust*, p. 29; Mae Huettig, *Economic Control of the Motion Picture Industry* (Philadelphia: University of Pennsylvania Press, 1944); Francis Klingender and David Legg, *Money Behind the Screen* (London: Lawrence and Wisehart, 1937).
3. Conant, *Antitrust*, p. 30.
4. Huettig, *Economic Control*, pp. 106–107.
5. Louis Nizer, *New Courts of Industry: Self-Regulation Under the Motion Picture Code* (New York: The Longacre Press, Inc., 1935), p. 245.
6. Ibid.
7. Conant, *Antitrust*, p. 94.
8. Ibid., p. 95.
9. Hank Messick, *Lansky* (New York: G.P. Putnam's Sons, 1971), pp. 75–76.
10. Hank Messick, "Gigolos and Gorillas," in *Beauties and the Beast: The Mob in Show Business* (New York: David McKay and Co., 1973).
11. Will Hays, *President's Report to the Motion Picture Producers and Distributors' Association* (New York, 1932), p. 21.
12. Quoted in Messick, *Beauties*, p. 99.
13. Ibid.
14. Ibid., p. 100.

15. Ibid., p. 89.

16. "Frank Nitti, Phil D'Andrea, former Capone body-guard and official head of the Mafia in Chicago; Paul "the waiter" Ricca, ally of Meyer Lansky and Lucky Luciano; Charles "Cherry Nose" Gioe, a top Capone lieutenant; and Louis "Little New York" Compagna. . . ." Messick, *Beauties*, p. 90.

Chapter 9

1. U.S. Bureau of the Census, *Historical Statistics of the United States* (Washington, D.C.: 1965), p. 73; also, Philip Eden, "For More Adequate Measurement of Unemployment," *Current Economic Comment*, Bureau of Economic and Business Research, University of Illinois, November 1959.

2. Edmund Wilson, *The American Jitters* (New York and London: Charles Scribner's Sons, 1932).

3. Gilbert Seldes, *Years of the Locust (America 1929–1932)* (Boston: Little, Brown and Co., 1932), p. 70.

4. Jack Salzman and Barry Wallenstein, eds., *Years of Protest* (New York: Western Publishing Co., 1967), pp. 10, 14.

5. Erik Barnouw, *The Golden Web: A History of Broadcasting in the United States*, Vol. I (New York: Oxford University Press, 1966–1970).

6. Robert and Helen S. Lynd, *Middletown in Transition* (New York: Harcourt, Brace and Co., 1937).

7. Quoted in William Stott, *Documentary Expression and Thirties America* (New York: Oxford University Press, 1973).

8. Will Hays, *Annual Report* (New York: 1934), p. 2.

9. Quoted in NET Playhouse Series on the thirties, 1976.

10. Gladys Hall, "James Cagney Confesses He Couldn't Be a Doctor," *Movie Classic*, January 1934, pp. 26, 60–61.

11. Letter from Floyd Casebolt, Waxahachie, Texas, *Movie Classic*, Mar. 19, 1933, p. 6.

12. Letter from Clifton Ray, Miami, Florida, *Movie Mirror*, August 1932, p. 36.

13. Letter from "A Faithful *Movie Mirror* Reader," New York, *Movie Mirror*, June 1932, p. 36.

14. Letter from Esther M. Spare, Sandusky, Ohio, *Screenland*, August 1933, p. 6.

15. Letter from M.T. Rucker, Jr., San Angelo, Texas, *Screenland*, July 1930, p. 8.

16. Seldes, *Years of the Locust*, p. 65.

17. Letter from F. Clinton Spooner, Brooklyn, New York, *Screenland*, April 1930, p. 8.

18. Hall, "James Cagney Confesses," p. 60.

19. Charles Grayson, "They've Battled the Depression—That's Why They're Stars," *Motion Picture Magazine* January 1933.

20. Letter from Stanley H. Briggs, Inglewood, California, *Motion Picture Magazine*, January 1932, p. 6.

21. Helen Louise Walker, "Hunting for a Hero," *Motion Picture Magazine*, July, 1931.

22. Letter from Stanley H. Briggs, *Motion Picture Magazine*, January 1932, p. 6.

23. Letter from Bernie C. Browne, Hollywood, Calif., *New Movie Magazine*, September 1931, p. 8.

24. Letter from Anita Mackland, Los Angeles, *Motion Picture Magazine*, December 1931, p. 6.

25. Herb Howe, "Hollywood Boulevardier," *New Movie Magazine*, April 1931, p. 9.

26. *Modern Screen Magazine*, June 1931, p. 5.

27. Letter from John O'Hara, Santa Rosa, California, *Movie Classic*, October 1934.

28. Egbert Donald and Stow Persons, *Socialism and American Life;* Granville Hicks, "How Red Was the Red Decade," *Harpers*, July 1953.

29. Interview with Gladys Hall, "Little Caesar Tosses Some Verbal Bombs," *Movie Classic*, November 1931, pp. 41, 81.

30. William E. Leuchtenburg, *Franklin D. Roosevelt and the New Deal* (New York: Harper and Row, 1963), p. 22.

31. Ibid., p. 30.

32. *Fortune*, July 1934.

33. Warshow, "The Gangster as Tragic Hero," in *The Immediate Experience* (New York: Anchor Books, 1962), p. 85.

34. *Gunsmoke*, Paramount Pictures, 1931.

35. Meyer Lansky sent his son to West Point.

36. Speech to American Legion Convention, Connecticut, Aug. 21, 1931. Quoted in Jules Archer, *The Plot To Seize the White House* (New York: Hawthorne Books, 1973).

Chapter 10

1. Evelyn Gerstein, "The Man Who Can Weep," *Modern Screen Magazine*, July 1932, p. 64.

2. Interview with Katherine Hartley, "I'm Going To Sandpaper Jimmy Cagney's Neck, Says Jimmy Cagney," *Movie Classic*, October 1934, p. 47.

3. Ida Zeitlin, "Robinson's Life Story as Told by E.G. Robinson to Ida Zeitlin," *Screenland*, July 1933, pp. 25, 71.

4. Harry Long, "Up from the East Side: The True Story of James Cagney as Told by Jimmy Cagney Himself," *Movie Mirror*, April 1932, p. 60.

5. Gladys Hall, "James Cagney Confesses He

Couldn't Be A Doctor,'' *Movie Classic,* January 1934, pp. 26, 60.

6. Letter from Dorothy Warshow, Crawfordsville, Arkansas, *Movie Classic,* February 1932, p. 6.

7. Richard Watts, Jr., Review, New York *Herald-Tribune,* Apr. 24, 1931; James Shelley Hamilton, *The National Board of Review Magazine,* May 1931.

8. Lincoln Kirsten, ''James Cagney and the American Hero,'' *Hound and Horn,* April/June 1932, p. 53.

9. Actors who subsequently played gangsters were not always short or as snappy in their delivery and acting. Gary Cooper in **City Streets** is laconic and occasionally boyishly exuberant, but this is excusable because he plays a Westerner who becomes a gangster, as opposed to a character who was urban. Paul Muni and Clark Gable did give their characters a street-wise tone and characterization marked by vitality. Muni's Tony Camonte in **Scarface** is perhaps the best performance in the entire history of the genre (with Cagney's Cody Jarrett in **White Heat** a close second). But Muni was able to move quickly on to other challenging roles and was not identified by audiences, critics, and studio heads as a type-cast gangster. Also, Muni played a gangster at the height of the craze, and he built his characterization on what Cagney and Robinson had already established.

10. Museum of Modern Art Lecture, #12 in a series. Source, Museum of Modern Art transcript, no date.

11. Kirsten, *Hound and Horn.*

12. Kenneth MacGowan, *Behind the Screen* (New York: Delacorte Press, 1965), p. 425.

13. *Motion Picture Magazine,* June 1932, p. 63.

14. Letter from Robert H. Quinn, Mechanicsville, New York, *Screenland,* August 1932, p. 98.

Chapter 11

1. Robert Eichberg, ''What They Think of Censorship,'' *Modern Screen Magazine,* October 1934, p. 88.

2. *Commonweal,* June 10, 1931, pp. 143–144; *The Nation,* Jan. 21, 1931, p. 8.

3. Letter from Jean Saturn, Terryville, Connecticut, *Modern Screen Magazine,* June 1931, p. 114.

4. Lewis Lawes, ''Convicts and the Movies,'' *Movie Screen Magazine,* February 1933, p. 29.

5. W.W. Charters, *Motion Pictures and Youth;* P.W. Holaday, *Getting Ideas from the Movies;* R.C. Peterson and L.L. Thurstone, *Motion Pictures and the Social Attitudes of Children;* S.K. Shuttleworth

and M.A. May, *The Social Conduct of Attitudes of Movie Fans;* W.S. Dysinger and C.A. Ruckmick, *The Emotional Responses of Children to the Motion Picture Situation;* C.C. Peters, *Motion Pictures and Standards of Morality;* Samuel Renshaw et al., *Children's Sleep;* Herbert Blumer, *Movies and Conduct;* Edgar Dale, *Children's Attendance at Motion Pictures;* Edgar Dale, *The Content of Motion Pictures;* Herbert Blumer and Philip Hauser, *Movies, Delinquency and Crime;* P.G. Cressey and F.M. Thrasher, *Boys, Movies and City Streets;* Edgar Dale, *How To Appreciate Motion Pictures.*

6. Ruth Inglis, *Freedom of the Movies* (Chicago: University of Chicago Press, 1947), pp. 114–116.

7. *Motion Picture Herald,* Apr. 4, 1930, p. 12.

8. Will Hays, *President's Report,* Los Angeles, 1932, pp. 21–22.

9. Ibid.

10. Warner Brothers, *Press Sheet on Little Caesar,* New York, 1930.

11. Letter from H. Pat, Rochester, New York, *Motion Picture Magazine,* October 1931, p. 6.

12. John Spivak, *America Faces the Barricades* (New York: Covici Friede, 1935).

13. Quoted in William Stott, *Documentary Expression and Thirties America,* (New York: Oxford University Press, 1973), p. 135.

14. Radio address at Fortress Monroe, Virginia, Oct. 18, 1931. Quoted in Edward Angly, *Oh Yeah?* (New York: The Viking Press, 1931), p. 19.

15. New York Motion Picture Commission records. Letter to First National Distribution Corporation.

16. Howard T. Lewis, *The Motion Picture Industry* (New York: Van Nostrand, 1933), p. 388.

17. Inglis, *Freedom of the Movies,* p. 119.

18. Ibid., p. 122.

19. Ibid., p. 124.

20. Ibid., p. 125.

21. Letter from Ira Billag, Yonkers, New York, *Movie Classic,* September 1931, p. 8.

22. Letter from J.W. Smith, Fort Stanton, New Mexico, *Motion Picture Magazine,* August 1932, p. 6.

23. New York *Times,* Oct. 13, 1931, pp. 1, 3.

24. Records of New York Motion Picture Commission, script for radio broadcast.

25. Milton Meyer, ''The Myth of the G-Men,'' *The Forum,* September 1935, p. 145.

26. Will Hays, *President's Report* (New York: 1936), p. 2.

27. Andrew Bergman, *We're in the Money* (New York: 1971), p. 87.

28. Meyer, "The Myth of the G-Men."

Chapter 12

1. Quoted in Raymond Lee and B.C. Van Hecke, *Gangsters and Hoodlums: The Underworld in the Cinema* (New York: A.S. Barnes & Co., 1971), p. 7.
2. Quoted in John Baxter, *The Gangster Film* (London and New York: Zwemmer and A.S. Barnes, 1970), p. 27.
3. Quoted in Lewis Yablonsky, *George Raft* (New York: McGraw-Hill Book Co., 1974), p. 240.
4. Antony Jay, *Corporation Man* (London: Cape, 1972), p. 183.

Chapter 13

1. Jim Bishop, *The Mark Hellinger Story* (New York: Appleton-Century-Crofts, 1952), p. 231.

Chapter 14

1. See Estes Kefauver, *Crime in America* (Garden City, N.Y.: Doubleday, 1951); Hank Messick, *Lansky* (New York: G.P. Putnam's Sons, 1971).
2. Hank Messick, *Lansky,* and Lowell Bergman and Jeff Gerth, "*La Costa,*" *Penthouse,* March 1975.
3. Joey, with Dave Fisher, *Killer: Autobiography of a Mafia Hit Man* (New York: Playboy Press, 1973).
4. Jeff Gerth, "Nixon and the Mafia," *Sundance,* vol. 1, no. 3, p. 30.
5. Ibid.
6. Ibid.
7. Seymour Melman, *The Permanant War Economy* (New York: Simon & Schuster, 1974).
8. Cathy Perkus, ed. *Cointelpro: The FBI's Secret War on Political Freedom* (New York: Monad Press, 1975).

9. Philip Agee, *Inside the Co.: A CIA Diary* (London: Stonehill Publishing, 1975).
10. *U.S. News and World Report,* Dec. 1975 and *The Pentagon Papers* as published by the *New York Times* (New York: Bantam Books, 1975).
11. Alfred McCoy, *The Politics of Heroin in Southeast Asia* (New York: Harper & Row, 1972).
12. New York *Times,* August 14, p. 1.
13. Jerzy Toeplitz, "The New Pattern," in *Hollywood and After* (London: Allen & Unwin, 1974).
14. Quoted in William Fadiman, *Hollywood Now* (New York: Liveright Press, 1972), p. 23.
15. Hank Messick, *Beauties and the Beast: The Mob in Show Business,* p. 95.
16. Fadiman, op. cit., p. 21.
17. Lewis Yablonsky, *George Raft* (New York: McGraw-Hill, 1974), p. 75.
18. Ibid., p. 176.
19. Messick, *Beauties and the Beast,* p. 95, and *Lansky.*
20. Yablonsky, op. cit., p. 181.
21. Ibid., p. 188.
22. Messick, op. cit., p. 103.
23. James A. Bishop, *The Mark Hellinger Story* (New York: Appleton-Century-Crofts, 1952), p. 95.
24. Messick, op. cit., p. 101.
25. Bishop, op. cit., p. 284.
26. New York *Times,* June 27, 1976, p. 120. See also Messick, in *Beauties and the Beast.*
27. Ibid.
28. New York *Times,* June 29, 1976, p. 1.
29. Ibid., p. 16.
30. New York *Times,* June 27, 1976, p. 20.
31. Ibid.
32. Ibid.
33. Ibid.
34. Ibid.
35. New York *Times,* June 28, 1976, p. 20.
36. New York *Times,* June 30, 1976, p. 14.
37. Pauline Kael, *Deeper into Movies* (Boston: Little, Brown and Co., 1973), p. 430.

BIBLIOGRAPHY

BOOKS

Adams, J.T. *Our Business Civilization*. New York: 1929.

Allen, Frederick Lewis. *Only Yesterday*. New York: 1931.

Alloway, Lawrence. *Violent America: The Movies 1946–1964*. New York: 1971.

Archer, Jules. *The Plot To Seize the White House*. New York: 1973.

Arnheim, Rudolph. *Film*. London: 1933.

Asbury, Herbert. *The Gangs of New York*. New York: 1927.

Atkins, Thomas, ed. *Sexuality in the Movies*. Bloomington: 1975.

Bardeche, Maurice, and Robert Brasillach. *The History of Motion Pictures*. Translated by Iris Barry. New York: 1938.

Barnouw, Erik. *The Golden Web: A History of Broadcasting in the United States*. New York: 1968.

Baxter, John. *The Gangster Film*. London: 1970.

Bazin, André. *What Is Cinema? Essays Selected and Translated by Hugh Gray*. 2 Vols. Berkeley: 1967.

Bergman, Andrew. *We're in the Money*. New York: 1971.

Bernstein, Irving. *The Lean Years*. Baltimore: 1966 ed.

Bitzer, G.W. *Billy Bitzer, His Story*. New York: 1973.

Bloem, Walter S. *The Soul of the Moving Picture*. New York: 1924.

Bluestone, George. *Novels into Film*. Baltimore: 1957.

Blumer, Herbert. *Movies and Conduct*. New York: 1933.

Bogdanovich, Peter. *Fritz Lang in America*. New York: 1969.

Boyer, Richard, and Herbert Morais. *Labor's Untold Story*. New York: 1955.

Borde, R., and E. Chaumeton. *Panorama du Film Noir Americain*. Paris: 1955.

Burnette, W.R. *Little Caesar*. New York: 1929.

Butterfield, R. *The American Past*. New York: 1947.

Campbell, Joseph. *Hero With a Thousand Faces*. New York: 1956.

Carmen, Ira. *Movies, Censorship and the Law*. Ann Arbor: 1966.

Cassirer, Ernst. *Language and Myth*. New York: 1956.

Cauliez, R. *Le Film Criminel et Le Film Policier*. Paris: 1956.

Cawelti, John G. *The Six Gun Mystique*. Bowling Green: 1968.

Chase, Stuart. *Men and Machines*. New York: 1929.

Cochran, Thomas, and William E. Miller. *The Age of Enterprise*. New York: 1942.

Croffut, William A. *The Vanderbilts and the Story of Their Fortune*. Chicago: 1886.

Crowther, Bosley. *The Lion's Share*. New York: 1946.

———. *Hollywood Rajah*. New York: 1960.

Croy, Homer. *Jesse James Was My Neighbor*. New York: 1960.

Dale, Edgar. *The Content of Motion Pictures*. New York: 1933.

Department of Commerce, Bureau of Foreign and Domestic Commerce, Motion Picture Division. *Bulletins*. Washington, D.C.

————. Bureau of the Census. *Distribution of Motion Picture Films, 1929*. Washington, D.C.

————. Bureau of the Census, Census of Manufacturers, 1939. *Motion Pictures, Not Including Projection in Theaters*. Washington, D.C.

DeCoulteray, Geaze. *Sadism in the Movies*. Translated by Steve Hult. New York: 1965.

Drinkwater, John. *The Life and Adventures of Carl Laemmle*. New York and London: 1931.

Egbert, Donald, and Stow Persons. *Socialism and American Life*.

Ernst, Morris, and Pare Lorentz. *Censored*. New York: 1930.

————. *The Censor Marches On*. New York: 1940.

Everson, William K., and George Fenin. *The Western*. New York: 1962.

Fadiman, Wilham. *Hollywood Now*. New York: 1972.

Franklin, Benjamin. *Autobiography and Other Writings*. Edited by Jesse Lemish. New York: 1961.

French, Phillip. *The Movie Moguls*. London: 1969.

Gabree, John. *Gangsters: From* Little Caesar *to* The Godfather. New York: 1973.

Gabriel, Ralph. *The Course of Democratic Thought*. New York, 1956.

Galbraith, John Kenneth. *The Great Crash*. New York: 1955.

Gish, Lillian, with Ann Pinchot. *The Movies, Mr. Griffith, and Me*. Englewood Cliffs, N.J.: 1969.

Goodman, Ezra. *The Fifty Year Decline and Fall of Hollywood*. New York: 1962.

Gurko, Leo. *The Angry Decade*. New York: 1947.

Hampton, Benjamin. *A History of the American Film Industry*. New York: 1970 ed.

Handel, Leo. *Hollywood Looks at Its Audience*. Urbana: 1950.

Hays, Will. *See and Hear*. New York: 1929.

————. *President's Report to the Motion Picture Producers and Distributors Association*. New York: 1932.

————. *The Memoirs of Will Hays*. Garden City: 1955.

Hecht, Ben. *A Child of the Century*. New York: 1954.

Higham, John. *Strangers in the Land*. New York: 1955.

Hobsbawm, E.J. *Bandits*. London: 1969.

————. *Primitive Rebels*. London: 1963.

Hofstadter, Richard. *Age of Reform*. New York: 1955.

————. *Social Darwinism in American Thought*. Boston: 1964.

Howe, Irving, and Lewis Coser. *The American Communist Party*. Boston: 1957.

Huettig, Mae. *Economic Control of the Motion Picture Industry*. Philadelphia: 1944.

Ince, Thomas. *History of the Motion Picture*. Museum of Modern Art Film Library. New York.

Inglis, Ruth. *Freedom of the Movies*. Chicago: 1947.

Jacobs, Lewis. *The Rise of the American Film*. New York: 1939.

James, Henry. *The American Scene*. New York: 1964 ed.

Josephson, Mathew. *The Politicos*. New York: 1938.

————. *The Robber Barons*. New York: 1934.

Kael, Pauline. *Kiss Kiss, Bang Bang*. New York: 1968.

Kanin, Garson. *Hollywood*. New York: 1974.

Kauffmann, Stanley, with Bruce Henstell. *American Film Criticism: Reviews of Significant Films at the Time They First Appeared*. New York: 1974.

Kennedy, Joseph P., ed. *The Story of the Films*. Chicago: 1927.

Kirchway, Freda, ed. *Our Changing Morality: A Symposium*. New York: 1924.

Kitses, Jim. *Horizons West*. London: 1969.

Klingender Francis, and Donald Legg. *Money Behind the Screen*. London: 1937.

Kobler, John. *Al Capone*. New York: 1971.

Koenigil, Mark. *Movies in Society*. New York: 1962.

Kracauer, Siegfried. *From Caligari to Hitler*. Princeton: 1966 ed.

Leab, Daniel. *From Sambo to Superspade*. Boston: 1975.

Leighton, Isabel, ed. *The Aspirin Age*. New York: 1949.

Leroy, Mervyn, and Dick Kleiner. *Mervyn LeRoy: Take One*. New York: 1974.

Leuchtenburg, William E. *The Perils of Prosperity, 1914–1932*. New York: 1962.

Lévi-Strauss, C. *Structural Anthropology*. New York: 1967.

Lewis, Howard. *The Motion Picture Industry*. New York: 1933.

Lindsay, Vachel. *The Art of the Moving Picture*. New York: 1915.

Litwack, Leon. *The American Labor Movement*. Englewood Cliffs, N.J.: 1962.

Lord, Daniel A., S.J. *The Motion Pictures Betray America*. St. Louis: 1934.

Lowenthal, Leo, and Norbert Guterman. *Prophets of Deceit*. New York: 1949.

Lynd, Robert and Helen. *Middletown*. New York: 1929.

————. *Middletown in Transition*. New York: 1937.

MacCann, R.D., ed. *Film and Society*. New York: 1964.

MacGowan, Kenneth. *Behind the Screen*. New York: 1965.

McArthur, Colin. *Underworld USA*. New York: 1972.

Marx, Leo. *The Machine in the Garden*. New York: 1964.

Marx, Samuel. *Mayer and Thalberg: The Make-Believe Saints*. New York: 1975.

May, Henry. *The End of American Innocence*. New York: 1959.

————, and Charles Sellers. *A Synopsis of American History*. Chicago: 1960.

Mayer, J.D. *Sociology of the Film: Studies and Documents*. London: 1946.

Mayersberg, Paul. *Hollywood: The Haunted House*. London: 1967.

Merz, Charles. *The Dry Decade*. New York: 1931.

Messick, Hank. *Lansky*. New York: 1971.

————. *Beauties and the Beast: The Mob in Show Business*. New York: 1973.

Miller, William E. *Men in Business*. Cambridge: 1952.

Mills, C. Wright. *White Collar*. New York: 1951.

————. *The Power Elite*. New York: 1956.

Mitchell, Broadus. *Depression Decade*. New York: 1947.

Moley, Raymond. *The Hays Office*. New York: 1945.

Mowry, George. *Theodore Roosevelt and the Progressive Movement*. New York: 1946.

Muensterberg, Hugo. *The Photoplay*. New York: 1916.

Nathan, George Jean. *Art of the Night (Notes on the Movies)*. New York: 1928.

Naumberg, Nancy, ed. *We Make the Movies*. New York: 1937.

Nizer, Louis. *New Courts of Industry: Self Regulation Under the Motion Picture Code*. New York: 1935.

Offen, Ron. *Cagney*. Chicago: 1972.

Ogburn, William, ed. *Social Changes During Depression and Recovery*. Chicago: 1935.

Pasley, Fred. *Al Capone: The Biography of a Self Made Man*. London: 1931.

Perlman, William J. *The Movies on Trial*. New York: 1936.

Potemkin, Harry Alan. *The Eyes of the Movies*. New York: 1934.

Powdermaker, Hortense. *Hollywood, the Dream Factory*. Boston: 1950.

President's Research Committee on Recent Social Trends. *Recent Social Trends in the United States*. Washington, D.C.: 1933.

Quigley, Martin. *Decency in Motion Pictures*. New York: 1937.

Ramsaye, Terry. *A Million and One Nights*. New York: 1926.

Riesman, David. *The Lonely Crowd*. New Haven: 1950.

Rieupeyrant, J.L. *La Grande Aventure du Western (1894–1964)*. Paris: 1964.

Riis, Jacob. *Battle With the Slums*. New York: 1902.

————. *How the Other Half Lives*. Cambridge: 1972.

Riordin, William L. *Plunkett of Tammany Hall*. New York: 1948.

Ripley, W.Z. *Main Street and Wall Street*. New York: 1927.

Rischin, Moses. *The American Gospel of Success*. Chicago: 1965.

————. *The Promised City*. Cambridge: 1962.

Robinson, David. *Hollywood in the Twenties*. London: 1968.

Robinson, Edward G., with Leonard Spiegelglass. *All My Yesterdays*. New York: 1975.

Rosenberg, Nathan, and David White. *Mass Culture*. Glencoe: 1957.

Ross, Lillian. *Picture*. New York: 1952.

Rosten, Leo C. *Hollywood: The Movie Colony, The Movie Makers*. New York: 1941.

Rother, Paul, and Richard Griffith. *The Film Til Now*. New York: 1951 ed.

Sadoul, Georges. *Histoire Generale du Cinema*. 6 Vols. Paris: 1947.

Salzman, Jack, and Barry Wallenstein, eds. *Years of Protest*. New York: 1967.

Sann, Paul. *Kill the Dutchman: The Story of Dutch Schultz*. New York: 1971.

Sarris, Andrew. *The American Cinema: Directors and Directions, 1929–1968*. New York: 1968.

Schlesinger, Arthur M. *The Rise of the City*. New York: 1933.

Schramm, Wilbur. *The Process and Effects of Mass Communications*. Chicago: 1954.

Seabury, William M. *The Public and the Motion Picture Industry*. New York: 1926.

————. *Motion Picture Problems*. New York: 1929.

Seldes, Gilbert. *The Movies Come from America*. New York: 1931.

————. *Years of the Locust (America, 1929–1932)*. Boston: 1932.

Sinclair, Andrew. *Age of Excess*. New York: 1964 ed.

Sinclair, Upton. *Upton Sinclair Presents William Fox*. Los Angeles: 1933.

Smith, Henry Nash. *Popular Culture in Industrial Society*. New York: 1967.

————. *Virgin Land: The American West as Symbol and Myth*. New York: 1950.

Soule, George. *Prosperity Decade*. New York: 1947.

Spivak, John. *America Faces the Barricades*. New York: 1935.

Steckmesser, Kent L. *The Western Hero in History and Legend*. Norman, Oklahoma: 1965.

Steffens, Lincoln. *The Autobiography of Lincoln Steffens*. New York: 1931.

Sternberg, Charles, ed. *Mass Media and Communications*. New York: 1964.

Stott, William. *Documentary Expression and Thirties America*. New York: 1973.

Tarbell, Ida M. *The History of Standard Oil*. New York: 1904.

Thomas, Bob. *King Cohn*. New York: 1967.

———. *Selznick*. New York: 1970.

Thorp, Margaret. *America at the Movies*. New Haven: 1939.

Tolles, Frederick. *Meeting House and Counting House*. Chapel Hill: 1948.

Tunnerd, Christopher, and Hope Reed. *American Skyline*. New York: 1956.

Turkus, Burton, and Sid Feder. *Murder, Inc.* New York: 1951.

Turner, Frederick Jackson. *The Frontier in American History*. New York: 1920 ed.

Tyler, Parker. *The Hollywood Hallucination*. New York: 1944.

Vidor, King. *A Tree Is a Tree*. New York: 1953.

Von Sternberg, Josef. *Fun in a Chinese Laundry*. New York: 1965.

Wagenknecht, Edward. *Movies in the Age of Innocence*. Norman, Oklahoma: 1962.

Warner, Jack. *My First 100 Years in Hollywood*. New York: 1965.

Warner, W. Lloyd. *American Life: Dream and Reality*. Chicago: 1953.

Warshow, Robert. *The Immediate Experience*. New York: 1962.

Waters, Frank. *Book of the Hopi*. New York: 1963.

White, David, and Richard Averson. *The Celluloid Weapon*. Boston: 1972.

Wilson, Edmund. *The American Jitters*. New York and London: 1932.

Wolfenstein, Martha, and Nathan Leites. *Movies, A Psychological Study*. Glencoe: 1950.

Wollen, Peter. *Signs and Meaning in the Cinema*. London: 1969.

Zierold, Norman. *The Hollywood Tycoons*. London: 1969.

Zukor, Adolph. *The Public Is Never Wrong*. New York: 1953.

ARTICLES

Adler, Nathan. "The Screen," *The New Masses*, Feb. 6, 1934.

Bakshy, Alexander. "The Talkies," *The Nation*, February 20, 1929.

———. "Concerning Dialogue," *The Nation*, Aug. 19, 1932.

Business Week. "Came the (Movie) Dawn," Nov. 9, 1935.

Cassady, Ralph, Jr. "Some Aspects of Motion Picture Production and Marketing," *Journal of Business of the University of Chicago*, April 1933.

Cawelti, John. "From Rags to Respectability: Horatio Alger," in Lawrence Levine and Robert Middlekauff, eds., *The National Temper*. New York: 1968.

Chapin, John R. "Hollywood Goes Closed Shop," *The Nation*, Feb. 19, 1936.

Commonweal. "Gang Films," June 10, 1931.

Davis, David Brion. "Ten Gallon Hero," *American Quarterly*, Summer 1954.

Durgnat, Raymond. "The Family Tree of Film Noir," *Cinema*, August 1970.

"Genre: Populism and Social Realism," *Film Comment*, July–August 1975.

Eaton, W.P. "The Menace of the Movies," *American Magazine*, September 1913.

Elkin, Frederick. "The Psychological Appeal of the Hollywood Western," *Journal of Educational Psychology*, 1950.

———. "Value Implications of Popular Films," *Sociology and Social Research*, May/June 1954.

Faith, Joel. "Will Hays: Film Enemy No. 1," *New Theatre*, December 1936.

Ferguson, Otis. "Cops and Robbers," *The New Republic*, May 15, 1935.

Crau, R. "Fortunes in the Moving Picture Field," *The Overland Monthly*, April 1911.

Hager, Alice. "Movies Reflect Our Moods," *New York Times Magazine*, Apr. 22, 1934.

Harrison, Louis Reeves. "The Fascinating Criminal," *Moving Picture World*, Apr. 26, 1913.

Hecht, Ben. "My Testimony to the Movies," *Theatre*, June 1929.

Hurwitz, Leo. "Hisses, Boos and Bouquets," *New Theatre*, July-August 1934.

Josephson, Mathew. "Masters of the Motion Picture," *Movie Classic*, August 1926.

Kaminsky, Stuart. "*Little Caesar* and Its Role in The Gangster Film Genre," *Journal of Popular Film*, Summer 1972.

Kirsten, Lincoln. "James Cagney and the American Hero," *Hound and Horn*, April/June 1932.

Lazarsfeld, P.F. "Audience Research in the Movie Field," *Annals of the American Academy*, November 1947.

Lerner, Irving. "The Situation Now," *The New Masses,* August 1933.

Literary Digest. "Are Gang Films Wholesome?" Mar. 4, 1933.

————. " 'G-Men' Wage Unending War," August 3, 1935.

Mayer, Milton. "The Myth of the G-Man," *Forum,* September 1935.

Pitkin, Walter B. "Screen Crime vs. Press Crime," *The Outlook,* July 29, 1931.

Ward, John W. "The Meaning of Lindbergh's Flight," *American Quarterly,* Spring 1958.

Warner, Alan. "Gangster Heroes," *Films and Filming,* November 1971.

Whitehall, Richard. "Crime, Inc.: A Three Part Dossier on the American Gangster Film," *Films and Filming,* January 1964.

————. "Some Thoughts on Fifties Gangster Films," *The Velvet Light Trap,* Winter 1974.

PERIODICALS

Biograph Bulletins
Film Daily Yearbook
Hollywood Quarterly
Modern Screen Magazine
Motion Picture Herald
Moving Picture World
Screenland
Variety
Views and Film Index

ANNOTATED FILMOGRAPHY

AL CAPONE (Allied Artists, 1959)

Prod John H. Burrows, Leonard J. Ackerman; *dir* Richard Wilson; *scr* Marvin Wald, Henry Greenberg; *mus* David Raksin; *art dir* Hilyard Brown; *ph* Lucian Ballard; *ed* Walter Hannemann; *cast* Rod Steiger (Al Capone); Fay Spain (Maureen Flannery); Murvyn Vye (Bugs Moran); James Gregory (Sergeant Schaeffer); Nehemiah Persoff (Johnny Torrio); Lewis Charles (Hymie Weiss); Joe De Santis (Big Jim Colosimo); Martin Balsam (Mack Keely).

Al Capone is typical of the spate of gangster biographies that appeared in the late 1950's. The film blended an iconographic nostalgia for the period of the Roaring Twenties and the classic gangster films of the early thirties with some documentary techniques (the use of a narrator, for example) that had become popular during the fifties.

Rod Steiger's emotional depiction of Capone is one of the most powerful gangster portrayals on the screen. Like Paul Muni in **Scarface,** Steiger projected the gangster's combination of sly, ruthless cunning and extremely violent nature. Lucian Ballard's crisply lit photography is an elegant descendant of the classic gangster film style, and the montage sequences, particularly those of rum-running and the manufacture of bootleg liquor, are finely crafted and true to the genre, as are the scenes of Big Jim Colosimo's funeral and the Cicero election in which the Capone mob takes over the local government of the Chicago suburb.

The story picks up Big Al's career when he starts out in Chicago as a bouncer for gambler Johnny Torrio, who had been a boyhood pal back in Brooklyn. They both work for Big Jim Colosimo, an old-fashioned, stylish gangster who has achieved his ambition of being the boss of the First Ward. Capone convinces Torrio that it is necessary to get rid of his uncle so that the young gambler can "be Mr. Big—that's the man in charge." Big Al has the older gangster shot down while they are singing opera together. A waiter who rushes up is also killed. Capone goes to the waiter's widow with his condolences and falls for her because she is different from all the other dames he knows. Torrio and Capone become partners and go into the liquor business with the advent of Prohibition. They are quite successful, but the competition is violent, and when Torrio is wounded he decides to go into retirement and turn the business over to Al. Capone takes over and battles gangsters Bugs Moran and Hymie Weiss for control of the city. He eliminates his rivals in a series of killings that were based on actual Chicago gangland incidents. The flower shop assassination of Dion O'Banion, the convoy of cars that machine-guns Capone's headquarters, the St. Valentine's Day massacre, and the killing of a reporter (Jake Lingel) infatuated with gangsters have developed by the late fifties into stations of the cross of the movie gangster's bloody rise to success. The story concludes, as it did in history, with the arrest and imprisonment of Capone on income tax violations and with his death from syphilis.

ALIBI (United Artists 1929)

Prod-dir Roland West; based on the play *Nightstick* by John Griffith Wray, J.C. Nugent, Elaine S. Carrington; *scr* Roland West, C. Gardner Sullivan; *art dir* William Cameron Menzies; *ph* Ray June; *ed* Hal Kern; *cast* Chester Morris (Chick Williams); Harry Stubbs (Buck Backman); Mae Busch (Daisy Thomas); Eleanor Griffith (Joan Manning); Irma Harrison (Totts, the cabaret dancer); Regis Toomey (Danny McGunn); Al Hill (Brown); James Bradbury, Jr. (Blake); Elmer Ballard (Sort Malone, the cab driver); Kernan Cripps (Trask, the plainclothesman); Purnell B. Pratt (Pete Manning, the police sergeant); Pat O'Malley (Detective Tommy Glennon); DeWitt Jennings (Policeman O'Brien); Edward Brady (George Stanislaus David); Edward Jardon, Virginia Flohri (singers in theater).

Alibi was one of the first sound gangster pictures to appear in the late twenties. The movie has an odd combination of qualities; there is a woodenness typical of many films that are based on plays (**Alibi** was based on the popular play *Nightstick*) and a fluidity of sound and image that was rare in the early days of talkies. The cacophonous crescendo of nightsticks in the opening prison sequence; and nighttime robbery of a fur store, with its first-person point-of-view getaway through the brightly lit city streets, which in turn dissolves into a tracking shot that leads the viewer into a posh nightclub, are imaginative exceptions to the stiff actions typical of gangster films contemporary with *Alibi*. Roland West was a true independent who financed, produced, and directed pictures for United Artists.

Suave Chester Morris, a Broadway actor who achieved movie popularity in the thirties, plays Chick Williams, a gangster who marries the daughter of a police captain. The policeman is suspicious of his new son-in-law, but the girl stoutly defends him. When Chick takes part in a robbery, during which a cop is killed, his young wife provides an alibi. When the police send an agent to penetrate the gang, Chick discovers his true identity and kills him, but not before the gangster's activities and identity are revealed. In a desperate attempt to escape, Chick Williams plummets to his death from the top of a skyscraper.

ALL THROUGH THE NIGHT (Warner Bros., 1942)

Prod Jerry Wald; *dir* Vincent Sherman; *scr* Leonard Q. Ross, Leonard Spigelglass, *ph* Sid Hickox; *art dir* Max Parker; *ed* Rudi Fehr; *cast* Humphrey Bogart (Gloves Donahue); Conrad Veidt (Hall Ebbing); Karen Verne (Leda Hamilton); Jane Darwell (Ma Donahue); Frank McHugh (Barney); Peter Lorre (Pepi); Judith Anderson (Madame); William Demarest (Sunshine); Jackie Gleason (Starchie); Phil Silvers (Waiter); Wallace Ford (Spats Hunter); Barton MacLane (Marty Callahan); Edward S. Brophy (Joe Denning); Martin Kosleck (Steindorff); Jean Ames (Annabelle); James Burke (Forbes); Ludwig Stossel (Mr. Miller); Ben Welden (Smitty); Charles Cane (Spence); Frank Sully (Sage); Irene Seidner (Mrs. Miller); Hand Schumann (Anton); Sam McDaniel (Deccar).

All Through the Night is one of the gangster pictures in which the hoodlum was enlisted to fight even more despicable Nazi criminals who operate on a larger scale and who, according to Gloves Donahue, "are strictly no

good from way down deep." As in *Lucky Jordan*, (1942), the murder of an innocent victim becomes the catalyst that turns the gangster against the Nazis. The picture blends comedy, mystery, and the gangster milieu with a strong sense of patriotism and noble purpose.

Gloves Donahue is a big-shot Broadway gambler with an insatiable appetite for a special brand of cheesecake prepared by a German baker in his old East Side neighborhood. When the baker, who is also a friend of Gloves's mother, is mysteriously murdered, the gambler and his gang go after the killers. When they discover a Nazi spy ring is responsible, the Nazis pin another murder on Gloves, who in turn becomes hunted by the police. Gloves and his boys track down the spies in their warehouse headquarters and manage to capture the Nazis in time to prevent them from blowing up a battleship with a motorboat full of explosives.

ANGELS WITH DIRTY FACES (Warner Bros. 1938)

Prod Sam Bischoff; *dir* Michel Curtiz; *story* Rowland Brown; *scr* John Wexley, Warren Duff; *art dir* Robert Hass; *mus* Max Steiner; *sound* Everett A. Brown; *ph* Sol Polito; *ed* Owen Marks; *cast* James Cagney (Rocky Sullivan); Pat O'Brien (Jerry Connelly); Humphrey Bogart (James Frazier); Ann Sheridan (Laury Martin); George Bancroft (Mac Keefer); Billy Halop (Soapy); Bobby Jordan (Swing); Leo Gorcey (Bim); Bernard Punsley (Hunky); Gabriel Dell (Pasty); Huntz Hall (Crab); Frankie Burke (Rocky as a boy); William Tracy (Jerry as a boy); Marilyn Knowlden (Laury as a girl); Joe Downing (Steve); Adrean Morris (Blackie); Oscar O'Shea (Guard Kennedy); William Pawley (Bugs, the gunman); Edward Pawley (Guard Edwards); Earl Dwire (priest); John Hamilton (police captain); Theodore Rand, Charles Sullivan (gunmen); William Worthington (warden).

Angels with Dirty Faces is one of the most powerful and beautifully crafted gangster films of the late thirties. It was also a financial and critical success. The picture has one of the liveliest casts of any gangster picture, with James Cagney, Humphrey Bogart, Anne Sheridan, Pat O'Brien, George Bancroft (who played Bull Weed in **Underworld**), and the Dead End Kids turning in particularly effective performances. The melodramatic plot deals directly with the phenomenon of the glorification of the gangster, as in **Manhattan Melodrama.** The good-versus-evil theme goes back to the pre-twenties gangster film, but rarely—and the thanks go mainly to Roland Brown's script—has it been so sophisticated. The film exhibits the sociological emphasis on environment that had appeared with **Public Enemy** and re-emerged strongly in the films of the late thirties.

Two boys break into a box car. Jerry Connelly escapes and grows up to become the neighborhood priest on New York's Lower East Side. Rocky Sullivan is caught and sent to reform school, from where he begins a life of crime that appears to be successful. When he is paroled after a short stretch in prison, he returns to his old neighborhood, where he is regarded as a hero by the local gang of kids. Father Connelly is trying to save them from the criminal career he knows to be a real possibility for ghetto kids, but Rocky threatens to upset his work by teaching them other skills—for example, not to knock anybody over in your own block. Rocky also spends time with Laury Martin, who used to pal around with Jerry and Rocky when they were kids.

Rocky tries to get $100,000 that his lawyer, James Frazier, and a crooked politician, Mac Keefer, owe on the job for which Rocky went to prison. When they refuse to pay up, Rocky kidnaps Keefer and threatens to expose his former partners in crime. They reluctantly give Rocky what they owe him, and he tries to give some of the money to Connelly's church to help the boys out. But Father Connelly refuses the money and warns his old pal that he intends to drive the gangsters out of the city with a reform movement. When his campaign proves effective, the gangsters decide to bump off Connelly. Rocky kills them instead, to save his old pal, and is sentenced to die for murder. Connelly asks Rocky to do something to try to convince the gang to go straight, but Rocky refuses. The gangster hero breaks down on the way to the electric chair, either to show the kids that he is afraid of dying or because he truly is afraid. The boys think he was a coward at the end, and the priest retains his influence over them, knowing that if he hadn't escaped when both were boys he could have ended up like Rocky.

THE ASPHALT JUNGLE (MGM 1950)

Prod Arthur Hornblow, Jr.; *dir* John Huston; based on the novel by W.R. Burnett; *scr* Ben Maddow, Huston; *art dir* Cedric Gibbons, Randall Duell; *ph* Harold Rosson; *ed* George Boemler; *cast* Sterling Hayden (Dix Handley); Louis Calhern (Alonzo D. Emmerich); Jean Hagen (Doll Conovan); James Whitmore (Gus Minissi); Sam Jaffe (Dr. Erwin Riedenschneider); John McIntire (Commissioner Hardy); Marc Lawrence (Cobby); Barry

Kelley (Lieutenant Dietrich); Anthony Caruso (Louis Ciavelli); Teresa Celli (Maria Ciavelli) Marilyn Monroe (Angela Phinlay); William Davis (Timmons); Dorothy Tree (May Emmerich); Brad Dexter (Bob Brannon); Alex Gerry (Maxwell).

The Asphalt Jungle is a heist or caper film that, like many a gangster movie, can trace its criminal lineage back to *The Great Train Robbery* (1902). The underworld characters and milieu render this and other robbery films a sub-genre of gangster films or one can argue, a separate genre altogether. *The Killing* (1969), *They Came To Rob Las Vegas* (1972), *Cool Breeze* (1972; based on **The Asphalt Jungle**) are more recent examples of this type of film.

Written by W.R. Burnett, who also penned **Little Caesar,** and forcefully directed by John Huston, the film is distinguished by a speedy pace, gritty quality, and the performances of Sterling Hayden, Jean Hagen, and Marilyn Monroe. The sharply etched underworld characters and the mounting tension of the heist and escape have become requirements for this type of film, as has the double cross that defeats the caper.

Dix Handley is a gunman who needs money to get back the family farm in Kentucky. He assembles a gang of specialists, each of whom has a specific role to perform in stealing jewels from an elaborately protected vault. The plot weaves together the story of hiring the gang, planning the execution of the robbery, and the successful efforts of the police to hunt down the criminals, when the latter are betrayed by the shyster lawyer, Emmerich, who acts as the gang's fence.

BABY FACE NELSON (United Artists 1957)

Prod Al Zimbalist; *dir* Donald Siegel; *scr* Daniel Mainwaring; *ph* Hal Mohr; *ed* Leon Barschke; *cast* Mickey Rooney (Lester Gillis/Baby Face Nelson); Carolyn Jones (Sue); Sir Cedric Hardwicke (Doc Saunders); Chris Dark (Jerry); Ted de Corsia (Rocca); Emile Meyer (Mac); Anthony Caruso (Hamilton); Leo Gordon (John Dillinger); Dan Terranova (Miller).

Baby Face Nelson is one of the more powerful gangster biographies to appear in the late fifties. Donald Siegel's direction and Mickey Rooney's intense portrayal of the pint-sized killer made the picture considerably more powerful than other gangster biographies. The film is also noteworthy for its presentation of the gangster as a psychotic character who becomes progressively crazier throughout the story. It is also typical of the gangster biographies in combining a documentary style with a nostalgic re-creation of the thirties.

Baby Face Nelson gets out of prison and is offered a contract by crime boss Rocca to assassinate a union leader. Nelson turns down the offer and looks up his girl friend, Sue. Rocca has the union leader killed by someone else and pins the crime on Nelson, who is sent back to prison. Sue helps Baby Face escape, and he kills Rocca for revenge. When he is wounded in a robbery, he is sent to the hospital by Doc Saunders, who has a yen for Sue. There the gangster meets one of the Dillinger gang, who introduces him to Dillinger. They pull a number of robberies masterminded by a character called Fatso, while Nelson grows more crazy and bloodthirsty. Nelson takes over the gang after Dillinger dies. He kills Doc Saunders in a jealous rage and stages a series of holdups during which several people are killed. When the F.B.I. finally closes in, Nelson convinces Sue that unless she shoots him, he will kill some children. Sue reluctantly complies and kills the crazed hoodlum.

THE BIG HOUSE (MGM 1930)

Dir George Hill; *story-scr* Frances Marion; *additional dialog* Joe Farnham, Martin Flavin; *art dir* Cedric Gibbons; *sound* Robert Shirley, Douglas Shearer; *ph* Harold Wenstrom; *ed* Blanche Sewell; *cast* Chester Morris (Morgan); Wallace Beery (Butch); Lewis Stone (Warden); Robert Montgomery (Kent); Leila Hyams (Anne); George F. Marion (Pop); J.C. Nugent (Mr. Marlowe); Karl Dane (Olsen); Claire McDowell (Mrs. Marlowe); Robert Emmett O'Connor (Donlin); Tom Kennedy (Uncle Jed); Tom Wilson (Sandy); Eddie Foyer (Dopey); Roscoe Ates (Putnam); Fletcher Norton (Oliver).

The Big House is a 1930 trend-setting prison picture that was produced during the golden age of gangster movies. Like many a prison picture to follow, it emphasized the oppressive and degrading conditions of prison life, using a story about three cons who are buddies. The theme of unjust conditions in prison was to receive its most powerful expression a short time later in *I Am a Fugitive from a Chain Gang* (1932). **The Big House** is characterized by a powerful script written by Frances Marion and particularly evocative sound work and art direction. The film has remained one of the most successful prison movies ever made, spawning dozens of prison pictures, such as *20,000 Years in Sing Sing* (1933). The lighting and the prison riot are particularly noteworthy in **The Big House.**

Butch, Morgan, and Kent are three cons who are in prison for murder, forgery, and manslaughter, respectively. The three are cellmates, and when Morgan escapes he goes to Kent's sister, Anne, for help. The two fall in love, and Kent decides to go straight, but he is captured and sent back to prison, where conditions have deteriorated. Butch is planning a breakout with a number of other cons. But Kent squeals to the warden, and when the escape is stopped, there is a riot against the rotten conditions, which Morgan manages to stop. He is paroled for his action in stopping the riot and is free to go straight and marry Anne.

THE BIG HEAT (Columbia 1953)

Prod Robert Arthur; *dir* Fritz Lang; based on the novel by William P. McGivern; *scr* Sidney Boehm; *art dir* Robert Peterson; *mus* Daniele Amfitheatrof; *ph* Charles Lang, Jr.; *ed* Charles Nelson; *cast* Glenn Ford (Sergeant Dave Bannion); Gloria Grahame (Debby Marsh); Jocelyn Brando (Datie Bannion); Alexander Scourby (Mike Lagana); Lee Marvin (Vince Stone); Jeanette Nolan (Bertha Duncan); Peter Whitney (Tierney); Willis Bouchey (Lieutenant Ted Wilkes); Robert Burton (Gus Burke); Adam Williams (Larry Gordon); Howard Wendell (Commissioner Higgins); Chris Alcaide (George Rose); Michael Granger (Hugo, the cop); Carolyn Jones (Doris); Dorothy Green (Lucy Champan); Ric Roman (Baldy); Dan Seymour (Atkins); Edith Evanson (Selma Parker); Donald Kerr (Cabby); Laura Mason (B-girl).

The Big Heat is one of Fritz Lang's most powerful and sinister American films. The picture uses the gangster milieu to tell the story of a cop who is forced into becoming a renegade in order to do his job. The situation was to reappear time and again in films like **Dirty Harry** and television police dramas. Lang emphasizes the themes of official corruption and revenge in describing Bannion's dogged determination to solve a series of crimes and avenge the death of his wife.

Dave Bannion is a hard-working, honest detective with a happy home life. When he investigates another policeman's suicide, he approaches a B-girl as a potential witness. The girl is savagely tortured and murdered shortly thereafter. Despite pressure from his captain, Bannion continues his investigation but discovers that the suicide victim's wife also wants the investigation stopped. Bannion's own wife agrees that he should continue but is blown up by a bomb intended for the detective. The cop is now out for revenge as well as the truth about the earlier crimes. Although he is suspended from the police force, he continues to follow the trail, which leads to business racketeer Mike Lagana. When Lagana's sadistic goon, Vince Stone, throws boiling coffee in his moll's face, she agrees to help the renegade cop close down the whole operation. Bannion also receives some help from his brother-in-law's war buddies. He discovers that the wife of the detective who committed suicide had been in cahoots with Lagana to prevent the cop from admitting that he was on the take. In the climax, Bannion forces Vince Stone to confess, the moll dies, and Lagana is brought to justice. Bannion is re-instated and begins to work on another case.

THE BIG SHOT (Warner Bros. 1942)

Prod Walter MacEwen; *dir* Lewis Seiler; *scr* Bertram Millhauser, Abel Finkel, Daniel Fuchs; *art dir* John Hughes; *mus* Adolph Deutsch; *sound* Stanley Jones; *ph* Sid Hickox; *ed* Jack Killifer; *cast* Humphrey Bogart (Duke Berne); Irene Manning (Lorna Flemming); Richard Travis (George Anderson); Susan Peters (Ruth Carter); Stanley Ridges (Martin Fleming); Minor Watson (Warden Booth); Chick Chanuler (Dancer); Joseph Downing (Frenchy); Howard da Silva (Sandor); Murray Alper (Quinto); Roland Drew (Faye); John Ridgely (Tim); Joseph King (Toohey); John Hamilton (Judge); Virginia Brissac (Mrs. Booth); William Edmuns (Sarto); Virginia Sale (Mrs. Miggs); Ken Christy (Kat); Wallace Scott (Rusty).

"He used to be a big shot" is a line that applies to many of the gangster pictures made in the late thirties and early forties, which feature a former gangster who tries to go straight, usually after a stretch in prison. As in **The Last Gangster,** the main character is sympathetically portrayed but doomed despite his good intentions and heroic actions. **The Big Shot** is particularly well photographed and contains one of the more exciting car chases in the gangster genre.

Duke Berne has spent enough time in prison to want to go straight. He attempts to live an honest life but ends up joining a holdup gang, whose chief is crooked lawyer Martin Flemming. The lawyer's wife used to be Duke's girl friend, and she still loves her old beau enough to keep him from joining the gang. Flemming becomes jealous and frames Duke for murder. The frame-up is enough to send Duke back to prison, from where he quickly escapes to meet Lorna in a mountain retreat. When he hears that his pal, Travis, has been indicted for a murder that Duke had committed, he heads back to clear him. But the police attack the gangster's car and kill Lorna, though Duke escapes. The gangster kills

Flemming and, though mortally wounded, is able to clear his buddy's name.

BLACK CAESAR (American International 1973)

Prod Larry Cohen; *dir-scr* Larry Cohen; *des* Larry Lurin; *mus* James Brown; *sound* Alex Vanderkar; *ph* Fenton Hamilton, James Signorelli; *ed* George Golsey, Jr.; *cast* Fred Williamson (Tommy Gibbs); D'Urville Martin (Reverend Rufus); Gloria Hendry (Helen); Art Lund (John McKinney); Val Avery (Cardoza); Minnie Gentry (Mama Gibbs); Julius W. Harris (Mr. Gibbs); Phillip Roye (Joe Washington); William Wellman, Jr. (Alfred Coleman); Myrna Hansen (Virginia Coleman); Omer Jeffrey (Tommy, as a boy); James Dixon (Bryant); Cecil Alonso (Motor); Allen Bailey (Sport); Larry Lurin (Carlos).

Black Caesar was typical of the black exploitation picture that pitted black gangsters against the Mafia, as in *Across 110th Street* (1974). The black gangster represented a determination to fight back in the same way **Little Caesar** had during the Depression, and the picture is distinguished by good use of Harlem locations, a musical track by James Brown, and a fine performance by Fred Williamson.

The film shows the rise and fall of Tommy Gibbs, a black gangster who was partially crippled by a sadistic, corrupt cop. When he rises to the top, he gets a set of ledgers that prove the Mafia's control of the police. The cop orders other policemen to kill Gibbs, who manages to escape. After he takes on the Mafia in a series of brutal murders, Gibbs believes that as a black man, he should control crime in Harlem instead of letting the Mafia take the money out of the community. He declares war on the Italian mobsters and takes over the organization in the black ghetto. But the more powerful Gibbs becomes, the more corrupt and personally dishonest he becomes, too, until he in turn, is shot down by a police assassin, who is caught by a neighborhood youth gang and beaten to death.

BLONDIE JOHNSON (Warner Bros. 1933)

Dir Ray Enright; *scr* Earl Baldwin; *ph* Tony Gaudio; *Supervisor* Lucien Hubbard; *cast* Joan Blondell (Blondie); Chester Morris (Curley); Allen Jenkins (Louie); Earle Foxe (Soannel); Mae Musch (Mae); Arthur Vinton (Max Wagner); Toshia Mori (Lulu); Sterling Holloway (Red); Claire Dodd, Joe Cawthorne, Olin Howland, Donald Kirke (gang members).

Blondie Johnson is one of those rare films in which a woman had the starring gangster role (along with *Madame Racketeer* (1932) or *Lady Scarface* (1941) *Bloody Mama* (1970), *Ma Barker's Killer Brood* (1960)). In **Blondie Johnson** the heroine gets to the top via the familiar route carved out by the genre in the early thirties. The film contains some scenes that express savage indictments of Depression conditions that were also expressed in such films as *I Am a Fugitive from a Chain Gang* (1932) and *Heroes for Sale* (1933). Joan Blondell gives the title role a strong and street-wise dimension angrily appropriate to the tough Depression mood.

Blondie and her sick mother are tossed out into a street when they can't pay the rent. The mother dies of pneumonia. Blondie goes to a lawyer and then a priest for help. Both of them offer her only platitudes of oily optimism and greedy cynicism. Blondie resolves to live by her wits. She begins her life of crime as a small-time con artist in cahoots with a cab driver who admires her brains and remains her friend. When she makes a sucker out of Curley, a smooth, small-time gangster, he follows her and asks if she would like to work with him. Blondie plans and executes a complicated jewelry swindle with her new gang. She loves Curley but is determined to take care of business before pleasure. When the boss she has helped to free tries to take over her new outfit, Blondie's boys finish him off. After the chrome coffin funeral (one of the funnier and more interesting scenes of its kind), Blondie decides it's time to go straight and sets her boy friend up as a front for the gang. Curley starts to take his role too seriously and puts on airs. He falls for an actress who has attracted him with her upper-class act. When he decides to star the actress in a show that he intends to produce with the gang's money, there is a showdown in which Blondie makes it clear who is running the gang. When Curley reacts, the gang urges her to agree to his assasination. Blondie very reluctantly agrees with the sentence but has a sudden change of heart and rushes (with the help of her cab driver friend) off to the rescue. The gang wounds Curley, and the police round everybody up. At the trial, Blondie and her beau indicate that when they get out of jail they will get together . . . and go straight.

BODY AND SOUL (United Artists 1947)

Dir Robert Rossen; *scr* Abraham Polonsky; *art dir* Nathan Juran; *mus* Hugo Friedhofer; *sound* Frank Webster; *ph* James Wong Howe; *ed* Francis Lyon; *cast* John Garfield (Charlie Davis); Lilli Palmer (Peg Born);

Hazel Brooks (Alice); Anne Revere (Anna Davis); William Conrad (Quinn); Joseph Pevney (Shorty Polaski); Canada Lee (Ben Chaplin); Lloyd Gregg (Irma); Peter Virgo (Drummer); Joe Devlin (Prince); Shimen Ruskin (Grocer); Mary Currier (Miss Tedder); Milton Kibbee (Dan); Tim Ryan (Shelton); Artie Dorrell (Jack Marlowe); Cy Ring II (Victor); Glen Lee (Marine); John Indrisano (Referee); Dan Tobey (fight announcer); Wheaton Chambers (doctor).

Gangsters and the boxing world have often been linked in the gangster genre. In films like *Kid Galahad* (1937 and 1972), or **Body and Soul,** the theme has been the struggle of honest fighters and managers to resist underworld control. As with gangster films, *Body and Soul* was filmed shortly after an investigation of the underworld's involvement in the fight game. Occasionally, as in *The Harder They Fall* (1956), the thorough exploitation is practically a call to abolish the fight game completely. Edward G. Robinson plays a fight promoter in *Kid Galahad* who in many ways resembles a gangster, although he ultimately revolts against underworld domination. Often the fight game has merely provided another locale, as in **The Killers. Body and Soul** is notable for the socially conscious script of Polonsky, John Garfield's powerhouse portrayal of the fighter, and the cinematography of James Wong Howe.

Body and Soul tells the story of Charlie Davis, a fighter whom the mob uses for money and political gain when he becomes a champion. The story includes a romance with Alice, a social-climbing girl friend who abandons the boxer for a playboy, and Peg Born, a girl who encourages Davis to be honest. Davis realizes the dangers and the extent of criminal involvement in the boxing business when a black boxer who is his friend and trainer dies of an earlier beating. Davis is angry enough to defy the underworld and win a fight he is ordered to lose, thereby earning the respect of his mother and girl.

THE BOSS (United Artists 1956)

Prod Frank N. Seltzer; *dir.* Byron Haskin; *scr* Ben Perry; *art dir* Frank P. Syles; *mus* Albert Glasser; *ph* Hal Mohr; *ed* Ralph Dawson; *cast* John Payne (Matt Brady); William Bishop (Bob Herrick); Doe Avedon (Elsie Reynolds); Roy Roberts (Tim Brady); Rhys Williams (Stanley Millard); Robing Morse (Johnny Mazia); Gil Lamb (Henry); Joe Flynn (Ernie Jackson); Bill Phipps (Stitch); Bob Morgan (Hamhead) Alex Frazer (Roy Millard); John Mansfield (Lazetti); George Lynn (Tom Masterson); Harry Chesire (Governor Beck).

The Boss emphasizes the political dimensions of the ganster genre. Political corruption and its monetary rewards are linked to emotional bankruptcy, a theme that runs throughout the genre. John Payne's portrayal of the political powerhouse is one of the better performances of an underrated actor who was for the most part confined to B pictures. **The Boss** was based on the notorious Pendergast regime of Kansas City.

Matt Brady returns from World War I to the city where his brother is a political boss. When he gets drunk and stands up his girl friend, she throws him out, saying that she will never marry him. Brady grabs a stranger in a bar and convinces her to get married. His older brother finds out, and after the two fight over the marriage, Tim Brady dies of a heart attack. Matt becomes the new boss and allies himself with a war buddy who has become a lawyer and who marries Matt's old girl. Brady's machine is soon much more powerful and lucrative than his borther's, but his marriage, which is for appearance's sake only, falls apart as the boss treats his wife as though she doesn't exist. His methods soon become too outrageous for the city as well as his own lawyer, and a reform campaign develops. At the same time, the gangsters, for whom the boss has only contempt, begin to exert more and more control over the boss, who is finally sent to prison for income tax evasion.

BONNIE AND CLYDE (Warner Bros-Seven Arts 1967)

Prod Warren Beatty; *dir* Arthur Penn; *scr* David Newman, Robert Benton; *art dir* Dean Tavoularis; *mus* Charles Strouse; *sound* Francis E. Stahl; *sp eff* Danny Lee; *ph* Burnett Guffey; *ed* Dede Allen; *cast* Warren Beatty (Clyde Barrow); Faye Dunaway (Bonnie Parker); Gene Hackman (Buck Marrow); Michael J. Pollard (C.W. Moss); Estelle Parsons (Blanche); Denver Pyle (Frank Hamer); Gene Wilder (Eugene Grizzard); Evans Evans (Velma Davis); Dub Taylor (Moss); James Stiver (grocery store owner); Clyde Howdy (deputy); Garry Goodgion (Billy); Ken Mayer (Sheriff Smoot).

Bonnie and Clyde is less a gangster film than an outlaw romance in which the bandit couple are sympathetically portrayed as Robin Hood figures during the period of the Great Depression. Rural outlaw pictures, which are usually considered gangster stories, form a distinct sub-genre of their own. As with **Bonnie and Clyde,** they often exploit the gunplay, car chases, and tone of complete rebellion against authority usually associated with the genre. **Bonnie and Clyde** was preceded by **Gun Crazy,** *You Only Live Once* (1937), and *The Bonnie Parker Story,* all of which drew on the legend of the outlaw couple and which in various ways are more interesting pictures than the more recent popular version of the outlaw story. Dorothy Provine's portrayal of Bonnie in the *The Bonnie Parker Story* (1958) is perhaps the strongest of the three. **Bonnie and Clyde** particularly exploited and ritualized violence by elaborate slow motion and special effects techniques, as well as by the story of gun-crazy Clyde's sexual problems.

Bonnie Parker is a small-town waitress going nowhere when she meets Clyde Barrow, who is just out of prison. The ex-con holds up the local store to prove himself, and the couple begins a crime wave. They are joined by C.W. Moss, a bored country mechanic, who fixes their car and helps them in the holdups. They soon join Clyde's brother, Buck, and his hysterical wife, Blanche. The gang becomes notorious, and Texas Ranger Frank Hamer closes in. After a couple of ambushes, Buck is killed and Blanche captured. Hamer finally traps the trio when Moss's father betrays them. Bonnie and Clyde are shot down in an ambush.

BORN RECKLESS (Fox 1930)

Dir John Ford; based on the novel *Louis Beretti,* by Donald Henderson Clarke; *scr* Dudley Nichols; *art dir* Jack Schulze; *sound* W.W. Lindsay; *ph* George Schneiderman; *ed* Frank E. Hull; *cast* Edmund Lowe (Louis Beretti); Catherine Dale Owen (Jean Sheldon); Warren Hymer (Big Shot); Marguerite Churchill (Rosa Beretti); Lee Tracy (Bill O'Brien); William Harrigan (Good News Brophy); Frank Albertson (Grank Sheldon); Paul Page (Ritzy Reilly); Ferike Boros (Ma Beretti); Paul Porcasi (Pa Beretti); Joe Brown (Needle Beer Grogan); Eddie Gribbon (Bugs); J. Farrell MacDonald or Roy Stewart (District Attorney Cardigan); Yola D'Avril (French girl).

Fox Film Studio used the story of **Born Reckless** twice. Based on the popular gangster novel *Louis Beretti,* the 1930 film is the more memorable and is noteworthy for the excellent depiction of underworld settings and an interesting cast of underworld characters. Edmund Lowe gave the gangster character a suave veneer more characteristic of the movie gangsters of the late twenties than the better-known brash quality associated with Cagney and Robinson. The 1937 version changed the plot considerably to tell the story of racketeers taking over a city's taxi fleet.

Louis Beretti is caught and convicted for a holdup. He

is sent to join the army to fight in World War I instead of going to prison. The gangster resumes his career after the war and falls for Jean Sheldon, a society woman. When Big Shot, a rival gangster, kidnaps Sheldon's little boy, Beretti saves the child and kills his rival.

BROADWAY (Universal 1929)

Prod Carl Laemmle, Jr.; *dir* Paul Fejos; based on the play by Jed Harris, Philip Dunning, George Abbott; *scr* Edward T. Lowe, Jr., Charles Furthman; *dialog,* Edward T. Lowe, Jr.; *art dir* Charles D. Hall; *sound* C. Roy Hunter; *sp eff* Grank H. Booth; *ph* Hal Mohr; *ed* Robert Carlisle, Edward Cahn; *cast* Glenn Tryon (Roy Lane); Evelyn Brent (Pear); Merna Kennedy (Billie Moore); Thomas Jackson (Dan McCom); Robert Ellis (Steve Crandall); Otis Harlan (Porky Thompson); Paul Porcasi (Nick Verdis); Marion Lord (Lil Rice); Fritz Feld (Mose Levett); Betty Francisco (Mazie); Edythe Flynn (Ruby); Florence Dudley (Ann); Ruby McCoy (Grace).

The mixture of musical and gangster genres has been successful since the appearance of *The Lights of New York* (1928), the first sound picture with dialogue. **Broadway** was another twenties musical with a gangster milieu. It was based on a successful long-run musical, and like most other gangster musicals, it offers a pleasant and fascinated view of gangster and nightclub life compared with more realistic and gritty pictures, such as *Applause* (1930). **Broadway** is particularly interesting for the fantastic Art Deco nightclub interiors. The film also included some color sequences. It was remade in 1942.

Bootlegger Steve Crandall kills his rival, Nick Verdis, who owns the Paradise Club. Dancer Billie Moore has witnessed the killing and agrees not to say anything, but then the gangster tries to pin the murder on her dancing partner, Roy Lane. She then tells the police, who free Lane. When Crandall kidnaps Billie for revenge, he is shot by Verdis's mistress, who has found out from Billie that Crandall had murdered her lover. Billie is free and marries her dancing partner.

BROTHER ORCHID (Warner Bros. 1940)

Exec prod Hal B. Wallis; *dir* Lloyd Bacon; *story* Richard Connell; *scr* Earl Baldwin; *art dir* Max Parker; *mus* Heins Roemheld; *sp eff* Byron Haskin, Willard Van Enger; *ph* Tony Gaudio; *ed* William Holmes; *cast* Edward G. Robinson (Little John Sarto); Ann Sothern (Flo Adams); Humphrey Bogart (Jack Muck); Ralph Bellamy (Clarence Fletcher); Donald Crisp (Brother Superior); Allen Jenkins (Willie "The Knife" Corson); Charles D. Brown (Brother Wren); Cecil Kellaway (Brother MacDonald); Morgan Conway (Philadelphia Powell); Richard Lane (Mugsy O'Day); John Ridgeley (Texas Pearson); Dick Wessel (Buffalo Burns); Tom Tyler (Curley Mathews); Paul Phillips (French Frank); Dan Rowan (Al Muller); Granville Bates (Pattonsville Superintendent); Nanette Vallon (Fifi); Paul Guilfoyle (Red Martin); Tim Ryan (Turkey Malone); Joe Caits (Handsome Harry Edwards); Pat Gleason (Dopey Perkins); Tommy Baker (Joseph); John Qualen (Mr. Pigeon).

Brother Orchid demonstrates the use of comedy in the genre, much as **The Little Giant, A Slight Case of Murder,** or **Some Like It Hot** have. The story of a gangster becoming a monk produces as farcical a tale as the genre has ever created.

Little John Sarto takes the familiar jaunt to Europe to acquire "culture" as the crown of his success. His rival within the gang, Jack Buck, uses his absence to take over the gang. When Sarto organizes another gang in order to destroy his rival, he is captured. He miraculously survives a one-way ride and hides out in a monastery. The monks, who grow flowers and give the money to the poor, have no idea of the actual identity of their new little brother. The gangster recovers and begins to enjoy the life of quiet contemplation and growing flowers, although he doesn't quite understand the benevolent generosity of his religious hosts. He leaves the monastery when he hears that his girl friend (who believes that he has died) plans to marry somebody else. Outside the monastery, he learns that his gangster rival, Buck, intends to shake down the monks for a piece of the flower business. Little John decides to take care of Buck once and for all. He finishes his rival off and returns to the monastery, where the monks have invited him to live permanently despite his occasional lapses of decorum. The gangster decides that the monks have "real class" and becomes Brother John.

THE BROTHERHOOD (Paramount, 1968)

Prod Kirk Douglas; *dir* Martin Ritt; *scr* Lewis John Carlino; *art dir* Tambi Larsen, Toni Sarzi-Braga; *mus* Lalo Schifrin; *sound* Jack C. Jacobsen; *ph* Boris Kaufman; Frank Bracht; *cast* Kirk Douglas (Grank Ginetta); Alex Cord (Vince Genetta); Irene Papas (Ida Ginetta); Luther Adler (Dominick Bertolo); Susan Strasberg (Emma Ginetta); Murray Hamilton (Jim

Egan); Eduardo Cianelli (Don Peppino); Joe De Santis (Pietro Riszi); Connie Scott (Camrela Ginetta); Val Avery (Jake Rotherman); Val Bisoglio (Cheech); Alan Hewitt (Sol Levin); Barry Primus (Vido); Michele Cimarosa (Toto); Louis Badolati (Don Turridu).

The Brotherhood dramatizes the process by which the ethnic underworld has been transformed into a business-like organization with little room or tolerance for ethnic traditions, no matter how colorful. The theme has been especially developed in **The Godfather.** Kirk Douglas's performance is one of the best of his career as a man who can understand the traditional codes of the Mafia but not the syndicate's need to invest in the electronics industry of the space age.

Frank Ginetta is a gangster in the godfather mold. He cares about traditions and family honor and about the ethnic community in which he is honored and respected. When his organization decides to become more busi-nesslike and operate like a modern corporation in joining up with the national syndicate, Frank opposes the plan. His younger, well-educated brother under-stands the need for the mob's new direction but can't convince Frank. Finally the syndicate forces Vince to kill his older brother—an act the latter teaches the younger man to perform with proper concern for traditions.

THE BROTHERS RICO (Columbia 1957)

Prod Lewis J. Rackmil; *dir* Phil Karlson; based on the novel by Georges Simenon; *scr* Lewis Meltzer, Ben Perry; *art dir* Roberty Boyle; *mus* George Duning; *ph* Burnett Guffey; *ed* Charles Nelson; *cast* Richard Conte (Eddie Rico); Dianne Foster (Alice Rico); Kathryn Grant (Norah); Larry Gates (Sid Kubik); James Darren (Johnny Rico); Argentina Brunetti (Mr. Rico); Lamont Johnson (Peter Malaks); Harry Bellaver (Mike La-motta); Paul Picerni (Gino Rico); Paul Dubov (Phil); Rudy Bond (Gonzales); Richard Bakalyan (Vic Tucci); William Phipps (Joe Wesson); Mimi Aguglia (Julia Rico); Maggie O'Byrne (Mr. Felici); George Cisar (Dude Cowboy); Peggy Maley (Jean); Jane Easton (Nellie).

The Brothers Rico is a slick, sleazy underworld drama whose tone is typical of the fifties. A good story based on a Simenon novel gives the film dramatic integrity. Its sinister *film noir* outlook is also combined with good gangster action. Phil Karlson's action-oriented direction keeps the film moving along.

When mob boss Sid Kubik asks Eddie Rico where his brother is, the ex-accountant for the syndicate doesn't realize that the mob has marked his brother for death. When he tries to find his brother, he is tailed everywhere by a mob hit-man. His other brother, Gino, is killed by the syndicate, so Eddie goes to the district attorney. This is the only way he can protect his wife and children—by striking back at the syndicate with what he knows about their activities. His own mother had saved Kubik's life, making the mobster's war on the brothers particularly heinous.

BRUTE FORCE (Universal, 1947)

Pro Mark Hellinger; *dir* Jules Dassin; *story* Robert Patterson; *scr* Richard Brooks; *art dir* Bernard Herz-brun, John F. De Cuir; *mus* Miklos Rozsa; *sound* Charles Felstead, Robert Pritchard; *ph* William Daniels; *ed* Edward Curtiss; *cast* Burt Lancaster (Joe Collins); Hume Cronyn (Captain Munsey); Charles Bickford (Gallagher); Sam Levene (Louis); Howard Duff (''Sol-dier''); Roman Bohnen (Warden Barnes); Art Smith (Dr. Walters); John Hoyt (Spencer); Richard Gaines (McCallum); Frank Puglie (Ferrara); Jeff Corey (''Freshman''); Vince Barnett (Muggsy); James Bell (Crenshaw); Yvonne De Carlo (Gina); Ann Blyth (Ruth); Ella Raines (Cora); Anita Colby (Flossie); Jack Overman (Kid Coy); Whit Bissell (Tom Lister); Sir Lancelot (''Calypso'').

Brute Force is typical of prison films, which can be seen as a sub-genre of gangster movies. Prison sequences have been integral to gangster movies since the late teens, and prison stories (e.g., *The Convict, 1906*) provided plots for early crime dramas. Prison stories flourished in the golden age of gangster movies in the thirties. *20,000 years in Sing Sing* (1931) or **The Big House** crystallized many of the prison movies' basic qualities as did the gangster films of the early thrities: prisoners behind bars; cell blocks; mess halls; stone walls, topped with barbed wire, watched by machine-gun towers with searchlight eyes; the escape scene; the prison riot; at least one mean, sadistic guard who plays Wagner while beating prisoners; a warden pictured as well-intentioned; a helpful priest; and a boozy prison doctor.

Gangsters are on their way to or from prison throughout the genre. The prison rarely moved directly into the foreground, as in pictures like **Brute Force,** *The Criminal Code* (1931), or *I Am a Fugitive from a Chain Gang.* (1932). Occasionally films were about women in prison, as in *Ladies of the Big House* (1931) or *Caged*

Heat (1975). Prison dramas offered an interesting vehicle for social criticism in American movies. **Brute Force,** like *I am a Fugitive From a Chain Gang,* was basically a condemnation of brutalizing prison conditions.

Brute Force was interesting in presenting the stories of several different convicts through flashbacks to reveal how they landed in prison, where they have to confront a brutally sadistic captain of the guards, Munsey, a drunken, irresponsible prison doctor, and a feeble warden. Goaded beyond endurance, the convicts riot to get even with the authorities, leading to the killing of a number of convicts.

BULLETS OR BALLOTS (Warner Bros. 1936)

Assoc prod Louis F. Edelman; *dir* William Keighley; *story* Martin Mooney, Seton I Miller; *scr* Miller; *art dir* Carl Jules Weyl; *mus* Heinz Roehmheld; *sound* Oliver S. Garretson; *sp eff* Fred Jackman, Jr., Warren E. Lynch; *ph* Hal Mohr; *ed* Jack Killifer; *cast* Edward G. Robinson (Johnny Blake); Joan Blondell (Lee Morgan); Barton MacLane (Al Durger); Humphrey Bogart (Nick "Bugs" Genner); Frank McHugh (Herman); Joseph King (Captain Dan McLaren); Richard Purcell (Ed Driscoll); George E. Stone (Wires); Louise Beavers (Nellie LaFleur); Joseph Crehan (grand jury spokesman); Henry O'Neill (Bryant); Gilbert Emery (Thorndyke); Henry Kolker (Hollister); Herbert Rawlinson (Caldwell); Rosalind Marquis (Specialty); Norman Willis (Vinci); Frank Faylen (Gatley).

Bullets or Ballots is a classic example of the gangster story in which a cop must become a hoodlum to clean out the gangsters. William Keighley uses the Warner Brothers cinematic gangster traditions admirably, and the film displays the skill and pacing that made the studio famous and that particularly characterized its gangster films in the late thirties. The film is also noteworthy for the vehemence with which it presents the Big Boys as bankers and creates the strong implication that the rich are the ultimate villains in society.

Policeman Johnny Blake is apparently booted off the force when he joins a gang. The gangsters overcome their original distrust of the ex-cop when he shows them a new racket—the numbers racket, which Blake's girl friend, Lee Morgan, has introduced to him. Blake rises in the gang when trigger-happy lieutenant Nick Fenner, who distrusts the ex-cop, kills the old gang leader. Blake takes over the gang and is on the verge of discovering the names of the Big Boys who control crime in New

York when Fenner discovers Blake's true identity. Blake kills Fenner in their final shootout. Mortally wounded, he finds out the identity of the crooked bankers, which he reports to the special crime investigator for whom he has been working. Blake dies happy in the knowledge that he has done his job.

CAGED (Warner Bros. 1950)

Prod Jerry Wald; *dir* John Cromwell; *story-scr* Virginia Kellogg, Bernard C. Schoenfeld; *art dir* Charles H. Clarke; *mus* Max Steiner; *ph* Carl Guthrie; *ed* Owen Marks; *cast* Eleanor Parker (Marie Allen); Agnes Moorehead (Ruth Benton); Ellen Corby (Emma); Hope Emerson (Evelyn Harper); Betty Garde (Kitty Stark); Jan Sterling (Smoochie); Lee Patrick (Elvira Powell); Olive Deering (June); Jane Darwell (isolation matron); Gertrude Michel (Georgia); Sheila Stevens (Helen); Gertrude Hoffman (Millie); Queenie Smith (Mrs. Warren); Esther Howard (Grace); Edith Evanson (Miss Barker); Ann Tyrell (Edna); Taylor Holmes (Senator Donnolly); Ruth Warren (Miss Lyons).

Caged is a prison picture about women in the tradition of *Ladies of the Big House* (1931). It emphasizes the point of view that prisons produce criminals rather than reform them. The film is also one of the few that places the gangsters' girl friends at the center of the drama. It has a realistic quality derived from screenwriter Virginia Kellogg's research behind bars as an inmate in several prisons, as well as a sense of the corrupt situation into which many inmates were forced. The bleak process by which a first offender is turned into a hardened criminal and has a breakdown makes **Caged** one of the most relentlessly plausible pictures of American prison life.

Marie Allen is an inmate who was sent to prison for participating in a gas-station robbery in which her husband was killed. The girl is a good-hearted, generous person who is transformed into a toughened, cynical inmate by sadistic guards and other prisoners. Despite the feebly benign attempts by the warden to alleviate conditions in the prison, Marie Allen becomes a hardened criminal. She has a baby in prison which she has to give up for adoption, and is paroled only when a vice syndicate pays her way in exchange for her agreement to work as a prostitute.

CITY STREETS (Paramount 1931)

Prod E. Lloyd Sheldon; *dir* Rouben Mamoulian; *story* Dashiell Hammett; *scr* Oliver H.P. Garrett, Max Marcin; *mus* Sidney Cutner; *sound* J.A. Goodrich, M.M. Paggi; *ph* Lee Garmes, William Shea; *ed* Viola Lawrence; *cast* Gary Cooper (The Kid); Sylvia Sidney (Nan Cooley); Paul Lukas (Big Fellow Maskal); William ''Stage'' Boyd (McCoy); Guy Kibbee (Pop Cooley); Stanley Fields (Blackie); Wynne Gibson (Aggie); Betty Sinclair (Pansy); Terry Carroll (Esther March); Bob Kortman (servant).

If **City Streets** is the most stylish and artistically interesting gangster film produced in the early thirties, it is also the least realistic. Rouben Mamoulian brought an imaginative—even operatic—sensibility to Dashiell Hammett's original screenplay. The picture is particularly remarkable for the startlingly beautiful and innovative cinematography of Lee Garmes and the imaginative use of sound. It is more melodramatic than most gangster films of the period but also more artistically modern.

Gary Cooper is appropriately cast in the role of the Kid, a carnival sharpshooter from out West who is stranded for a while in the East. Nan Cooley is the stepdaughter of a member of a gang of bootleggers who falls in love with the Kid and suggests that he join the gang to make some money so that they can get married. The Kid refuses, saying that it would be no better than being a cop. When Big Fellow Maskal has Nan's stepfather murder another gang member, whose girl friend the boss covets, Nan is involved and sent to prison as an accomplice because she won't talk. The Kid finally agrees to join the gang in order to raise the money to get Nan an expensive lawyer. The Kid makes money, likes his work, and becomes an appropriately flashy dresser. Nan realizes that her stepfather and the gang are not helping to secure her release, and she grows alarmed at the Kid's new career.

When Nan gets out she tries to get the Kid to quit, but he doesn't understand her change of mind and likes his new life too much. The Big Fellow has grown tired of his girl friend and gets a yen for Nan, who has realized what may happen to the Kid. She agrees to meet the Big Fellow at his mansion if he won't kill the Kid. The Big Fellow hires two assassins anyway, whom the Kid outwits and sends back to Chicago. Aggie, the Big Fellow's girl friend, becomes insanely jealous and shoots the gangster—an act that the gang blames on Nan. The Kid takes over the gang at this point and says that he will prove Nan innocent. The gang members, however, are determined to have their revenge, and take Nan and the Kid for a ride. The Kid takes the wheel and drives faster and faster, barely missing a train and zooming around dangerous mountain curves, threaten-

ing to kill them all unless the gunmen surrender. The Kid and Nan drive off into the sunset, as free as the flock of birds that burst into the sky in the final shot of the movie.

CORSAIR (United Artists 1931)

Prod-dir Roland West; *scr* Walton Green, *ph* Ray June; *ed* Hal Kern; *cast* Chester Morris (John Hawks); Alison Loyd (Alison Corning); William Austin (Richard Bentinck); Frank McHugh (''Club'' Hopping); Emmett Corrigan (Stephen Corning); Fred Kohler (Big John); Frank Rice (Fish Face); Ned Sparks (Slim); Mayo Methot (Sophie).

Corsair is interesting primarily for drawing an explicit parallel between rum-running and the stock manipulations of big business and for providing an ending in which the crooks get away with their crimes without bowing to the film censors' demand to show that crime doesn't pay and that criminals suffer punishment in the end.

John Hawks is a tough college football hero who is rejected by society gadabout Alison Corning. Hawks works for her father, Stephen Corning, a Wall Street stock swindler who finances a large bootleg operation. The footballer quits his job in disgust and becomes a hijacker who preys primarily on the banker's bootleg operation. He sells the liquor back to Corning, to earn the old man's respect by proving that he can outswindle him. The girl again falls in love with Hawks when she realizes that he is a criminal after her own heart, and Hawks convinces the family to go straight in the future.

CRAZY JOE (Columbia 1973)

Presenter, Dino De Laurentiis; *exec prod* Nino E. Kriksman; *dir* Carlo Lizzani; *story* Nicholas Gage; *scr* Lewis John Carlino; *art dir* Robert Dundlach; *sound* Dennis Maitland; *ph* Aaldo Tonti; *cast* Peter Boyle (Crazy Joey Gallo); Paula Prentiss (Anne); Fred Williamson (Willy); Charles Cioffi (Coletti); Rip Torn (Richie); Luther Adler (Galco); Fausto Tozzi (Frank); Franco Lantieri (Nunzio); Eli Wallach (Don Vittorio).

Crazy Joe is an Italian/American co-production typical of several such B-movie efforts. The film capitalizes on the fame of Brooklyn mobster Joey Gallo, who was gunned down in Umberto's Clam House in New York's Little Italy in 1972 for threatening the established Mafia hierarchy and who had become a minor cult figure during the late sixties and early seventies as a gangster who read Sartre.

Crazy Joe begins with Joey Gallo forming an alliance in Attica Prison with black criminals led by his con buddy, Willy. Gallo negotiates an end to a riot and receives a pardon. Once out, he is determined to get back territory that had been whittled away by his rival, Coletti. He is assured by Mafia leader Don Vittorio that he can keep whatever he can grab, which seems like an empty offer, as Gallo has few "soldiers" for a war. When the young turk proves that he has the muscle, thanks to his alliance with the blacks, the older Don grows worried. Gallo takes back his own lost territory and then tries to expand his criminal domain. His alliance with the blacks alarms the older Mafia leaders, who decide that Gallo must go. He is gunned down just when victory seems within his grasp.

DEAD END (United Artists 1937)

Prod Samuel Goldwyn; *dir* William Wyler; based on the play by Sidney Kingsley; *scr* Lillian Hellman; *art dir* Richard Day; *mus* Alfred Newman; *sound* Frank Maher; *sp eff* James Basevi; *ph* Gregg Toland; *ed* Daniel Mandell; *cast* Joel McCrea (Dave Connell); Sylvia Sidney (Drina Gordon); Humphrey Bogart (Joe "Baby Face" Martin); Allen Jenkins (Hunk); Wendy Barrie (Kay Burton); Claire Trevor (Francey); Gabriel Dell (T.B.); Billy Halop (Tommy Gordon); Huntz Hall (Dippy); Bobby Jordan (Angel); Leo Gorcey (Spit); Bertnard Punsley (Milty); Charles Peck (Philip Griswold); Minor Watson (Mr. Griswold); Marjorie Main (Mrs. Martin); James Burke (Mulligan, the cop); Marcelle Corday (governess); Ward Bond (doorman); George Humbert (Pascagli); Esther Dale (Mrs. Feneer, the janitress); Elisabeth Risdon (Mrs. Connell).

Dead End was the picture that most forcefully presented an environmental theory of the formation of criminals by slum conditions. The film is particularly notable for the relatively strong contrasting of rich and poor and for presenting the unrelenting pressure of urban poverty. The sets evoke the confining quality of ghetto life and the temptations to despair over restricted opportunities. The film launched the careers of the Dead End Kids and reflects a concern for production values rarely seen in gangster movies, with Samuel Goldwyn producing and William Wyler directing. Lillian Hellman's screenplay dignifies the genre with realistic expression of social classes and democratic idealism rare in gangster movies.

Baby Face Martin returns to his old neighborhood to see his mother and his former girl friend, Francey. He impresses the local gang, much to the dismay of Dave, an idealistic architect who wants to tear down the slums and replace them with decent housing. Dave is attracted to two women: Kay, who is the mistress of a wealthy man, and Drina, who works in a store and whose ambition is to get her younger brother, Tommy, out of the slums. When Martin is rejected by his mother and finds that Francey has become a streetwalker, he is disgusted and decides to kidnap a local rich kid before leaving forever. Meanwhile, Tommy Gordon knifes the rich boy's father when the latter starts to hit him for beating the boy up. Tommy goes into hiding, and Drina resolves that they will go away together. Martin decides that he can't live with a rich woman, so Kay goes off to Europe without him. When Martin tries to kidnap the rich boy, Dave stops him but is wounded and left for dead. The architect struggles back and shoots the gangster, thereby earning reward money. One of the gang betrays Tommy, who is arrested for the knifing. Dave decides to stay with Drina and use the reward money for Tommy's legal defense.

DILLINGER (Monogram 1945)

Prod Maurice and Franklin King; *dir* Max Nosseck; *scr* Phil Yordan; *mus* Dimitri Tiomkin; *tech dir* Herman King; *sound* Thomas Lambert; *ph* Jackson Rose; *ed* Edward Mann; *cast* Edmund Lowe (Specs); Anne Jeffreys (Helen); Lawrence Tierney (Dillinger); Eduardo Cianelli (Murph); Mard Lawrence (Doc); Elisha Cook, Jr. (Kirk); Ralph Lewis (Tony); Ludwig Stossel (Otto); Else Jannsen (Mrs. Otto).

Dillinger was the first explicit gangster biography. Other films were purportedly based on the lives of actual criminals—e.g., **Scarface**—and screenwriters had frequently used actual gangsters as models, but **Dillinger** was the first to do so directly. Monogram successfully exploited the Dillinger legend with the claim that the film was based on Dillinger's actual life story, which it was not.

Dillinger robs a store to show a girl how daring he is. He is captured and sent to jail, where he meets Specks, a convict gang leader. After being paroled, Dillinger helps bust Specks and some other convicts out of jail. During a series of robberies, Dillinger takes over the gang and meets Helen, who encourages the bandit's criminal inclinations. When the law begins to close in on the gang, they hide out in the country, where Dillinger kills Specks for double-crossing him. Dillinger hides out in a seedy hotel with Helen, who betrays him to the police. The cops kill the notorious bandit in front of a movie theater.

DILLINGER (American International 1973)

Prod Buzz Feitshans; *dir-scr* John Milius; *art dir* Trevor Williams; *mus* Barry Devorzon; *sound* Don Johnson, Kenny Schwarz; *sp eff* A.D. Flowers, Cliff Wenger; *ph* Jules Brenner; *ed* Fred Feitshans, Jr.; *cast* Warren Oates (John Dillinger); Ben Johnson (Melvin Purvis); Michelle Phillips (Billie Frechette); Cloris Leachman (Anna Sagel); Harry Dean Stanton (Homer Van Meter); Steve Kanaly (Lester ''Pretty Boy'' Floyd); Richard Dreyfuss (George ''Baby Face'' Nelson); Geoffrey Lewis (Harry Pierpont); John Ryan (Charles Mackley); Roy Jenson (Samuel Cowley); John Martino (Eddie Youngblood); Jerry Summers (Tommy Carroll); Terry Leonard (Theodore ''Handsome Jack'' Klutas); Bob Harris (Ed Fulton).

The 1973 AIP version includes Dillinger's meeting with Pretty Boy Floyd, Homer Van Meter, and Baby Face Nelson, as well as his famous escape from an Indiana jail with a gun carved out of wood. The latter version treats the period much more realistically, and with reverential attention to details and to the Dillinger legend.

DIRTY HARRY (Warner Bros. 1971)

Exec prod Robert Daley; *prod* Don Siegel; *dir* Siegel; *story* Harry Julian Fink, Rita M. Fink; *scr* Harry Julian Fink, Rita M. Fink, Dean Riesner; *art dir* Dale Hennesy; *mus* Lalo Schifrin; *sound* William Randall; *ph* Bruce Surtees; *ed* Carl Pingitore; *cast* Clint Eastwood (Harry Callahan); Harry Guardino (Lieutenant Bressler); Reni Santoni (Chico); John Vernon (the mayor); Andy Robinson (killer); John Larch (chief); John Mitchum (De Geordio); Mae Mercer (Mrs. Russell); Lyn Edgington (Norma); Ruth Kobart (bus driver); Woodrow Parfrey (Mr. Jaffe); Josef Sommer (Rothko); Maurice S. Argent (Sid Kleinman); Jo de Winter (Miss Willis); Craig G. Kelly (Sergeant Reinke).

Dirty Harry is a cop movie that amplifies a vigilante attitude clearly discernible in the gangster films of the early thirties—e.g., *Beast of the City* (1932) or *This Day and Age* (1933). The film's point of view is that cops have to behave like criminals in order to defend the public adequately. In **Dirty Harry** the cop is the same type of character as the gangster, the only difference being that he is motivated by a professional pride rather than by greed. The film exploits the action and viciousness of gangster films in a rabid advocacy of law and order at any price. The successful film was followed up by other Dirty Harry pictures.

A psychotic sniper shoots a number of innocent people and threatens to continue unless the city pays him a ransom. Dirty Harry and his partner are assigned to the case. Harry stops a bank robbery in spectacular fashion, while the killer shoots another boy and kidnaps a girl, whom he holds for an even greater ransom. The mayor asks Harry to deliver the money, which he does after a complicated runaround. When he arrives, the killer stomps him and tells the battered cop that he has killed the girl anyway. Harry tracks the fiend to his room in the park, where he works as a grounds keeper, and captures the killer after shooting him and beating him up. The court lets the killer go, since Harry violated his rights in making the arrest. The killer pays someone to beat him up and blames Dirty Harry, who is suspended long enough to give the killer another chance to go into action, which he does by kidnapping a busload of schoolchildren. He threatens to kill them unless he is given money and a plane to use for a getaway. The mayor decides to give in to the killer's demands, but Dirty Harry has other ideas. He intercepts the bus and shoots the killer down like the dirty dog he is.

THE DOORWAY TO HELL (Warner Bros. 1930)

Dir Archie Mayo; based on the story *A Handful of Clouds,* by Rowland Brown; *scr* George Rosener; *mus* Leo F. Forbstein; *sound* David Forrest; *ph* Barney McGill; *ed* Robert Crandall; *cast* Lew Ayres (Louis Ricarno); Charles Judels (Sam Marconi); Dorothy Mathews (Doris); Leon Janney (Jackie Lamar); Robert Elliott (Captain O'Grady); James Cagney (Steve Mileway); Kenneth Thomson (Captain of military academy); Jerry Mandy (Joe); Noel Madison (Rocco); Bernard ''Bunny'' Granville (Bit).

Despite the miscasting of clean-cut Lew Ayers as gangster Louie Ricarno, **Doorway to Hell** is one of the more interesting gangster films of the early thirties, particularly because of its script, which stressed the gangster's identification with Napoleon. It also included such conventional gangster elements as the takeover scene, a machine-gun killing (complete with violin case), the ongoing bitter rivalry of bootleggers, and a clear statement of the theme that the gangster can never quit the gang alive. The riotous shootout at the Acme Brewery is a dated but interesting staging of this classic scene. The gangster writing his memoirs is also an unusual, intriguing addition to the genre.

Louis Ricarno is a bootlegger who is already powerful when the film begins. He has organized the city's bootlegging concerns "on a business basis" and puts himself in charge of the whole operation as the final arbiter of territorial disputes. Things are running so smoothly that Louis decides to quit the rackets, marry Doris, and go legitimate for the sake of his younger brother, who is in a military school and knows nothing of his big brother's business. Louis passes the organization leadership over to his best friend, Mileway, who has been having an affair with Doris, and the gangster and his bride go to Florida to retire in style, play golf, and write Louis's autobiography. When rival factions start fighting each other, Mileway cannot exert a strong enough hand to stop them, so he asks Louis to return. However, Louis refuses, even though Doris would like to get back to the big-city action. One faction decides to force Louis back by kidnapping his kid brother from the military school, but the boy is accidentally killed in the process. Louis returns and gets revenge by killing all of those involved in the kidnapping. He is arrested when Mileway talks. Rival gangsters arrange for Louis's escape so that they can kill him, which they do after the gangster has one farewell meeting with Captain O'Grady, the neighborhood cop who had tried to make him go straight.

EACH DAWN I DIE (Warner Bros. 1939)

Assoc prod David Lewis; *dir* William Keighley; based on the novel by Jerome Odlum; *scr* Norman Reilly Raine, Warren Duff, Charles Perry; *art dir* Max Parker; *mus* Max Steiner; *sound* E.A. Brown; *ph* Arthur Edeson; *ed* Thomas Richards; *cast* James Cagney (Frank Ross); George Raft ("Hood" Stacey); Jane Bryan (Joyce Conover); George Bancroft (Warden John Armstrong); Maxie Rosenbloom (Fargo Red); Stanley Ridges (Muller); Alan Baxter, (Polecat Carlisle); Victor Jory (J.J. Grayce); Willard Robertson (Lang); Paul Hurst (Garsky); John Wray (Peter Kassock); Louis Jean Heydt (Joe Lassiter); Ed Pawley (Dale); Joe Downing (Limpy Julien); Emma Dunn (Mrs. Ross); Thurston Hall (District Attorney Jesse Hanley); Clay Clement (Attorney Lockhart); William Davidson (Mill Mason); John Ridgely (Jerry Poague, a reporter); John Harron (Lew Keller, a reporter); Selmer Jackson (Patterson); Robert

Homans (Mac, the guard); Harry Cording (Temple); Abner Biberman (Shake Edwards); Napoleon Simpson (Mose).

Each Dawn I Die is typical of the various films that mix elements of gangster pictures with newspaper and prison dramas. Rather than crusading against the inequities of the prison system, **Each Dawn I Die** uses the prison as a setting for the story. The picture is notable for the interesting interacting of Cagney and Raft and for the bleakly sinister view of a crooked District Attorney.

Frank Ross is an investigative reporter who discovers that the District Attorney is in cahoots with racketeers in the building trade. When he publishes an exposé, the D.A. frames the reporter on a charge of drunk driving and manslaughter. The reporter is denied parole every time he applies, and so becomes progressively more bitter. He makes friends with gangster "Hood" Stacey and helps him escape on the condition that the latter work for him on the outside to get evidence that will free the reporter. Through a misunderstanding, the gangsters think that Ross has squealed on them, and Stacey, now on the outside, forgets about the imprisoned reporter. When Stacey finds out the true identity of the squealer, who is also the man who can clear Ross, he goes on to help his reporter pal and returns to prison to stage a breakout. The escape attempt fails and Stacey is killed, but he manages to clear the reporter before he dies. Ross is determined to work for prison reform upon his release.

THE ENFORCER (Warner Bros. 1951)

Prod Milton Sperling; *dir* (credited) Bretaigne Windust (actually Raoul Walsh); *scr* Martin Rackin; *art dir* Charles H. Clarke; *mus* David Buttolph; *sound* Dolph Thomas; *ph* Robert Burks; *ed* Fred Allen; *cast* Humphrey Bogart (Martin Ferguson); Zero Mostel (Big Babe Lazich); Ted De Corsia (Joseph Rico); Everett Sloane (Albert Mendoza); Roy Roberts (Captain Frank Nelson); Lawrence Telan (Duke Malley); King Donovan (Sergeant Whitlow); Bob Steele (Herman); Adelaide Klein (Olga Kirshen); Don Beddoe (Thomas O'Hara); Tito Vuolo (Tony Vetto); John Kellogg (Vince); Jack Lambert (Philadelphia Tom Zaca); Patricia Joiner (Angela Vetto); Susan Cabot (Nina Lombardo); Mario Siletti (Louis, the barber); Alan Foster (Shorty); Harry Wilson (B.J.).

The Enforcer, like **Murder Inc.**, is concerned with exposing an assassination squad operating within the world of organized crime. The picture has Bogart on the right side of the law as a crusading District Attorney whose investigations lead to the discovery and destruction of the mob's murderers. The picture was one of the earlier crime dramas to emphasize the terror and national scope of the organization that retained its power through murder and intimidation.

District Attorney Martin Ferguson thinks he has finally pinned a murder on mob big shot Albert Mendoza, but his star witness dies "accidentally." Ferguson forces an enforcer to confess to the existence of a network of killers, but all witnesses who can help the D.A. bring any convictions have disappeared. The organization is the idea of Mendoza, who reasons that as long as the killers have no identifiable motive, they cannot be effectively linked to their crimes, and indeed, the lack of motive keeps the D.A. stymied. When Ferguson discovers the existence and whereabouts of a young woman who had witnessed one of the mob's earlier killings, Mendoza also gets that information and sends another assassin, Herman, to kill the girl. Ferguson shoots the would-be killer and saves the girl, whose testimony sends the head of the murder mob to the electric chair.

FORCE OF EVIL (MGM 1948)

Prod Bob Roberts; *dir* Abraham Polonsky; *scr* Abraham Polonsky and Ira Wolfert; based on the novel *Tucker's People,* by Ira Wolfert. *ph* George Barnes; *art dir* Richard Day; *mus* Rudolph Polk; *sound* Frank Webster; *cast* John Garfield (Joe Morse); Beatrice Pearson (Doris Lowry); Thomas Gomez (Leo Morse); Roy Roberts (Ben Tucker); Marie Windsor (Edna Tucker); Howland Chamberlin (Freddy Bauer); Paul McVey (Hoke Wheelook), Jack Overman (Juice); Tim Ryan (Johnson); Barbara Woodell (receptionist); Raymond Largay (Bunte); Stanley Prager (Wally); Beau Bridges (Frankie Tucker); Allan Mathews (Badgley); Barry Kelley (Egan); Sheldon Leonard (Ficce); Jan Dennis (Mrs. Bauer); Georgia Bachus (Sylvia Morse); Sid Tomack (Two and Two Taylor).

Force of Evil is one of the few gangster films to explore directly the moral relationship between business and crime and to detail the day-to-day operation of a racket—in this case, the numbers racket. The film has a particularly effective script and forceful acting by Garfield and Gomez.

Joe Morse is a smart lawyer who decides that he can strike it rich by manipulating the numbers racket for his boss, racketeer Ben Tucker. His brother, Leo, has slaved away running an honest numbers bank to send Joe through school and wants him to stay away from the rackets. But the younger man finds a method to bankrupt all the independent banks so that Tucker can control the entire numbers racket. Morse also has big plans to turn the numbers into a legitimate racket as a public lottery which the gangsters would secretly control. When his brother opposes the plan, he is murdered by gangster goons, and Joe swears revenge. He avenges his brother's death by killing the heads of the syndicate, whom he was helping to gain control over the numbers racket.

THE FRIENDS OF EDDIE COYLE (Paramount 1973)

Prod Paul Monash; *dir* Peter Yates; based on the novel by George V. Higgins; *scr* Monash; *des* Gene Callahan; *mus* Dave Grusing; *sound* Dick Raguse; *ph* Victor J. Kemper; *ed* Pat Jaffe; *cast* Robert Mitchum (Eddie Coyle); Peter Boyle (Dillon); Richard Jordan (Dave Foley); Steven Keats (Jackie); Alex Rocco (Scalise); Joe Santos (Artie Van); Mitchell Ryan (Waters); Peter MacLean (Partridge); Kevin Morrison (manager of second bank); Marvin Lichterman (Vernon); Carolyn Pickman (Nancy); James Tolkan (The Man's contact man); Margaret Ladd (Andrea); Matthew Cowles (Pete); Helena Carroll (Sheila Coyle); Jane House (Wanda); Michael McCleery (The Kid); Alan Koss (Phil); Dennis McMullen (Webber); Judith Ogden Cabot (Mrs. Partridge); Jan Egleson (Pale Kid); Jack Kegoe (The Beard); Robert Anthony (Moran); Gus Johnson (Ames); Ted Maynard (Sauter); Sheldon Feldner (Ferris).

The Friends of Eddie Coyle is an interesting film in its portrayal of a small-time crook forced into becoming a stoolie. Similar in plot to **The Kiss of Death,** the film succeeds in conveying the seedy quality of the treacherous Boston underworld. Author George Higgins was a Massachusetts assistant district attorney who presented a thoroughly authentic account of the finks, killers, and detectives who inhabit the sinister world of low-echelon hoods. The movie preserves this quality.

Eddie Coyle is a three-time loser faced with another term in prison, which will cause his family to go on welfare. Boston police official Dave Foley agrees to put in a good word with the court if the aging hood helps get evidence on a gang of bank robbers. Coyle gets guns for the gang to use in a robbery and then informs the police. But the cops aren't satisfied and demand that he help turn the gang in. When Scalise, the gang's boss, is arrested, the underworld figures that Coyle is responsible and orders him killed. His friend, bartender Dillon, is given the job—though he is the actual informant. It is clear that the cops don't care what happens to Eddie Coyle.

GANGS OF NEW YORK (Republic 1938)

Assoc prod Armand Schaefer; *dir* James Cruze; *scr* Wellyn Totman, Sam Fuller, Charles Francis; based on an original story by Sam Fuller, the latter suggested by Herbert Asbury's book, *Gangs of New York; ph* Ernest Miller; *art dir* John Victor Mackay; *mus* Alberto Columbo; *ed* William Morgan; *cast* Charles Bickford (John Franklin/Rocky Thorpe); Ann Dvorak (Connie); Alan Baxter (Dapper); Wynne Gibson (Orchid).

Having little in common with Herbert Asbury's book about the history of New York gangs, the Republic picture is interesting primarily for its use of a dual role played by Bickford as police agent and gang leader. There is plenty of action, in the Republic tradition, and the film is typical of the B-movie crime stories that the studio produced for years.

Rocky Thorpe directs his gang's activities from his cell in prison, using a short-wave radio. Just prior to his release, he is put in solitary away from his radio. Policeman John Franklin, who looks exactly like the mobster, is sent out in his place. The cop takes over the rival gangs and convinces them to adopt "business methods." Franklin tells the other gangsters that this will require them to write reports and keep ledgers, which they should turn over to him so that they can more efficiently pool their operations for greater profits. Meanwhile, Franklin and Connie have a romance, inviting the jealous suspicions of Orchid, another moll. The cop is about to gather enough evidence to put away all the gangs in the city when Rocky Thorpe escapes to destroy his plan for a peaceful roundup, requiring the police to shoot it out with the gangsters in order to capture them.

THE GANGSTER (Allied Artists 1947)

Prod Maurice King, Frank King; *dir* Gordon Wiles; based on the novel *Low Company*, by Daniel Fuchs; *scr* Fuchs; *art dir* F. Paul Sylos; *mus* Louis Gruenberg; *sound* William Randall; *sp eff* Roy W. Seawright; *ph* Paul Ivano; *ed* Walter Thompson; *cast* Barry Sullivan (Shubunka); Belita (Nancy Starr); Joan Loring (Dorothy); Akim Tamiroff (Nick Jammey); Henry "Harry"

Morgan (Shorty); John Ireland (Karty); Fifi D'Orsay (Mrs. Ostroleng); Virginia Christine (Mrs. Karty); Sheldon Leonard (Cornall); Charles McGraw (Dugas); John Kellogg (Sterling); Elisha Cook Jr. (Obal); Ted Hecht (Swain); Jeff Corey, Peter Whitney, Clancy Cooper (Brothers-in-Law); Murray Alper (Eddie); Shelley Winters (Hazel).

There are a few films that are devoted to the dissolution of the movie gangster and his slide to obscurity and defeat. **The Gangster** is atypical in that it deals with a hoodlum's failure of nerve. Barry Sullivan does a remarkable job of portraying the gangster whose desire to go legitimate ultimately leads to his destruction.

Shubunka is a successful hoodlum who wants to go straight with his girl friend, who is a nightclub singer. He grows obsessively jealous and is unable to concentrate on his business when a new rival gang begins to extort money from businesses supposedly under Shubunka's protection. When the gangster tries to get the members of his gang to fight off the interlopers, his hoods realize that the gangster has lost his nerve. One by one, they desert him, and his rivals take over his territory. His girl leaves, and Shubunka goes to his death at the hands of his rivals.

THE GANGSTERS AND THE GIRL (K-B 1914)

Dir Thomas Ince; *cast* Charles Ray, Elizabeth Burbridge, Arthur Jarret, Margaret Thompson.

The Gangsters and the Girl is a good example of the early gangster films that followed **The Musketeers of Pig Alley**. The film is characterized by a melodramatic tone and a good deal of action. The Girl of the title is "Molly, a girl of the slums" (a moralistic echo of Stephen Crane's "Maggie"), whose boy friend, Jim, is the head of the neighborhood gang. Jim gives part of their loot to Maggie, whose father is in prison, and when Maggie herself is sent to prison unjustly, the gang breaks her out. The police, who are determined to stop the gang, send in an agent, Detective Scott, whose job is to infiltrate the gang and then turn its members in to the police. Molly falls for the new member. When one gang member gets less than he thinks is his fair share of the loot, he turns informer. Jim thinks that Molly is the guilty one when the police raid their hideout, but before he can get to her, Scott kills the gangster and marries the girl.

The film is stiff and slow moving, but the blend of outdoor locations and sets has remained a fairly constant ratio of reality and make-believe throughout the genre. The robbery of an apartment house, with its systematic looting, chase up to the roof, rooftop shootout, and escape back down to the street, is one of the most interesting early sequences of its type. Another classic scene is the division of the loot, in which the underpaid member decides to become a squealer. Ince, who produced and supervised the picture, was a powerhouse of independent film production.

G-MEN (Warner Bros. 1935)

Dir William Keighley; based on the book *Public Enemy No. 1,* by Gregory Rogers; *scr* Seton I. Miller; *art dir* John J. Hughes; *mus* Leo F. Forbstein; *ph* Sol Polite; *ed* Jack Killifer; *cast* James Cagney (James "Brick" Davis); Ann Dvorak (Jean Morgan); Margaret Lindsay (Kay McCord); Robert Armstrong (Jeff McCord); Barton MacLane (Brad Collins); Lloyd Nolan (Hugh Farrell); William Harrigan (McKay); Edward Pawley (Danny Leggett); Russell Hopton (Gerard); Noel Madison (Durfee); Regis Toomey (Eddie Buchanan); Addison Richards (Bruce J. Gregory); Harold Huber (Venke); Raymond Hatton (The Man); Monte Blue (analyst); Mary Treen (Gregory's secretary); Adreain Morris (accomplice); Emmett Vogan (Bill, the ballistics expert); James Flavin (agent); Stanley Blystone, Pat Flaherty (cops); James T. Mack (agent); Jonathan Hale (congressman).

G-Men is the key film in which the movie gangster was reincarnated as a cop. The film spawned a new cycle of gangster films in which tough, honest cops who grew up in the same environment as the gangsters prove to be the only force capable of stopping the hoods. **G-Men** was made on a fairly lavish budget for gangster pictures and contained even more action than its predecessors that favored the hoodlums. The shootout at the railroad station, in which the gangsters rescue their henchman, and at the lodge which the hoods use as a hideout are spectacular examples of such scenes in the genre. The film was powerful and durable enough to be re-released in 1949 with a new prologue.

James "Brick" Davis is a poor but honest lawyer who is having a tough time making ends meet. When his best friend, who has become an F.B.I. agent (unarmed), is shot down by hoods, Davis decides to join the F.B.I. to seek revenge. He gets the approval of a benevolent crime boss who had sent him to law school, says goodbye to his dancer girl friend, and goes off to Washington. The F.B.I. agents at first are skeptical of this young lawyer with a Ph.D., but Davis proves

himself adept enough at shooting and fighting to win acceptance. When the agents discover his connection to McKay, the crime boss, and think about Davis's knowledge of the underworld, they begin to suspect him as a spy for the hoodlums. Davis, however, proves his worth in helping to round up his old underworld acquaintances and avenge his pal's death. In the meantime, the young G-man falls for the sister of his chief. After a shootout with the gang in which his benefactor is accidentally killed, Davis decides to quit the F.B.I. When the last gangster kidnaps the sister of F.B.I. Chief McCord, Davis goes back into action to rescue her, kill the last and most notorious member of the gang, and win the girl's hand.

THE GODFATHER (Paramount 1972)

Prod Albert S. Ruddy; *dir* Francis Ford Coppola; based on the novel by Mario Puzo; *scr* Puzo, Coppola; *des* Dean Tavoularis; *art dir* Warren Clymer; *mus* Nino Rota; *sound* Bud Grenzbach, Richard Portman, Christopher Newman; *sp eff* A.D. Flowers, Joe Lombardi, Sass Bedig; *ph* Gordon Willis; *ed* William Reynolds, Peter Zinner, Marc Laub, Murray Solomon; *cast* Marlon Brando (Don Vito Corleone); Al Pacino (Michael Corleone); James Caan (Sonny Corleone); Richard Castellano (Clemenza); Robert Duvall (Tom Hagen); Sterling Hayden (McCluskey); John Marley (Jack Woltz); Richard Conte (Barzinz); Diane Keaton (Kay Adams); Al Lettieri (Sollezzo); Abe Vigoda (Tessio); Talia Shire (Connie Rizzi); Gianni Russo (Carlo Rizzi); John Cazale (Fredo Corleone); Rudy Bond (Cuneo); Al Martino (Johnny Fontane); Mergana King (Mama Corleone); John Martino (Paulie Gatto); Lenny Montana (Luca Brasi); Alex Rocco (Moe Greene); Tony Giorgio (Bruno Tattaglia); Vito Scotti (Nazorine); Victor Livrano (Phillip Tattaglia); Jeannie Linero (Lucy Mancini); Julie Gregg (Sandra Corleone); Ardell Sheridan (Mrs. Clemenza); Corrado Gaipa (Don Tommasino); Angelo Infanti (Fabrizio); Saro Urzi (Vitelli); Franco Citti (Calo).

The Godfather is the most successful and expensive gangster movie ever produced. Based on Mario Puzo's best seller (10 million copies) of the same name, it is a blockbuster, with every advantage in production values a high-budget picture can offer; an enormous cast, many scenes, and a wide variety of locations, with a marvelous re-creation of the past. Ninety percent of the movie was shot on location, with particularly effective use of New York's Little Italy and Staten Island. The production drew criticism from the Italian-American Civil Rights League, along with anonymous threats and some violence for depicting the Mafia. Producer Albert Ruddy agreed to delete every mention of the words "Mafia" or "Cosa Nostra" in response to the pressure, to donate some money from the production to a community hospital, and to give some jobs to members of the League.

The Godfather is a gangster picture of epic proportions that uses the mythological raw material established by the genre in the preceding sixty years. Coppola made the gangster film a self-conscious metaphor of American capitalist thinking and behavior. The tribal/corporate warfare of the feuding families, the recognition of power, and the glorification of its use in a society in which the individual and family grow increasingly powerless re-echo a theme that made gangster pictures popular in the thirties. In some ways **The Godfather** is a gangster soap opera on a grand scale. Appropriately nostalgic in its reverence for the family and appropriately cynical in its depiction of the business of murder, **The Godfather** is most of all a monumental testimonial to the enduring popularity of gangster movies in America.

The Godfather in particularly noteworthy for its number and variety of excellent performances. Brando's tour de force portrayal of Don Vito Corleone, Al Pacino's beautifully modulated performance, Robert Duvall's excellent job of playing the adopted son who becomes the family *consiglieri,* and James Caan's portrayal of the virile and impetuous Sonny combine with the many fine character studies to make **The Godfather** one of the best acted gangster films in the genre.

The story concerns the powerful Corleone family and focuses on the patriarch, Don Vito Corleone, an aging crime boss, and his youngest son, Michael, whom the father hopes will attain legitimate eminence ("a senator or something"). Michael, a college graduate and war hero, returns home on the day of his sister's wedding, an event during which various guests come to pay their respects to Don Corleone and ask him for special favors. Among them are singer Johnny Fontane, who needs a part in a Hollywood movie to save his ailing career, and Sollozzo, a mobster allied with a rival family, who needs Don Corleone's political connections for the mob's entry into the narcotics business. The Godfather gets Fontane the coveted part by making the recalcitrant studio boss "an offer he can't refuse." Corleone's refusal to help establish the narcotics business provokes Sollozzo, in cahoots with the Tataglia family, to attempt to kill the aging Don. The plotters succeed in killing the

Don's trusted bodyguard, Luca Brasi, but the Don himself survives an attempt on his life. Michael is drawn into the events and proves his worth when he saves his father from a second attempt in the hospital. He realizes that he must play a larger role to prevent a gang war that is developing. He suggests that he kill Sollozzo himself under the guise of a truce meeting, since no one believes that the youngest son is involved with the family business. Like his father, Michael Corleone proves his manhood with murder, and is sent to Sicily to hide out until circumstances allow him to return. During his time in the old country, Michael falls in love with a Sicilian girl, whom he marries. Soon afterward, she is blown up by a bomb intended for him. Michael returns to New York to seek revenge and enter the family business. He marries Kay Adams, his former sweetheart. This time, the Barzini family is pushing the Corleone clan toward the narcotics business, and a new plot and gang war are brewing, in which brother Sonny is killed. Don Vito Corleone accepts the fact that his youngest son has entered the family business and advises him what to expect from his rivals. Michael has already begun to think and act like his father when he guides the family's takeover of Moe Green's casino in Las Vegas. When the Godfather dies of a heart attack, the Barzini clan makes its move, using Tessio, one of the Don's most trusted lieutenants, to set up an assassination attempt on Michael. But the young Don outmaneuvers his enemies and has them all killed (while also avenging the murder of his Sicilian wife) on the day of the baptism of his godson. In the process, he has his brother-in-law, Carlo Rizzi, killed for being a traitor to the family and setting up his brother Sonny. Michael Corleone lies about this deed to his wife and assumes the lonely burden and mantle of power of the new Don.

THE GODFATHER, PART II (Paramount 1974)

Prod Francis Ford Coppola; *co-prod* Gary Frederickson, Fred Goos; *dir* Coppola; based on the novel by Mario Puzo; *scr* Coppola, Puzo; *des* Dean Tavoularis; *art dir* Angelo Graham; *mus* Nino Rota; *sound* Walter Murch; *sp eff* A.D. Flowers, Joe Lombardi; *ph* Gordon Willis; *ed* Peter Zinner, Barry Malkin, Richard Marks; *cast* Al Pacino (Michael Corleone); Robert Duvall (Tom Hagen); Diane Keaton (Kay); Robert De Niro (Vito Corleone); John Cazale (Fredo Corleone); Talia Shire (Connie Corleone); Lee Strasberg (Hyman Roth); Michael V. Gazzo (Frankie Pentangeli); G.D. Apradlin (Senator Pat Geary); Richard Bright (Al Neri); Gaston Moschin (Fanutti); Tom Rosqui (Rocco Lampone); B.

Kirby, Jr. (Young Clemenza); Frank Svero (Genco); Francesc de Sapio (young Mama Corleone); Morgana King (Mama Corleone); Mariana Hill (Deanna Corleone); Leopaldo Triste (Signer Roberto); Dominic Chianese (Johnny Ola); John Aprea (young Tessio); Abe Vigoda (Tessio); Tere Livrano (Theresa Hagen); Gianni Russo (Carlo); Joe Spinell (Willi Cicci); Maria Carta (Vite's mother); Oreste Baldini (Victor Andolini as a boy); Guiseppe Sillato (Don Frencesco); Mario Cotone (Don Tommasino); James Gounaris (Anthony Corleone); Fay Spain (Marcia Roth); Harry Dean Stanton, David Baker (F.B.I. men); Ezio Flagello (impresario); Peter Donat (Questadt); Roger Corman (Senator); James Caan (Sonny).

The Godfather, Part II was not as popular or dramatically successful as its predecessor but is in many ways more ambitious and interesting in terms of the evolution of the genre. The picture broadens the scope of **The Godfather** by telling the story of the Corleone dynasty's adjustment to America and by relocating the classic rise-and-fall story in terms of its effect on the family and character. As Michael's acquisition of power was appreciated, if not glorified outright, in the earlier film, his final ascendancy in Part II is in fact a fall into a gutter of corporate success which is every bit as life-denying as the pavement to which Scarface falls in an earlier era. There is a rise and fall of respect depicted simultaneously in Vito's (the Godfather as a young man) early career and Michael's continued story that is unique in the genre. The settings and historical sweep are much more lavish than in **The Godfather**, as are the broadly stated implications that the gangsters in Cuba were as much an accurate metaphor of American corporate imperialism (I.T.T., Coca-Cola, and United Fruit) as a symbol of business practice and thinking in America. As in **The Godfather**, the direction, acting (particularly of De Niro and Pacino), and camerawork are excellent. Normally, sequels of popular pictures are inferior to the originals. **The Godfather, Part II**, is a fascinating exception to the rule.

The **Godfather, Part II**, tells first the story of Vito Corleone, who becomes the Don in the preceding **Godfather**. The picture opens in a Sicilian village, from which young Vito flees after the murder of his family. He goes to America, where he rises to power in New York after he kills a local Black Hand extorter, Fanutti. He eventually returns to Sicily to avenge the death of his family by killing Silatto, the local Mafia powerhouse, who had killed them. This story is intercut with that of Michael Corleone, which begins in 1958 in Lake Tahoe,

where Corleone has re-located his family. With longtime family *consiglieri* Tom Hagen, he gains influence over corrupt Senator Pat Geary, and outmaneuvers Miami powerhouse Hyman Roth and turncoat family friend Frank Pentangeli. Sister Connie Corleone weds playboy Merle Johnson against her brother's wishes, and brother Fredo unwittingly betrays Michael, while his wife destroys their marriage by having an abortion rather than raise another child in the criminal environment of the Corleone clan. Michael uses his influence to avoid an indictment after a Senate investigating committee looks into his business. He eliminates Roth, brother Fredo, and Pentangeli, but winds up an empty man with no family or friends to share in his business success.

GUN CRAZY (DEADLY IS THE FEMALE)
(United Artists 1949)

Prod Frank and Maurice King; *dir* Joseph H. Lewis; based on the story *Gun Crazy*, by MacKinlay Kantor; *scr* Kantor, Millard Kaufman; *mus* Victor Young; *ph* Russell Harlan; *ed* Harry Gerstad; *cast* Peggy Cummings (Annie Laurie Starr); John Dall (Bart Tare); Barry Kroeger (Packett); Morris Carnovsky (Judge Willoughby); Anabel Shaw (Ruby Tare); Harry Lewis (Clyde Boston); Hedrick Young (Dave Allister); Trevor Bardette (Sheriff Boston); Mickey Little (Bart Tare at age seven); Rusty Tamblyn (Bart Tare at age fourteen); Paul Frison (Clyde Boston at age fourteen); Dave Bair (Dave Allister at age fourteen); Stanley Prager (Bluey-Bluey); Virginia Farmer (Miss Wynn); Anne O'Neal (Miss Sifert); Frances Irwin (Danceland singer); Don Beddow (man from Chicago); Simen Ruskin (cab driver); Harry Hayden (Mr. Mallenberg).

The fascination with a gun as a symbol of manhood and power has never received treatment as effectively as in **Gun Crazy**. The portrait of a devious, manipulative woman is also memorable, comparable to *Out of the Past* (1947). A low-budget film that has seldom been shown since, it is nonetheless one of the better-directed gangster stories in the hands of Joseph Lewis. The story was loosely based on the career of Bonnie Parker and Clyde Barrow and is worth comparing with *You Only Live Once* (1937) and **Bonnie and Clyde.**

Bart Tare is a sharpshooting World World II veteran who has always been fascinated with guns. He meets Annie Starr, a shapely carnival sharpshooter who is impressed with Tare's marksmanship. The two gun nuts fall in love, and Annie convinces Bart to stage a series of holdups, which ultimately results in their killing somebody during a robbery. The action and risks give the lovers something to live for, and they recklessly continue their crime wave. Bart becomes increasingly paranoid and Annie increasingly ruthless as their reputation grows. The cops finally track the two down and shoot them to death in a swamp.

HIGH SIERRA (Warner Bros. 1941)

Exec prod Hal B. Wallis; *dir* Raoul Walsh; based on the novel by W.R. Burnett; *scr* John Huston, Burnett; *art dir* Ted Smith; *mus* Adolph Deutsch; *sound* Dolph Thomas; *sp eff* Byron Haskin, H.F. Koenekamp; *ph* Tony Gaudio; *ed* Jack Killifer; *cast* Humphrey Bogart (Roy Earle); Ida Lupino (Marie Garson); Alan Curtis (Babe Kozak); Arthur Kennedy (Red Hattery); Joan Leslie (Velma); Henry Jull ("Doc" Banton); Barton MacLane (Jake Kranmer); Henry Travers (Pa); Elisabeth Risdon (Ma); Cornel Wilde (Louis Mendoza); Minna Gombell (Mrs. Gaughman); Paul Harvey (Mr. Baughman); Donald MacBride (Mig Mac); Jerome Cowan (Healy); John Eldredge (Lou Preisser) Isabel Jewell (Blonde); Willie Best (Algeron); Arthur Aylesworth (auto court owner); Robert Strange (Art); Wade Boteler (sheriff); Sam Hayes (radio commentator); Spencer Charters (Ed); Cliff Saum (Shaw).

From **Little Caesar** to **The Big Shot,** the road had grown increasingly rocky for the movie gangster's last stand. **High Sierra** is a brilliant example of the passing of the heroic gangster. The film is interesting in placing a gangster picture in the mountains and in rooting the drama in character development rather than plot. Bogart and Ida Lupino give powerful portrayals of a couple of social losers whose dignity remains intact despite the tragic conclusion.

The picture opens with Roy "Mad Dog" Earle stepping out of prison to breathe the air of freedom. He heads for the mountains, where he meets two young hoods and the girl they have brought with them. Earle has been sprung in exchange for leading the robbery of an expensive resort. The older gangster earns the grudging respect of the younger gangsters and the girl falls for him, despite Earle's early hostility and desire to send her away. When the gangster goes to case the resort hotel, he runs into a poor farm couple whose pretty granddaughter is crippled. Earle resolves to get medical help for the girl from the gang's old doctor. The gang holds up the resort, during which a local cop and one of the gang members are killed. Earle and the girl head for Los Angeles, where they will deliver the loot

and get their share. Earl arranges an operation for the crippled girl, but his romantic hopes are dashed when she becomes engaged to a Babbitt-like boyfriend. Earle receives another blow when his old boss, Big Mac, dies (or is murdered) and ex-cop Jake Kranmer tries unsuccessfully to steal the loot. Earle tries to fence the jewels as the police close in. He is betrayed and barely escapes into the mountains, where he is shot down by a country sharpshooter.

HOODLUM EMPIRE (Republic 1952)

Prod J. Yates; *dir* Joseph Kane; *story* Bob Considine; *scr* Bruce Manning, Considine; *art dir* Frank Arrigo; *mus* Nathan Scott; *ph* Reggie Lanning; *ed* Richard L. Van Enger; *cast* Brian Donlevy (Senator Bill Stephens); Claire Trevor (Connie Williams); Forrest Tucker (Charley Fignatalli); Vera Ralston (Marte Dufour); Luther Adler (Nicky Mancani); John Russell (Joe Gray); Gene Lockhart (Senator Tower); Grant Withers (Reverend Andrews); Taylor Holmes (Benjamin Lawton); Roy Barcroft (Louie Draper); William Murphy (Pete Daily); Richard Jaeckel (Ted Dawson); Don Beddoe (Senator Blake); Roy Roberts (Chief Taylor); Richard Benedict (Tanner); Phillip Pine (Louis Barcetti); Damian O'Flynn (Foster); Pat Flaherty (Mikkelson); Ric Roman (Fergus); Douglas Kennedy (Brinkley); Don Haggerty (Mark Flynn); Francis Pierlot (Uncle Jean); Sarah Spencer (Mrs. Stephens); Thomas Browne Henry (Commodore Mermant); Jack Pennick (Tracey).

Hoodlum Empire reflects the postwar climate of searing exposé, sparked by the Kefauver investigations of 1950–1951 and a tone of righteous governmental pursuit of the gangsters. The film was one of the first to acknowledge the scope of racketeering but failed to explore seriously its meaning or actual activities. It was supposedly based on the life of Frank Costello, but the connection between the final film and the life of the mobster was tenuous at best. **Hoodlum Empire** is significant for introducing the scene in which a powerful hood has to face a governmental committee hearing. Luther Adler does an excellent portrayal of a syndicate racketeer. The personal drama narrowed the dramatic focus of the exposé effectively but, in turn, obscured the facts of organized crime in the United States. The use of flashbacks is particularly effective and unusual.

Joe Gray quits the mob after his patriotic wartime experience and tries to disappear and go straight. But the syndicate, led by gangster Nicky Mancani, can't let him go, since they have been using Gray's name as part of a complicated scheme to launder money. Gray owns a gas station with two war buddies, and he is discovered there by the mob after a widespread search which has been closely watched by government investigators. They frame Gray as the boss of all crime in his community. He becomes an outcast, defended only by his army chaplain. After several murders and a lot of action, Gray, his army pals, and the chaplain defeat the hoods and destroy the hoodlum empire.

INVISIBLE STRIPES (Warner Bros 1939)

Exec prod Hal B. Wallis; *dir* Lloyd Bacon; based on the book by Warden Lewis E. Wawes; *story* Jonathan Finn; *scr* Warren Duff; *art dir* Max Parker; *mus* Heinz Roehmheld; *sound* Dolph Thomas; *sp eff* Byron Haskin; *ph* Ernest Haller; *ed* James Gibbons; *cast* George Raft (Cliff Taylor); Jane Bryan (Peggy); William Holden (Tim Taylor); Humphrey Bogart (Chuck Martin); Flora Robson (Mrs. Taylor); Paul Kelly (Ed Kruger); Lee Patrick (Molly Daniels); Henry O'Neill (Parole Officer Masters); Frankie Thomas (Tommy); Moroni Olsen (Warden); Margot Stevenson (Sue); Marc Lawrence (Lefty); Joseph Downing (Johnny); Leo Gorcey (Jimmy); William Haade (Shrank); Tully Marshall (Old Peter); Chester Clute (Mr. Butler); Bruno (Smitty, a prisoner).

The "invisible stripes" are the social and psychological scars that ex-cons must wear after their release from prison. **Invisible Stripes** is typical of those gangster films that focused on the transition from life in prison to life on the outside. The basic dramatic situation for such films remains one that involves the choice of living a straight life or of returning to crime. The film is particularly noteworthy for the interacting of Raft, Bogart, and William Holden and for its expression of the unrelenting tone of the desperate pressures of urban poverty, a theme that had also characterized some of the films of the early thirties.

Ex-con Cliff Taylor finds life difficult when he gets out of prison. He can find only menial jobs, which he has trouble holding on to, and the cops harass him continually. Taylor's younger brother, Tim, becomes attracted to a criminal career in order to make enough money to live with his girl friend. But brother Cliff is adamantly opposed and joins Chuck Martin's gang himself in order to get enough money for the brother to go straight. Several robberies later, Cliff has enough money to buy a gas station, so he quits the gang. The gang, however, uses the gas station in a getaway, and although Cliff is angry, he helps the wounded gang leader. When the cops move in on the gang, they believe that Cliff has squealed, so they gun him down. He has succeeded, however, in keeping his younger brother honest.

KEY LARGO (Warner Bros. 1948)

Prod Jerry Wald; *dir* John Huston; based on the play by Maxwell Anderson; *scr* Richard Brooks; *art dir* Leo K. Kuter; *mus* Max Steiner; *sound* Dolph Thomas; *sp eff* William McGann, Robert Burks; *ph* Karl Freund; *ed* Rudi Fehr, *cast* Humphrey Bogart (Frank McCloud); Edward G. Robinson (Johnny Rocco); Lauren Bacall (Nora Temple) Lionel Barrymore (James Temple); Claire Trevor (Gaye Dawn); Thomas Gomez (Curley); Harry Lewis (Toots); John Rodney (Deputy Clyde Sawyer); Marc Lawrence (Ziggy); Dan Seymore (Angel Garcia); Monte Blue (Sheriff Ben Wade); Jay Silverheels (John Osceola); Rodric Redwing (Tom Osceola); William Haade (Ralph Feeney).

Key Largo is one of the most interesting gangster pictures in sharply etching the characters rather than emphasizing action and the normal iconography of gangster movies. The picture has a static quality, due in part to its origin as a play. Still, though it is somewhat wordy, it overflows with good acting by Bogart, Bacall, Robinson, Lionel Barrymore, Claire Trevor, and Thomas Gomez. The postwar melodrama pitted good guy Bogart against a powerfully evil aging gangster, played by Robinson, to pose the larger question of whether the war had been fought to allow gangsters and what they represented to flourish in a democratic society. A hurricane is effectively used to heighten the tension as the picture moves to a climax. The opening shot of gangster Johnny Rocco in his bath with a cigar is the epitome of the gangster at ease.

Frank McCloud pays a visit to the father and wife of his wartime buddy, who has died in action. The pair run a hotel on Key Largo which is being used as headquarters for Johnny Rocco and his gang. The former big-time mobster had been deported and is trying to sneak back into the country. He is waiting at the hotel for a bundle of counterfeit money which will finance his re-entry. When a local deputy sheriff grows suspicious, the gang kills him and blames the deed on local Indians, who seek shelter at the hotel from a coming hurricane. When things don't work out for Rocco, he forces McCloud to take the gang off the island to Cuba.

McCloud shoots it out with the gang at sea and heads back to Key Largo, where he will stay with Nora and James Temple.

THE KILLERS (Universal 1946, 1964)

1964: *Prod-dir* Donald Siegel; based on the story by Ernest Hemingway; *scr* Gene L. Coon; *art dir* Frank Arrigo, George Chan; *mus* Johnny Williams; *sound* David H. Moriarty; *ph* Richard L. Rawlings; *ed* Richard Belding; *cast* Lee Marvin (Charlie); Angie Dickinson (Sheila Farr); John Cassavetes (Johnny North); Ronald Reagan (Browning); Clu Gulager (Lee); Claude Akins (Earl Sylvester); Norman Fell (Mickey); Virginia Christine (Miss Watson); Don Haggerty (mail truck driver); Robert (gym assistant); Irvin Mosley (mail truck guard) Jimmy Joyce (salesman); Seymour Cassel (desk clerk). 1946: *Prod* Mark Hellinger; *dir* Robert Siodmak; based on the story by Ernest Hemingway; *scr* Anthony Veiller; *art dir* Jack Otterson, Martin Obzina; *mus* Miklos Rosza; *sound* Bernard B. Brown, William Hedgcock; *ph* Woody Bredell; *ed* Arthur Hilton; *cast* Edmond O'Brien (Riordan); Ava Gardner (Kittly Collins); Burt Lancaster (Swede); Albert Dekker (Colfax); Sam Levene (Lubinsky); John Miljan (Jake); Virginia Christine (Lilly); Vince Barnett (Charleston); Charles D. Brown (Packy); Donald MacBride (Kenyon); Phil Smith (Queenie); Garry Owen (Joe); Harry Hayden (George); Bill Walker (Sam); Jack Lambert (Dum Dum); Jeff Corey (Blinky).

There were two versions of Hemingway's story that reached the screen. They are both strong crime dramas that depicted a sense of the physical and moral dimensions of the underworld milieu. Mark Hellinger produced the 1946 version (directed by Robert Siodmak), which introduced Burt Lancaster to stardom in the role of the over-the-hill boxer marked for death by hoods who have double-crossed him. Whereas the forties version was famous, the 1964 version is the more powerful version and remains one of director Don Siegel's most exciting films.

Charlie and Lee, two hired killers, assassinate Johnny North, a former race-car driver and mechanic, in the school for the blind where he teaches (and is hiding out). Johnny offers no resistance, and the killers begin to wonder why he dies without putting up a fight. They reconstruct the circumstances that led up to the killing, to discover that their victim had been involved in an elaborate mail-truck robbery. Johnny was enticed to join the gang by Sheila Farr, the beautiful girl friend of Browning, a businessman who plans the job. Sheila and Browning plan on keeping all the loot, and so blame the betrayal on North. But the driver discovers the plot and escapes with the loot, Sheila, and a bullet wound. Sheila returns to Browning with the money, and the businessman hires the killers to murder North. The assassins decide to collect some of the loot themselves after they kill Johnny. Both Charlie and Browning die in a suburban shootout as the police arrive.

KISS OF DEATH (Twentieth Century-Fox 1947)

Prod Fred Kohlmar; *dir* Henry Hathaway; *story* Eleazar Lipsky; *scr* Ben Hecht, Charles Lederer; *art dir* Lyle Wheeler, Leland Fuller; *mus* David Buttolph; *sound* W.D. Flick, Rober Heman; *ph* Norbert Brodine; *ed* J. Watson Webb, Jr.; *cast* Victor Mature (Nick Bianco); Brian Donlevy (D'Angelo); Colleen Gray (Nettie); Richard Widmark (Tom Udo); Taylor Holmes (Earl Howser); Howard Smith (Warden); Karl Malden (Sergeant William Cullen); Anthony Ross (Williams); Mildred Dunnock (Ma Rizzo); Millard Mitchell (Max Schulte); Temple Texas (Blondie); J. Scott Smart (Skeets); Wendel Phillips (Pep Mangone); Lew Herbert, Harry Kadison (policemen).

Kiss of Death is a late-forties thriller/melodrama with an underworld setting. The film is graced with a fierce script by Hecht and Lederer, location shooting, giving a documentary feeling, artfully mixed with sets, and beautiful camerawork. The picture is characterized by a feeling of how the underworld is a netherworld beyond the law whose helplessness forces the *film noir* protagonist back on his own resources. Richard Widmark's portrayal of sadistic Tom Udo set the mold for such characters in gangster pictures.

Nick Bianco is a second-generation stickup man who tries to go straight after his release from prison. He marries, has two kids, and sticks to the straight and narrow until his wife dies. Then Bianco joins a gang in order to support his children. But he is nabbed and sent back to prison, where he makes a deal with the District Attorney, D'Angelo, to help get evidence on the gang. He meets Nettie, whom he loves but does not want involved in what may become a tragedy. Bianco succeeds in getting the evidence and has to testify in court, but the rap doesn't stick and the gang goes after the informant. Rather than wait in terror, Bianco goes after Tom Udo and kills him. The film is particularly strong in depicting the existential situation of a protagonist who has to become an informer to gain his self-respect as well as his freedom. The scene in which sadistic Tom Udo shoves Rizzo's crippled mother down a flight of stairs is a particularly grotesque moment in the history of the genre.

THE LAST GANGSTER (MGM 1937)

Dir Edward Ludwig; *story* William A. Wellman, Robert Carson; *scr* John Lee Mahin; *art dir* Cedric Gibbons, Daniel Cathcart; *montages* Slavko Vorkapich; *ph* William Daniels; *ed* Ben Lewis; *cast* Edward G. Robinson (Joe Drozac); James Stewart (Paul North); Rose Stradner (Talya Krozac); Lionel Stander (Curly); Douglas Scott (Paul North, Jr.); John Carradine (Casper); Sidney Blackmer (San Francisco editor); Edward Brophy (Gats Garvey); Alan Baxter ("Acey" Kile); Edward Marr (Frankie Kile); Grant Mitchell (warden); Frank Conroy (Sid Gorman); Moroni Olson (Shea); Ivan Miller (Wilson); Willard Robertson (Broderick); Louise Beafers (Gloria); Donald Barry (Billy Ernst); Ben Welden (Bottles Bailey); Horace McMahon (Limpy) Edward Pawley (Brockett); John Kelly (Red).

The Last Gangster emphasized (prematurely!) the movie gangster as a vanishing species. Every gangster that died in the late thirties was in some way presented as the last gangster, and the films of this period display a twinge of nostalgia for the movie gangsters who were so popular earlier in the decade. The movie industry tried to exploit character while acknowledging that the gangsters were somehow dinosaurs doomed to extinction. **The Last Gangster** re-echoes the recognition of the end of individualism and the sacrifice of the individual for the good of society (the family in **The Last Gangster**). The M.G.M. production lacks the snap of the Warner Brothers films but the camerawork, montage sequences, and art work are noteworthy. The teaming of gangster Robinson and James Stewart as the family man is successful and interesting.

When gangster Joe Krozac returns from his honeymoon in Europe, he finds that he himself has become a victim of a gang takeover. His revenge and return to power are cut short when he is betrayed and sent to prison. His new wife divorces him and marries a reporter, who adopts the gangster's son. Ten years later, Joe gets out of prison and sets out to find his ex-wife and son. But Joe is out of touch and no longer his old powerful self. He is captured by members of his former gang, who force him to tell where he has hidden the loot from their previous activities. He goes to kill his ex-wife and her new husband but gives up his plan of bloody revenge when he sees that his son will lead a better life by staying with his reporter stepfather and ex-wife. Joe leaves and dies in a shootout with rival gangster "Acey" Kile.

LEPKE (Warner Bros. 1975)

Prod-dir Menachem Golan; *exec prod* Yoram Globus; *scr* Wesley Lau, Tamar Hoffs, from a story by Lau; *sound* Bob Casey; *ph* Andrew Davis; *ed* Dov Hoenig; *cast* Tony Curtis (Louis "Lepke" Buchalter); Anjanette Comer (Bernice Buchalter); Michael Callan (Robert Kane); Warren Berlinger (Gurrah Shapiro); Gianni Russo (Albert Anastasia); Vic Tayback (Lucky Luciano); Milton Berle (Mr. Meyer).

Lepke is the story of a Jewish gangster who rises from the Lower East Side slums to syndicate success. The film uses the long-established gangster movie iconography with a post-**Godfather** emphasis on ethnicity. As a relatively inexpensive feature, **Lepke** returns gangster pictures to the low-budget mainstream typical of most of the genre.

Lepke Buchalter grows up in the streets of New York's Lower East Side, where he soon becomes adept as a pickpocket and a petty thief. He is caught and sent to prison, where he spends his adolescence. Upon his release, Lepke joins a gang of strike breakers with his friend, Gurrah Shapiro. Lepke quickly becomes head of the gang, who expand their enforcement work and become Murder Inc. after moving to Brooklyn. Another boyhood pal becomes Lepke's legal adviser and introduces the hood to a young widow with a little boy whom he marries. Lepke becomes part of the syndicate's governing board, along with Lucky Luciano and Albert Anastasia, and enters the narcotics trade, which makes him a millionaire. When politically ambitious District Attorney Thomas E. Dewey manages to indict Lepke on a minor rap, the gangster orders the execution of a witness in a fit of anger in front of other witnesses. He is arrested but jumps bail and goes into hiding. Lepke's gang starts to fall apart, and the syndicate, under pressure from the government, tells Lepke that he should give up or die. He sets up a deal with F.B.I. Director J. Edgar Hoover, using columnist Walter Winchell as a go-between. The federal government double-crosses Lepke and convicts him on the testimony of his own men. Lepke is electrocuted despite the efforts of his wife and lawyer to save him.

LITTLE CAESAR (First National 1930)

Dir Mervyn LeRoy; based on the novel by W.R. Burnett; *scr* Francis Faragon; *ph* Tony Gaudio; *cast*

Edward G. Robinson (Caesar Enrico Bandello); Douglas Fairbanks, Jr. (Joe Massara); Glenda Farrell (Olga Stassoff); William Collier, Jr. (Tony Passo); Ralph Ince (Diamond Pete Montana); George E. Stone (Otero); Thomas Jackson (Lieutenant Tom Flaherty); Stanley Fields (Sam Vettori); Armand Kaliz (DeVoss); Sidney Blackmer (The Big Boy); Landers Stevens (Commissioner McClure); Maurice Black (Little Arnie Lorch); Noel Madison (Peppi); Nick Bela (Ritz Colonna); Lucille La Verne (Ma Magdelena); Ben Hendricks, Jr. (Kid Bean).

Little Caesar is deservedly regarded as a landmark in the history of gangster movies. Robinson's powerhouse portrayal of the ambitious and trigger-happy gangster is memorable. The picture, like **Public Enemy** and **Scarface,** has all the essential scenes of the gangster's rise and fall. Some still stand out after all these decades. The introduction to the gang, the takeover, the nightclub robbery, the meeting with the Big Boy, the success banquet, and Rico's final pathetic shootout are particularly well done. While the picture is not as stylistically interesting as **Public Enemy** or **Scarface,** it is nonetheless significant as the movie that spearheaded gangster movie popularity in the early thirties.

    Little Caesar tells the rise-and-fall story of a small-time hood. The picture opens with a gas station holdup, in which the attendant is gunned down by Rico, after which the future Little Caesar and his partner, Joe Massara, decide to go East "where things break big." Rico joins Sam Vettori's mob, and to his disgust, Joe becomes a dancer. Rico begins to work his way up and develop a reputation as a trigger-happy gunsel. Although he is warned to cut down on the gunplay by Diamond Pete Montana, a higher-ranking hood, Rico kills the police commissioner during an elaborately staged New Year's Eve holdup of a nightclub. He then takes over the gang from Sam Vettori, who "can dish it out but can't take it anymore." Little Caesar is honored with a success banquet, at which the gang presents him with a stolen watch, and the newspapers take his picture to acknowledge that he is a man on the way up. Rico survives an assassination attempt by a rival gang and returns to run his rival (Little Arnie Lorch) out of town. Wealthy, well-dressed and powerful, Little Caesar goes up to the Big Boy's mansion, where the city's most powerful gangster tells Rico that he is to get Diamond Pete Montana's territory as well as Little Arnie's part of the city. Little Caesar begins to think about taking over the Big Boy's spot at the top and calls in his old pal, Joe Massara, to help him and to tell him that the dancer has

to rejoin the gang "or else." Joe, who has become a successful dancer, refuses, saying that he wants to marry his dancing partner (Olga Stassoff) and go straight. Olga realizes that Joe knows Little Caesar has killed the police commissioner and calls in the police in order to save her fiancé. Rico and Otero, his new right-hand man, come to kill Joe, but Rico is unable to shoot his old pal. When the police arrive, Little Caesar escapes, but Otero is shot and killed. His gang is rounded up and Sam Vettori executed as Little Caesar hides out in skid-row flophouses. When the newspapers quote the police description of Rico as yellow, the down-and-out gangster phones in a death threat to Flaherty, the cop who insulted him. The police trace the call and gun down Little Caesar on a cold, rainy night underneath a billboard advertising Joe and Olga's dance act. The gangster dies gasping, "Mother of Mercy . . . is this the end of Rico!!??"

THE LITTLE GIANT (First National, 1933)

Dir Roy Del Ruth; *story* Robert Lord; *scr* Lord and Wilson Mizner; *art dir* Robert Hass; *mus* Leo F. Forbstein; *ph* Sid Wickor; *ed* George Marks; *cast* Edward G. Robinson (James Francis "Bugs" Ahearn); Helen Vinson (Polly Case); Mary Astor (Ruth Wayburn); Kenneth Thomson (John Stanley); Russell Hopton (Al Daniels); Shirly Grey (Edith Merrian); Donald Dillaway (Gordon Cass); Louise Mackintosh (Mrs. Cass); Berton Churchill (Donald Hadley Cass); Helen Mann (Frankie); Dewey Robinson (Butch Zanquotoski); John Kelly (Ed).

The Little Giant is one of the funnier pictures that used the gangster genre as a springboard for comedy. It satirized social-climbing gangsters and had a certain bite in depicting how wealthy bankers—the socially "acceptable"—were responsible for hundreds of poor and middle-class people going broke. There are a number of remarkably funny scenes depicting the gangster's rise in society, particularly when he begins to read Plato ("Say! Those Greeks do plenty besides shining shoes and running lunch rooms",) listen to Wagner, and buy modern art ("a genuine Kaputzovich"). There were several gangster comedies in the early thirties, like *Rackety Rax* or *What! No Beer!?* but **The Little Giant** was the most successful—particularly because of Edward G. Robinson's ability to satirize effectively the role that he had helped make so popular.

    When Franklin D. Roosevelt is elected President and Prohibition ends, bootleg kingpin Bugs Ahearn decides that it's time to retire. The gangster pays off his gang, and his moll and decides to move to Santa Barbara in order to mingle with society people. He buys a mortgaged mansion from an impoverished society girl, who helps the crude gangster learn the social ropes of the polo set. At first, the social set will have little to do with the new "Sportsman" in their midst. But Bugs perseveres, buys a yacht, and painfully learns how to play polo. A social family of swindlers decide to take the ex-gangster in a stock swindle. Bugs falls for the daughter of these high-class crooks, and the father unloads millions of phony securities on the bedazzled hoodlum by turning a local bank over to Bugs. When small shareholders angrily demand their money back and go to the district attorney, Bugs is left holding the bag. The gangster talks the D.A. into postponing prosecution long enough for him to settle the matter himself and pay back the small investors who have been swindled. He calls together his old gang and institutes the "Chicago Plan," whereby the crooked bankers are forced to pay back all those who have been defrauded. Bugs marries the impoverished society girl as the gang plays polo in their own particular shoot-em-up fashion.

LOVE ME OR LEAVE ME (MGM 1955)

Prod Joe Pasternak; *dir* Charles Vidor; *story* Daniel Fuchs; *scr* Fuchs, Isobel Lennart; *art dir* Cedric Gibbons, Urie McCleary; *mus* George Stoll; *sound* Wesley C. Miller; *sp eff* Warren Newcombe; *ph* Arthur E. Arling; *ed* Ralph E. Winters; *cast* Doris Day (Ruth Etting); James Cagney (Martin "The Gimp" Snyder); Cameron Mitchell (Johnny Alderman); Robert Keith (Bernard V. Loomis); Tom Tully (Frobisher); Harry Bellaver (Georgie); Richard Gaines (Paul Hunter); Peter Leeds (Fred Taylor); Claude Stroud (Eddie Fulton); Audrey Young (Jingle Girl); John Harding (Greg Trent); Dorothy Abbott (dancer); Phil Schumacher, Otto Reichow, Henry Kulky (bouncers); Jady Adler (Orry); Maurity Hugo (irate customer); Veda Ann Borg (hostess); Claire Calreton (Claire).

Love Me or Leave Me brings crime and show business together in the grand tradition that goes back to the twenties in such films as **Broadway.** The film was part of a cycle of musical biographies about songwriters and entertainers. Martin "The Gimp" Snyder's attempt to control singer Ruth Etting is also the story of independence and creative honesty versus the soul of exploitation—economic, sexual, and psychological. The picture harks back to the twenties for an appropriate jazz setting

and is especially notable for Cagney's powerful portrayal (with an amazing limp) of Snyder. The film is also effective because Cagney played a character in a relationship that he had begun to develop back in **The Roaring Twenties.** A good script provides the solid foundation for this very effective picture. The film is an example of the successful fusion of the musical genre with the gangster genre, for the musical sequences arise out of the dramatic structure of the story. Many period songs actually sung by or identified with Ruth Etting are used in the film.

Thrush Ruth Etting is a farm girl who becomes the protégé of "Gimp" Snyder, a racketeer whose territory is the laundry industry. Snyder makes the girl a star, forces her into marriage, and drives her to drink. After twelve years Etting has had enough, and she leaves to resume her career. The irate mobster shoots her accompanist, Johnny Alderman, whom he suspects of having an affair with the singer. Doris Day's portrayal of Ruth Etting is one of her best roles.

MACHINE GUN KELLY (American International 1958)

Exec prod James H. Nicholson, Samuel Z. Arkoff; *prod-dir* Roger Corman; *scr* R. Wright Campbell; *mus* Gerald Fried; *art dir* Dan Haller; *sound* Philip Mitchell; *ph* Floyd Crosby; *ed* Ronald Sinclair; *cast* Charles Bronson (Machine Gun Kelly); Susan Cabot (Flo); Morey Amsterdam (Fandango); Jack Lambert (Howard); Wally Campo (Maize); Bob Griffin (Vito); Barboura Morris (Lynn); Richard Devon (Apple); Ted Thorp (Teddy); Mitzi McCall (Harriet); Frank De Kova (Clinton); Larry Thor (Drummond); George Archambeault (Frank); Jay Sayer (Philip Ashton).

Machine Gun Kelly is typical of the spate of gangster biographies that appeared in the late fifties. Like **Baby Face Nelson, Portrait of a Mobster** (about Dutch Schultz), or **The Rise and Fall of Legs Diamond,** the film purported to be the real-life story of a famous criminal. These outlaw biographies generally became vehicles for stringing together scenes and icons that had come to typify gangster pictures. Like the other biographies, **Machine Gun Kelly** is a low-budget, fast-moving potboiler with pretensions at historicity. Charles Bronson was particularly well cast as killer Kelly, a man in love with his Thompson sub-machine gun.

When the end of Prohibition puts bootlegger Kelly out of business, he turns to bank robbery as a new career. His fame spreads, and the bank jobs become more difficult. Kelly's girl, as is typical of many a gangster's moll, gets tired of life on the road. Kelly decides that one more job will make them rich, so he plans to kidnap the daughter of an extremely wealthy industrialist. Kelly becomes progressively crazier and more ruthless in his ambitions and jealous of his girl Flo's friendship with Fandango, a member of the gang. He forces Fandango out of the gang, and the latter tells the cops about the planned kidnapping. When Kelly falls into a police trap, he loses his courage and is captured.

MANHATTAN MELODRAMA (MGM 1934)

Prod David O. Selznick; *dir* W.S. Van Dyke, II; *story* Arthur Caesar; *scr* Oliver H.P. Garrett, Joseph L. Mankiewicz; *ph* James Wong Howe; *ed* Ben Lewis; *cast* Clark Gable (Blackie Gallagher); William Powell (Jim Wade); Myrna Loy (Eleanor Packer); Leo Carrillo (Father Pat); Nat Pendleton (Spud); George Sidney (Poppa Rosen); Isabel Jewell (Annabelle); Muriel Evans (Tootsie Malone); Claudelle Kaye (Miss Adams); Frank Conroy (Blackie's attorney); Jimmy Butler (Jim as a boy); Mickey Rooney (Blackie as a boy); Landers Stevens (inspector of police); Harry Seymour (piano player); William N. Bailey, King Mojave, W.R. Walsh (croupiers); Charles R. Moore (black boy in speakeasy); John Marston (Coates); Lew Harvey (craps dealer); Billy Arnold (black jack dealer); Jim James (chemin de fer dealer); Stanley Taylor (police interne); James Curtis (party leader); Herman Bing (German proprietor); Edward Van Sloan (yacht skipper).

Like dozens of other pictures of the late twenties and early thirties, **Manhattan Melodrama** used a gangster setting and character to tell a personal drama. The plot and characters were to appear often in future gangster and prison pictures, most notably **Angels with Dirty Faces.** The M.G.M. picture is noteworthy for the script, acting, and cinematography, which display the characteristic M.G.M. polish, lavish production values, and large cast. Clark Gable's portrayal of Blackie Gallagher, like his gangster character in *The Finger Points* (1931), is memorable, as are the performances of William Powell and Myrna Loy. The radical demonstration that turns into a riot in which the boys' stepfather is killed by rampaging police is particularly effective and realistic, as is much of the dialogue.

Blackie Gallagher, Jim Wade, and Father Pat had grown up together. Blackie becomes a gangster, Jim a lawyer/politician, and Father Pat the familiar neighborhood priest. Blackie's girl, Eleanor Packer, wants him to quit his criminal career, and when the gangster refuses she leaves him. Eleanor falls for Jim, and they marry. Jim becomes the District Attorney and begins a reform campaign by firing an assistant who is on the take. When the assistant attempts to blackmail Jim in order to get even, Eleanor goes to Blackie to see what he can do. Blackie kills the blackmailer and Jim prosecutes him, knowing nothing of the motive. The gangster is sentenced to death, and Jim wins an election for governor on his record as a prosecutor. When Eleanor tells Jim the situation, he goes to the prison to commute Blackie's sentence, but the gangster refuses, knowing that it would ruin the new governor's career. He goes off to the electric chair, with Father Pat praying for hs soul.

MARKED WOMAN (Warner Bros. 1937)

Exec prod Jack L. Warner, Hal B. Wallis; *prod* Lou Edelman; *dir* Lloyd Bacon; *scr* Robert Rossen, Abem Finkel; *mus* Bernard Kaum, Heinz Roehmheld; *songs,* Harry Warren; *art dir* Max Parker; *ph* George Barnes; *ed* Jack Killifer; *cast* Bette Davis (Mary Dwight Strauber); Humphrey Bogart (Special Prosecutor David Graham); Jane Bryan (Betty Strauber); Eduardo Ciannelli (Johnny Vanning); Isabel Jewell (Emmy Lou Egan); Allen Jenkins (Louis); Mayo Methot (Estelle Porter); Lola Lane (Gabby Marvin); Ben Welden (Charley Delaney); Henry O'Neill (District Attorney Arthur Sheldon).

The Marked Woman, like a prism, reflects several conflicts and contradictions of American society as it slid toward a second Depression in the late thirties: rich and poor, male and female, country and city, socialist and fascist. The film is based on the trial of Lucky Luciano, one of the kingpins of the national crime syndicate, who was tried and jailed on a prostitution charge when prosecuted by Thomas E. Dewey. With strong roles for both men and women, the film has a dramatic power enhanced by the editing of Jack Killifer and the remarkable performance by Bette Davis as the woman marked by the terrors of raw exploitation in the big city at night. The script is very successful, in part because it was based on actual court testimony of the Luciano trial.

Mary Strauber works for gangster Johnny Vanning. When the hood has a gambler killed for not paying his debts, he is brought to trial by crusading District Attorney David Graham. Mary has witnessed the killing, but she clears her boss after being threatened by his goons. When Mary's younger sister comes to the city, the girl wants the same life as her older sister, but Mary tries to keep her away from nightclubs and gangsters. When the girl ignores her sister's advice, she is killed by a gangster whose advances she has resisted and who works for Vanning, who helps cover up the incident. When Mary threatens to go to the District Attorney, Vanning has her branded on the face as a warning. But the angry girl courageously turns state's evidence, helps send Vanning away for life, and makes a hero out of the ambitious young District Attorney.

MURDER INC. (Twentieth Century-Fox 1960)

Prod Burt Balaban; *dir* Balaban, Stuart Rosenberg; based on the book by Burton Turkus, Sid Feder; *scr* Irv Tunick, Mel Barr; *art dir* Tony LeMarca; *sound* Emil Kolisch; *ph* Gaine Rescher; *ed* Ralph Rosenblum; *cast* Stuart Whitman (Joey Collins); May Britt (Eadie Collins); Henry Morgan (Burton Turkus); Peter Falk (Abe Reles); David J. Stewart (Louis "Lepke" Buchalter); Simon Oakland (Detective Tobin); Morey Amsterdam (Walter Sage); Sarah Vaughan (nightclub singer); Warren Fennerty (The Bug); Joseph Bernard (Mendy Weiss); Eli Mintz (Joe Rosen); Vincent Gardenia (Lawyer Laslo); Howard L. Smith (Albert Anastasia); Joseph Campanella (Panto); Seymour Cassell, Paul Porter (teenagers).

Like other films that purported to tell the inside story of the mob (e.g., **The Valachi Papers**), **Murder Inc.** is based upon a popular book about gangsters. Assistant District Attorney Burton Turkus's investigations uncovered a special assassination squad operating within the world of organized crime, and provided the basis for the film, which has a documentary flavor that is typical of such films. **Murder Inc.,** however, reveals little about the actual operation of the specialists in assassination, though based on the actual testimony of Abe Reles (who is excellently portrayed by Peter Falk) and despite using the names of the actual gangsters involved.

The film focuses on the story of a couple, Joey and Eadie Collins, whose lives are made a living hell by their involvement with the mob. Joey is deep in debt when his "friend" Abe Reles helps him out. In return, Reles, who is pictured here as a psychotic killer, demands that Joey Collins help finger a victim, establish alibis for Reles, and maintain an apartment to be used for mob meetings and for Lepke Buchalter to hide out. Reles forces sexual favors from Eadie Collins. The couple finally has enough money, but Eadie is fed up and convinces Joey

to work with the District Attorney to get them out of their predicament. After the police arrest Reles, who agrees to talk in exchange for immunity from prosecution, the star witness is thrown out of the sixteenth-floor window of the Blue Moon Hotel, where he was being "protected" by the police. Eadie is killed and Joey finally gives the District Attorney enough evidence to bust up the murder mob.

THE MUSKETEERS OF PIG ALLEY (Biograph 1912)

Dir D.W. Griffith; *ph* Billy Bitzer; *cast* Lillian Gish (The Little Lady); Walter Miller (The Musician); Elmer Booth (The Snapper Kid); Harry Carey, Lionel Barrymore, Jack Dillon, Alfred Paget, W.C. Robinson, Robert Harron (gangsters). (See pages 67–70, 72, 75, 79 for discussion.)

NAKED CITY (Universal 1948)

Prod Mark Hellinger; *dir* Jules Dassin; *story* Malvin Wald; *scr* Albert Maltz, Wald; *art dir* John F. DeCuir; *mus* Miklos Rozsa, Frank Skinner; *sound* Leslie I. Carey, Vernon W. Kramer; *ph* William Daniels; *ed* Paul Weatherwax; *cast* Barry Fitzgerald (Lieutenant Dan Muldoon); Howard Duff (Frank Niles); Dorothy Hart (Ruth Morrison); Don Taylor (Jimmy Halloren); Ted DeCorsia (Willie Garzah); Jean Adair (Little Old Lady); Nicholas Joy (McCormick); House Jameson (Dr. Lawrence Stoneman); Anne Sargent (Mrs. Halloran); Adelaide Klein (Mrs. Batory); Grover Burgess (Mr. Batery); Tom Pedi (Detective Perelli); Enid Markey (Mrs. Hylton); Frank Conroy (Captain Sam Donahue); Mark Hellinger (narrator); Walter Burke (Peter Backalis); David Opatoshu (Ben Miller); John McQuade (Constantine); Hester Sondergaard (nurse); Paul Ford (Henry Fowler); Ralph Bunker (Dr. Hoffman); Curt Conway (Nick); Arthur O'Connell (Shaeffer); Beverly Bayne (Mrs. Stoneman); James Gregory (Officer Hicks); Elliott Sullivan (trainer); John Marley (managing editor); Ray Greenleaf (city editor).

Perhaps more than any other film in the genre, **Naked City** emphasized the documentary approach. Shot entirely and imaginatively on location in New York, the film effectively brings to life the streets, subways, tenements, alleyways, and neighborhoods of the city and in so doing builds on maintaining the documentary tradition first established by **The Musketeers of Pig Alley.** The climactic chase across the bridge is particularly noteworthy as a dramatic use of realistic settings. The camerawork of William Daniels is masterful. In many ways, **Naked City** pointed to the future of feature film production on location. Few films have handled New York City locations as well, even though today location shooting has become the rule rather than the exception.

Naked City is the story of the police tracking down a murderer through the city. Led by experienced Lieutenant Dan Muldoon and rookie cop Jimmy Halloran, the police find the killer through arduous, painstaking investigation, coupled with Muldoon's skillful hunches based on years of police work. They finally narrow down their investigation to a small-time wrestler, Willie Garzah; whom they trap after a long chase on foot through the East Side and across the Brooklyn Bridge.

ON THE WATERFRONT (Columbia 1954)

Prod Sam Spiegel; *dir* Elia Kazan; based on articles by Malcolm Johnson; *scr* Budd Schulberg; *art dir* Richard Day; *mus* Leonard Bernstein; *ph* Boris Kaufmann; *ed* Gene Milford; *cast* Marlon Brando (Terry Malloy); Karl Malden (Father Barry); Lee J. Cobb (Johnny Friendly); Rod Steiger (Charley Malloy); Pat Henning (Kayo Dugan); Eva Marie Saint (Edie Doyle); Leif Erickson (Glover); James Westerfield (Big Mac); Tony Galento (Truck); Tami Mauriello (Tillio); John Hamilton (Pop Doyle); Heldabrand (Mott); Rudy Bond (Moose); Don Blackman (Luke); Arthur Keegan (Jimmy); Martin Balsam (Gilette); Fred Gwynne (Slim); Anne Hegira (Mrs. Collins); Thomas Handley (Tommy).

On the Waterfront is the most powerful film made about gangster infiltration of labor unions. It displays the documentary techniques popular at the time, especially in its excellent use of the waterfront and city locations. The acting of Marlon Brando, Eva Marie Saint, Karl Malden, Rod Steiger, and Lee J. Cobb was particularly effective, and Budd Schulberg's script is noteworthy for capturing the feel and rhythm of life on the docks. Academy awards went to the film, Kazan, Brando, and Bernstein.

Terry Malloy is a dock worker who has ambitions to be a champion boxer. His ability, however, is not up to this ambition. Racketeer Johnny Friendly, who controls the longshoremen's union, encourages the boxer but is more interested in using him as a thug. Terry's brother, Charley, is a union lawyer who works for Friendly. After Terry is used to set up a longshoreman who is killed for talking too much about gangster control of the union, he meets the dead worker's sister. As they fall in

love, she begins to make him understand the extent of the gangsters' control of the union. Along with Father Barry, the girl convinces Terry to help expose the gangsters to the law. Charley tries to warn his younger brother that they are both in grave danger if he continues his activities. Terry ignores the warning, and, when Charley is brutally murdered, he goes to the Federal Crime Commission to testify. After the testimony, Friendly and Terry fight it out in a climactic brawl that signals the end of the racketeer's control over the workers.

The scene in which Steiger tries to convince Brando not to turn state's evidence deserves special mention for the excellent interaction between two particularly gifted actors.

THE PETRIFIED FOREST (Warner Bros. 1936)

Assoc prod Henry Blanke; *dir* Archie Mayo; based on the play by Robert E. Sherwood; *scr* Charles Kenyon, Delmer Daves; *art dir* John Hughes; *mus* Bernhard Kaun; *sound* Charles Lang; *sp eff* Warren E. Lynch, Fred Jackman, Willard Van Enger; *ph* Sol Polito; *ed* Owen Marks; *cast* Leslie Howard (Alan Squire); Bette Davis (Gabrielle Maple); Genevieve Tobin (Mrs. Chisholm); Dick Foran (Boze Hertzlinger); Humphrey Bogart (Duke Mantee); Joe Sawyer (Jackie); Porter Hall (Jason Maple); Charley Grapewin (Gramp Maple); Paul Harvey (Mr. Chisholm); Eddie Acuff (Lineman); Adrian Morris (Ruby); Nina Campana (Paula); Slim Thompson (Slim); John Alexander (Joseph); Arthur Aylesworth (commander of Black Horse Troopers); George Guhl (trooper); James Farley (sheriff); Jack Cheatham (deputy); Addison Richards (radio announcer).

The Petrified Forest is a stage-stuck movie that is interesting primarily in its relation to the gangster genre for the allegorical depiction of gangster Duke Mantee as a primitive product of an acquisitive, materialistic society. Gramp Maple, however, sees the gangster as inheriting the mantle of Billy the Kid. Duke Mantee is depicted as an irrational, elemental force who represents the destructive and power-mad lowbrow aspects of civilization, in contrast to Alan Squire's rational, sensitive evocation of highbrow culture with a tradition of ineffective intellectuality. Squire views the gangster as a relic of a lawless age.

Vagabond Alan Squire wanders into a remote gas station and restaurant on the edge of the Arizona desert. There he meets the Maple family, who own and operate the place. The father's only passion is for the Black Horse Troopers, while Grandpa Maple's is for bloodthirsty stories of ancient outlaws. Daughter Gabby is a vital, sensitive girl who reads poetry and hungers for art and culture but who is burdened with loneliness and a loutish boy friend. Squire excites Gabby's longing to get away from her bleak life (as well as her boy friend's jealousy). Duke Mantee and his gang arrive, on their way to the Mexican border. They stop briefly so that Duke can meet his girl. Squire decides that he will help get the girl to Paris, which he does by manipulating the gangster into shooting him so that the girl will collect on his insurance policy. In portraying a role he had played successfully on Broadway, Bogart launched his career as a movie gangster.

PICKUP ON SOUTH STREET (Twentieth Century Fox 1953)

Prod Jules Schermer; *dir* Samuel Fuller; *scr* Samuel Fuller; from a Story by Dwight Taylor; *mus* Leigh Harline; *ph* Joe MacDonald; *art dir* Lyle Wheeler, George Patrick; *sound* Winston H. Leverett, Harry M. Leonard; *ed* Nick De Maggio; *cast* Richard Widmark (Skip McCoy); Jean Peters (Candy); Thelma Ritter (Moe); Murvyn Vye (Capt. Dan Tiger); Richard Kiley (Joey); Willis B. Bouchey (Zara); Milburn Stone (Winoki); Henry Slate (MacGregor); Jerry O'Sullivan (Dietrich); George E. Stone (clerk at police station); George Eldredge (Fenton); Stuart Randall (Police Commissioner); Frank Kumagh (Lum); Victor Perry (Lightning Louis).

Pickup on South Street is an underworld melodrama characterized by the red-baiting fervor typical of the McCarthy era. The cold war crime thriller displays Samuel Fuller's hard-boiled individual stamp as writer, producer, and director. It is particularly evident in his depiction of minor underworld characters like Lightning Louie, and Moe, played by Thelma Ritter. The latter is an ex-pickpocket who makes her living as a street peddler of second-hand ties and a stool pigeon whose only goal in life is to save enough money for a decent burial. Fuller typically handles violence and tension for shocking effect, along with a sordid view of a back-alley world.

Skip McCoy is a small-time pickpocket whose ambition is to make one big score. When he picks the purse of a girl named Candy, he discovers some microfilm among the loot. When the girl reports the theft to her boss, a Communist spy named Joey (whom she thinks is a patents lawyer), he sends her back out to find the pickpocket with the help of other Communist agents.

The agents close in on Skip after murdering Moe. When the F.B.I. agents find Skip and tell him what they are after, he figures that the microfilm is worth a lot of money. Candy falls in love with Skip, and when she discovers that she was a Communist dupe, she tries to stir Skip's patriotic sentiments. The pickpocket decides to fight the spies because they murdered Moe and beat up Candy. He helps turn the spies over to the federal agents after a climactic gun battle and settles down with Candy.

THE PHENIX CITY STORY (Allied Artists 1955)

Prod Samuel Bischoff, David Diamond; *dir* Phil Karlson; *scr* Crane Wilbur, Daniel Mainwaring; *mus* Harry Sukman; *ph* Harry Neumann; *ed* George White; *cast* John McIntire (Albert Patterson); Richard Kiley (John Patterson); Kathryn Grant (Ellie Rhodes); Edward Andrews (Rhett Tanner); Lenka Paterson (Mary Jo Patterson); Biff McGuire (Fred Gage); Truman Smith (Ed Gage); Jean Carson (Cassie); John Larch (Clem Wilson); James Edwards (Zeke Ward); Otto Hulett (Hugh Bentley); Ma Beachie, James Seymour (themselves).

Phenix City Story is particularly interesting for the use of interviews at the beginning of the picture, in which people describe how terrible conditions were in Phenix City. The documentary footage was optional for theater owners to use or not. It roots the film's story in the actual events that occurred at Phenix City, Alabama, when some organized hoods gave the place a reputation as "the wickedest city in the U.S." The picture was typical of several midfifties exposés of citywide crime— e.g., *Portland Exposé* (1957) and *Kansas City Confidential* (1952) or *The Houston Story* (1956). The muckraking point of view of the film, combined with location shooting and a cast without major stars, gave the picture a gritty realism that was rare even with the documentary pretension that runs throughout the gangster genre.

When G.I. lawyer John Patterson returns to his hometown, things are as bad as ever. Patterson is tough and honest. His father, who has been a lawyer for gamblers, is distressed at the lawless turn that the quality of life has taken in the gambling mecca of the south near Fort Benning, Georgia, where the games of chance are played with crooked dice and a crooked wheel. After his pals are beaten and his father is killed when he runs for office on a reform ticket, Patterson accepts the job of attorney general and goes after boss Rhett Tanner, who was responsible for his father's death. He allies himself with a black janitor and a female croupier who revolt against the hoodlums' control of the city. When the crooks show that they can rig elections anc control the police, vigilante action becomes the only viable alternative for the outraged citizens.

POINT BLANK (MGM 1967)

Prod Judd Bernard, Robert Chartoff; *dir* John Boorman; based on the novel *The Hunter,* by Richard Stark; *scr* Alexander Jacobs, David Newhouse, Rafe Newhouse; *art dir* George W. Davis, Albert Brenner; *mus* Johnny Mandel; *sound* Franklin Milton; *sp eff* J. McMillan Johnson; *ph* Philip H. Lathrop; *ed* Henry Berman; *cast* Lee Marvin (Walker); Angie Dickinson (Chris); Keenan Wynn (Yost/Fairfax); Carroll O'Connor (Brewster); Lloyd Bochner (Frederick Carter); Michael Strom (Stegman); John Vernon (Mal Reese); Sharon Acker (Lynne).

Point Blank reveals a contemporary flavor in its tough and determined protagonist who seeks revenge and money from a betraying friend and an impersonal crime corporation. The film effectively uses San Francisco (Alcatraz) and Los Angeles (a car lot) locations. It demonstrates the plasticity of the medium through editing (as in the flashbacks), slow-motion techniques, and a particularly imaginative use of sound. There is a swift pace and abundance of action for a story that is basically a bleak, powerful character study of a gangster as an existential gladiator at work in the modern world.

Walker agrees to hijack an illegal cash shipment when a pal, Mal Reese, pleads for help at a crowded and noisy reunion. After they successfully grab the money, Reese shoots Walker and runs off with his wife, Lynne, who has helped in the hijacking and betrayal. Though left for dead, Walker manages to swim ashore, where some time later he meets a mysterious stranger, Yost, who offers him help in getting revenge as well as recovering his share of the loot. Yost starts Walker on the trail by telling him where to find his wife. The latter, drugged and deserted by Reese, kills herself without helping Walker get any closer to revenge or money. Walker then approaches her sister, Chris, who helps Walker get into Reese's well-guarded penthouse. After a scuffle, Reese plunges to his death. Walker still wants his $20,000. Yost again proves helpful by telling Walker who and where Reese's boss is—a man called Carter, who tries to trap Walker but is caught in his own trap and killed by the assassin he had hired. Walker goes after the next man in the organization, Brewster, and in the process realizes that Yost is actually the mob's bookkeeper

(whose real name is Fairfax), who is using Walker to help him take over the organization. When Yost/Fairfax finally agrees to pay Walker, the latter senses another trap and walks away from the money and the mob.

PORTRAIT OF A MOBSTER (Warner Bros. 1961)

Dir Joseph Pevney; *scr* Howard Browne; from the book by Garry Grey; *art dir* Jack Poplin; *sound* M.A. Merrick; *ed* Lee H. Shreve; *mus* Max Steiner; *ph* Eugene Polite; *cast* Vic Morrow (Dutch Schultz/A. Fleigenheimer); Leslie Parrish (Iris Murphy); Peter Breck (Frank Brennan); Norman Alden (Bo Wetzel); Robert McQueeney (Michael Ferris); Ken Lynch (Lieutenant D. Corbin); Frank de Kova (Anthony Parazzo); Steven Roberts (Guthrie); Evan McCord (Vincent Coll); Arthur Tenen (Steve Matryck); Frances Morris (Louise Murphy); Larry Blake (John Murphy); Joseph Turkel (Joe Noe); Eddie Hanley (Matty Krause); John Korval (Lou Rhodes); George Werier (Thompson); Ray Danton ("Legs"Diamond).

Portrait of a Mobster is a gangster biography done in semi-documentary style that combines nostalgia for the Roaring Twenties with a direct account of the gangster's rise and fall. Vic Morrow's portrayal of Dutch Schultz is one of the best acting performances in gangster biographies, conveying a character both ruthless and sentimental. Ray Danton's portrayal of Legs Diamond in this film is interesting because he starred in the role in the earlier gangster biography, **The Rise and Fall of Legs Diamond.**

Dutch Schultz is a petty criminal who goes to work as a goon for Legs Diamond. He falls for the daughter of a bootlegger he has killed, but she marries a police detective. Schultz traps the policeman in a web of corruption, and the girl moves in with the mobster for a while. Schultz eliminates Legs when the latter becomes an obstacle to his rise to the top. Iris Murphy leaves Dutch and returns to her husband after tipping off Dutch's gang that their leader intends to double-cross them. The gang exacts revenge by shooting down Dutch in a wild gun battle that is the climax of the film.

PUBLIC ENEMY (Warner Bros. 1931)

Dir William A. Wellman; based on the story *Beer and Blood,* by John Bright; *scr* Kubec Glasmon, Bright; *art dir* Max Parker; *mus* David Mendoza; *ph* Dev Jennings; *ed* Ed McCormick; *cast* James Cagney (Tom Powers);

Jean Harlow (Gwen Allen); Edward Woods (Matt Doyle); Joan Blondell (Mamie); Beryl Mercer (Ma Powers); Donald Cook (Mike Powers); Mae Clark (Kitty); Mia Marvin (Jane); Leslie Fenton (Nails Nathan); Robert Emmet O'Connor (Paddy Ryan); Rita Flynn (Molly Doyle); Murray Kinnell (Putty Nose); Ben Hendricks, Jr. (Bugs Moran); Adele Watson (Mrs. Doyle); Frank Coghlan, Jr. (Tommy as a boy); Frankie Darro (Matt as a boy); Robert E. Homans (Pat Burke); Dorothy Gee (Nails Girl); Purnell Pratt, Helen Parrish, Dorothy Gray (little girls); Ben Hendricks, III (Bugs as a boy).

Public Enemy and **Little Caesar** were long considered to be the movies that started the gangster genre. **Public Enemy** makes a particularly strong case for environment as the crucial element in molding criminals. Part of the film's power comes from its structure of a series of episodes, as opposed to a story, that convey the process by which a ghetto kid became a gangster. The effective evocation of the bootleg era was combined with a cynical toughness appropriate to the Depression period when the film was produced and distributed. **Public Enemy** catapulted Cagney to stardom. Too, its major scenes and themes have come to typify the genre ever since. The film was particularly effective in describing the beer racket from the onset of Prohibition to bitter gang warfare. There are several remarkable and memorable scenes: the beautifully lit robbery of a fur warehouse; the scene of Tom and Matt secretly siphoning beer from a padlocked brewery—all without dialogue; the notorious scene in which Cagney pushes a grapefruit into Mae Clark's face; and the gruesome finish, where Tom Powers's mummified body falls through the door.

Tom Powers and Matt Doyle are two tough kids who become petty crooks fencing their stolen goods with Putty Nose, who runs a neighborhood "boys club." They graduate to larger crimes and kill a cop in an armed robbery of a fur warehouse. Though he gave them their guns, Putty Nose refuses to help the boys hide from the police. They go to work as truck drivers and find work with Paddy Ryan running liquor when Prohibition begins. Soon they ally themselves with Nails Nathan, siphoning liquor out of a closed-down brewery. The money rolls in, and the boys get clothes, a car, and girls suitable to their higher station in life. They find and kill Putty Nose, thereby evening an old score. Their job is now to sell beer and expand their Chicago territory. Tom Powers drops Kitty (he pushes the grapefruit in her face to let her know) and takes up with Gwen Allen, a moll with some blue-blood pretensions. When a horse throws and kills Nails Nathan (Tom and Matt shoot the horse), a gang war begins. Paddy tells the boys to lay low for a while, but when Tom goes stir crazy and leaves with Matt, his pal is shot and killed. Tom assaults the rival gang's headquarters singlehandedly and is wounded on the way out. The rivals kidnap Tom from the hospital and push his bullet-riddled body through the front door of his mother's house, as a record player spins, "I'm Forever Blowing Bubbles."

QUICK MILLIONS (Fox 1931)

Dir Rowland Brown; *story* Courtney Terrett, Rowland Brown; *scr* Terrett and Brown; *art dir* Duncan Cramer; *sound* W.W. Lindsay, Jr.; *ph* Joseph August; *cast* Spencer Tracy (Bugs Raymond); Marguerite Churchill (Dorothy Stone); Sally Eilers (Daisy de Lisle); Robert Burns (Arkansas Smith); John Wray (Kenneth Stone); Warner Richmond (Nails Markey); George Raft (Jimmy Kirk).

Quick Millions is one of several gangster films—**Dead End, The Little Giant,** or **Bullets or Ballots** are others— that convey strong sense of social classes in America. Spencer Tracy's gangster role never received the same attention as those of E.G. Robinson or Cagney and Muni, but his performance as Bugs Ahearn is in many ways equally powerful. Roland Brown's direction is masterful and grounded in a sense of realism rare in Hollywood film-making. The film is a subtle denial of the promise of social mobility in Depression America, and a frank expression of the upward mobility of those willing to be criminally ruthless in their pursuit of success.

The film has many fascinating small touches, as in the scene in which George Raft does a deft soft-shoe routine at a party where one gangster, an expert in stolen jewelry, cooks the spaghetti al dente and pays for a ring with $10,000 in cash that he carries in his pocket. In another scene, the gangsters, sitting around just before giving Bugs his final ride, listen to one of their number singing a ballad, "You're All Right Til You're Caught." The montage sequences are particularly fast and furious and well choreographed, and the costuming is particularly appropriate.

A train loaded with steel hurtles into the city's industrial section, where Bugs Ahearn is working as a truck driver. After brawling with a cop for ramming a limousine, Bugs receives a $50 fine and then gets into a fight with his girl friend, who threatens to leave him. Bugs decides to "stop fighting these cops and be nice to them." He figures out the various criminal angles open to an ambitious truck driver. First he begins to work a protection racket by vandalizing cars parked in city streets and taking a percentage of the garage-owners' profits. Then he moves on to extort street peddlers, independent truckers, and building contractors. Another young hood in the trucking business is approached with the proposal that, "If we controlled all the trucks, we could put this town in our vest pocket." Bugs falls for a society girl, Dorothy Stone, and shakes down her father to become his partner. He moves up in the world to an appropriately ornate office and apartment, but his goal becomes one of marrying into society and achieving respectability. When his pal, Jimmy, kills a reformer without Bugs's approval, the angry ganglord has his pal killed. His old gang questions Bugs's overwhelming desire for respectability. When Dorothy Stone turns down the gangster's marriage proposal, Bugs decides to kidnap her from the church steps on her wedding day. The gang takes Bugs for a ride instead.

THE RACKET (Paramount Famous Lasky/Corp. Caddo Co. 1928)

Prod. Howard Hughes; *dir* Lewis Milestone; *scr* Harry Behn; Del Andrews; from the play *The Racket,* by Bartlett Cormack; *ph* Tony Gaudio; *ed* Tom Miranda; *cast* Thomas Meighan (Captain McQuigg); Marie Prevost (Helen Hayes, an entertainer); Louis Wolhiem (Nick Scarsi); George Stone (Joe Scarsi); John Darrow (Ames, a cub reporter); Skeets Gallagher (Miller, a reporter); Lee Moran (Pratt, a reporter); Lucien Prival (Chick, a gangster); Tony Marlo (Chick's chauffeur); Henry Sedley (Corcan, a bootlegger); Sam De Grasse (district attorney).

The Racket was a popular play about gangsters that created such a sensation that it was banned in Chicago for being too explicit about gangster involvement in political corruption. Nick Sarsi was patterned after Al Capone, and the political bedfellow was clearly Chicago Mayor Big Bill Thompson. The film was remade in 1951, again produced by Howard Hughes, to take advantage of the publicity surrounding the Kefauver investigations.

Nick Scarsi is a powerful bootlegger who brazenly defies the police by openly transporting liquor throughout the city. When the gang is caught, a politician who needs the votes that the gangster controls intercedes to secure their release. Scarsi kills a patrolman with apparent impunity, but he is caught by honest Police Captain McQuigg, who had long resisted the gangsters'

efforts to control him. When Scarsi tries to escape, Captain McQuigg kills him, for McQuigg knows that the courts will only let him go again.

RACKET BUSTERS (Warner Bros. 1938)

Assoc prod Samuel Bischoff; *dir* Lloyd Bacon; *scr* Robert Rossen, Leonardo Bercovici; *mus* Adolph Deutsch; *sound* Robert B. Lee; *ph* Arthur Edeson; *ed* James Gibbon; *cast* George Brett (Denny Jordan); Humphrey Bogart (John "Czar" Martin); Gloria Dickson (Nora Jordan); Allen Jenkins (Skeets Wilson); Walter Abel (Hugh Allison); Penny Singleton (Gladys Christie); Henry O'Neill (governor); Oscar O'Shea (Pop); Elliot Sullivan (Charlie Smith); Fay Helm (Mrs. Smith); Joe Downing (Joe); Norman Willis (Gus); Don Rowan (Cliff Kimball); Anthony Averill (Dave Crane); Mary Currier (Mrs. Allison).

Racket Busters is typical of films that detailed the way in which gangsters turned an industry into a racket that threatened the public welfare. Combining G-man elements with union racketeering, the film is particularly effective in its use of the warehouse locales of the produce industry and in its use of trucks in action sequences.

When independent trucker Denny Jordan resists a mob takeover of a trucking company led by gangster John Martin, his truck is burned. Jordan breaks into the company office in desperation in order to support his pregnant wife, but he is caught. Special Prosecutor Hugh Abel offers the unlucky trucker a deal: he can go free if he will help get the goods on the mob that threatens to monopolize the trucking industry and take over the produce market. When Martin organizes a strike, trucker Skeets Wilson tries to prevent it but is murdered by Martin's men. Jordan seeks revenge for his dead buddy and leads the truckers into a climactic battle with the gangsters. In the process, Jordan stomps Martin and turns him over to the cops with the evidence that will put him away.

THE RISE AND FALL OF LEGS DIAMOND (Warner Bros. 1960)

Prod Milton Sperling; *dir* Budd Boetticher, *scr* Joseph Landon; *art dir* Jack Poplin; *mus* Leonard Rosenman; *sound* Samuel F. Goode; *ph* Lucian Ballard; *ed* Folmar Blangsted; *cast* Ray Danton (Jack "Legs" Diamond); Karen Steele (Alice Shiffers); Elaine Stewart (Monica Crake); Jesse White (Leo Bremer); (Simon Oakland

(Lieutenant Moody); Robert Lowery (Arnold Roth-stein); Judson Pratt (Fats Walsh); Warren Oates (Eddie Diamond); Frank De Kova (Chairman); Gordon Jones (Sergeant Cassidy); Joseph Ruskin (Matt Moran); Dyan Cannon (Dixie); Richard Gardner (Vince Coll); Sid Melton (Little Augie); Nesdon Booth (Fende).

The Rise and Fall of Legs Diamond is still another biographical film that uses the story of an individual gangster to re-create a hallowed period of gangster history—the twenties and thirties. The inherent tragedy of the inevitable alienation of the individual's drive for success is well expressed. As Diamond's wife put it at the end of the picture, "A lotta people loved my husband but he never loved anybody; that's why he's dead." Like **The St. Valentine's Day Massacre, The Rise and Fall of Legs Diamond** is suffused with nostalgia for a lawless era, and at times the film seems to be a parade of front-page crimes across the screen.

Legs Diamond is an ambitious dancer and con artist who is always looking to make a buck in whatever way he can. He robs a jewelry store in order to show his kid brother how smart he is and to get his girl some diamonds. But ambitious Legs wants to get close to the famous criminal Arnold Rothstein so that he can really learn how to make money. He robs a fence and heads for Miami, where he gets a job as one of Rothstein's bodyguards. When rivals shoot the head bodyguard and wound Legs, he goes to his old army sergeant, who teaches him how to shoot accurately. He gets his revenge on the gangsters who shot him and earns the job of Rothstein's chief bodyguard and collector. Legs learns the whole setup—bootlegging, gambling, narcotics, brothels. When Rothstein is mysteriously murdered, the gang carves up the business, and Legs sells them protection. When gang war breaks out, Legs sends his drunken brother off to Denver so that he won't be vulnerable. Legs takes over 50 percent of the gang's business and takes a trip to Europe, where he watches newsreels that describe the end of Prohibition and of the bootleg era. When the gangster gets back, a nationwide syndicate has taken over, which Legs resolves to fight. His wife walks out, and Rothstein's former girl friend fingers him in order to avenge Rothstein's death. Isolated, without friends or love, Legs Diamond dies the gangster's lonely death.

THE ROARING TWENTIES (Warner Bros. 1939)

Exec prod Hal B. Wallis; *dir* Raoul Walsh, Anatole Litvak; *story-foreward* Mark Hellinger; *scr* Jerry Wald, Richard Macaulay, Robert Rossen; *mus* Heinz Roemheld, Ray Heindorf; *art dir* Max Parker; *sound* Everett A. Brown; *sp eff* Byron Haskin, Edwin B. Du Par; *ph* Ernest Haller; *ed* Jack Killifer; *cast* James Cagney (Eddie Bartlett); Priscilla Lane (Jean Sherman); Humphrey Bogart (George Hally); Jeffrey Lynn (Lloyd Gart); Gladys George (Panama Smith); Frank McHugh (Danny Green); Paul Kelly (Nick Brown); Elisabeth Risdon (Mrs. Sherman); Ed Keane (Pete Henderson); Joseph Sawyer (Sergeant Pete Jones); Abner Biberman (Lefty); John Deering (commentator).

Like **Angels with Dirty Faces, The Roaring Twenties** was a slickly powerful and nostalgic recapitulation of the gangster films of the early thirties. The film is characterized by the epic sweep of the script, the fluid staging of the action, and the performances of Bogart and Cagney, each of whom had fully developed his own essential gangster character by the time they made film together. The use of jazz for the sound track, especially the tunes of Noble Sissle and Eubie Blake, and the period sets and costumes, produced a realistic and nostalgic re-creation of the twenties. Mark Hellinger based his original story on what he knew about the twenties as a New York columnist who covered the underworld. Cagney's role closely paralleled the career of gangster Larry Fay, and Gladys George gives a memorable portrayal of a nightclub hostess modeled in the famous "Texas" Guinan.

The film aptly places the origins of **The Roaring Twenties** in World War I. Three buddies who survive the war go off in different directions. Eddie Bartlett operates a fleet of cabs; George Hally becomes a bootlegger; and Lloyd Hart becomes a lawyer. Eddie enters the bootleg business himself by becoming partners with nightclub owner Panama Smith. She supplies, and he delivers with his fleet of cabs. Lloyd becomes their lawyer. Eddie falls for a young singer, Jean Sherman, who sings in Panama's club, and helps her with her career. Eddie precipitates a gang war when he hijacks a load of liquor from one of Hally's allies, Nick Brown. Hally sees a chance to grab Brown's business and temporarily allies himself with Eddie. They soon fall out and become rivals. Meanwhile, Jean falls in love with lawyer Lloyd, and they get married. The Wall Street crash wipes out Eddie, who winds up with one cab, while Hally has the rest of the fleet. Several years later, Jean comes to an alcoholic Eddie for help because Lloyd, who is now District Attorney, is on the verge of prosecuting Hally, who in return has threatened to kill him if he continues. Eddie tells Hally to lay off but realizes that the only way to stop him is with a bullet. In the final shootout, Eddie kills Hally and is mortally wounded by the latter's gang. He dies in Panama's arms on the snow-covered steps of a church.

THE ST. VALENTINE'S DAY MASSACRE
(Twentieth Century-Fox 1967)

Prod Roger Corman; *dir* Corman; *scr* Howard Browne; *art dir* Jack Martin Smith, Philip Jefferies; *mus* Fred Steiner; *sound* Herman Lewis, David Dockendorf; *sp eff* L.B. Abbott, Art Cruickshank, Emil Kosa, Jr.; *ph* Milton; Krasner; *ed* William B. Murphy; *cast* Jason Robards (Al Capone); George Segal (Peter Gusenberg); Ralph Meeker (George "Bugs" Moran); Jean Hale (Myrtle Nelson); Clint Ritchie (Machine Gun Jack McGurn); Frank Silvera (Nicholas Sorello); Joseph Campanella (Al Wienshank); Richard Bakalyan (John Scalisi); David Canary (Frank Gusenberg); Bruce Dern (Johnny May); Harold J. Stone (Frank Nitti); Joseph Turkel (Jake Guzik); Milton Frome (Adam Heyer); Mickey Deeps (Reinhart Schwimmer); John Agar (Dion O'Banion); Celia Lovsky (Josephine Schwimmer); Tom Reese (Ted Newberry; Jan Merlin (Willie Marks); Alex D'Arcy (Hymie Weiss); Gus Trikonis (Rio); Charles Dierkop (Salvanti); Tom Signorele (Bobo Borotte); Rico Cattani (Albert Anelmi); Alex Rocco (Diamond); Leo Gordon (James Morton).

The St. Valentine's Day Massacre is constructed almost completely of the iconography of gangster pictures. It is a film that is concerned less with story and character than with an articulation of gangster mythology surrounding the actual St. Valentine's Day mass murder of members of Bugs Moran's gang by Capone gangsters. The settings and characters, cars, guns, radios, and magazines, and the emphasis on the ethnicity of the Chicago underworld, all recall the surfaces of gangster history. Other icons, such as the soft sock on the chin for friendship (from Cagney in **Public Enemy**), refer directly to gangster films of the early thirties. The film uses the documentary technique of narration. A veritable compendium of gangster lore, some coming from movies, some from the actual history of the battles between the Capone and Moran mobs, and the events leading up to the infamous killings, the film is essentially a story of hunters stalking each other, with each killing treated as a ritual of gang warfare, as in the murder of Dion O'Banion in his flower shop or the machine-gun attack by a convoy of cars on Capone's headquarters.

SCARFACE, SHAME OF A NATION (United Artists 1932)

Prod Howard Hughes; *dir* Howard Hawks; based on the novel by Armitage Trail; *scr* Ben Hecht, Seton I. Miller, John Lee Mahin, W.R. Burnett, Fred Pasley; *mus* Adolph Tandler, Gus Arnheim; *sound* William Snyder; *ph* Lee Garmes, L. William O'Connell; *ed* Edward D. Curtiss; *cast* Paul Muni (Tony Camonte); Ann Dvorak (Cesca Camonte); Karen Morley (Poppy) Osgood Perkins (Johnny Lovo); Boris Karloff (Gaffney); C. Henry Gordon (Guarino); George Raft (Guido Rinaldo); Purnell Pratt (Publisher); Vince Barnett (Angelo); Inez Palange (Mrs. Camonte); Harry J. Vejar (Costillo); Edwin Maxwell (Chief of Detectives); Tully Marshall (Managing Editor); Henry Ametta (Pietro).

(See pages 203, 209–210 for discussion.)

THE SECRET SIX (MGM 1931)

Dir George Hill; *story-scr* Frances Marion; *sound* Robert Shirley; *ph* Harold Wenstrom; *ed* Blanche Sewell; *cast* Wallace Beery (Louis Scorpio); Lewis Stone (Newton); John Mack Brown (Hank Rogers); Jean Harlow (Anne Courtland); Marjorie Rambeau (Peaches); Paul Hurst (Nick Mizoski, the Gouger); Clark Gable (Carl Luckner); Ralph Bellamy (Johnny Franks); John Miljan (Joe Colimo); DeWitt Jennings (Chief Donlin); Murray Kinnell (Dummy Metz); Fletcher Norton (Jimmy Delano); Louis Natheaux (Eddie).

The Secret Six was one of the earlier films to suggest vigilante action as a means of dealing with gangsters. The masked vigilante businessmen are particularly sinister, a precursor of the various crime-fighting superheroes who appeared at the end of the decade. The picture is an interesting contrast to the gangster pictures produced at Warner Brothers in that the story moves at a more leisurely and elegant pace, with better dialogue and more attention to production values. The theme of the gangster as a scapegoat for America's troubles was one that was to appear again and again.

The Secret Six is a group of anonymous businessmen who hire tough crime reporters Hank Rogers and Carl Luckner to investigate a gang of bootleggers led by Louis Scorpio, whose lawyer, Newton, has managed to keep the gangster well protected. The reporters set out to gather evidence in the middle of a gang war that has resulted in several murders. Scorpio finds out what the reporters are up to and asks Anne Courtland to keep the snoopers away from his activities. When the girl falls in love with Rogers, Scorpio has the reporter killed. Anne seeks revenge by giving evidence that brings Scorpio to trial. Newton fixes the trial, so the gangster gets off scott free. Scorpio kidnaps the girl, but she is rescued by Carl Luckner. The picture ends when Scorpio and Newton kill each other in a fight over the gang's profits.

SLAUGHTER ON TENTH AVENUE (Universal 1957)

Prod Albert Zugsmith; *dir* Arnold Laven; based on the book *The Man Who Rocked the Boat,* by William J. Keating and Richard Carter; *scr* Lawrence Roman; *mus* Joseph Gershenson; *art dire* Alexander Golitzen, Robert E. Smith; *ph* Fred Jackman; *ed* Russell F. Schoengarth; *cast* Richard Egan (William Keating); Jan Sterling (Madge Pitts); Dan Duryea (John Jacob Masters); Julie Adams (Dee); Walter Matthau (Al Dahlke) Charles McGraw (Lieutenant Anthony Vosnick); Sam Levene (Howard Rysdale); Mickey Shaughnessy (Solly Pitts); Harry Bellaver (Benjy Karp); Nick Dennis (Midget); Ned Weaver (Eddie "Cockeye" Cook); Billy M. Greene ("Monk" Mohler); Johnny McNamara (Judge); Amzie Strickland (Mrs. Cavanagh); Mickey Hargitay (Big John).

Slaughter on Tenth Avenue is another picture concerned with labor racketering. Like *The Garment Jungle* (1957), **On the Waterfront,** or the earlier **Racket Busters,** the film makes use of the New York waterfront as a setting. It also emphasizes the way gangsters subvert organizations meant to protect and defend workers from exploitation. Finally, it has a remarkably good musical score.

When labor leader Mickey Shaughnessy is murdered, the District Attorney's office suspects that the crime is associated with labor racketeering on the docks. Assistant District Attorney William Keating is unable to discover what happened, for the murdered man's family is too frightened to talk. When Keating does begin to gather evidence, he finds that the suspect is protected by a corrupt labor leader and that the District Attorney is unwilling to prosecute the case fully because the killer is defended by the District Attorney's friend. After a courtroom drama reveals that the racketeers were behind Shaughnessy's murder, the longshoremen resolve to run the gangsters off the docks, which they do in a spectacular waterfront battle.

A SLIGHT CASE OF MURDER (Warner Bros. 1938)

Prod Hal B. Wallis; *dir* Lloyd Bacon; based on the play by Damon Runyon, Howard Lindsay; *scr* Earl Baldwin, Joseph Schrank; *art dir* Max Parker; *ph* Sid Hickox; *ed*

James Gibbons; *cast* Edward G. Robinson (Remy Marco); Jane Bryan (Mary Marco); Willard Parker (Dick Whitewood); Ruth Donnelly (Mora Marco); Allen Jenkins (Mike); John Litel (Post); Eric Stanley (Ritter); Harold Huber (Giuseppe); Edward Brophy (Lefty); Paul Harvey (Mr. Whitewood); Margaret Hamilton (Mrs. Cagle); George E. Stone (ex-jockey Kirk); Bert Hanlon (Sad Sam); Jean Benedict (Remy's secretary); Betty Compson (Loretta); Harry Seymour (the singer); George Lloyd (Little Butch); John Harmon (Blackhead Hallagher); Duke York (Champ).

There have been few successful gangster comedies, though the genre has been spoofed since the twenties. The few successful ones have inverted standard gangster iconography and have relied on actors, here like Robinson, who have so successfully played gangster roles before satirizing them.

Remy Marco is a beer baron whose beer was palatable only as long as it was illegal. The gangster himself has never tasted the stuff and has no idea how bad it is. He begins to lose money at the same time that he tries to crash high society. On the way to his new country home, Marco picks up a tough orphan whom he will teach the qualities necessary to be a success. Upon arrival, his gang discovers a number of corpses in the house, the result of a murder over the loot from a race track robbery that rival gangsters are trying to pin on Marco before they have a falling out among themselves. The loot is hidden in the house by the killer, who is unable to get away before Marco arrives with his retinue. To complicate matters, bankers are closing in on Marco's losing brewery business, which they threaten to close down unless he can give them money. Perhaps the worst blow is that his daughter's boy friend has found a job as a cop, which embarrasses and outrages the retired gangster. The tough orphan finds the loot and the hiding killer. Marco uses the money to prevent foreclosure, and the cop is made a hero for capturing the killer. Marco finally tastes his own beer, realizes why nobody drinks it, and orders the recipe changed.

SMART MONEY (Warner Bros. 1931)

Dir Alfred E. Green; based on the story *The Idol,* by Lucian Hubbard, Joseph Jackson; *scr* Kubec Glasmon, John Bright, Hubbard, Jackson; *ph* Robert Kurrle; *ed* Jack Killifer; *cast* Edward G. Robinson (Nick "The Barber" Venizelos); James Cagney (Jack); Evelyn Knapp (Irene Graham); Ralf Harolde (Sleepy Sam);

Noel Francis (Marie); Margaret Livingston (District Attorney's girl); Maurice Black (the Greek barber); Boris Karloff (Sport Williams); Morgan Wallace (District Attorney Black); Billy House (salesman-gambler); Paul Porcasi (Alexander Amenoppopolus); Polly Waters (Lola); Gladys Lloyd (cigar stand clerk); Clark Burroughs (Back-to-Back Schultz); Edwin Argus (Two-Time Phil); John Larkin (Snake Eyes).

Smart Money is of particular interest as the only film in which James Cagney and Edward G. Robinson acted together. The film emphasized the theme of the predicament of the rube in the city. Hoping to capitalize on the success of **Little Caesar** and **Public Enemy,** Warner Brothers combined the stars from both movies with the writers of the latter. The picture is a drama of small-time crooks rather than a full-fledged gangster picture.

Nick Venizelos is a small-time barber who is a passionate and lucky gambler. His pals, who hang out around the barber shop, convince him that he should head for the city, where the winnings will be bigger. With the help of his pal, Jack, they raise a stake of $10,000 and send Nick off. In the city, Nick is steered by Marie to a crooked game, where the small-time gambler is cheated out of his money by syndicate city slickers. Nick determines to get even and asks Jack to come to the city and help him out. He goes back to cutting hair and begins to make another pile of money by playing the horses. He bankrupts Sleepy Sam, who had cheated him at cards, and opens his own lavish gambling joint. Nick's activities attract the attention of the District Attorney, who may be in cahoots with the syndicate. The D.A. frames Nick with the help of blonde seductress Irene Graham. Nick goes to prison for six months without knowing that Irene helped send him there. When Jack tries to tell him about her behavior, they fight and Nick accidentally kills his pal. The gambler goes back to prison, while Irene, who has grown to regret her actions, says that she'll wait for him.

SOME LIKE IT HOT (United Artists 1959)

Prod Billy Wilder; *dir* Wilder; based on an unpublished story by R. Thoeren, M. Logan; *scr* Wilder, I.A.L. Diamond; *art dir* Ted Haworth; *mus* Adolph Deutsch; *sound* Fred Lau; *ph* Charles Lang, Jr.; *ed* Arthur Schmidt; *cast* Marilyn Monroe (Sugar Kane); Tony Curtis (Joe); Jack Lemmon (Jerry); George Raft (Spats Columbe); Pat O'Brien (Mulligan); Joe E. Brown (Osgood Fielding III); Nehemiah Persoff (Little Bonaparte); John Shawlee (Sweet Sue); Billy Gray (Sig

Pliakoff); George E. Stone (Toothpick); Dave Barry (Beinstock); Mike Mazurki, Harry Wilson (Spat's Henchmen); Beverly Wills (Dolores); Barbara Drew (Nellie); Edward G. Robinson, Jr. (Paradise).

Some Like It Hot is one of the best and funniest comedies to use the gangster genre. The picture is a wonderful blend of slapstick, nostalgia for gangster films, music, and action. The picture effectively used such long-time gangster actors as George Raft and George E. Stone to root the comedy in the tradition of gangster pictures. It also re-creates such famous gangster episodes as the Saint Valentine's Day Massacre scene and the triumphal banquet. The opening scene, in which a group of gangsters disguised as undertakers escort a coffin full of liquor, is typical of the comic blend of gangster iconography that characterizes the entire film.

Jerry and Joe, two musicians working in a gangster-run nightclub, witness the St. Valentine's Day Massacre and immediately become hot property. When the gangsters and the police discover that the musicians are the only witnesses, the pair realize they must escape the manhunt set up for them, so they flee to Miami disguised as chorus girls. They are befriended by singer Sugar Kane, who wants to find and marry a Miami millionaire. Millionaire Osgood Fielding III falls for Jerry (disguised as Daphne), while Joe disguises himself as a wealthy bachelor with a Cary Grant accent, to woo Sugar. When Spats Columbo and his gang show up for an underworld conclave at the hotel where the musicians are staying, they recognize the witnesses, but Spats and his gang are eliminated by rivals at a banquet in their honor, and the musicians are off the hook.

SUPERFLY (Warner Bros. 1972)

Prod Sig Shore; *dir* Gordon Parks, Jr.; *scr* Phillip Fenty; *ph* James Signorelli; *mus* Curtis Mayfield; *sound* Harry Lapham; *ed* Bob Brady; *cast* Ron O'Neal (Priest); Carl Lee (Eddie); Sheila Frazier (Georgia); Julius W. Harris (Scatter); Charles McGregor (Fat Freddie); Nate Adams (Dealer); Polly Niles (Cynthia); Yvonne Delainore (Mrs. Freddie).

Superfly is a gangster picture that emphasizes the black gangster's stylistic assertion of individual worth and the black junkie's oppression in a corrupt world dominated by whites. The film emphasizes that crime is the only route out of the ghetto and that the dope dealer, like the bootlegger of the twenties, has the respect and envy of the community for his activities. The film is interesting for its use of Harlem locations and particularly for Curtis Mayfield's musical score.

Priest (Superfly) is a cocaine dealer who is already on top of the heap when the film begins. A stylish dresser with a fancy customized car and a couple of beautiful girl friends, Superfly wants to quit the racket with one last million-dollar score. To do so, he has to outwit and outfight the corrupt white cops who actually control the city's cocaine connection, and who have been responsible for the murder of Priest's pal. Superfly sets up his last big deal and escapes with his favorite girl friend.

THUNDERBOLT (Paramount 1929)

Dir Josef von Sternberg; *story* Jules Furthman, Charles Furthman; *scr* Charles Furthman; *art dir* Hans Drier; *ph* Henry Gerrard; *ed* Helen Lewis; *cast* George Bancroft (Jim Lang/Thunderbolt); Richard Arlen (Bob Moran); Fay Wray (Mary/Ritzy); Tully Marshall (Warden); Eugene Besserer (Mrs. Moran); James Spottswood (Snapper O'Shea); Fred Kohler (Bad Al Frieberg); Mike Donlin (Kentucky Sampson).

Thunderbolt is typical of the late twenties gangster pictures that followed **Underworld. Thunderbolt** (1929) and *Dragnet* (1928), both directed by Josef von Sternberg and starring George Bancroft, were an effort to duplicate the formula for success established by **Underworld.** *Dragnet* was based on the play *Nightstick* and starred Bancroft as a tough ex-cop, Two Gun Nolan, who is pitted against bootleggers and racketeers and who must overcome his own alcoholism. **Thunderbolt,** the moe interesting of the two films, was a sound film.

Thunderbolt is a bank robber whose mistress falls for Bob Moran, a young banker. When she tells Thunderbolt that she wants to marry the banker, he says that he will kill his rival if she does. The police have followed the girl to Thunderbolt's hideout, and they arrest the bank robber. Bob Moran is fired when the police tell the manager of the bank where he works that Mary is part of a gang of bank robbers. Thunderbolt's gang thinks that Bob and Mary were responsible for sending their leader to prison, so they frame the young banker for murder. He soon joins Thunderbolt on death row. The gangster jealously vows to kill the banker, but when he finds out that the young man and the girl were childhood sweethearts, he has a change of heart, clears the banker, and goes to his death a satisfied man.

UNDERWORLD (Paramount 1927)

Pres Adolph Zukor, Jesse L. Lasky; *prod* Hector Turnbull; *dir* Josef von Sternberg; *story* Ben Hecht; *adaptor* Charles Furthman; *scr* Robert N. Lee; *ph* Bert Glennon; *cast* George Bancroft (Bull Weed); Clive Brook (Rolls Royce); Evelyn Brent (Feathers); Larry Semon (Slippery Lewis); Fred Kohler (Buck Mulligan); Helen Lynch (Mulligan's girl); Jerry Mandy (Paloma); Karl Morse (High Collar Sam).

Underworld is the best-known gangster picture from the 1920's. The picture used many of the devices established by gangster pictures earlier in the decade. Its enormous popularity created a vogue for gangster films that paved the way for the golden age of gangster pictures in the thirties. The film cast the gangster in a romantic mold typical of director Josef von Sternberg, as well as reflecting the twenties trend of gangster idolatry. (See pages 00–00 for discussion.)

UNDERWORLD USA (Columbia 1961)

Prod-dir-scr Samuel Fuller; *art dir* Robert Peterson; *mus* Harry Sukman; *ph* Hal Mohr; *ed* Jerome Thomas; *cast* Cliff Robertson (Tolly Devlin); Dolores Dorn (Cuddles); Beatrice Kay (Sandy); Paul Dubov (Gela); Robert Emhardt (Connors); Larry Gates (Driscoll); Richard Rust (Gus); Gerald Milton (Gunther); Allan Gruener (Smith); David Kent (Tolly at age twelve); Tina Rome (woman); Sally Mills (Connie); Robert P. Lieb (officer); Neyle Morrow (Barney); Henry Norell (prison doctor).

Underworld USA is a federal agents-versus-the-syndicate battle typical of the G-man/gangster warfare that has remained important to the genre since the mid-thirties. This time the bleak world of a small-time crook seeking revenge is the dramatic device used to illuminate the war. Writer/producer/director Samuel Fuller's distinctive depiction of the underworld establishes a tone of realistic ruthlessness blended with a romanticism that is also typical of the genre in general.

Tolly Devlin is a small-time crook who is determined to avenge the death of his father at the hands of three men who have become leaders of the crime syndicate. Devlin agrees to infiltrate the organization for the Federal Crime Commission so that he can use their help in destroying his father's murderers. Once in the organization, Devlin manages to kill mobsters Gunther and Smith, after sowing discord among the crime bosses and feeding information to the investigators. When special investigator Driscoll tells Devlin to ease off, the revenger pits Gela, the remaining mobster, against Connors, the syndicate head, and kills Gela for the syndicate. Devlin is ready to quit, but when Connors threatens his girl, Cuddles, Devlin kills the mob boss and, mortally wounded, staggers from penthouse to gutter, where he dies among the garbage cans.

WHITE HEAT (Warner Bros. 1949)

Prod Louis F. Edelman; *dir* Raoul Walsh; based on the story by Virginia Kellogg; *scr* Ivan Goff, Ben Roberts; *art dir* Fred M. MacLean; *mus* Max Steiner; *sound* Leslie Hewitt; *sp eff* Roy Davidson, H.G. Koenekamp; *ph* Sid Hickok; *ed* Owen Marks; *cast* James Cagney (Arthur Cody Jarrett); Virginia Mayo (Verna Jarrett); Edmund O'Brien (Hank Fallon); Margaret Wycherly (Ma Jarrett); Steve Cochran (Big Ed Somers); John Archer (Phillip Evans); Wally Cassell (Cotton Valett); Fred Clark (Daniel Winston—The Trader); Ford Rainey (Zuckie Hommell); Fred Coby (Happy Taylor); G. Pat Collins (Gerbert, the reader); Mickey Knox (Het Kohler); Paul Guilfoyle (Roy Parker); Robert Osterloh (Tommy Ryley); Ian MacDonald (Bo Creel); Ray Montgomery (Ernie Trent); Jim Toney (brakeman); Leo Cleary (fireman); Marshall Bradford (Chief of Police); Milton Parsons (Willie Rolf, the Steelie); Sherry Hall (clerk); Bob Foul (plant guard); Jim Thorpe (con); Harry Lauter (radio patrolman of Car A)

White Heat brought the psychotic hero to the gangster film. There have been other gangster films that presented psychological insights into the gangster character, but none with the dramatic intensity of Cagney's portrayal of Cody Jarrett. *The Dark Past* (1949), for example, examined the gangster's psychology through the device of having the gangster hold a psychiatrist hostage, thereby forcing the latter to correctly diagnose his captor in order to outwit him. **White Heat** was typical of the films in the late forties, in which the gangster as an individual died his tragic and lonely death. An emphasis on syndicate films during the next decade regularly pictured the gangster as a businessman whose career was tied to an organization, as in *New York Confidential* (1955). The tradition of the aberrant gangster was clearly established by Paul Muni's portrayal of Tony Camonte in **Scarface** in the early thirties. Cagney's Cody Jarrett amplified the psychotic elements of the character to their full potential. His oedipal complex and outbursts of uncontrolled violence were climaxed by the film's appropriately explosive ending.

Cody Jarrett is the leader of a holdup gang whose first job is the robbery of a train's payroll car. Smart and utterly ruthless, Jarrett orders the death of one gang member who has been wounded in the robbery and later guns down another who tries to steal his girl and take over the gang. When the police move in on the gangster, he turns himself in on a lesser false charge, which will give him an alibi for the killing. The federal agents plant Hank Fallon in prison in order to get evidence against the killer. Fallon befriends Jarrett and joins his gang when they get out of prison. He informs the feds of the gang's activities and thwarts an elaborate heist of a large factory payroll. Jarrett escapes into the chemical plant and shoots it out with the police from on top of a giant gasoline storage tank. Mortally wounded, he hollers his famous line, "Top of the world, Ma!" and puts a bullet into the tank, thereby ending his life and the film with a gigantic explosion.

THE VALACHI PAPERS (Columbia 1972)

Exec prod Nino E. Krisman; *prod* Dino De Laurentiis; *dir* Terence Young; based on the book by Peter Maas; *scr* Stephen Geller; *art dir* Mario Carbuglia; *mus* Rix Ortolani; *sound* Roy Mangano; *sp eff* Eros Baciucchi; *ph* Aldo Tonti; *ed* John Dwyre; *cast* Mario Pilar (Salerno); Charles Bronson (Joseph Valachi); Fred Valleca (Johnny Beck); Giacomino De Michelle (Little Augie); Arny Freeman (Warden at Atlanta Penitentiary); Gerald S. O'Loughlin (F.B.I. Special Agent Ryan); Lino Ventura (Vito Genovese); Sylvester Lamont (Commander at Fort Mammouth); Guido Leontini (Tony Bender); Walter Chiari (Dominick "The Gap" Petrilli); Amedeo Nazzari (Gaetano Reina); Joseph Wiseman (Salvatore Maranzano); Franco Corelli (Buster from Chicago); Alessandro Sperli (Giuseppe "Joe the Boss" Masseria); Angelo Infanti (Charles "Lucky" Luciano); John Alarimo (Ferrigno); Jill Ireland (Maria Valachi); Pupella Maggio (Rosanna Reina).

The Valachi Papers is an Italian-American co-production based on Peter Maas's book of the same title. The material is based on the testimony of Mafia lieutenant Joseph Valachi, who provided the federal authorities with a considerable amount of information on the workings of the Italian-American underworld. Charles Bronson did a good job of portraying the underworld stoolie, though the film is rather stiff and wooden in comparison with American gangster biographies.

The film is structured by a series of flashbacks from an interview that Valachi gives to an F.B.I. agent after the

Mafia places a $20,000 contract on him. Valachi agrees to tell all he knows about the Cosa Nostra (Mafia) in exchange for a guarantee of maximum security in another prison. Valachi goes to work for Mafia Don Gaetano Reina until that boss is killed by Vito Genovese and Lucky Luciano, for whom Valachi then goes to work. His pal Dominick Petrilli is appointed bodyguard to Genovese's mistress after the gangster chief is deported and Luciano imprisoned. When Genovese finds out, he orders Petrilli castrated, so Valachi puts his pal out of his misery. Valachi continues to work his way up in the organization until he and Genovese are arrested at the big Mafia conference in Appalachia, New York. Genovese blames the bust on Valachi and arranges a contract to kill Valachi, which he raises to $100,000 after Valachi appears before the Senate subcommittee investigating organized crime. Valachi tries to hang himself after he squeals and then decides to live on to spite Genovese. He dies six months after Genovese of a heart attack in prison.

FILMOGRAPHY

The dates of Filmography listings are the release dates. Films are included because of a gangster protagonist, story, or setting. These films have been researched, and in each case an attempt was made to view the film.

1912 *The Musketeers of Pig Alley*
1914 *The Gangsters and the Girl*
    The Gangsters of New York
    Resurrection
1916– *Intolerance (The Modern Story)*
1921 *Outside the Law*
    The Penalty
    Play Square
    There Are No Villains
    Voices of the City
1922 *The Bootlegger's Daughter*
    Broad Daylight
    Fair Lady
    Fools First
    A Wide Open Town
1923 *The Exciters*
    Missing Millions
    The Soul Harvest
    Souls in Bondage
1924 *The Beautiful Sinner*
    Grit
    Jack O'Clubs
    The Law and the Lady
    Poison
    Racing Luck
    Those Who Dance
1925 *Contraband*
    Go Straight
    The People versus Nancy Preston
    That Royle Girl
    Three Wise Crooks
    Tuned Up
1926 *The Highbinders*
    Robes of Sin
1927 *Boy of the Streets*
    The Cheaters

    The City Gone Wild
    The Girl from Chicago
    Midnight Rose
    Underworld
1928 *The Big City*
    Crooks Can't Win
    Danger Street
    The Dragnet
    Dressed To Kill
    Feel My Pulse
    Four Walls
    Gang War
    Ladies of the Mob
    The Lights of New York
    Me Gangster
    Midnight Life
    Protection
    The Racket
    Side Street Sadie
    Stool Pigeon
    Tenderloin
    Tenth Avenue
    Walking Back
    While the City Sleeps
1929 *Alibi*
    Broadway
    The Carnation Kid
    Come Across
    Dark Streets
    Fast Company
    Kid Gloves
    The Mighty
    The Racketeer
    Romance of the Underworld
    Side Street
    Thunderbolt

Voice of the City
Weary River
Welcome Danger
1930 *The Big Fight*
Big Money
Born Reckless
The Costello Case
The Czar of Broadway
The Doorway to Hell
Double Cross Roads
Framed
Hide Out
Hook, Line and Sinker
Ladies Love Brutes
Little Caesar
Man Trouble
Night Ride
Outside the Law
The Pay Off
Playing Around
Roadhouse Nights
See America Thirst
Shooting Straight
Sinner's Holiday
The Squealer
Street of Chance
Those Who Dance
The Widow from Chicago
1931 *Bad Company*
City Streets
Dance Fools Dance
Enemies of the Law
The Finger Points
A Free Soul
The Gang Buster
Gentleman's Fate
The Good Bad Girl
The Guilty Generation
Gunsmoke
Hell Bound
Homicide Squad
Hush Money
The Last Parade
The Lawless Woman
The Maltese Falcon
The Public Enemy
Quick Millions
Reckless Living
The Ruling Voice
The Secret Six
Smart Money

The Star Witness
The Tip Off
Three on a Match
1932 *Afraid To Talk*
The Beast of the City
Big City Shadows
The Big Shot
Broadway to Cheyenne
Central Park
Corsair
The Crooked Circle
Dragnet Patrol
Guilty as Hell
The Hatchet Man
Heart of New York
High Pressure
Illegal
Jewel Robbery
Madame Racketeer
Man Wanted
Missing Witness
Night After Night
Night Beat
Night World
The Public Be Damned
Purchase Price
Rackety Rax
Radio Patrol
The Roadhouse Murder
The Ruling Voice
Scarface
70,000 Witnesses
Soul of the Slums
Street of Women
Streets of Shadows
Taxi
Under Cover Man
The Wet Parade
Winner Take All
The Wiser Sex
1933 *The Big Payoff*
Blondie Johnson
Blood Money
Broadway Through a Keyhole
Gambling Ship
The Important Witness
The Little Giant
Mayor of Hell
This Day and Age
What! No Beer?
The World Gone Mad

1934 *The Big Shakedown*
Fog over Frisco
He Was Her Man
Heat Lightning
Hide Out
Jimmy the Gent
Lady Killer
The Last Trail
Manhattan Melodrama
Million Dollar Ransom
Sing and Like It
Straight Is the Way
Whirlpool

1935 *Doctor Socrates*
False Faces
G-Men
The Glass Key
Let 'em Have It
Mary Burns, Fugitive
Men Without Names
The People's Enemy
Public Hero #1
Special Agent
Stolen Harmony
The Whole Town Is Talking

1936 *Big Brown Eyes*
Bullets or Ballots
Counterfeit
Crime Patrol
Dragnet
F-Men
Man Hunt
Murder in the Big House
Petrified Forest
Special Investigator
Sworn Enemy
We're Only Human
Whipsaw
Winterset
Woman Trap

1937 *Armored Car*
Counsel for Crime
Criminal Lawyer
Dead End
Dick Tracy
The Frame Up
The Gangster's Bride
King of the Gamblers
The Last Gangster
Man of the People
Marked Woman

Parole Racket
Racketeers in Exile
Smart Blonde
Tainted Money
They Gave Him a Gun
The 13th Man
Trapped by G-Men
You Only Live Once

1938 *Angels with Dirty Faces*
Border G-Men
Boy of the Streets
Crime School
Dangerous To Know
Fast Company
Fugitive Lady
Gangs of New York
Gangster's Boy
I Am the Law
The King of Alcatraz
Little Tough Guy
Racket Busters
A Slight Case of Murder
Smashing the Rackets
When G-Men Step In
You and Me

1939 *Angels Wash Their Faces*
Big Town Czar
Blind Alley
Code of the Streets
The Devil's Party
Earl of Chicago
Hells Kitchen
I Am a Criminal
I Stand Accused
I Stole a Million
Illegal Traffic
Invisible Stripes
King of the Underworld
The Lady and the Mob
My Son Is a Criminal
Persons in Hiding
They Made Me a Criminal
Undercover Doctor
You Can't Get Away with Murder

1940 *Black Friday*
Brother Orchid
Castle on the Hudson
City for Conquest
Criminal Cargo
East of the River
Gangs of Chicago

It All Came True
Johnny Apollo
Parole Fixer
Queen of the Mob
Roaring Twenties
Wolf of New York
1941 *The Big Shot*
Buy Me That Town
Citadel of Crime
The Gay Falcon
High Sierra
Lady Scarface
The Maltese Falcon
Miracle on Main Street
Mr. D.A.
The Penalty
1942 *Across the Pacific*
Baby Face Morgan
Broadway
A Close Call
Confessions
Eyes of the Underworld
Gang Busters
The Glass Key
Grand Central Murder
Hot Spot
Johnny Eager
Kid Glove Killer
Lady Gangster
Larceny Inc.
The Man Who Wouldn't Die
Seven Miles from Alcatraz
Strange Alibi
The Strange Case of Dr. Rx
This Gun for Hire
1943 *All Through the Night*
Boss of Big Town
Bullet Scars
Double Indemnity
Lucky Jordan
Mask of Dimitrios
Mr. Lucky
The Whistler
1944 *Gangsters of the Frontier*
1945 *Conflict*
Crime Inc.
Dillinger .
Farewell My Lovely
Gangs of the Waterfront
House on 92nd Street
The Last Gangster

The Missing Juror
Roger Touhy, Gangster
Salty O'Rourke
Woman in the Window
1946 *Angel on My Shoulder*
The Big Sleep
The Blue Dahlia
Cornered
Dark Corner
Gilda
The Killers
Somewhere in the Night
1947 *Brute Force*
Dead Reckoning
Desperate
The Gangster
I Walk Alone
Johnny O'Clock
Lady in the Lake
Nocturne
Out of the Past
1948 *The Big Clock*
Body and Soul
Call Northside 777
Crossfire
Cry of the City
Dark Passage
G-Men Never Forget
Key Largo
Kiss of Death
Raw Deal
T-Men
1949 *Border Incident*
City Across the River
Criss Cross
The Dark Past
Force of Evil
He Walked by Night
Johnny Stool Pigeon
Knock on Any Door
Panic in the Streets
Race Street
Side Street
Sleeping City
They Live by Night
Thieves Highway
Undercover Man
White Heat
1950 *The Asphalt Jungle*
The Black Hand
Caged

D.O.A.
The Damned Don't Cry
Dark City
Deported
Gun Crazy
Highway 301
Kiss Tomorrow Goodbye
Love That Brute
Mystery Street
Night and the City
Port of New York
Where the Sidewalk Ends

1951 *Armored Car Robbery*
Captive City
Detective Story
The Enforcer
The Hoodlum
Hoodlum Empire
I Was a Con for the FBI
Lucky Nick Cain
The Mob
People vs. O'Hara
The Racket
St. Benny the Dip
711 Ocean Drive
Stop, You're Killing Me
The Strip

1953 *The Big Heat*
The City Is Dark
Crime Wave
On Dangerous Ground
Kansas City Confidential
Pick Up on South Street

1954 *Down Three Dark Streets*
Dragnet
I, the Jury
The Long Wait
The Miami Story
Naked Alibi
Riot in Cell Block 11
Rogue Cop
On the Waterfront

1955 *The Big Combo*
Black Tuesday
A Bullet for Joey
Chicago Syndicate
City of Shadows
The Desperate Hours
Five Against the House
Gangbusters
Guys and Dolls

House of Bamboo
I Cover the Underworld
I Died a Thousand Times
Joe Macbeth
Kiss Me Deadly
Love Me or Leave Me
The Naked Street
New York Confidential
Pete Kelly's Blues
Shield for Murder
Six Bridges To Cross
Tight Spot
Violent Saturday

1956 *Beyond a Reasonable Doubt*
Cry Vengeance
The Harder They Fall
Hell on Frisco Bay
The Houston Story
Illegal
Inside Detroit
Killer's Kiss
The Killing
Phenix City Story
Toughest Man Alive
While the City Sleeps

1957 *Accused of Murder*
The Boss
The Brothers Rico
Calling Homicide
Chain of Evidence
Crime in the Streets
Crime of Passion
A Face in the Crowd
Footsteps in the Night
The Garment Jungle
The Joker Is Wild
Nightfall
Short Cut to Hell
Slaughter on 10th Ave.

1958 *Baby Face Nelson*
The Bonnie Parker Story
The Case Against Brooklyn
Chicago Confidential
Cop Hater
Damn Citizen
Gang War USA
The Lineup
Machine Gun Kelly
The Mobster
My Gun Is Quick

1959 *The Big Operator*

City of Fear
The Crimson Kimono
Cry Tough
The FBI Story
I, Mobster
Inside the Mafia
The Law vs. Gangsters
Murder by Contract
Never Steal Anything Small
Odds Against Tomorrow
Party Girl
Pretty Boy Floyd
The Purple Gang
The Rise and Fall of Legs Diamond
Some Like It Hot
Stakeout on Dope Street
Twelve Hours To Kill
Vice Raid

1960 *Al Capone*
High Powered Rifle
King of the Roaring Twenties
Ma Barker's Killer Brood
The Mobster
Murder Inc.
Oceans 11
Pay or Die
Pretty Boy Floyd
Seven Thieves
The Threat
Three Came To Kill

1961 *Blast of Silence*
The George Raft Story
The Hoodlum Priest
Law Breakers
Mad Dog Coll
Portrait of a Mobster
True Gang Murders
Underworld USA

1962 *The Scarface Mob*
1963 *Johnny Cool*
1964 *Robin and the Seven Hoods*
1965 *Young Dillinger*
1966 *Dead Heat on a Merry-Go-Round*
Harper
The Silencers

1967 *Bonnie and Clyde*
Gunn
Point Blank
The St. Valentine's Day Massacre
Tony Rome

1968 *The Biggest Bundle of Them All*

The Brotherhood
Bullitt
Coogan's Bluff
Madigan
The Split

1969 *Mafia*
Marlowe
They Came To Rob Las Vegas

1970 *The Anderson Tapes*
Bloody Mama
A Bullet for Pretty Boy
Cotton Comes to Harlem

1971 *Bunny O'Hare*
Dirty Harry
The Gang That Couldn't Shoot Straight
The Grissom Gang
Shaft

1972 *Come Back Charleston Blue*
Cool Breeze
Every Crook and Nanny
The French Connection
The Godfather
The Mechanic
Prime Cut
Shaft's Big Score
Superfly
Sweet Sweetback's Baddasssss Song
The Valachi Papers

1973 *Black Caesar*
Coffy
Crazy Joe
Dillinger
The Don Is Dead
The Friends of Eddie Coyle
Hell up in Harlem
Hit!
The Outfit
Serpico
Shaft in Africa
Shamus
The Stone Killer

1974 *Big Bad Mamam*
The Godfather Part II
McQ
Melvin Purvis
Newman's Law

1975 *Mean Streets*
1976 *Al Capone*
Farewell My Lovely
Lepke

PICTURE SOURCES

29   Newsboy—on the road to success?
      Courtesy Library of Congress.
      Photograph by Lewis Hine.
31   Harrison Gray Fiske dinner.
      Photograph by Byron. The Byron
      Collection. Courtesy Museum of the
      City of New York.
33   Immigrant children learning about
      America. Photograph by Jacob A.
      Riis. The Jacob A. Riis Collection.
      Courtesy Museum of the City of New
      York.
35   Dime novel cover. Courtesy New
      York Public Library.
36   *The Naked City*. Courtesy Museum of
      Modern Art Film Stills Archive.
38   The Flatiron Building. Courtesy
      Library of Congress.
39   Wall Street. Photograph by Berenice
      Abbott. Federal Arts Project,
      "Changing New York." Courtesy
      Museum of the City of New York.
40   Broadway. Courtesy Museum of the
      City of New York.
41   Arriving immigrants. Photograph by
      Edward Levick. Courtesy Library of
      Congress.
42   Orchard Street. Photograph by Byron.
      The Byron Collection. Courtesy
      Museum of the City of New York.
44   Playground. Courtesy Library of
      Congress.
46   Bandit's Roost. Photograph by Jacob
      A. Riis. The Jacob A. Riis Collection.
      Courtesy Museum of the City of New
      York.
47   Stale Beer Dive in Cellar on Mulberry
      Bend. Photograph by Jacob A. Riis.
      The Jacob A. Riis Collection.
      Courtesy Museum of the City of New
      York.
49   Bottle Alley, Mulberry Bend.
      Headquarters of the Whyo Gang.

      Photograph by Jacob A. Riis. The
      Jacob A. Riis Collection. Courtesy
      Museum of the City of New York.
50   Some famous members of the Whyo
      Gang. Courtesy Museum of the City of
      New York. From Herbert Asbury, *The
      Gangs of New York*.
51   The Montgovery Guards. Photograph
      by Jacob A. Riis. The Jacob A. Riis
      Collection. Courtesy Museum of the
      City of New York.
53   The Short Tail Gang. Photograph by
      Jacob A. Riis. The Jacob A. Riis
      Collection. Courtesy Museum of the
      City of New York.
54   Automatic 1¢ vaudeville, exterior.
      Photograph by Byron. The Byron
      Collection. Courtesy Museum of the
      City of New York.
56   Automatic 1¢ vaudeville, interior.
      Photograph by Byron. The Byron
      Collection. Courtesy Museum of the
      City of New York.
57   The Comet nickelodeon. Courtesy
      Quigley Photographic Archive.
      Georgetown University Library.
58   Loew's first run. Courtesy Quigley
      Photographic Archive. Georgetown
      University Library.
59   Vitagraph Studios. Courtesy Quigley
      Photographic Archive. Georgetown
      University Library.
62   Ince's burned-out editing room. Cour-
      tesy Quigley Photographic Archive.
      Georgetown University Library.
64   Charles Bauman. Courtesy Quigley
      Photographic Archive. Georgetown
      University Library.
66   *The Great Bank Robbery*. Both
      photographs Courtesy Library of
      Congress.
68   Nickelodeon marquee. Courtesy
      Library of Congress.

69 Griffith, Bitzer, and the Biograph business representatives. Courtesy Museum of Modern Art Film Stills Archive. *Musketeers of Pig Alley,* title card. Courtesy Library of Congress.

70 The Snapper Kid. Courtesy Library of Congress.

71 Street scene. Alleyway. Saloon. *Musketeers of Pig Alley.* Courtesy Library of Congress.

72 The rival gang. *Musketeers of Pig Alley.* Courtesy Library of Congress.

73 Title: "The Little Lady Meets the Snapper Kid." *Musketeers of Pig Alley.* Courtesy Library of Congress. The little lady meets the Snapper Kid. *Musketeers of Pig Alley.* Courtesy Library of Congress.

74 Title: "The Little Lady at the Gangsters' Ball." *Musketeers of Pig Alley.* Still: The little lady at the gangsters' ball. Courtesy Library of Congress.

76 Title: "The Gangsters' Feudal War." *The Musketeers of Pig Alley.* Still: The Snapper Kid and gang. *The Musketeers of Pig Alley.* Still: Rival gang retreats. *The Musketeers of Pig Alley.* Courtesy Library of Congress.

77 Still: Gun shots. *Musketeers of Pig Alley.* Still: Gang shoots. *Musketeers of Pig Alley.* Courtesy Library of Congress.

78 Title: "Links in the System." Courtesy Library of Congress. Still: The Snapper Kid with cop. *Musketeers of Pig Alley.* Courtesy Academy of Motion Picture Arts and Sciences Library.

79 Thomas Ince. Courtesy Museum of Modern Art Film Stills Archive.

80 *Intolerance.* Courtesy Academy of Motion Picture Arts and Sciences Library.

81 Good vs. Evil in Ince production. Courtesy Museum of Modern Art Film Stills Archive.

85 *The Penalty.* Lon Chaney "The Buzzard." Courtesy Academy of Motion Picture Arts and Sciences Library.

86 *The Penalty.* Lon Chaney. Courtesy Academy of Motion Picture Arts and Sciences Library.

87 Wall Street bomb explosion, 1920. Courtesy Museum of the City of New York.

88 *Gang War.* Courtesy Museum of the City of New York.

89 *Big Money.* Courtesy Museum of Modern Art Film Stills Archive.

90 *The Racketeer.* Courtesy Museum of Modern Art Film Stills Archive.

91 *The Big City.* Courtesy Academy of Motion Picture Arts and Sciences Library.

93 *The Racketeer.* Courtesy Academy of Motion Picture Arts and Sciences Library *Four Walls.* Courtesy Academy of Motion Picture Arts and Sciences Library.

94 *Thunderbolt.* *Dressed To Kill.* *Four Walls.* All Courtesy Museum of Modern Art Film Stills Archive.

95 *Born Reckless.* Courtesy Museum of Modern Art Film Stills Archive.

96 *The Bootlegger's Daughter.* Courtesy Museum of Modern Art Film Stills Archive. *Romance of the Underworld.* Author's collection.

97 Hold of rum-runner's ship. Courtesy Library of Congress.

98 Al Capone. United Press International photo.

99   Harry Daugherty. Bettmann Archive, Inc. Albert Fall. Courtesy Library of Congress.

100   Will Hays. Author's collection.

102   Ku Klux Klan meeting, 1924. Courtesy Library of Congress.

104   *Grit*. Courtesy Museum of Modern Art Film Stills Archive.

105   *Four Walls*. Courtesy Academy of Motion Picture Arts and Sciences Library.

106   *Kid Gloves*. Courtesy Academy of Motion Picture Arts and Sciences Library.
      Those Who Dance. Courtesy Museum of Modern Art Film Stills Archive.

107   *While the City Sleeps*. Courtesy State Historical Society of Wisconsin.

108   Ford factory. Courtesy Library of Congress.

109   *The Racket* (chase). Courtesy Museum of Modern Art Film Stills Archive.
      The Racket (crash). Courtesy Academy of Motion Picture Arts and Sciences Library.

110   Angelo Genna funeral. Courtesy Chicago Historical Society.

112   Lindbergh and airplane. Courtesy Library of Congress.

113   Listening to the radio. Courtesy Library of Congress.

114   Newstand. Courtesy Museum of the City of New York.

115   *Little Caesar*. Courtesy Museum of Modern Art Film Stills Archive.

116   Bull Weed reads. *Underworld*. Courtesy Academy of Motion Picture Arts and Sciences Library.

117   Ben Hecht and Arthur Rossen. Courtesy Museum of Modern Art Film Stills Archive.

119   George Bancroft. *Underworld*. Courtesy Academy of Motion Picture Arts and Sciences Library.

120   George Bancroft and Evelyn Brent. *Underworld*. Courtesy Academy of Motion Picture Arts and Sciences Library.

121   Fred Kohler. *Underworld*. Courtesy Academy of Motion Picture Arts and Sciences Library.
      George Bancroft and Clive Brook. *Underworld*. Courtesy Academy of Motion Picture Arts and Sciences Library.
      George Bancroft and Clive Brook. *Underworld*. Courtesy Academy of Motion Picture Arts and Sciences Film Stills Archive.

122   Bull's hideout. *Underworld*. Courtesy Academy of Motion Picture Arts and Sciences Library.

123   The gangsters' ball. *Underworld*. Courtesy Academy of Motion Picture Arts and Sciences Library.

125   *Voices of the City*. Courtesy Museum of Modern Art Film Stills Library.
      The Mighty. Courtesy Academy of Motion Picture Arts and Sciences Library.

126   *Four Walls*. Courtesy Academy of Motion Picture Arts and Sciences Library.

127   *The Big City*. Courtesy Academy of Motion Picture Arts and Sciences Library.

128   *Fools First*. Courtesy Museum of Modern Art Film Stills Archive.
      Four Walls. Courtesy Academy of Motion Picture Arts and Sciences Library.
      Midnight Life. Author's collection.

129   *Broadway*. Courtesy Academy of Motion Picture Arts and Sciences Library.

130 *Sinner's Holiday*. Courtesy State Historical Society of Wisconsin Film and Theater Collection. Edward G. Robinson in *The Racket*. Courtesy New York Public Library, Lincoln Center for the Performing Arts. *The Racket*. Courtesy New York Public Library, Lincoln Center for the Performing Arts.

131 *The Racketeer*. Courtesy Academy of Motion Picture Arts and Sciences Library.

132 *While the City Sleeps*. Los Angeles location. Courtesy Museum of Modern Art Film Stills Archive.

134 George Bancroft. *Underworld*. Courtesy Academy of Motion Picture Arts and Sciences Library.

136 Paramount Studios. Courtesy Museum of Modern Art Film Stills Archive.

137 Paramount Studios. Courtesy Museum of Modern Art Film Stills Archive.

138 *Lights of New York*. Courtesy State Historical Society of Wisconsin.

139 *Lights of New York* premiere. Courtesy Museum of Modern Art Film Stills Archive.

140 Roxy Theater, interior. Courtesy Museum of Modern Art Film Stills Archive.

145 *Little Caesar*. Courtesy Museum of Modern Art Film Stills Archive.

147 *Homicide Squad*. Courtesy Academy of Motion Picture Arts and Sciences Library. *Doorway to Hell*. State Historical Society of Wisconsin. *City Streets*. Courtesy Academy of Motion Picture Arts and Sciences Library.

148 Warner Brothers Studio, 1932. Courtesy Museum of Modern Art Film Stills Archive.

150 Warner Brothers' production shot. Courtesy Museum of Modern Art Film Stills Archive. *Public Enemy*. Courtesy Museum of Modern Art Film Stills Archive.

152 Harry Cohn. Courtesy Quigley Photographic Archive. Georgetown University Library.

153 Tony Accardo, 7/11/58. United Press International photo.

154 Breadline. Courtesy Library of Congress.

156 "Depression." Courtesy Library of Congress.

157 James Cagney and Jean Harlow. *Public Enemy*. Courtesy Museum of Modern Art Film Stills Archive.

158 *Big Town Czar*. Courtesy Museum of Modern Art Film Stills Archive.

159 *Doorway to Hell*. Courtesy Museum of Modern Art Film Stills Archive.

160 James Cagney. *Public Enemy*. Courtesy Bob Kushman.

161 *Quick Millions*. Courtesy Museum of Modern Art Film Stills Archive.

162 Wisconsin farmers spill milk. Courtesy Library of Congress.

163 Unemployed demonstrate. Courtesy Library of Congress.

164 Unemployed fight police. Courtesy Library of Congress.

165 *Ladies Love Brutes*. Courtesy Academy of Motion Picture Arts and Sciences Library.

166 Al Capone's soup kitchen. Courtesy National Archives.

167 *Blondie Johnson*. Courtesy State Historical Society of Wisconsin.

168 *Mayor of Hell*. Courtesy Museum of Modern Art Film Stills Archive.

169 *Mayor of Hell*. Courtesy Museum of Modern Art Film Stills Archive.

170   *Public Enemy*. Courtesy Museum of Modern Art Film Stills Archive.

171   *Public Enemy*. Courtesy Museum of Modern Art Film Stills Archive.

172   *Public Enemy*. Courtesy Museum of Modern Art Film Stills Archive.
      Little Caesar. Courtesy Museum of Modern Art Film Stills Archive.
      Quick Millions. Courtesy Academy of Motion Picture Arts and Sciences Library.

173   *Public Enemy*. Courtesy Museum of Modern Art Film Stills Archive.
      Doorway to Hell. Courtesy State Historical Society of Wisconsin.
      Little Giant. Courtesy State Historical Society of Wisconsin.

174   *A Free Soul*. Courtesy Academy of Motion Picture Arts and Sciences Library.

175   *Little Caesar*. Courtesy Museum of Modern Art Film Stills Archive.

177   *Public Enemy*. Courtesy Academy of Motion Picture Arts and Sciences Library.
      Lady Killer. Courtesy Academy of Motion Picture Arts and Sciences Library.

178   *Sing and Like It*. Courtesy Museum of Modern Art Film Stills Archive.

180   *Public Enemy* poster. Courtesy State Historical Society of Wisconsin.

182   *Little Caesar* poster. Courtesy State Historical Society of Wisconsin.

183   *Little Caesar*. Author's collection.

184   James Cagney. Courtesy Bob Kushman.

185   *Street of Chance*. Courtesy Academy of Motion Picture Arts and Sciences Library.

186   *Little Caesar*. Courtesy Museum of Modern Art Film Stills Archive.

187   *Scarface*. Courtesy Academy of Motion Picture Arts and Sciences Library.

188   *Public Enemy*. Courtesy Academy of Motion Picture Arts and Sciences Library.

190   *Quick Millions*. Spencer Tracy and Sally Eilers. Courtesy Academy of Motion Picture Arts and Sciences Library.

191   *Quick Millions*. Spencer Tracy and Marguerite Churchill. Courtesy Academy of Motion Picture Arts and Sciences Library.

192   *Ladies Love Brutes*.
      Little Caesar. Both Courtesy Museum of Modern Art Film Stills Archive.

193   *Little Caesar*. Courtesy State Historical Society of Wisconsin.

194   *Beast of the City*. Courtesy Academy of Motion Picture Arts and Sciences Library.

195   *Czar of Broadway*.
      Night Ride. Both Courtesy Museum of Modern Art Film Stills Archive.

196   *Scarface*.
      Beast of the City. Both Courtesy Academy of Motion Picture Arts and Sciences Library.

197   *Little Caesar*. Courtesy State Historical Society of Wisconsin.
      Scarface. Author's collection.

198   *What! No Beer?* Courtesy Academy of Motion Picture Arts and Sciences Library.

199   *High Pressure*. Author's collection.

201   *G-Men*. Author's collection.

202   *Little Caesar*. Courtesy Academy of Motion Picture Arts and Sciences Library.

204   *Scarface*. Courtesy Academy of Motion Picture Arts and Sciences Library.
      Scarface. Author's collection.

205 *Scarface*. Author's collection.
Scarface. Courtesy State Historical Society of Wisconsin.

206 *Scarface*. Courtesy Academy of Motion Picture Arts and Sciences Library.
Scarface. Author's collection.

207 *Scarface*. Author's collection.

208 *Scarface*. Author's collection.

209 *Scarface*. Courtesy Museum of Modern Art Film Stills Archive.

211 *Scarface*. Author's collection.

212 *G-Men*. Courtesy Museum of Modern Art Film Stills Archive.

214 *Little Caesar*. Courtesy Museum of Modern Art Film Stills Archive.
King of the Roaring 20's. Courtesy Museum of Modern Art Film Stills Archive.
Scarface. Author's collection.

215 *Odds Against Tomorrow*. Courtesy Museum of Modern Art Film Stills Archive.

216 *The Roaring Twenties*. Courtesy Museum of Modern Art Film Stills Archive.

218 *Special Agent*. Author's collection.

219 *Star Witness*. Courtesy Academy of Motion Picture Arts and Sciences Library.

222 *Beast of the City*. Courtesy Academy of Motion Picture Arts and Sciences Library.

223 *G-Men* poster. Courtesy State Historical Society of Wisconsin.

224 *G-Men*. Courtesy State Historical Society of Wisconsin.
G-Men. Courtesy State Historical Society of Wisconsin.
Special Agent. Courtesy Museum of Modern Art Film Stills Archive.

225 FBI files. Courtesy Federal Bureau of Investigation.

226 J. Edgar Hoover and unidentified employee. Courtesy Federal Bureau of Investigation.

227 Magazine cover. *Operator #5*. Author's collection.

231 *The Roaring Twenties* poster. Courtesy State Historical Society of Wisconsin.

232 *The Roaring Twenties*. Courtesy Museum of Modern Art Film Stills Archive.

234 *High Sierra*. Courtesy Academy of Motion Picture Arts and Sciences Library.

235 *East of the River*. Courtesy State Historical Society of Wisconsin.

236 *White Heat*. Courtesy Bob Kushman.
The Brotherhood. Courtesy Academy of Motion Picture Arts and Sciences Library.

237 *Machine Gun Kelly*. Courtesy Museum of Modern Art Film Stills Archive.

238 *Lepke*.
The Friends of Eddie Coyle.
Shaft's Big Score. All Courtesy Academy of Motion Picture Arts and Sciences Library.

239 *The Godfather Part II*.
The Godfather. Both Courtesy Academy of Motion Picture Arts and Sciences Library.

240 Artwork for *Angels with Dirty Faces*. Courtesy State Historical Society of Wisconsin.

241 *Key Largo*. Courtesy Bob Kushman.
Key Largo. Courtesy State Historical Society of Wisconsin.
The Biggest Bundle of Them All. Courtesy Museum of Modern Art Film Stills Archive.

242 *G-Men*. Courtesy State Historical Society of Wisconsin.

Never Steal Anything Small. Courtesy Museum of Modern Art Film Stills Archive.

244 *The Petrified Forest.* Courtesy Academy of Motion Picture Arts and Sciences.

245 *Dead End.* Courtesy Museum of Modern Art Film Stills Archive.
The Maltese Falcon. Courtesy Academy of Motion Picture Arts and Sciences Library.
The Desperate Hours. Courtesy Museum of Modern Art Film Stills Archive.

246 George Raft. Courtesy Bob Kushman. George Raft and Sylvia Sidney. Courtesy Museum of Modern Art Film Stills Archive.

247 *Brother Orchid.* Courtesy State Historical Society of Wisconsin.

248 *Bullets or Ballots.* Author's collection.

249 *Al Capone.* Courtesy Museum of Modern Art Film Stills Archive.
Dillinger. Courtesy Academy of Motion Picture Arts and Sciences Library.

250 *Mad Dog Coll.* Courtesy Academy of Motion Picture Arts and Sciences Library.

251 *The Rise and Fall of Legs Diamond.* Author's collection.

252 *T-Men.* Courtesy Academy of Motion Picture Arts and Sciences Library.
The Big Heat. Glen Ford and Lee Marvin. Author's collection.
The Valachi Papers. Courtesy University of California at Los Angeles Theater Arts Library.

254 *The Godfather, Part II.* Robert De Niro and Guiseppe Sillato.
The Godfather. Lenny Montana.
The Detective. Kirk Douglas and William Bendix. All Courtesy

Academy of Motion Picture Arts and Sciences Library.

255 *Some Like It Hot.* Courtesy Museum of Modern Art Film Stills Archive.
Johnny Stool Pigeon. Courtesy Academy of Motion Picture Arts and Sciences Library.
The St. Valentine's Day Massacre. Author's collection.

256 *On the Waterfront.* Rod Steiger.
A Bullet for Pretty Boy. Fabian Forte.
The St. Valentine's Day Massacre. All Courtesy Academy of Motion Picture Arts and Sciences Library.

257 *The Lineup.* Eli Wallach. Courtesy Academy of Motion Picture Arts and Sciences Library.
The Glass Key. William Bendix, George Meader, and Joseph Calleia. Courtesy Museum of Modern Art Film Stills Archive.
The French Connection. Gene Hackman and Marcel Bozzutti. Courtesy Academy of Motion Picture Arts and Sciences Library.

258 *Key Largo.* Edward G. Robinson and Lauren Bacall.
Dirty Harry. Clint Eastwood and Tisha Sterling. Both Courtesy Academy of Motion Picture Arts and Sciences Library.

259 *The Damned Don't Cry.*
Short Cut to Hell. Both Courtesy Academy of Motion Picture Arts and Sciences Library.

260 *The Big Heat.* Courtesy Museum of Modern Art Film Stills Archive.

261 *On the Waterfront.* Courtesy Academy of Motion Picture Arts and Sciences Library.

262 *The Roaring Twenties.* Courtesy Academy of Motion Picture Arts and Sciences Library.

263 *Point Blank*. Author's collection.
264 *The Lineup*. Courtesy Museum of Modern Art Film Stills Archive. *Public Enemy*. Author's collection.
265 *Scarface*. Author's collection. *Bonnie and Clyde*. Courtesy Academy of Motion Picture Arts and Sciences Library. *The Purple Gang*. Courtesy Museum of Modern Art Film Stills Archive.
266 *Dirty Harry*. *Shaft in Africa*. Both Courtesy Academy of Motion Picture Arts and Sciences Library.
267 *Shaft's Big Score*. Courtesy Academy of Motion Picture Arts and Sciences Library.
268 *Angels with Dirty Faces*. Courtesy Academy of Motion Picture Arts and Sciences Library.
269 *Dead End*. Courtesy Academy of Motion Picture Arts and Sciences Library.
270 *The Gang That Couldn't Shoot Straight*. *Superfly*. Both Courtesy Academy of Motion Picture Arts and Sciences Library.
271 *The Godfather*. Courtesy Academy of Motion Picture Arts and Sciences Library.
272 *The Killers*. Courtesy Academy of Motion Picture Arts and Sciences Library.
273 *Force of Evil*. *Bullets or Ballots*. *New York Confidential*. All Courtesy Museum of Modern Art Film Stills Archive.
274 *The Brotherhood*. Courtesy Academy of Motion Picture Arts and Sciences Library.
275 *Slaughter on 10th Avenue*. Courtesy Museum of Modern Art Film Stills Archive.
276 *Point Blank*. Courtesy Museum of Modern Art Film Stills Archive.
277 *The Asphalt Jungle*. Courtesy Academy of Motion Picture Arts and Sciences Library. *The Friends of Eddie Coyle*. Courtesy Academy of Motion Picture Arts and Sciences Library.
278 *Cool Breeze*. *Superfly*. Both Courtesy Academy of Motion Picture Arts and Sciences Library.
281 *Racket Busters*. Courtesy Museum of Modern Art Film Stills Archive.
283 *Key Largo*. *Crazy Joe*. *Hell up in Harlem*. All Courtesy Academy of Motion Picture Arts and Sciences Library.
284 *Dead End*. Courtesy Academy of Motion Picture Arts and Sciences Library. *White Heat*. Courtesy Museum of Modern Art Film Stills Archive.
285 *Marked Woman*. *Love Me or Leave Me*. Both Courtesy Academy of Motion Picture Arts and Sciences Library.
286 *Gilda*. *Some Like It Hot*. Both Courtesy Academy of Motion Picture Arts and Sciences Library.
287 *The Killers*. *The Big Heat*. Both Courtesy Academy of Motion Picture Arts and Sciences Library.
288 *City Across the River*. Courtesy Academy of Motion Picture Arts and Sciences Library. *Hoodlum Empire*. Author's collection.
289 *The Godfather*. Courtesy Academy of

Motion Picture Arts and Sciences Library.

290 *Deadline*. Courtesy University of California at Los Angeles Theater Arts Library.
A Face in the Crowd. Courtesy Academy of Motion Picture Arts and Sciences Library.

291 *Al Capone*. Author's collection.
Naked City. Courtesy Academy of Motion Picture Arts and Sciences Library.
Ma Barker. Courtesy Academy of Motion Picture Arts and Sciences Library.

292 *Racket Busters*. Courtesy State Historical Society of Wisconsin.

293 *On the Waterfront*. Courtesy Academy of Motion Picture Arts and Sciences Library.
Al Capone. Courtesy Museum of Modern Art Film Stills Archive.
Office. Title of film unknown. Author's collection.

294 *Angels with Dirty Faces*. Courtesy State Historical Society of Wisconsin.
The Killers. Courtesy Academy of Motion Picture Arts and Sciences Library.
Bullitt. Courtesy Academy of Motion Picture Arts and Sciences Library.

295 *Dead End*. Courtesy Museum of Modern Art Film Stills Archive.

296 *Cry Tough*. Author's collection.

297 *7-11 Ocean Drive*. Courtesy Academy of Motion Picture Arts and Sciences Library.

298 *You Only Live Once*. Courtesy Academy of Motion Picture Arts and Sciences Library.

299 *On the Waterfront*. Courtesy Academy of Motion Picture Arts and Sciences Library.

300 *The Racket*.
D.O.A. Both Courtesy Academy of Motion Picture Arts and Sciences Library.

301 Filming *Naked City*. Courtesy Academy of Motion Picture Arts and Sciences Library.

302 *Naked City*. Courtesy Academy of Motion Picture Arts and Sciences Library.

303 *Party Girl*. Author's collection.

304 *Lepke*. Courtesy Academy of Motion Picture Arts and Sciences Library.
Title unknown. Author's collection.
Title unknown. Author's collection.

306 *St. Valentine's Day Massacre*. Courtesy Chicago Historical Society.

307 *Al Capone*.
Some Like It Hot.
Al Capone. All Courtesy Museum of Modern Art Film Stills Archive.

308 *Little Caesar*. Author's collection.

309 *Johnny O'Clock*. Courtesy Academy of Motion Picture Arts and Sciences Library.

311 *Hoodlum Empire*. Courtesy Museum of Modern Art Film Stills Archive.

312 Joseph Valachi testifies. United Press International photo.

313 *Johnny Allegro*. Courtesy Academy of Motion Picture Arts and Sciences Library.

316 *The Racket*. Courtesy Academy of Motion Picture Arts and Sciences Library.
Body and Soul. Courtesy Museum of Modern Art Film Stills Archive.

315 United Press International photo.

317 *Marked Woman*. Author's collection.
Willie Dynamite. Courtesy Academy of Motion Picture Arts and Sciences Library.

318 *Five Against the House*.
Phenix City Story.

Guys and Dolls. All Courtesy Academy of Motion Picture Arts and Sciences Library.

320 *On the Waterfront*. Courtesy Museum of Modern Art Film Stills Archive. *The Brotherhood*. Courtesy Academy of Motion Picture Arts and Sciences Library.

321 Title unknown. Author's collection.

322 A-bomb. Courtesy Quigley Photographic Archive, Georgetown University Library.

323 United Press International photo.

324 The Untouchables. Robert Stack. Author's collection.

325 *The French Connection*. Courtesy Academy of Motion Picture Arts and Sciences Library.

326 John Roselli. United Press International photo.

328 Howard Hughes. Courtesy Bob Kushman.

329 Gulf and Western Plaza. Courtesy Gulf and Western.

333 Benjamin Siegel and George Raft. United Press International photo.

334 Mark Hellinger and Jules Dassin. Courtesy Museum of Modern Art Film Stills Archive. Photo by WeeGee.

335 Mr. and Mrs. Hellinger, Mr. and Mrs. Warner. Author's collection.

337 United Press International photo.

338 *The Godfather Part II*. Courtesy Academy of Motion Picture Arts and Sciences Library.

INDEX